FAME AND FAILURE 1720–1800

Adam Rounce presents a colourful and unusual history of eighteenth-century British literature, exploring ideas of fame through writers who failed to achieve the literary success they so desired. Recounting the experiences of less canonical writers, including Richard Savage, Anna Seward, and Percival Stockdale, Rounce discusses the inefficacy of apparent literary success, the forms of vanity and folly often found in failed authorship, and the changing perception of literary reputation from the beginning of the eighteenth century to the emergence of Romanticism. The book opens up new ways of thinking about the nature of literary success and failure, given the post-Romantic idea of the doomed creative genius, and provides an alternative narrative to critical accounts of the famous and successful.

ADAM ROUNCE is a Lecturer at the University of Nottingham. He has written on various seventeenth- and eighteenth-century writers, including Dryden, Johnson, Pope, Akenside, Cowper, Warburton, and Wilkes. He is also co-editing two volumes for the Cambridge Edition of the Works of Jonathan Swift.

FAME AND FAILURE 1720–1800

The Unfulfilled Literary Life

ADAM ROUNCE

CAMBRIDGE UNIVERSITY PRESS

CAMBRIDGE
UNIVERSITY PRESS

University Printing House, Cambridge CB2 8BS, United Kingdom

Published in the United States of America by Cambridge University Press, New York

Cambridge University Press is part of the University of Cambridge.

It furthers the University's mission by disseminating knowledge in the pursuit of education, learning and research at the highest international levels of excellence.

www.cambridge.org
Information on this title: www.cambridge.org/9781107042223

© Adam Rounce 2013

This publication is in copyright. Subject to statutory exception and to the provisions of relevant collective licensing agreements, no reproduction of any part may take place without the written permission of Cambridge University Press.

First published 2013

Printed in the United Kingdom by Clays, St Ives plc

A catalogue record for this publication is available from the British Library

Library of Congress Cataloguing in Publication data
Rounce, Adam.
Fame and failure 1720–1800 : the unfulfilled literary life / Adam Rounce.
    pages cm
Includes bibliographical references.
ISBN 978-1-107-04222-3 (Hardback)
1. English literature–18th century–History and criticism.   2. Authors, English–18th century–Psychology.   3. Fame–History–18th century.   4. Literature and society–England–History–18th century.   5. Authorship–Public opinion–Great Britain–History–18th century.   6. Failure (Psychology)   I. Title.
PR441.R67 2013
820.9′006–dc23

ISBN 978-1-107-04222-3 Hardback

Cambridge University Press has no responsibility for the persistence or accuracy of URLs for external or third-party internet websites referred to in this publication, and does not guarantee that any content on such websites is, or will remain, accurate or appropriate.

Contents

Acknowledgements	*page* vi
Introduction: motion without progress	1
1 An author to be let	28
2 The exemplary failure of Dr Dodd	69
3 Anna Seward's cruel times	109
4 Percival Stockdale's alternative literary history	154
Conclusion	194
Notes	208
Bibliography	237
Index	245

Acknowledgements

A book about failure (as I've been reminded more than once over the last few years) is a considerable hostage to fortune; thanks are due to many for its eventual completion and arrival into the world, not least to Linda Bree and Maartje Scheltens at Cambridge University Press, for their good advice and splendid company over the period of its composition and publication. I have been helped by the librarians at the University of Bristol Library; the Bodleian Library, Oxford; The British Library; and the Houghton Library, Harvard; and by the anonymous readers of the manuscript for Cambridge University Press. Parts of this book were given at research seminars at the Universities of Birmingham, Central England, Exeter, Glasgow, Nottingham Trent, and Oxford, and at assorted meetings of the British and American Societies for Eighteenth-Century Studies. Parts of Chapters 3 and 4 appear in a different context in my essay, 'Toil and Envy: Some Responses to the *Lives of the Poets*', in *Samuel Johnson After 300 Years*, edited by Greg Clingham and Philip Smallwood (Cambridge University Press, 2009).

As well as colleagues, former and present, at Bristol, Keele, and Manchester Metropolitan Universities who may have added to the book (wittingly or otherwise), I am indebted to the following people for their various forms of help over the years: Hugh Adlington, Paul Baines, Rebecca Barr, Andrew Bennett, Andrew Biswell, the late Skip Brack, Paddy Bullard, Michael Bundock, Steven Cheeke, Stephen Clarke, Marcus Dahl, Robert DeMaria, Helen Deutsch, Nikolai Duffy, Jess Edwards, Tim Fulford, Paul Fuller, Christine Gerrard, Stuart Gillespie, Nick Groom, Ben Hawes, David Hopkins, Steven James, Freya Johnston, Robert Jones, Jacob Sider Jost, Antti Karjalainen, Steve Karian, Simon Kovesi, Richard Lambert, Emma Liggins, Roger Lonsdale, Jack Lynch, Dafydd Moore, Lucy Munro, James Noggle, Adam Potkay, Juan Pellicer, Mark Pedreira, Henry Power, Paul Price, Claude Rawson, Alice Reeves, John Richetti, Tim Saunders, John Scanlan, Steve Scherwatzky, Phil Smallwood, Richard

Terry, Christopher Vilmar, David Venturo, Howard Weinbrot (the other member of the Stockdale club), Dinah Wood, and James Woolley.

The most important contributions of all have come from John Lucas (for the initial idea, and the invaluable example of Iain Fletcher's interest in the poets of the 1890s); Jim McLaverty, Tom Mason, and Abigail Williams, who all read parts of the book, even at its most baggy and wearisome, suggested how it could be improved, and encouraged me to finish it; and lastly from Louise, who ensured its completion.

Introduction: motion without progress

The official end of Walter Scott's often barely concealed anonymity as a novelist came with his putting his name to the 'Introduction' of the first volume of his *Chronicles of the Canongate* in 1827, where 'The Author of *Waverley*' and its successors finally dropped his mask and admitted what so many of his readers had long known. After admitting no obvious reason for his choice of remaining anonymous (and thus ensuring that speculations on his motives would continue into posterity), Scott announces what seems to be an extenuating factor:

> I hope it will not be construed into ingratitude to the public, to whose indulgence I have owed much more than to any merit of my own, if I confess that I am, and have been, more indifferent to success, or to failure, as an author, than may be the case with others, who feel more strongly the passion for literary fame, probably because they are justly conscious of a better title to it.[1]

It is easy to see this sort of declaration of modesty as disingenuous, or at least somewhat ironic, given that Scott would have seen many devotees passionate for literary fame who were less than just in their sense of entitlement, in terms of talent alone. And what would justice in such matters mean? The suggestion is of authors who are convinced that literary fame is their inherent right. In distancing himself from such people, Scott seems to mean what he says – success and failure are matters of relative indifference to him, perhaps for the very salient reason that he had experienced both. In his *Journal* two months later, after negative responses to *Chronicles of the Canongate*, he reiterated his feelings:

> Reconsidered the probable downfall of my literary reputation. I am so constitutionally indifferent to the censure or praise of the world, that having never abandoned myself to the feelings of self-conceit which my great success was calculated to inspire, I can look with the most unshaken firmness upon the event as far as my own feelings are concerned. If there

be any great advantage in literary reputation, I have had it, and I certainly do not care for losing it.[2]

It is not, it would seem, in Scott's nature to be affected by the extremes of success or failure. Of course, the gravity of Scott's situation – he had since 1826 lost his wife, and was undergoing the grim battle with insolvency that would dominate the rest of his life – would have helped him to be above such matters, yet such obliviousness to the prospects of fame or ignominy is rare indeed. Scott's response is complicated, when read against his earlier 'Introduction', where he follows his indifference to success or failure with the recollection that when he

> became aware that literary pursuits were likely to engage in future a considerable portion of my time, I felt some alarm that I might acquire those habits of jealousy and fretfulness which have lessened, and even degraded, the character of the children of imagination, and rendered them, by petty squabbles and mutual irritability, the laughing-stock of the people in the world. I resolved, therefore, in this respect to guard my breast ... and as much as possible to avoid resting my thoughts and wishes upon literary success, lest I should endanger my own peace of mind and tranquillity by literary failure.[3]

Here, apparent constitutional indifference is replaced by the very acute realisation that the desire for literary success had too often persecuted the mind of the aspirants, caused them to become figures of scorn, and culminated in their failure, which they could in no way tolerate. There is, accordingly, a change in emphasis, with Scott not able to stand back from such follies, by virtue of his equanimity, but having instead to guard himself from involvement in this selfish and destructive cycle. The latent fear that the 'children of imagination' always humiliate and torment themselves leads to the necessity of placing yourself above such a career if you are to be even moderately happy; the alternative is a life of perpetual metaphorical warfare, whether with those critics and readers who do not do your work justice, or with your own sense of expectations and needs. For Scott, it is not possible to dream of success without escaping the consequences of failure – the two concepts are interdependent. Moreover, the 'self-conceit' that demands success can only lead to failure, it is implied, because its own imaginings cannot be easily satisfied.

The inefficacy of apparent literary success, and the forms of vanity and folly often found in failed authorship, are central to the concerns of this book. It offers a survey of literary failure in the last eighty years of the eighteenth century, an all-consuming and even degrading area of culture that is nonetheless rarely, if ever referred to specifically: failure tends to elide a narrative, or cut it short, rather than encourage further investigation. Failure is an almost completely unexamined subject; it takes many forms, and can be found as a subtext in almost every example of a writer who succeeded, let alone as the keynote in the lives of those who did not. This book will examine why different writers failed, and for what different reasons, and will therefore try to determine what exactly is meant by literary failure (or, for that matter, success) in the period, and what conclusions can be drawn from it, with regard to such disparate matters as literary value, canon formation, and the social construction and progression of ideas of authorship.

Examining a period specifically through the idea of failure casts a new and illuminating light on some familiar and some obscure byways of the literature of the period. It offers a perspective on literary fame and under-achievement before the emergence of Romanticism, and a different, more modern understanding of authorial individualism – one where failure becomes acceptable or even welcomed as a sign of genius – and offers a description of eighteenth-century authorship in different guises, from the bohemian attractions of the failed life in posterity, to the public celebrity of an otherwise nondescript author, the case of an author not being able to satisfy their own needs with regard to fame, and a long career of self-destructive mediocrity.

In the instances explored in the chapters that follow, literary failure will often seem to be the result of a judgement on character, and its supposed weaknesses, whether these be the egocentricity hinted at by Scott (such as the inherent belief that literary fame is your due), or partiality and excesses that have obscured otherwise intellectually estimable reputations. Examples of failure are sometimes a comment upon the wider morals of a society, or on the inability of writers to integrate themselves within such a social system.

Above all, literary failure in the period covered by this book has its own style. The types of failure examined here thus range from instances where literary productions were roundly criticised or ignored, to ostensible successes that still, in the manner in which they were achieved, produced a level of hostility and ridicule that represents a failure. A style or aesthetic of failure sounds contradictory, but it merely means the unique qualities – whether of vociferous argument, ostentation, or misguided assumptions of grandeur – by which particular failures distinguished themselves. It is a premise of this book that such distinctiveness makes such figures stand out to posterity, and suggest, through their resonant examples, much evidence of a literary culture that has never been properly examined: many artists failed and disappeared into total obscurity, yet the figures with which I am concerned showed such individuality of manner as to be remembered, even if often as bywords for eccentricity and hubris, rather than genuine achievement. It would be relatively simple to explore the concept of failure in the literary world of the eighteenth century by looking at the scantily documented non-careers of writers that were almost completely unsuccessful. It seems more worthwhile, profitable, and provocative to examine the idea of literary failure against a wider range of eighteenth-century literary experiences, including those which are not obviously failures in material terms.

It is undoubtedly the case that failure eludes any specific definition to such an extent that any material or critical attempt at one would founder on its inclusions and exceptions. The most failed of all writers would be those who (even in years of such burgeoning publication of all types of writing) failed to leave any evidence of having reached the initial stage of being published, even for a short interval before their pages were reconstituted into the linings for pastries or other less salubrious matter. As Swift put it in his mocking address to 'Prince Posterity' in *A Tale of a Tub*, 'Books, like Men their Authors, have no more than one Way of coming into the World, but there are ten Thousand to go out of it, and return no more.'[4] Therefore, for the good reason that nothing of such writers has come down to us, they cannot merit as much attention as authors who left behind a more considerable body of work, either in their own writings or in their reception. Equally, it is not hard to find problems at the other end of the scale, in looking at writers who are failures less for material than for more metaphysical reasons. The very considerable achievements of William Cowper, for example, make him one of the most important poets of the second half of the century. Yet, on his own terms, most of his adult life was cursed by his failure to reconcile himself to God's judgement, after a number of serious breakdowns.[5] The religious intensity of Cowper's perceived failure is not easily separated from his poetry, but neither is it reducible to the more secular desires for fame and recognition that mark all of the subjects of this book, as Cowper was, in important and damaging ways, beyond either.[6] In the absence of a standard of measurement that is adequately inclusive, it has seemed more effective to explore a range of authors that, in different ways, illustrate the individuality of failure, in terms of the perceptions of their own need for success being unsatisfied, as well as their reception by contemporary and posthumous audiences. Failure in this sense is taken to be a cumulative lack of a level of success or recognition in a writer's career, measured in material terms, by the reaction of posterity, or by the author's own sense that they have not received their due. Whilst such levels of success or failure vary (all of the figures covered in this book had some notable works or some recognition), their literary careers gave them neither the material nor intellectual satisfactions that they required.

A large part of the interest of the careers chosen is that they all exhibit, in very individual ways, both the desire for success and fame, and the results of the complications of following that desire, no matter how unlikely or impossible its achievement, in a fashion that suggests both the inevitability of the need for literary fame, and the impossibility of its ever satisfying its aspirants. Another connection between the subjects of this book can be found in their relations to Samuel Johnson, which range from intimate friendship to antagonism. It is no surprise that Johnson, the writer who succeeded in spite of the many possibilities of material failure that surrounded him for so long, recurs in the lives of all these writers, not just because of the variety of his acquaintance and intellectual involvements, but also because of his own mutable status within the world of letters. Johnson's place as the archetypal literary figure by the end of the century was a reproof to other, less successful writers, yet it also showed the uncertainties of a literary world where he had been on a level footing with the subjects of this book for most of his career.

The first chapter deals with the life, works, and reception of Richard Savage, a figure immortalised in Grub Street folklore by the time of his death in 1743. Savage was an extraordinary case, being a figure who demanded that public fame and fortune were his due, mainly because of his claims to be the illegitimate product of a liaison between Earl Rivers and Lady Macclesfield. His literary works are tied in with very public announcements of this supposed birthright – to an almost unique degree for the time, Savage is the subject of his work. He represents an older, aristocratic model of the author as gentleman-amateur, though his personal difficulties and egocentricity made his fate analogous to that of the penurious modern hack. Furthermore, he was the subject of a crucial work of literary biography, his friend Samuel Johnson's *Life of Savage* (1744), an account that is of the first importance in debates on literary failure, the motives and needs of the aspirant author, the grim realities of their lack of success, and the delusions inherent in their search for fame. Savage's other peculiarity was his adoption (often through necessity) of different types of persona in his writing: he is sometimes a high-minded satirist, at others an inspirational bard, a defiant (*soi-disant*) nobleman, or a typically cynical Grub Street scribbler. What emerges from a reading of his works and reputation is a tragic narrative of self-delusion: Savage repeatedly conspires in his own downfall, by his deliberate lack of perspective or self-awareness, so that his life becomes a metonym for literary failure even before its squalid end, and he is more celebrated for his bohemianism than for the often perfunctory poems that he thought would win him fame. Indeed, the story of his tortuous career can act as a template for later doomed Romantic figures, and for the ever-prevalent celebrity and notoriety of the starving, penniless artist, destroyed by a malicious fate.

Chapter 2 is concerned with a very different sort of life, albeit one that also ended prematurely. William Dodd was the author of a number of unsuccessful literary works, who gained no little fame and many desirable connections as a clergyman. He became well known for his ostentatious sermons, which gained him many connections to an exclusive world of nobility. Unable financially to sustain his place in such a milieu, Dodd forged a bond on his former pupil, the Earl of Chesterfield, and (after being sentenced to death) became a celebrity – the subject of a huge and ultimately unsuccessful campaign for clemency waged, amongst others, by Samuel Johnson, that touched many levels of society that would otherwise have remained unaware of this meretricious, if charismatic preacher and literary hack. After his execution in 1777, the earlier writings of Dodd, along with his homiletic and ponderous works composed in prison, found very great success, thus reversing the failure of Dodd's literary ambitions, and indicating how Dodd's ultimate and absolute failure had recreated him as the sort of literary personality he had strived to become in his life. A reading of his works alongside the often melodramatic accounts of his time in prison and execution shows how Dodd was refashioned and represented as an important type of the age – a 'man of feeling' – and how the narrative of his life was revised as a sentimental fiction, with Dodd as unfortunate hero. This strange career of posthumous success indicates how the narrow boundaries of literary failure could be moved very easily, given the necessary celebrity, and how an apparently negligible literary achievement could be cast into a very different light, given the obscuring filter of publicity. Failure is not an absolute state but a concept that can shift according to the most unlikely circumstances. Moreover, Dodd's case shows how the understanding of a literary life is transfigured and refashioned utterly, once exposed to wider, more suggestive, and less discriminating media than literary criticism. The posthumous success of Dodd's career was entirely due to publicity, revealing the dichotomy of a literary world where genuine literary appreciation was hard to come by, and always overshadowed by notoriety.

The support of Samuel Johnson played no small part in the memorialising of Dodd. He was also central to the subject of Chapter 3, for very different reasons. Although Anna Seward, the 'Swan of Lichfield', shared a provincial birthplace with Johnson, she was also considerably provoked by his literary judgements, particularly in the *Lives of the Poets*, and spent a great deal of time and energy trying to undermine what she saw as the pernicious influence of Johnson's criticism. Seeing Johnson as the reactionary defender of a narrow and obsolete idea of poetry, Seward wrote repeatedly of a type of 'new poetry', embodied in the example of Thomas Gray, and much of her own early poetry shows this abiding influence. What Seward never achieved, though, was any widespread acceptance of her own critical views, and the purpose of this chapter is to show, through accounts of her voluminous writings (including a correspondence extensively rewritten for publication), why she was perceived to be an eccentric and provocative character in the literary world, and why her work never found the acclaim that she thought it deserved. Seward left some notable poems, and her critical writings (for all their somewhat rhapsodic nature) won some approbation; on the other hand, her failure to fully achieve her poetic and critical ends is evinced by the melancholy tone of much of her writing, both in prose and verse, which indicates a lack, signalled also by her restless reaching into argument and dispute, which was often deleterious to her reputation. For all her very real success, Seward failed to find the degree of acclaim and approbation she thought commensurate with her talents. Furthermore, she is indicative of a shift in representing a literary life, albeit one that works against her: the increased opportunities to memorialise her career (given the burgeoning interest of publishers in collected editions and correspondence) worked against her, and exaggerated her image as a literary eccentric. Access to more avenues of publication, for Seward, merely meant more exposure for her perceived lack of fulfilment – the opposite impression to that she wished to make.

Chapter 4 is concerned with a writer whose peculiar and verbose desire to recount his literary failure made his long career something of a tragicomedy for his contemporaries. Percival Stockdale (1736–1811) was born whilst Richard Savage was still alive, and just outlived Anna Seward. His many publications included poems, a play, much literary criticism, accounts of exceedingly trivial personal arguments, sermons, pamphlets against slavery, and voluminous memoirs. What all had in common (though in different degrees) was lack of success. Unlike many authors who faded into obscurity, Stockdale recorded these defeats and (inevitably) argued that their fate should have been otherwise. He did so with such little proportion as to overshadow even the minor successes, such as his perfectly respectable edition of Edmund Waller (1772) which produced in Stockdale the same somewhat turgid story of a conspiracy against him on the part of the literary establishment as the fate of the more wildly eccentric of his works (such as the self-published *Lectures on the Truly Eminent English Poets* (1807), a reply to what he saw as the calumny of Johnson's *Lives*), which were unread for far more obvious reasons. Consumed with resentment, and unable to admit the vast variations in quality and the problems in terms of tone and temperament of his writings, Stockdale is a fascinating example of an eighteenth-century literary failure, continually revising and justifying his role in terms of how he feels he should be remembered, and even wishing to emulate the miserable (yet memorable) homelessness of Richard Savage, if it might gain him his desired fame. Not the least valuable part of a reading of Stockdale's motley career is that his idea of literary success emerges as an important (and widely held) delusion, whereby the successful writer is removed into a kind of pastoral scene, and is remote from the vicissitudes of normal existence. This fallacy not only explains Stockdale's ceaseless and ineffectual striving; it also gives some indication of what the idea of fame represents to the aspiring author, and why they are so often disappointed with its results, no matter how meagre or apparently substantial. For Stockdale, literary fame needs to be more life-changing than is possible, and his example goes some way to show why literary failure is a necessary concomitant to our understanding of artistic success, as well as a prefiguring of how similar cases would be reinvented by a different, post-Romantic view of artistry, where failure is not hapless or redolent of pity, but a type of achievement in its authenticity. Stockdale's example shows how the eighteenth-century literary world adapted and changed very greatly in a few decades, until his final years saw him almost as a relic from a forgotten past.

The Conclusion compares these analogous and yet disparate careers, the contrast they make with the figure of Johnson (the central example in the century of literary fulfilment against very considerable odds), and looks at how the notion of literary failure at the end of the eighteenth century is transfigured into the more modern idea of the doomed Romantic artist, a shift that can be traced through the reputation of Thomas Chatterton, amongst others. The Romantic identification with the nobility of suffering and the ignorance of the public in the face of genius superficially covers the same ground as writers such as Savage and Stockdale, in their clamours to be afforded the respect due to their talents. Yet, in legitimising the struggling artist as a failure who will only be given their due by a kinder posterity, the effect of Romanticism is to make such literary careers as followed by the figures in this book seem mainstream and typical, rather than the exceptional instances of injustice that are the claim of their subjects.

In offering a range of experiences (from a would-be aristocrat to an extravagant and spendthrift clergyman, a provincial poet-critic, and an author obsessed with success in literary London) the book represents the shared experiences and tribulations of eighteenth-century authorship. Furthermore, it does so by taking works rarely if ever examined, let alone read closely, and in doing so describes a composite literary history of the century, looking at different qualities, values, styles, and judgements but from something approaching the bottom up; it gives an innovative reading of the familiar, from an angle that is usually ignored, and contributes to scholarship on writers that are important figures in their own right: all created substantial bodies of work, and became part, directly or otherwise, of significant cultural debates, even when their contributions were not fully recognised. It also, cumulatively, opens up new ways of thinking about a familiar period of literary life and history. Failure is far from being a new species of writing, but its wider significance to eighteenth-century British literary culture has never before been acknowledged, or examined.

The idea of failure

Amongst the millions of words published in English in the years from 1720 to 1800, there are a great many about failure. The remainder of this Introduction will look at some characteristic discussions of ideas of failure in the period from disparate sources, in order to provide a context for the chapters that follow, and to suggest how the subject of failure was, if not often addressed directly, a familiar undercurrent in all forms of literary culture.

Discussions of failure in the eighteenth century often begin (and end) with examinations of those monoliths of satire, *A Tale of a Tub* and *The Dunciad*. In the present study, Grub Street and its products are examined in relation to the works of Pope's friend and confidant, Richard Savage (who imitated Pope and, less consciously, Swift's hack writer), in Chapter 1. Grub Street, and its mythology, also has a latent effect upon much of the matter of this book; the proliferation of print so antithetical to the cultural ideals of Pope has consequences for almost every failed author, from Savage insisting on the powers of patronage in a professional age, to Percival Stockdale, who would later be mocked in terms that often deliberately recall Pope's sallies against the dunces.

The background to the emergence of Grub Street is a shift in the understanding of authorship during the early eighteenth century, from something approaching a vocation, usually supported by patronage, to the conflicting status of a commercial trade, which opened the author to all the exigencies that this entailed. Like almost everything, the idea of such a shift in the eighteenth-century British author has been questioned in recent decades: the more aesthetic argument concerns the larger role of the author as artist, which encompasses a change described (perhaps somewhat proto-Romantically) by Martha Woodmansee, who begins with the Renaissance idea of '"author" [as] an unstable marriage of two distinct concepts', being both a 'craftsman', a 'master of a body of rules, or techniques, preserved and handed down in rhetoric and poetics', and 'inspired' by muses, or by God. The change in eighteenth-century theorists is that 'They minimized the element of craftsmanship ... and they internalized the source of that inspiration.'[7] As Woodmansee goes on to point out, the greater related change of the period is in the material conditions of authorship. The traditional narrative that found (or more often assumed) in the eighteenth century an orderly movement of authorship from patronage to professionalism has been criticised as overly teleological and Whiggish: Dustin Griffin, to support his own thesis on the subject, has suggested that 'there was no rapid or complete changeover during the century from an aristocratic culture to a commercial culture, no sudden change from a patronage economy to a literary marketplace'.[8] Instead, there was a gradual, often contradictory movement, in which patronage continued alongside the increasing attempts of professional authors to earn a commercial living.

In an influential work, Brean Hammond has examined how 'In this period, conflicts between an older, patronage-based model of authorship as the result of prolonged study and immersion in the classics, and a newer model of professionalism gradually being constituted, are at their most dramatic.' Specifically, this drama is concerned with the struggles of commercial literary authorship to become accepted and viable: 'Authorship could only develop as a profession when it became respectable for individuals to live off their wits.'[9] Hence Hammond's investigation of the ways in which, from the Restoration, the fight to own (and be rewarded for selling) literary property becomes central to the profession of authorship.

As Mark Rose describes it in a monograph on the subject, the long arguments over copyright in the period are fundamental to understanding the authorial role: 'the representation of the author as a creator who is entitled to profit from his intellectual labour came into being through a blending of literary and legal discourses in the context of the contest over perpetual copyright'. It is therefore futile to attempt to separate the idea of the writer, in any simple aesthetic terms, from the material substance of their creations: 'the sense of the commodity value of writing is often just beneath the surface of eighteenth-century discussions of literary worth'.[10]

Rose relates the mid-eighteenth-century contrast between genius and mechanical writing with the contemporary copyright debates, where 'the task was to differentiate true authorship from mechanical invention and to mystify and valorize the former'. Linda Zionkowski has argued pointedly (in a manner akin to Hammond's project, though with broader brushstrokes) that this process of differentiation was very actively pursued by figures accepted by posterity as the centre of mid-century literature: 'instead of developing as a natural result of writers' financial independence, the idea of a literary profession was devised amid a context of debate ... on the formation of a literary canon'. The emergence of the literary profession 'had its roots in exclusionary concepts of literary labor and value concepts resting on the denial of certain features inherent to commodified print'.[11] Zionkowski's perhaps somewhat uncomplicated argument is that the writings of Fielding, Johnson, and Goldsmith about modern authorship are 'attempts to institute a guardianship over print', neglecting the lack of cultural hegemony, and the material and sometimes intellectual insecurity of these writers at different times, which makes it hard to view their plans as so deliberately designed to further their ideological ends. Similarly, Zionkowski's blanket description of 'theories of writing that restrict or limit composition' reduces and simplifies the mixture of observation, worry, and genuine bemusement about the burgeoning numbers of authors, expressed by Goldsmith, Johnson, and others in the mid-century.[12] Looking at the question from another perspective, that of reviews in periodicals, Frank Donoghue argues that it was not authors who made such decisions about canonicity: by the middle of the century, authors lacked 'a clear index of literary fame (such as affiliation with a patron had once bestowed)', so 'readers, an expanding consumer market, indirectly exerted considerable influence on the shape of the literary commerce; and reviewers sought to police both the production and consumption of literature'.[13] The emergent canon is malleable and controlled, in part, by its readership.

Such questions of authorial exclusivity are a reminder of an important general point concerning Grub Street and failure. In the famous works of Pope and Swift, and the less well-known satires that accompanied them, discussion of failure (in the representations of 'dulness' or duncery) often presupposes an inherent lack of talent in the writers concerned, allied to a mercenary bent that obviates whatever little skill may have been involved. Moreover, there is the tendency, followed up in many subsequent accounts that draw upon Pope and Swift, to place the impecunious and failed authors of Grub Street in something of a void, whereby their works become of increasing irrelevance to the infamous misery of their lives. The necessarily exaggerated fictions of Swift and Pope are thus taken as real, and their metaphoric creation of the area enters into the language as fact. The result is what Pat Rogers described as 'a picturesque story masquerading as truth', in which writers serve alternately as vehicles for sentimental pathos or thinly submerged voyeurism.[14] The fascination with the grotesque misfortunes of Grub Street produces a series of variations on Hogarth's 'Distressed Poet' which obscure any critical sense of the reality of writing; instead, authors mount, shine, evaporate, and fall in a moment, as if they were born in a garret with their rejected manuscript in hand, rather than the more complex patterns in which they endured and sometimes even triumphed over the vicissitudes of existence. Writers become not free agents of their own destiny, but slaves powerless to escape from the Grub Street miasma. The connection between the physical and mental discomfort of Grub Street and creative failure is nowhere better seen than in a staple of the myth, the poet and translator Samuel Boyse (1708–49), described in 1753 thus:

> It was about the year 1740 that Mr. Boyse, reduced to the last extremity of human wretchedness, had not a shirt, a coat, or any kind of apparel to put on; the sheets in which he lay were carried to the pawnbroker's, and he was obliged to be confined to bed, with no other covering than a blanket. He had little support but what he got by writing letters to his friends in the most abject style. He was perhaps ashamed to let this instance of distress be known to his friends, which might be the occasion of his remaining six weeks in that situation. During this time he had some employment in writing verses for the Magazines; and whoever had seen him in his study, must have thought the object singular enough. He sat up in bed with the blanket wrapt about him, through which he had cut a hole large enough to admit his arm, and placing the paper upon his knee, scribbled in the best manner the verses he was obliged to make.[15]

Boyse is the quintessential Grub Street failure, in that the story of his life (overshadowing brief mention of his works) regularly appeared through such accounts, into the twentieth century. A few small details are enough to suggest the tragicomedy: the hole in the blanket is the most well-known (as is Robert Shiels's claim, in the same account, that Boyse made imitation shirt collars and cuffs out of pieces of paper when he had to venture out), and is augmented by Johnson's description of his wasting 'the last half-guinea he possessed in truffles and mushrooms' to accompany his beef, 'eating them in bed too, for want of clothes, or even a shirt to sit up in'.[16] Boyse 'translated well from the French, but if any one employed him, by the time one sheet of the work was done he pawned the original', so that the exasperated employer would be perpetually chasing after his books.[17] As well as the familiar raising of subscriptions for volumes that did not exist, he also apparently pretended, Volpone-like, to be dying, whereupon his wife would collect money from concerned parties (a trick that inevitably wore thin rather quickly).[18]

Boyse and his shroud with its hole is a shorthand for all the iniquities of Grub Street, a morality tale where the vanities of the hapless author and the injustices of the hack-writing world alternate, as Boyse rolls darkling down towards the abyss. Narratives of his life are based around these extreme events. Yet even a brief account of the fuller picture of his life suggests that this mixture of tragedy and absurdity was only a small part of a difficult, but varied (and far from typical) career: born in Dublin, Boyse married at the age of twenty whilst at Glasgow University, and, after living off his father in Ireland, returned to Scotland, living for a time in Edinburgh, before setting off to London. As well as writing much verse, including *Deity*, a poem praised by Fielding in *Tom Jones*, he worked on George Ogle's modernised versions of *The Canterbury Tales* (1741). The moralistic strain of Robert Shiels's account of 1753 presents Boyse as a feckless and extravagant example of failure: it was alleged that the Duchess of Gordon found him a place in the Customs at Edinburgh, but he turned back from going to accept it, because it was raining, thus showing 'indolence of temper' and 'sluggish meanness of spirit'.[19] Boyse spent his time fawning around those who might give him some support, as he was 'abject in his disposition' (p. 167). His eating in a tavern on the proceeds of charity whilst his wife was 'starving at home' is 'an instance of base selfishness, for which no name is invented', and comparable only to the similar conduct of Richard Savage, 'with some variation of circumstance' (p. 168), in that Savage, at least, was not denying any family. Boyse is a selfish example of sensuality: 'if he could but gratify any appetite, he cared not at what expence, whether of the reputation, or purse of another' (p. 170). The moral warning reaches its height in pointing out that

'To such distresses must that man be driven, who is destitute of prudence to direct the effects of his genius' (p. 171). Not that Shiels admits of much genius in Boyse. Shiels's opinion of *Deity* is the same as his judgement on its creator: its 'shining lines' and 'elevated sentiments' are undermined by its being 'without a plan, or any connexion of parts, for it may be read either backwards or forwards, as the reader pleases' (p. 173). Shiels's condemnation of Boyse's wasteful and wretched career can only be read in one way, and its sense of condemnation of weakness of character as the explanation for failure is clear indeed. Shiels's account is a very simple assessment of failure, whereby weakness, selfishness, and the inability to deal with difficult circumstances become a way of simplifying the contingencies of a life, until judgement of personal qualities is the only significant factor.

Even with the uncertain veracity of such accounts, it would seem that the circumstances of Boyse's life were disastrous before he reached London, yet in later sentimental retellings of his tale the warning is lost amongst the concentration on the visceral miseries of Grub Street. Hence the most notable (and only lasting) anecdote concerning Boyse being that of his ingenious blanket, where the physical difficulty of Boyse in writing anything, sans clothes and money, removes all dignity or sense of control over what he produces; this, apparently, is the lowest point of failure, where the very materials of your art are only usable in such a bathetic manner. The problem with many accounts of Boyse is that, as Rogers says, 'he was as far from being representative' of Grub Street 'as Johnson himself', and that the 'absurdities which grew up around his name indicate a desire to make the hack figure at once stranger and yet more lovable than he was in reality'.[20]

Failure in the abstract and in practice

Tales of Boyse's misfortunes are the apogee of one way of talking about literary failure, which offers a very tangible and yet distorted manner of describing art: in such criticism, which is predominantly biographical, actual artistic creativity is placed in the background, and the major concern is instead a rather pious moralising over weaknesses of character or temperament in the failed writer; sometimes, too, such failings are made the subject of sentimental regret. This forms a contrast to other, more abstracted discussions of literary success and failure in the century. Whereas many different kinds of moral, philosophical, and critical work touch on failure, other than in outright denunciations, homilies, or specific studies (the most important of which, Johnson's *Life of Savage*, uses its example to make greater moral points), the issue of why and how writers fail either has a direct biographical element, or is side-stepped. One such common area in which failure is a latent presence is the idea of artistic ambition, already touched upon by Walter Scott's fears of the neurotically successful or the failed author being consumed by self-conceit. As will become clear in this study, self-awareness (or its absence) is a key element in understanding literature associated with failure. This can also be seen in more general comments about the ambitions of those who choose writing for a career.

An account of the workings of the literary world is provided by David Hume, in 'Of the Rise and Progress of the Arts and Sciences', an essay that has much suggestive matter about the nature of literary emulation of the ancients, and the need for native tradition. On the subject of literary ambition, Hume's views are as follows:

> A man's genius is always, in the beginning of life, as much unknown to himself as to others; and it is only after frequent trials, attended with success, that he dares think himself equal to those undertakings, in which those who have succeeded have fixed the admiration of mankind. If his own nation be already possessed of many models of eloquence, he naturally compares his own juvenile exercises with these, and, being sensible of the great disproportion, is discouraged from any further attempts, and never aims at a rivalship with those authors whom he so much admires. A noble emulation is the source of every excellence. Admiration and modesty naturally extinguish this emulation; and no one is so liable to an excess of admiration and modesty as a truly great genius.[21]

What is striking here is the assumption of literary authority as a fixed entity: the aspirant artist copies great predecessors, discovers the level of their own genius, and if it is lacking by comparison, is naturally 'discouraged' from further competition. There is an obvious contrast with Scriblerian mockery of the vanities of the perpetually self-deluded, where writers never know where to stop. (Equally, this refined process takes us a long way from the miseries of Samuel Boyse, even though it was published just two years after Robert Shiels had seen him struggle with his blanket.) For Hume, on the other hand, if a 'noble emulation' encourages writers to reach such great heights, this source of artistic ambition is then extinguished by the 'modesty' which is a hallmark of true artistic excellence. The more cynical reader might consider what happens to those who are not convinced of the 'disproportion' between their work and its greater predecessors, and who, far from being discouraged, are spurred on to try to affirm their supposed genius – those, in other words, who lack the equilibrium of the awareness of their own talents that Hume takes for granted. Such an idea of artistic progress is dependent upon a fixed idea of evaluation, an agreed standard of excellence that superannuates less gifted writers, and stops them from wasting their time. In positing a natural and consenting process of retirement by unsuccessful writers, Hume presents an artistic world that would seem very favourable to publishers suffering the vanities of unsuccessful authors, one where failure is recognised and absents itself, politely.

Such a consensual agreement about how artistic emulation would efface its less successful members is unlikely to have ever existed in any milieu, of course. A similar message concerning natural talent, but with a more hardened sense of the realities that ensue regarding its distribution, is found in a very different Scottish philosopher some forty years later. James Beattie's discussion of the imaginative powers (in his 'On Memory and Imagination' of 1783) includes a suggestive account of the origins and workings of genius, in all its worldly forms. For Beattie, genius is an imaginative 'talent for invention' that 'is not a common, but rather a rare accomplishment', and this is no bad thing:

> All men are teachable; but few possess the power of useful invention. Such is the will of our Creator. And it is right that it should be so. Life has oft been likened to a warfare: and civil society may in this respect be compared to an army; that in it there must be some to contrive and command, but that far the greater number have nothing to do but obey.[22]

These are not views that would find favour with modern sociologists, but they are pertinent in terms of what the limits of eighteenth-century ambition were felt to be for most, and show far more awareness of the likelihood of human agency upsetting the artistic scheme than Hume's. There are qualifications: Beattie envisages 'great genius' being 'exerted in improving the inventions of another' (p. 149), in, for example, producing an accessible account of Newton's theories; though this is a lesser example of imaginative power, it is no less valuable for that. The mistake, for him, is to pretend that everyone can do the same things to the equal degree of excellence:

> Arts there are, and sciences, wherein any man of sense, who is willing to be industrious, may make such proficiency as will enable him to perform in them with reputation... But to command a fleet, or an army, to preside in a court of justice, or lay down rules for improving commerce or agriculture, are offices, which can fall to the share of very few, and for which not one, perhaps, in a thousand is fully qualified, even though he receives a suitable education. (p. 150)

All do not all things well. Consequently, the genius of a Homer, Newton, Handel, or Raphael is not to be emulated by most: 'how many poets, painters, musicians, philosophers, and historians, and those too of considerable ingenuity, have endeavoured to reach the merits of these great masters, and found after all, that they were in pursuit of what they could never attain!' Accordingly, a 'man of moderate talents may learn to perform with applause in several arts', but will lack 'a particular and distinguishing Genius, which learning may improve, but cannot bestow' (pp. 152–3). Beattie notes something else about the pantheon of the great that is of pragmatic relevance:

> Genius and greatness are almost equally exposed to the assaults of envy: both must encounter mortifications, that are not known to the majority of mankind: and both are liable to the influence of a restless ambition, which is often fatal to happiness, and not always friendly to one's worldly interest. Mediocrity of talents, as well as of fortune, seems indeed to be the most desirable state, to those who have no other wish, than to be happy and useful (p. 154)

Instead of admiration and modesty marking the relationships of the talented with their lesser brethren, the 'assaults of envy' are compounded by the often destructive restlessness which makes even the successful apparently unhappy. This shows Beattie's acknowledgement that genius in itself neither provides happiness, nor insures against the restlessness of the sort of ambition which is not easily satisfied. (A further problem implied, though not addressed, is the fate of genius that may well have to wait some time before its successful recognition.) Beattie's solution is to not join in the game at all; unfortunately, this state of ignorance is something, for him, which you are born into, and cannot simply be acquired by the deliberate shedding of your self-consciousness or pretensions. As in the homily of Robinson Crusoe's father on the blessings of the 'middle state' of society, to be happy and useful are fine things, in the abstract, yet few choose mediocrity, or accept it as their lot. The unanswered question is what happens to those who are not content with such a middle station, but must advance their pretensions to greatness, howsoever limited their claims.

Both Hume and Beattie offer descriptions of how an artist should behave, and of what sort of relationship with their own abilities and vanity they should possess and maintain. It is not hard to locate contrary views of failure in the literary world, amongst authors with a more fundamental relationship with the subject. The world has never lacked warnings directed towards those wanting to write, suggesting that they might think again, and pursue a course of life more constant. Throughout the eighteenth century, it is possible to find such admonitions, usually delivered by those who have known the harsh results of literary failure. John Dunton (1659–1733), the bookseller and author who had found success in the 1690s with *The Athenian Mercury*, spent the last thirty years of his life writing odd works which are by turns apologias for his rectitude, complaints and jeremiads towards the injustice shown him by those who he had served, politically and otherwise, and screeds that denounce the literary world and its uncaring rulers. In his rambling autobiography, *The Life and Errors* (1705), Dunton expresses his belief that the life of a poet is entwined with a destiny of failure:

> But, alas! after all, when I see an Ingenious Man set up for a *meer Poet*, and steer his Course through Life, towards that Point of the Compass, I give him up as one *prick'd down by Fate, for misery and misfortune*. 'Tis something unaccountable, but one wou'd incline to think there's some indispensable Law, whereby Poverty and Disappointment are entail'd upon Poets.[23]

The fatalism that Dunton assumes towards literary culture means that he anticipates failure as the norm. Of course, there are specific enemies in this apocalyptic vision. In an even more peculiar work, the flyting and self-advertisement that passes by the name of *The Whipping-Post: Being a Satyr upon Every Body* (1706), Dunton has a vision of the republic of letters as a tyranny, ruled over by those who dare to judge and evaluate:

> Justice is administered by the Critics, frequently, with more severity than justice. The people groan under the tyranny of these governors, particularly when they are capricious and visionary. They rescind, they erase, or add, at their will and pleasure ... and no author can answer for his fate, when once he is fairly in their hands. Some of these are so unfortunate, that, through the cruelty of the treatment they receive, they lose not only their temper, but their sense and wits ... The Public are the distributors of glory; but, too often, the distribution is made with blindness, or undiscerning precipitation. It is this which causes loud complaints, and excites such murmurs throughout the republic ... The predominating vices of this state are presumption, vanity, pride, jealousy, and calumny. There is also a distemper peculiar to the inhabitants, which is denominated *hunger*, and which occasions frequent desolations throughout the country.[24]

For all his zany prose, Dunton does not represent literary failure as being a state where unfeelingly ignorant critics blindly punish idealistic and innocent authors; the writers themselves are no more free from 'presumption, vanity' and the other vices and prejudices than their critical masters, and contribute equally to the unhappiness of this arbitrary republic. It is the random and chaotic nature of its punishments and rewards (whether critical or by public reception) that is paramount – because of this inherent lack of justice, failure within it seems so inevitable and endemic as to make Dunton dissuade anyone from choosing to join it.

Such warnings are also found in a slightly later author who had written for years for his livelihood, often with diminishing returns. The main focus of James Ralph's *The Case of Authors by Profession* (1758) is on the status of an author: how the professional writer is looked down upon (unlike any other artisan), and is expected to live like an amateur, or, alternately, to be at the mercy of the market shaped by the booksellers and theatre managers. Ralph's argument is that of an experienced professional author, with considerable disillusionment about the cumulative lack of respect or remuneration he has achieved. The process of failure he describes is systematic, in that the literary market grinds down authors because it is in its nature to do so. The choice for an author is clear cut, if unappealing:

> Authors do not come as wise into the world, as they go out of it – Raw from the Schools, esteeming *Virgil* a far greater Man than *Augustus*, *Cæsar* the Writer than *Cæsar* the Dictator, and eager to inrol themselves on the same List, in Hope to be consider'd accordingly, they write, are flatter'd by their Friends; publish and are undone – Undone good and bad alike – These with Contempt, Those with Neglect; which is all the Difference between them.[25]

It is an outburst worthy of a literary trade unionist, even if Ralph's palette is not extensive: for all that he made an important claim for the dignity of professional authorship, his idea is that some are compelled to write, and are singularly unprepared to deal with the amassed cynical forces of commerce and criticism that await their publications. It has been claimed of Ralph that 'the very act of publishing such a vigorous defense indicated the beginning of a more independent position for the professional writer'.[26] For a study of failure, however, he is more notable for his pessimism; as a Jeremiah, Ralph shows the problem of the line of thought which expects failure to give up the game and go home. For, he argues, writers have no other profession, and have been warned before:

> But then alas! We *are* Writers; consequently incapable of taking up any other Trade; and consequently, instead of Examples, can only bequeath our Advices and Warnings to others. And, if Advice had any Power to convince or Warnings to deter, the Glut of Writing which has cloy'd the present Age, should be follow'd, like *Pharoahs* Years of Abundance, with a Dearth as durable. (pp. 64–5)

It is not as if the message has not been received, but still the number of people writing continues to grow, even when all the hazards of the literary life, and the likely prospect of failure are known.

One response to such an unhappy prognosis of the struggles of authors in an unfair world was offered by Oliver Goldsmith the following year, in his 'Introduction' to the *Enquiry into the Present State of Learning*. He claims that the prevalence of those complaining, as ever, about the decadence and barbarism of contemporary literary culture might well be assigned to more personal factors, rather than taken at face value:

> To deplore the prostitution of learning, and despise contemporary merit, it must be owned, have too often been the resource of the envious or disappointed, the dictates of resentment not impartiality. The writer, possessed of fame, is willing to enjoy it without a rival, by lessening every competitor; the unsuccessful author is desirous to turn upon others the contempt which is levelled at himself, and being convicted at the bar of literary justice, vainly hopes for pardon by accusing every brother of the same profession.[27]

This more adroitly identifies the motives behind complaints about the evils of the literary life. It combines the beliefs of Hume and Beattie in an absolute and (relatively) fair idea of evaluative literary justice, with a prosaic understanding of the actions of authors being not always high-minded, and often compromised by their own status, or bitter past experience. Goldsmith does not expect objectivity from a group of people who have spent their careers either criticising others, or being at the mercy of such criticism, having a dispassionate understanding of the reasons and frailties behind literary actions. In this, he echoes his friend Samuel Johnson.

The Johnsonian exemplum

Dunton's and Ralph's jaundiced practical descriptions of the literary world offer a different view of failure from its place in the abstracted definitions of genius offered by Hume and Beattie, where it seems unlikely that the failed artist will accept their necessary subordination to the great, or calmly channel their energies into a less attractive, but more socially useful direction. Many of the writings of Samuel Johnson are a corrective to such notions, not least because Johnson's discussions of ambition do not banish failure and limitation as oversights in a providential scheme, but rather view them as inherent problems for almost all human endeavour. There is no sense of any critical distance between Johnson (who had known his fair share of unfulfilled ambitions, and the difficulties of apparently straightforward accomplishments) and his subject, when writing upon failure and the limits of our powers. Moreover, in a practical sense, he offers a direct biographical link to the histories and anecdotes of the likes of Boyse and Savage. Thwarted ambition is the theme of some of his most celebrated (and most autobiographical) criticism. Indeed, some degree of failure, rather than being the disabling factor that stops mere mortals from pursuing the path of genius, is an inherent part of the creative act, as in the well-known ruminations from the 'Preface' to his *Dictionary* on what he has not achieved:

> Yet these failures, however frequent, may admit extenuation and apology. To have attempted much is always laudable, even when the enterprize is above the strength that undertakes it: To rest below his own aim is incident to every one whose fancy is active, and whose views are comprehensive; nor is any man satisfied with himself because he has done much, but because he can conceive little.[28]

The process of activity leads to failure, but this needs to be qualified, realistically, by an understanding that it is the original lofty aim that ensures even a partial achievement. The alternative is even less satisfaction than Johnson (who was harder on himself than most, particularly with regard to his own work ethic) allows. It is better to take what consolation you can from what has been done, than to waste time speculating on how you could fulfil the impossible, and reach (or surpass) your own aim: 'But these were the dreams of a poet doomed at last to wake a lexicographer. I soon found that it is too late to look for instruments, when the work calls for execution, and that whatever abilities I had brought to my task, with those I must finally perform it.' As in *Rasselas*, there are cases 'where something must be done, and where little can be said'.[29] Since, despite the necessity for action, whatever can be done will never be enough, all that is possible is the self-injunction to bear inevitable imperfection with patience:

> I may surely be contented without the praise of perfection, which, if I could obtain, in this gloom of solitude, what would it avail me? I have protracted my work till most of those whom I wished to please, have sunk into the grave, and success and miscarriage are empty sounds: I therefore dismiss it with frigid tranquillity, having little to fear or hope from censure or from praise.[30]

Not for the last time, it is of great significance that this acknowledgement of the inevitability of human failure is a result of profound personal awareness, and a refusal to countenance self-deception.

Such an understanding of the limits of what can be achieved, and what is necessarily lost between conception and fulfilment, means that Johnson is always able to forestall accusations of failure: by interrogating himself about the purposes and point of his endeavour, he moves beyond the narrow bounds of praise and censure. A writer with a less robust and self-critical understanding of human limitation would face the far more difficult problems of needing success and trying, unsuccessfully, to accept failure (to put the matter very baldly); the careers of the writers examined in this book all diverge from Johnson's, with none resulting in the very qualified satisfaction that he saw as his own accomplishment. What Johnson offers to the understanding of failure is precisely the idea that in acknowledging your limits, you can go some way towards tolerating them; this is not ideal, but the alternative is to delude yourself as to the real value of your work. To replace truth (however harsh) with the deceptions of the imagination is a far greater failure than the small one of not having achieved all that you set out to accomplish. Self-criticism is the greatest defence against such vanity, and for Johnson, it is combined with an inherent dislike of the cant that covers up its lack of meaning by resoundingly empty and vain claims. Hence his sincere dislike of Soame Jenyns's intellectual pretence of solving the impossible: 'I do not mean to reproach this author for not knowing what is equally hidden from learning and from ignorance. The shame is, to impose words, for ideas, upon ourselves or others. To imagine, that we are going forward, when we are only turning round.'[31] The tendency to assume more than we have achieved is a natural companion, for Johnson, to the desire to accomplish something of worth. And this, a regular theme of his periodical papers, he argues, is innate:

> He that compares what he has done with what he has left undone will feel the effect which must always follow the comparison of imagination with reality; he will look with contempt on his own unimportance, and wonder to what purpose he came into the world; he will repine that he shall leave behind him no evidence of his having been, that he has added nothing to the system of life, but has glided from youth to age among the crowd, without any effort for distinction

This natural state of limitation cannot be obviated by delusions of pride or the over-running of the imagination. The only answer is to take what small concrete results are offered: 'He that has improved the virtue or advanced the happiness of one fellow-creature, he that has ascertained a single moral proposition, or added one useful experiment to natural knowledge, may be contented with his own performance.'[32] These are similar to Beattie's terms of what constitutes achievement, but with an allowance for the apparently frustrated ambition to be rewarded in wide enough terms to retain individual dignity. The problem, of course, does not go away, and there are many times when Johnson's view of the wastages of 'confutation' in scholarly editing is a parable of all such wider striving: 'the human mind is kept in motion without progress. Thus sometimes truth and errour, and sometimes contrarieties of errour, take each others place by reciprocal invasion.'[33] Yet to face such unpalatable truths is in itself a sort of freedom from the more damaging delusions of the imagination.

Johnson's realistic understanding of failure draws attention to the very opposite state of mind, where a signal lack of self-consciousness is the most telling factor. It requires a great degree of humility to understand and try to resolve your failings, and the far easier (and more prevalent) solution is to blame other factors for your inadequacies. A great deal of this book will examine cases where such blame will be (often wildly) apportioned, and where Johnson's suggestion of calm realisation of what has been achieved, rather than what has been inevitably left undone, is ignored in favour of a childish belief in the absolute value or rightness of particular works. At its most extreme, in the monumental self-delusions of Richard Savage or Percival Stockdale, this self-righteous and egocentric view utterly rejects the thwartings and contradictions offered it, and supersedes a world of disappointment with its own version of reality, a kind of pastoral that rewrites and reinterprets a failed history. In Charlotte Lennox's *Female Quixote* (1752), the chapter supposedly written by Johnson, the argument of the clergyman who exposes the romantic fictions that have so affected Arabella, contains a comment meant to be taken further than its immediate context:

> It is the Fault of the best Fictions, that they teach young Minds to expect strange Adventures and sudden Vicissitudes, and therefore encourage them often to trust to Chance. A long Life may be passed without a single Occurrence that can cause much Surprize, or produce any unexpected Consequence of great Importance; the Order of the World is so established, that all human Affairs proceed in a regular Method, and very little opportunity is left for Sallies or Hazards, for Assault or Rescue; but the Brave and the Coward, the Sprightly and the Dull, suffer themselves to be carried alike down the Stream of Custom.[34]

As John Berryman so memorably put it, 'Life, friends, is boring', or at least monotonous enough in its necessarily regular patterns. The need for fantasy, like the urges of creativity, is in some ways an attempted escape from this unpalatable truth. 'I am afraid, Sir,' Arabella remarks soon after, 'that the Difference is not in Favour of the present World.' Indeed not: the wonders of the imaginary will of course be of greater appeal than the uncertainties of sublunary nature. But there is no question of choice – for the clergyman (a surrogate for Johnson's ideas), there is not a fantasy world to waste our time dreaming upon. Instead we must face our troubles in this one. Arabella's fashioning of a series of 'romantic' narratives to replace the inadequate variations of life is akin to the series of processes, which range from wish fulfilment to complete self-delusion, which compensates for the lack of the success which the failed artist feels to be their due. The imposing figure of Johnson stands as a corrective to such compensations, not without sympathy, but always with the reminder that these phantoms of the imagination will, if unchecked, cause more problems than they appear to solve.

It was nonetheless possible, during the eighteenth century, for a thoughtful and pragmatic writer to take some solace from a level of recognition and literary fame achieved, no matter how compromised, given that the arena of literature was becoming overcrowded at an almost exponential rate. The likelihood of literary failure was of course increased by the growth in the number of published and (unpublished) authors, and the concomitant number of these who could not expect to have any significant success. When, in *Adventurer* 115, Johnson styled the present as '*The Age of Authors*', he was in one sense only describing the modern truth that 'perhaps, there never was a time, in which men of all degrees of ability, of every kind of education, of every profession and employment, were posting with ardour so general to the press'. This endless search for 'literary praise', however, has a clear drawback: 'at all times more have been willing than have been able to write' and the 'dogmatical legions of the present race' seem to outnumber those of the past. In the absence of finding a reason for 'this epidemical conspiracy for the destruction of paper', all Johnson can do is hope that hopeful writers 'would fix their thoughts upon some salutary considerations, which might repress their ardour for that reputation which not one of many thousands is fated to obtain'.[35] To pretend otherwise would be to mislead. Johnson sees the boom in eager authorship as (in many respects) a waste and a misdirection of talents, which turns people away from their real abilities, even if he is less harsh about it than many.

Johnson's allowance for the necessity of both striving and failure is one kind of response to lack of literary success in the eighteenth century, yet for every reading that is nuanced, and understanding of the particular rarity of exceptional writing, and enormous odds against success, there can be found a dismissive riposte that sees failed authors as embodying the self-evident truth that lack of talent is, ultimately, its own form of definition. At certain points in the chapters that follow, it will be argued that an all too general lack of distinction is an explanation for the failure of particular works, but this is far from being the one convenient answer to the problem: a failure is not always generally accepted as such, in any evaluative or commercial sense. There is no such thing as a 'typical' failure, given that the factors behind such a description are themselves fluid and subjective; the unsuccessful writer may have had potential early on, or been popular for a season (as with the main subjects of this book), or their ostensible literary achievement, albeit minor, might have been compromised by their own insurmountable needs and goals. Moreover, a writer might have been tormented by perceived commercial and critical neglect, or more happy to suffer it, if in a comfortable station of life (as will be seen in the case of William Dodd, who always put money first).

Therefore, when an individual case is made to stand for a type (as in the case of a Boyse or a Savage), the very peculiarities of their lives give the lie to any predictive and easily intelligible pattern of failure. Yet, inevitably, the narratives of failed authors do show certain congruencies, including (in many cases) the inability to take criticism constructively, the all too common overestimation of personal abilities, and the exaggerated value of (and correspondent need for) literary success. This last shared quality becomes of signal importance in considering such careers: the question of why writers fail and what is at odds for them in so doing is intertwined with the almost metaphysical freedoms that success appears to offer, and why the very nature of such delusive vistas suggests a lack of individual fulfilment, and a greater absence of a belief in the worth and value of an individual life. To try to glimpse some of the reasons behind failure is thus a way of opening up some very large questions indeed about the real meaning and qualities of authorship in the eighteenth century.

One such prevalent question was asked by Isaac D'Israeli. In the 1790s, D'Israeli began his hugely successful anthologies of literary ana, and musings on the nature of authorship. Of independent means, an enthusiast for the literary life, and an avid collector of all materials pertaining to it, in *Curiosities of Literature* (1791) and *The Literary Character* of 1795 (both much augmented in subsequent editions) D'Israeli was keen to place the idea of literary genius on a pedestal, but not unwilling to notice when the talents of many leave them short of such eminence; nor does he rail against literary criticism as a necessarily corrupt and unjust institution. Perhaps as an enthusiast rather than a practitioner, it was easier for him to place the critical role in its perspective than the more embattled, who had experienced failure at first hand. *The Literary Character* does, however, have some pessimism: the literary establishment is not, for D'Israeli, a den of vicious and philistine critics, but is suffering some damage from the present over-abundance of writers. D'Israeli distinguishes the idea of the 'author' from 'those who intrude on the public notice without adequate talents, whose vanity listens to a few encomiasts whose politeness is greater than their discernment, or who applaud loudly and censure in whispers'.[36] If talent, as ever, is in the eye of the beholder, this disdain for ephemeral triflers is related to a subtext of much of his book (and of this one, for all its different aims): given that literary life is so inconstant and often unrewarding, who would choose to pursue it, lacking the ability to gain the consolations of renown that it offers? Surely, D'Israeli argues, 'no reasoning man would voluntarily place himself in a situation, fraught with burning anxieties, and with sickening disgusts; with hope mingling with despondence; with felicity so variable, that the utmost happiness of an author is as transient and rare, as those fine Italian skies we sometimes see in our unsettled climate' (p. 103). Yet such reasoning people did indeed continue to volunteer, sacrificing their personal happiness for the sake of a literary fame they would never achieve. Why they did so, having been warned against such a career repeatedly for the most part, invites speculation, but D'Israeli had already answered his own question, when in the preceding lines he had showed the (for him) very clear distinction between genius and normalcy: 'The modes of life of a man of genius are often tinctured with eccentricity and enthusiasm. These are in an eternal conflict with the usages of common life. His occupations, his amusements, and his ardour, are discordant to daily pursuits, and prudential habits. It is the characteristic of genius to display no talent to ordinary men' (p. 103). D'Israeli's idea of the difference between the genius and the norms of society is ostensibly Romantic in its separation of art and inspiration from the everyday, and its affirmation of such a divide. Yet all the evidence is against such a claim; it is a characteristic of many unsuccessful writers in the eighteenth century (including, as will become clear, the subjects of this book) to think themselves separated from the quotidian by their special talents. It was their misfortune to be writing before the nineteenth-century acceptance of the failed genius as a central cultural figure. Furthermore, D'Israeli's distinction is no less valid for a failure than a genius: for the former, belief in their own intrinsic artistic merit is in itself a way of life. The pursuit and affirmation of genius, of standing outside of the common herd, is often in failed writers laughably inappropriate, or destructive and delusive, as the following chapters show, but is also as prevalent as the confidence of genuine artistic achievement, and no less telling, in its details, about the nature of eighteenth-century literary culture. D'Israeli's demarcation unwittingly points out a key aspect of the sort of literary failure that I will discuss – the belief (which goes beyond and often contradicts reason) that the person is chosen, different, and special. For the subject of the first chapter, being separate from the norm, and belonging by birth and inherent right to a higher rank (both social and artistic) was the fundamental rationale of his life.

CHAPTER I

An author to be let

Very little about the career of Richard Savage (1697/8–1743), self-proclaimed 'Bastard' and supposed son of Richard Savage, the 4th Earl Rivers, and Lady Macclesfield, was ever understated. A pamphlet *Life of Savage* (written to gather support at the time of his trial for murder in 1727) attempts to make clear the uniqueness of his situation: 'Perhaps no History in the World, either ancient or modern, can produce an Instance of any one Man's Life fill'd with so many calamitous Circumstances'.[1] Hyperbole such as this, and the description of his birth, 'A Day, that he might very reasonably, in the Language of the despairing *Job*, have repented his ever seeing' (p. 5), ensured from very early on that Savage's public appearances would be viewed as a type, usually of the suffering and vindicated victim of treachery (on the part of his supposed mother). The success of Johnson's masterful *Life* of 1744 made Savage a different sort of emblem, with the naïve tragedy of Savage's pride a suggestion of a wider human failing, the inadequacy of most existences to match their expectations, or to accept their place with humility: 'Those are no proper Judges of his Conduct who have slumber'd away their Time on the Down of plenty, nor will a wise Man presume to say, "Had I been in *Savage's* Condition, I should have lived, or written, better than *Savage*."'[2] This ringing moral warning was ignored or misread, amongst what was perceived as Johnson's misplaced sympathy for his selfish and often ridiculous friend. Nine years later, Robert Shiels offered a corrective: 'However slightly the author of Savage's life passes over the less amiable characteristics of that unhappy man, yet we cannot but discover therein, that vanity and ingratitude were the principal ingredients in poor Savage's composition.'[3] As shall be shown, gratitude and its absence are usually at the heart of Savage's life, writings, and psychological engagement with the world; his demands for money and status and his obvious self-regard have often been simplified by his detractors into symptoms of his alleged imposture, yet these factors indicate something of the complexity of what exactly Savage felt he deserved.

Such condemnation bears witness to the fascination exerted by Savage's life in the eighteenth century and after (when he had become an exemplum of the romanticised squalor and iniquities of Grub Street). Even those who castigated him were forced to engage with the mixture of pathos and absurdity that surrounded him and his bohemian existence, to say nothing of the mystery over his real identity. Partly by dint of Johnson's *Life* (a novel and crucial aspect of which is its recording of a man who failed in almost every area of his life, and died a miserable death), Savage became the type of eighteenth-century literary failure writ large. His career offers tremendously compelling evidence of how a writer dealt with lack of success, and endeavoured to rise in significance, self-delusively, as their fortunes dwindled towards a penurious end. In Savage's writing, and in the many accounts of those who crossed this memorable man, is a record of a search for artistic legitimacy that was concomitant with the birthright that Savage hoped, in vain, to prove: his attempts to prove his status as an aristocrat (which took the surrogate form of a poet) show often very explicitly why he could not succeed in a literary marketplace that had shifted away from authorising the claims of the gentleman-poet, and instead placed a more mercantile slant on creativity. In this, as in many other respects, his is both a striking individual career, and suggestive of a wider trend. It is the business of this chapter to look at this career, both as a case study of literary failure, and as an attempt to discover the peculiar (and often overlooked) qualities of Savage and his literary work that made him the friend of Johnson, Pope, Thomson, and Aaron Hill, amongst others. These qualities are rarely consistent in his life or writing, and they often did Savage as much harm as good, but they made him a figure of great symbolic significance.

A power that fascinates

The influence of Johnson's *Life* on subsequent readings of Savage was profound, not least because of its managing to combine a real sympathy with subtle condemnation of Savage's actions. The result was a portrait that was a landmark in literary biography because of the roundedness of its attitudes towards its subject and implications.[4] Johnson's successors often fell short of such flexibility, and many commentators have never moved that far from a moral critique of Savage that resembles that of Robert Shiels, and overshadows Savage's writing, along with any pretensions that it can be taken seriously, other than as a reflection upon the posturing of an amoral charlatan. This has always been, in part, an incidental result of the extraordinary veneration for Johnson, which led his admirers to consider why such an embodiment of sense and moral rectitude should befriend a destitute poet whose name was so often a byword for scandal. Sir John Hawkins, never the last in the queue to condemn Johnson's more controversial acquaintances, was an important contributor to this critical trend, though his comments, a template for the easiest way of dismissing Savage, are unintentionally revealing about Savage's attractions. The key, for Hawkins, is that Savage had

> a character self-formed, as owing nothing to parental nurture, and scarce anything to moral tuition ... nature had endowed him with fine parts, and those he cultivated as well as he was able; but his mind had received no moral culture; and for want thereof, we find him to have been a stranger to humility, gratitude, and those other virtues that tend to conciliate the affections of men, and insure the continuance of friendship.[5]

Although it is couched in the tones of a sermon, this musing on the lack of moral inculcation of Savage draws attention to an important part of his legend – how his having, for whatever reason, no background of which to speak (other than a mysterious one) allowed him to emerge into literary and public life as a sort of antinomian force, a person freed from the normal social expectations and constraints of behaviour. It is obvious that Savage cultivated this idea of himself as a perpetual outsider, and it was equally cultivated by propagandists for his claims of birthright, but it remains of the utmost significance that his career was always viewed as one that could not be accommodated to (or judged by) existing models of behaviour or social norms. Aligned with this sense of necessary isolation is the reason most often put forward for Savage's charm – what can be called, in shorthand, Savage's charisma – which Hawkins tries (less than adequately) to describe:

> Doubtless there is in the demeanour and conversation of some men a power that fascinates, and suspends the operation of our own will: to this power in Savage, which consisted in the gentleness of his manners, the elegance of his discourse, and the vivacity of his imagination, we must attribute the ascendant which he maintained over the affections of Johnson, and the inability of the latter to pursue the suggestions of his own superior understanding. (p. 34)

Hawkins's priggishness cannot erode the impression of Savage's gifts, the elegance and attraction of his manner and conversation, which won him so many friends even when his loyalty towards them was repeatedly proved to be less than consistent (to use an understatement). Even this faintly absurd special plea, with the hypnotised Johnson powerless to resist the Svengali Savage, suggests why such a figure would find friends, even if he failed to keep them.

Consideration of such charisma leads to a more charitable view of Savage, one that sees his endless self-fashioning as part of his fantasy world (which may, or may not be an accurate description of his claim of origin). As his most authoritative biographer puts it, 'In his imagination he was by turns a peer of the realm, a divinely inspired bard, and a statesman of creative talent; and he wasted his life hoping for the millennium that never came.'[6] Moreover, Savage's imaginative shaping and projection of himself is the simplest way to understand his career, given that the evidence for his real identity and entitlement to his birthright has been exhaustively examined, and no one has been able to prove the question conclusively either way. The man himself never stopped claiming that his status, as the product of an affair between Earl Rivers and Lady Macclesfield, was revealed to him in his teens, by the finding of documents belonging to the woman who had helped to bring him up after he was removed from his mother at birth. The counter-argument of Lady Macclesfield is that whilst she indeed had two illegitimate children by Rivers, both died in childbirth. Other suggestions have been made to resolve these contradictory accounts, including that Savage was a child of poor parents who was convinced (or convinced himself) when very young of his 'true' nobility, and thus became a sort of unconscious, but not deliberate impostor.[7] This might explain what Clarence Tracy has described as the 'consistency and pertinacity' that Savage showed in upholding his story, 'to say nothing of his success in convincing almost all his contemporaries', which 'would have been possible only to a scoundrel of genius or to a man who honestly and deeply believed in himself' (p. 27). No one has ever questioned Savage's self-belief, though its source and its fruits are another matter.

If Savage's belief in his nobility did rely to some degree on imagination, then this has a more positive side. It is important to stress the imaginative faculty that many found so attractive in him, and that motivated Johnson in his very high praise of his poetry, concluding 'that his Works are the Productions of a Genius truly poetical; and, what many Writers who have been more lavishly applauded cannot boast, that they have an original Air, which has no Resemblance of any foregoing Work' (*Life*, p. 139). Such acclaim is so often overlooked that it is worth pointing out (as John Dussinger does, in a rare study of Savage's poetry), that Johnson's *Life* would be frustrated in its purpose in the absence of such judgement: 'without confidence in his friend's poetic talent [Johnson] would not have had a biographical hero at all, but merely a pathetic victim of delusion and misfortune'.[8] There have been many happy to accept the latter verdict, but the reader who goes further and engages with Savage's work, rather than the myth, finds it to be of a piece. The obvious characteristic of Savage's writings is that their 'original Air' co-exists alongside a dramatic quality, which takes the form of repeated attempts at the formation of identity and self-affirmation, in the teeth of criticism, censure, and the possibility of failure: there is hardly a line of Savage's work where he is not playing a part or trying on a role, and all such moments have the aim of vindicating his behaviour, or guaranteeing his own success by legitimating himself, artistically and otherwise.

In 1715, 'Mr Savage, natural son to the late Earl Rivers' was arrested for the possession of a treasonable Jacobite pamphlet.[9] This was the first public mention of such a son. Savage's first published reference to his birth came four years later in 1719, with the publication of his play *Love in a Veil* (taken from Calderón). In the dedication to Lord Lansdown, he remarks that 'It is my Misfortune to stand in such a Relation to the late Earl *Rivers*, by the Countess of —, as neither of us can be proud of Owning; but that is the smallest part of my Unhappiness, since I am one of those *Sons of Sorrow*, to whom he left nothing, to alleviate the *Sin* of my *Birth*.'[10] The mixture of deference and mordant wit (often at his own expense) is a feature of Savage's references to his case in incidental writings. Such references are designed to evoke real sympathy, making them close to the maudlin or self-pitying, though sometimes rescued by their sense of fatalism and self-depreciation, which gives a shrug of the shoulders at the injustices of the world. Yet the anger sometimes overcomes such intended urbanity, making them shrill, strident, and rarely as self-possessed as they initially seem. The question of agency is also very germane: this first description of his plight appeared when Savage was at least twenty-one, yet the effect of such hints and supplications was to make him seem, in the decade ahead, to be perpetually a young man incapable of controlling his own life (an ominous prediction for his future, in many ways). At the remove of three centuries and in a vastly more meritocratic era, it is indeed difficult to accept Savage's repeated plea that he has been deprived of every chance in life by the cruelty of his mother: Earl Rivers left him nothing, because he did not know of his alleged existence when he died, and the act that dissolved Lady Macclesfield's marriage in 1698 declared her children (though born in wedlock) to be illegitimate, because the product of adultery.[11] The catastrophic result of this was that Savage was supposedly denied not just his financial inheritance, but also the metaphorical (and practical) effects of nobility.

In many ways, it is this symbolic loss of power and influence that seems to come across most in his complaints. The height of wealth and influence to which he has been wrongly denied multiplies his sense of powerlessness. Significantly, the story of his 'true' origins would become in the future a release from and a justification for all his problems, providing an escape where he could explain his grievances away. It is noticeable how Savage indulges in metaphors that highlight his lack of control, so that he seems to enjoy such an absence of responsibility: there is something childish about Savage's expecting his care and income to be the concern of other people. The tone had not changed by the time of the collection of poems largely concerned with his cause that Savage collected and published in 1726, with the help of Aaron Hill and other friends; its original 'Preface' exposed the barely hidden purpose of the volume: Savage is 'thrown, friendless, on the World, without means of supporting *myself*; and without Authority to apply to Those, whose Duty I know it is to support me'. This powerlessness is extended into metaphor: 'So I came sported into the World, a kind of Shuttlecock, between Law and Nature: – If Law had not beaten me back, by the Stroke of an Act, on purpose, I had now been *above Wit*, by the Privilege of a Man of Quality.'[12] Two years later, having in the meantime been condemned for murder and pardoned, Savage's 'Preface' to his most famous poem, 'The Bastard', raises the stakes as to who should be responsible for him: '*when I am a little disposed to a gay turn of Thinking, I consider, as I was a* de-relict *from my Cradle, I have the Honour of a* lawful Claim *to the best Protection in* Europe. *For being a* Spot *of* Earth, *to which no Body* pretends *a* Title, *I devolve naturally upon the* KING, *as one of the* Rights *of his* Royalty' (*Poetical Works*, p. 88). Such sallies divided his posthumous audience, being received either as a witty mask for an understandable anger, or further irritating evidence for a lack of accountability.

A natural result of Savage's problems is his adoption (in lieu of his inheritance) of the status of writer and poet. The implicit idea is that his role as writer is a necessary substitute for the injustices he has faced, whereas his true 'Privilege' would place him above the need for such publications. This was hardly a unique position, as Dustin Griffin, in his survey of Savage's dealing with patronage, suggests: 'the idea that the poet is a gentleman, even an aristocrat, was a cultural convention still honored in Savage's day (although under pressure from the expanding class of authors) and within living memory a matter of fact'.[13] Yet conventions run their time, and the double bind was that Savage was in the dubious position of claiming a birthright that enabled him nothing; poetry was akin to that birthright, in that he would be successful at it, because he was (or should have been) a nobleman. As Griffin argues, 'he devoted his life to regaining what he thought was rightfully his, not money but title and regard. Furthermore, his attempt to reclaim his birthright and his *patrimony* was intimately linked, in his own mind and in that of his friends, with his obsessive claim on *patronage*' (p. 175). The many figures that helped Savage financially in his artistic aims were, for him, offering a proxy for the erstwhile rewards that his situation had denied him.

The natural aristocracy that placed Savage (in his own mind) above judgement would always be inherent in his poetic utterances, and made him (unlike the 'expanding class of authors' to which Griffin refers) expect success and recognition as a matter of course, in the same way as he expected to one day gain his true inheritance. In general, this self-righteousness had mixed effects on his literary career: it gave him an audience (an illegitimate nobleman was a valuable selling point), and energised his writing, though at the risk of turning him into more of a spectacle than a writer; in another, more damaging sense, it limited him, in his work's dependence on his life for its rationale: Savage declared that poetic recognition was in default of affirmation of his true dignity of birth, thus downgrading such praise as a necessary but limited substitute. The unhappy result was that Savage, whilst needing to be supported as an artist, perceived the role as a second-hand way of gaining his rightful place in the world. This explains a strange passage in the *Life* of 1727, which remarks that Savage

> threw himself upon the barren and unthriving Province of *Poetry*, a Science how ornamental a Flower soever it may be among the Qualifications of Men of Ease and Fortune, when display'd only for the Amusement of a leisure Hour, yet too frequently held in Contempt, when made the whole Business of a Man's Life, and set to Sale for Bread; and more especially from the Taste of the present Age, in which the Figure and Condition of the Author takes up a greater Share of the Reader's Enquiry, than his Parts or the Matter he writes upon. (p. 9)

The problem is that, for all the veracity of the misery of the life of the poet living by the pen, when compared to the dilettante productions of the men of 'Ease and Fortune', this distinction does not apply to Savage as simply as this (openly favourable) account would have it. Its suggestion that, being thwarted in his destiny, Savage chose the obscurity of honest artisanship in the form of poetry does not quite ring true. The complaint that style and appearance are valued over substance is hard to reconcile with the writings of one who so tirelessly declared himself 'son of the late Earl Rivers' in his works. Writings by Savage (and by his friends, in his support) are often directly concerned with 'the Figure and Condition of the Author', and very little else.

The description is also misleading because it implies that Savage, in joining the ranks of poets, entered into a world where the difficulties of making a living had to be met with resignation. Almost all evidence suggests that Savage responded to criticisms of his poetry as if they were extensions of attacks upon his birthright (which, in his own mind, they might as well have been), and as if his literary judgement was beyond question. In practical terms, this meant that any contradiction to his work was met with hauteur and incredulous disdain, as his writing was an expression of his nobility of spirit. It is a somewhat intransigent attitude.[14] Furthermore, if he could not legitimately claim either his 'true' identity, or be recognised for the genius of his poetry as an offshoot of it, his failure was compounded. In many ways, Savage demanded so much from the public personality that he cultivated that it is no surprise that it failed to either redeem his birthright, or enshrine his art.

The emotional Jacobite

The public persona of Richard Savage, 'son of the late Earl Rivers', does not appear in his first literary productions, unearthed in the 1930s.[15] These are five poems probably written in 1715, in support of the first Jacobite uprising. The extent to which the teenage Savage was genuinely attracted to Jacobitism is unclear, and the poetry that resulted is perfunctory. Political commitment was, later on, a matter of circumstance and expediunce for Savage, but these mediocre verses do relate to the crucial and all-encompassing need to authenticate himself. In this sense, it is less important whether Savage was a sincere opponent of the Hanoverian line, or a temporary enthusiast for the Stuarts, and more apposite that he was connecting himself with a mythology of injustice and the denial of rightful lineage. As Christine Gerrard summarises, 'Savage's convictions that blue blood ran in his veins, his fantasy that he was a "prince" wandering in disguise, forced to roam abroad until he could come into his own again and reclaim his rights, made him what can genuinely be described as an emotional Jacobite.'[16] It is an apt description of how Savage turned everything into a metaphor for his own plight, and adopted the worldview of the perpetual outsider, waiting (like the King over the water) for his time to come. It is more of a state of mind than a specific allegiance.

What comes across repeatedly in Savage's work is a strong attraction towards those who, like him, have been thwarted unfairly by evil fortune or the ill deeds of others. With Jacobitism, there is also a rich vein of recent history that allows for identification: as Gerrard puts it, 'Savage had also perpetuated his own personalized version of the Tory cult of Charles the Martyr' (p. 234), and it is through such identifications that Savage's later obsessions can be located within the Jacobite verses, as when he exhorts his countrymen:

> Shall the dear Native Prince from that King sprung,
> Like age accomplish'd, though in Years, but Young;
> The only Relick of the Royal Race;
> (Whose Angel's Nature would the Scepter Grace)
> Be forced to Wander through the World forlorne,
> And rue the time, he was your Monarch born?
> O think of Charles, and give the Youth his due,
> Think of that King that lost his Life for you.
> Think of the Uncle and the Sire Exil'd,
> Think of the Unhappy Parents and the child.
> ('Britannia's Miseries', *Poetical Works*, p. 21)

It is not the most convincing propaganda, and history has shown that not enough people thought as Savage wished. Although he does not envision himself directly in the martyrs of the past, the resonance of exile, injustice, and the denial of what is 'due' are the most memorable things about these performances. Hindsight lends itself too easily to such sentiments as 'Defend us Heaven, and to the Throne restore / The Rightfull Heir' ('A Littany for the Year', *Poetical Works*, p. 25), but the artistic emergence of Savage the 'Rightfull Heir' a few years later would be equally marked by instances of the betrayal of the legitimate, and the triumph of the treacherous.

Although it long ago disappeared from critical attention, Savage's play *Sir Thomas Overbury* (1723) was not the least regarded of his works in the eighteenth century. It was revived decades after his death, when Sheridan wrote a prologue and Richard Cumberland an epilogue for it, in 1777, which Tracy describes as 'virtually a Savage festival', as it also featured a second edition (by popular demand, it seems) of his works, which had been published in 1775. The play ran for eleven performances.[17] Its original appearance more than fifty years before was less successful, though notable for the playwright's own performance, as Johnson records:

> Mr. *Savage* was admitted to play the Part of Sir *Thomas Overbury*, by which he gained no great Reputation; the Theatre being a Province for which Nature seemed not to have designed him; for neither his Voice, Look, nor

Gesture, were such as are expected on the Stage, and he was himself so much ashamed of having been reduced to appear as a Player, that he always blotted out his Name from the List, when a Copy of his Tragedy was to be shown to his Friends. (*Life*, p. 24)

It is not the aesthetic incongruity of Savage's acting (which can be read between Johnson's tactful lines), so much as the indignity of having to appear as an actor that shames Savage. The author's erasure of his own name is a telling detail to Savage's peculiar mode of thought: doing something beneath you badly is irrelevant, compared with the embarrassment of having to do it at all.

The mysterious tale of Overbury (1581–1613), his opposition to the marriage of the divorced Lady Frances Howard, Countess of Essex, and his friend Robert Carr, Earl of Somerset, and his death in the Tower of London from poisoning, is a sordid and violent historical episode. Savage's telling of it suggests an interest in Overbury as a kind of failure – the righteous man destroyed by the selfish machinations of others – and his play is filled with echoes of the way that his own life had been manipulated (in his eyes) by the disingenuous actions of other people. He filled out the basic story of the plot against Overbury with touches typical of an heroic tragedy: an orphan, Isabella, is in love with Overbury; Lady Howard, despite her dark deeds against him, is also in love with Overbury (thus making her a potential surrogate for Lady Macclesfield, in ways that the play confirms); even Carr confesses his (platonic) love for the best and noblest of men, and his self-loathing at having helped to destroy him. Yet no number of plot contrivances can conceal the lifelessness of the play's verse and its distinct lack of characterisation. In a poem asking Aaron Hill to help tidy up the manuscript, Savage likens his anticipated alterations to the philosopher's stone.[18] Lavish even by his own standards, the compliment is not borne out in the final product. Its solemn action and depiction of suffering heroism shows the influence of Addison's *Cato*, but even more than that work, *Sir Thomas Overbury* represents not drama, but a series of mouthpieces for moral attitudes. When Lady Howard calls Overbury a 'Preaching Statue', there is an unintended truth to her words. As Tracy puts it, the characters of the play 'respond automatically to situations in the plot like puppets dangling on strings', and when they are 'crushed by their own errors the reader feels no pity, only relief at finding the stage finally rid of them'.[19] The play is neither risible nor absurd, but it is not in any sense dramatic.

Like many of Savage's more extended works, the play is not so much a cohesive whole as a collection of disparate extracts, some of which are especially noteworthy for his particular obsessions, such as the related ingratitude and treachery of the powerful. In this respect, the portrayal of Lady Howard is particularly suggestive. Lady Macclesfield was the target of some intemperate abuse from Johnson, whose loyalty to his friend led him to support Savage's unverifiable claims that, when he was a boy, she had tried to ensure his disinheritance by intending to have him kidnapped and removed to the West Indies: 'even those who had by a long Gradation of Guilt hardened their Hearts against the Sense of common Wickedness, would yet be shocked at the Design of a Mother to expose her Son to Slavery and Want'.[20] In *Sir Thomas Overbury*, Lady Howard becomes a substitute for Savage's supposed mother, and merits similar blame; the poisoning of Sir Thomas sees his friend Carr inveigh against his dishonest wife: 'Ten thousand plagues o'ertake her for the deed! / Oh! if she acted this unnatural guilt, / May all the woes of vengeance be her portion' (p. 181). Her crimes, like those of Lady Macclesfield, are a sin against nature. The play sets up a simple division between loyalty, love, and friendship, and the blackest ingratitude. The credulous Carr tells his wife that 'I must believe you' when she pretends that Overbury is trying to blackmail her, yet he then qualifies this:

> Believe you, said I! what must I believe?
> If you prove false! – if you traduce my friend!
> And wrong my faith! may sorrow blast thy beauties!
> May conscience rise in all her dreadful triumph!
> Scare every sense! and strike thee with distraction!
> (pp. 141–2)

As well as showing the play's somewhat gratuitous exclamatory tone, this is a signpost, telling any audience that she will indeed prove false, because such is the way with supposedly high-minded women of noble birth. For the follower of Savage's fortunes, the play exhibits a worldview where malice triumphs by punishing the claims of honesty and legitimate truth, with an almost exponential certainty. Thus, it is possible to compare Savage's own projected fall with the similar failure of the righteous Overbury:

> ... when the great man's glories shrink away,
> Shrubs, which grew under him, shoot up ungrateful,
> And brave him in declension – None assist him,
> No kind hand lifts him from engulphing ruin,
> But all join strength to press him lower still –
> (p. 145)

Consideration of the play's obsession with ingratitude, and the inevitable collusion by which the good are punished and their rights taken away, leads to a reading which finds traces of Savage's grievance even in Overbury's stilted lines of defiance: 'safe in innocence, I'll dare their malice. / To fly, wou'd be to leave my fame unclear'd, / My fame, much dearer to me than my life' (p. 161). That he is betrayed by those dearest to him, particularly his friend Carr, adds a sentimentality alien to the original story (to say the least), but it also touches upon Savage's bone of contention: being destroyed by those whose natural ties should guarantee their support. 'Name not forgiveness – nor expect my pity', Overbury tells Carr (p. 178), exclaiming somewhat implausibly that being imprisoned and poisoned by the actions of those dearest to you is worst of all: if 'any other thus contriv'd my ruin', he 'could have borne it with a manly patience', but as it comes 'from thy hand! my friend! my very self', the betrayal is the very height of misery (p. 179). In the unlikely event of the former Lady Macclesfield's attending any of the four performances of this stodgy drama in 1723, she would probably have seen in lines such as these that her alleged son's new profession of authorship was another channel for the main fixation of his life.

The muse's mansion

If works such as *Sir Thomas Overbury* contained hints of the overweening injustice of which Savage undoubtedly felt he had been a victim, the character of his poetry in the 1720s is more autobiographical, in that its ostensible subject either is, or becomes, the vicissitudes of the unfortunate son of the late Earl Rivers. This is complicated by Savage's adoption of the role of bohemian author, supposedly imposed upon him by the denial of his inheritance. This ensures that sometimes Savage will stress the absolute irrelevance of superficial status: 'But who to Birth *alone* would Honours owe? / Honours, if True, from Seeds of *Merit* grow', he exclaims to his friend, the poet and painter John Dyer.[21] Savage's praises of merit over inheritance may be less sincere utterances than reflections of his own frustrations, but this kind of inverted snobbery co-exists alongside the ostensible claim that unquestioned merit is due to nobility of spirit, which is a metonym for the more tangible aristocracy to which he belonged. He tried to square this particular circle by placing the idea of genius above adherence to the mechanics of art. In an earlier poem, he praises Dyer's skill at painting:

> Let the dull Artist puzzling Rules explore,
> Dwell on the Face, and gaze the Features o'er;
> You eye the Soul – there genuine Nature find,
> You, through the Meaning Muscles, strike the Mind.
> ('To a Young Gentleman, a Painter', *Poetical Works*, p. 54)

Here, the dichotomy between the sterility of the rule-driven and the freedom of Dyer's more instinctive inspiration is let down by the looseness of 'Meaning Muscles' in the last line, which gives little shape to the discovery of 'Nature' so confidently proclaimed. Such an assertion is of a piece with Savage's outspoken and antinomian attitude, which affirms the visceral idea of freedom from almost everything, yet this cannot be separated from his search for legitimacy, in that in praising 'Nature', he is also upholding the natural order, rather than the kind of arbitrary workings that deny 'Nature' its proper expression: natural law made him a nobleman, whilst the machinations of civil society made him a bastard. The problem comes when he declares poetry itself to be only a way-station for the greater things that nature has planned:

> Think not light Poetry, my Life's chief Care,
> The Muse's Mansion is at best but Air!
> Not sounding Verse can give great Souls their Aim,
> Action alone commands substantial Fame.
> Though with clip'd Wings I still lie flutt'ring here,
> I'd soar sublime and strike the Topmost Sphere.
>
> (p. 57)

Restrained, as always, by unfair circumstance, Savage does not mask the fact that his writing is only a temporary alternative for his more exalted place in the world, which seems here to involve some sort of statesmanship. Yet 'Nature' is profligate enough with her gifts for him to be a natural bard as a default for a natural lord: denied this entitled role, he took up that of the bohemian author, which, being often indigent, but equally often inspired and always charismatic, must have seemed the nearest thing, as it placed him beyond the norms of a society to which he believed himself superior.

Savage's failure as a poet was not absolute, and was more material than anything else, but it does often seem to have been a result of his peculiarly unhelpful attitude. It used to be easy to blame the unevenness of his writing on the extravagance of his behaviour, and to see this almost as a kind of masochism: thus, a distinguished biographer of Johnson could write that Savage 'constantly made his own troubles and obviously took pleasure in the experience'.[22] From Johnson onwards, images such as the vagrant Savage writing *Sir Thomas Overbury* by borrowing pen and paper from random shopkeepers have become part of a sentimental mythology, but, at any level of resemblance to truth, are no less telling about the effect of indigence on Savage's authorship.[23] On the other hand, what can be charitably described as Savage's self-confidence in his own poetic and aristocratic righteousness seems to have led to disastrous results, in terms of the quality of his work, and its reception. In a cogent summary, Dustin Griffin has argued that Savage 'tirelessly pursued literary patronage, enjoyed a considerable level of support, and lamented that he never received the recognition he so deeply desired and deserved'. In this sense, Savage was his own worst enemy, because he was caught between the idea of author as gentleman, and a more material way of judging literature: 'he didn't realize that continued success would require some entrepreneurial energy and application. Failing to adapt to an emerging market economy in which writing was something to be sold for a good price, he deployed an old rhetoric of entitlement, and wrote obsessively all his life about false patrons and deserving authors.' The key to this failure to adapt, for Griffin, is the old problem of Savage's expectations: 'What is most striking about Savage's reaction to his good fortune (despite the conventional professions of gratitude to his patrons) is that he considered a comfortable income simply to be his due'; his unusual strategy for patronage 'was to declare that he was literally the social equal of any patron in the land'. Ultimately, 'Savage seemed to think that he had no obligations', and it is not surprising to Griffin that in Savage's work, his failure is marked by familiar outrage, as 'the same figures appear again and again: the bountiful patron, the ungenerous tyrant of rank and wealth, the rewarded hack and the suffering true poet'.[24] Savage always dramatises the same parts in his writings (which are a reflection of the larger struggle of his life), and there is, as Griffin says, something unconvincing about seeing such stock figures held up to repeated blame or praise.

If Savage was prone to self-dramatisation, then a lasting role is that of the 'true poet', overlooked and betrayed by the acclaim given to works of less deserving and disingenuous others. If this role is a substitute for the entitlement due to a true gentleman, there is a logical problem with Savage's repeated poetic representations of overlooked worth and merit: the true aristocrat naturally received certain privileges and rewards, but the true poet cannot assume that his work is similarly self-evidently deserving. The consequence of such an assumption is the flavourlessness and lack of detail found in much of Savage's poetry, particularly when it is concerned with writing itself. A prominent example is *The Authors of the Town*, dedicated to Edward Young, and inspired by his four satires published as *The Universal Passion* – it appeared in the same year, 1725. It also anticipates *The Dunciad*, and Savage's providing Alexander Pope with Grub Street gossip. What it lacks, though, is specificity either in pointed satire, or in grounding an aesthetic in the sort of writing of which it approves.

In neither praise nor blame do its verse paragraphs connect or cohere, though (for someone with such a difficult personal reputation) Savage is best at describing his friends, such as Young:

> YOU, who delineate strong our Lust of Fame,
> These mimic Lays your kind Protection claim!
> My Frown, like your's, would to Improvement tend,
> You but assume the Foe, to act the Friend.
> Pleasing, yet wounding, you our Faults rehearse,
> Strong are your Thoughts! Inchanting rolls your Verse!
> Deep, clear, and sounding! decent, yet sincere;
> In Praise impartial, without Spleen severe.
> *(Poetical Works, p. 68)*

The allusion to Denham's famous passage in *Cooper's Hill* in the penultimate line has a precise sense of praise that is somewhat oppressed by the surrounding confusion: the meaning is obstructed rather than enabled by the local expression – why should Young be 'decent' and *yet* 'sincere', rather than one as a result of the other? And is it really a compliment to describe him as 'Pleasing, yet wounding'? Reversing the terms would at least sweeten the pill a little. A related problem concerns the moral high ground. It is vain to demand that a satirist be utterly consistent, but there were many reasons for the unpredictable Savage to refrain from attacking the very activities that were increasingly central to his Grub Street existence. The following passage from the poem indicates the problem:

> FIRST, let me view what noxious Nonsense reigns,
> While yet I loiter on Prosaic Plains;
> If Pens impartial active Annals trace,
> Others, with secret Hist'ry, Truth deface:
> Views and Reviews, and wild Memoirs appear,
> And Slander darkens each recorded Year.
> *(Poetical Works, p. 69)*

This gesture assumes a position that it should try to prove through its own example. The satiric authority he claims for himself is partly, however, a dramatic irony – as soon as the need for money grew, Savage would resort to these very slanders and secret histories himself. What becomes increasingly clear is that there is little middle ground in Savage's verse: writers are either noble historians or libellous Grub Street hacks, and the critics cited suffer from a similar lack of moderation, being 'Partial alike in Censure, and in Praise' and offering 'PHLEGM without Fire' (p. 71), the irony being that their lack of objectivity and inspiration finds its parallel in Savage's description.

The literary world described is a murky one, and a reflection of Savage's wider obsessions: in creating himself as an author, he engrafts the old struggle between the legitimate and the dissembling onto different models, including jealousy:

> Artists on Artists scoul with jealous Eyes,
> And Envy Emulation's place supplies.
> With Envy's Influence the dark Bosom's fraught,
> But Emulation brightens ev'ry Thought!
> Pale Envy pines, if Excellence aspires,
> And most she slanders what she most admires;
> Charm'd Emulation can, with Transport, gaze,
> Yet wou'd outsoar the Worth, she loves to praise.
> (*Poetical Works*, p. 76)

It is an interesting contrast: mean-spirited jealousy creeps into the place reserved for the high-minded ideal of artistic emulation. As so often, Savage presents a division between a platonic ideal of beings with nobility of spirit and sentiment, and an impossibly grubby world of baser passions in which they cannot exist. Ultimately, for all the claims made by himself for his poetry, Savage is too often unable to 'outsoar' the writers he emulates, such as Young and especially Pope: often Savage seems to put forward the outline of an idea, but does not flesh out its details. The result is the strangely directionless *Authors of the Town*, which joins itself to poetry of taste and discrimination through rather bald statements, rather than intrinsic poetic qualities. Having laboured over defining bad art, the poem can only somewhat superficially state what good art might be, in its conclusion:

> Here soften'd Virtue Rigours's Frown declines!
> Precept, enforc'd by just Example, shines!
> In each rais'd Tear a gen'rous Meaning flows!
> In each pleas'd Smile a fair Instruction grows!
> When we strike Nature, and improve the Mind,
> Those deathless Works a sweet Remembrance find
> (*Poetical Works*, p. 76)

This is more of a didactic plan for what good poetry should resemble than an instance of it. More generally, there is also a very particular lack of flexibility: whether writing to praise or blame, Savage is either unable to offer a balanced or pluralistic view, or unwilling to compromise the vehemence of his message.

The extremes of loyalty and treachery by which he often seems to judge literary acquaintances are perhaps related to his perceived familial disenfranchisement, yet what became something like persecution mania also produced a level of genuine praise that marks some of Savage's finest poetic moments. One such is a passage on Pope in the opening canto of *The Wanderer* (1729), Savage's longest and most interesting poem:

> Pope, the Monarch of the tuneful train!
> To whom be Nature's, and Britannia's Praise!
> All their bright honours rush into his Lays!
> And all that glorious Warmth his Lays reveal,
> Which only Poets, Kings, and Patriots feel!
> Though gay as Mirth, as curious Thought sedate,
> As Elegance polite, as Pow'r elate;
> Profound as Reason, and as Justice clear;
> Soft as Compassion, yet as Truth severe;
> As Bounty copious, as Persuasion sweet,
> Like Nature various, and like Art complete;
> So fine her Morals, so sublime her Views,
> His Life is almost equall'd by his Muse.
> (*Poetical Works*, p. 107)

Here, the parallelisms are less oblique or a hindrance than in Savage's other lines on the subject of poetry. Unfortunately, the material demands made on Savage's writing ensured that such sincere approbation would be somewhat diluted by the same level of praise appearing in more ephemeral contexts. In 1727, the demise of the same monarch whom the younger Savage had urged to quit his throne out of shame brought forth the following gushing sentiment:

> But why, O *Muse*! are songful Hours thy choice?
> Lost is the Life, whose glory lifts thy voice!
> GEORGE is no more! As at the doomful sound
> Of the last Trump, all *Nature* feels the wound!
> ('A Poem, Sacred to the Glorious Memory of Our Late Most Gracious
> Sovereign King George, Inscribed to the Right Honourable George
> Dodington', *Poetical Works*, p. 83)

The poem's attempt to gain patronage from George II and 'Bubb' Dodington, who had recently become very influential in Walpole's government, was a failure, but the writing of it prefigured the many future occasions when Savage would have to trim his opinions to suit his fortune, and let himself out as an author in ways contrary to previously held opinions and beliefs.[25] Shortly after this misguided effort at gaining some respectable income, both Savage's 'Fame and his Life were endangered' by what Johnson called 'an Event, of which it is not yet determined, whether it ought to be mentioned as a Crime or a Calamity' (*Life*, p. 30). Despite Johnson's neutral tone, as the result was Savage's imprisonment for murder, it should really be mentioned as both.

The *Bastard's* lot

The murder or manslaughter of one James Sinclair by Savage in a brawl in Charing Cross in November 1727 was the ironic catalyst for the fame that Savage had long sought. The circumstances behind the fight and the arguments over the responsibility for Sinclair's death have been very fully explored, with early supporters (along with Johnson) willing to extenuate every action of Savage and his drinking partners, and later critics being more circumspect.[26] The episode would lend Savage notoriety for his remaining sixteen years of life. In the short term, it won him the patronage of Lady Macclesfield's nephew, Lord Tyrconnel, and the apparent favour of Queen Caroline, who was supposed to be instrumental in the pardon Savage was given in 1728. The latter came at his lowest ebb, after his conviction, and was the product of the work of a wide network of well-wishers (including Aaron Hill) who were able to collaborate in their efforts; the anonymous *Life* of 1727, a key document for knowledge of Savage's narrative of his birth and origins, was written to help gain the pardon. Such concerted aid suggests the level of friendship that Savage could cultivate, and is a corrective to the legend of him as a perpetually rowdy and disagreeable spirit; as Tracy says, 'if Savage had actually been the sort of man modern readers usually assume he is, it would be impossible to account for the friends he was able to make among the most intelligent and respectable members of the community'.[27]

It is a point well made, but the support of Tyrconnel for Savage is a more complex issue: in some ways, it has been taken to indicate the former Lady Macclesfield's indirect guilt and a vindication of Savage's claims, in that Tyrconnel's subsequent support would be a way of ensuring that Savage's behaviour was monitored and his public statements demarcated. Alternately, Tyrconnel was breaking with his aunt because he either believed in Savage's story, or thought that he was at least deserving of patronage.[28] What is certain is that from some time in 1728 he provided Savage with accommodation at his London house, and an annuity of £200. There is no way of knowing how long this arrangement lasted, though the end of the friendship between the two can be dated to 1735, when Savage wrote a letter characteristic of a final breakdown in relations.[29] He had probably moved out of Tyrconnel's house before this, but it seems that, for a few years at least, what Johnson calls the 'Golden Part' of Savage's life gave him a secure income and dwelling: 'for some Time he had no Reason to complain of Fortune; his Appearance was splendid, his Expences large, and his Acquaintance extensive' (*Life*, p. 44). His pardon and subsequent security brought forth Savage's most interesting and accomplished poetry.

The only poem by Savage that in any way maintained its fame beyond the century of his life is 'The Bastard', written around or after the disaster of imprisonment and subsequent pardon, and published in 1728. Inscribed '*with all due Reverence to* Mrs BRET, *once Countess of* Macclesfield', it is the most substantial (and artistically successful) of all Savage's attempts to claim his rightful inheritance, going through five editions in its first year. The poem exploits his recent sensational circumstances to present Savage's case, which is essentially one of blameless accident: 'Is chance a guilt? that my disast'rous heart, / For mischief never meant must ever smart? / Can self-defence be sin?' he asks (*Poetical Works*, p. 91). It would seem that it could indeed, in the eyes of the court, but more important than such casuistry is the way that catastrophe had energised Savage's poetry, leading to the most celebrated lines that he ever wrote:

> Blest be the *Bastard's* birth! thro' wond'rous ways,
> He shines eccentric, like a Comet's blaze!
> No sickly fruit of faint compliance He!
> He! stampt in nature's mint of extasy!
> He lives to build, not boast a generous race:
> No tenth transmitter of a foolish face.
> His daring hope, no sire's example bounds;
> His first-born lights, no prejudice confounds.
> He, kindling from within, requires no flame;
> He glories in a *Bastard's* glowing name.
>
> (p. 89)

As well as their striking sense of boundless confidence, these lines sound like no one else, exemplifying the 'original Air' that Johnson found in Savage's verse. They offer an 'eccentric' but undeniably effective poetic expression. It is also perhaps significant that the idea expressed is one of independence – for the first time Savage does not lament the failure of his life and contested birth, but proposes to turn it to his advantage, finding a sense of liberation in not being confined in the wealthy but dull existence for which he had previously pined, where as a 'dull, domestic heir' he would 'Perhaps been poorly rich, and meanly great'. Instead, his ambitions will make a virtue of what has been forced upon him:

> Far nobler blessings wait the *Bastard's* lot;
> Conceiv'd in rapture, and with fire begot!
> Strong as necessity, he starts away,
> Climbs against wrongs, and brightens into day.
>
> (p. 90)

The idea that the antinomian Savage is made more powerful and substantial by his status and illicit origin than as a child of pampered wealth is one of

The Bastard's lot

Savage's most original dramatisations of his life, showing the influence of Edmund in *King Lear*. It is also a realisation (counter to all his previous debates on the matter) that the most effective challenge to the structures, institutions, and personalities that he had inveighed against was to break free of their influence, rather than seek to be absorbed within them. It is more appealing than his erstwhile attacks upon his mother and the injustices of the world. It does not last, of course – the poem begins by recalling such optimism, then moves towards its curtailment: 'Rashly deceiv'd, I saw no *pits* to shun, / But thought to *purpose*, and to *act* were *one*' (p. 90). The final sentiment indicates something of the poetic potential of Savage, when he shook off his obsession with personal injustice. The poem offers a glimpse of a more fulfilled writer, who did not confirm his failure by recurrent revisiting of the evils of the past, but who sought to fashion himself anew.

The major achievement of the period Savage spent under Tyrconnel's wing is *The Wanderer: A Vision*, his most ambitious poem, published in 1729 with fulsome thanks in its dedicatory matter to the 'Virtues' and 'kind Influence' of Tyrconnel, 'which has so lately been shed upon me' (*Poetical Works*, p. 96). It is not a work that lends itself to summary, though John Dussinger's is the best that has been offered: 'an unnamed traveller passes through a variety of landscape in winter and spring, and eventually learns from a hermit, transformed to a divine seer, the moral significance of his journey'.[30] If the poem had stuck to such a plan, it might well have found more readers, but the sublimity of its vision (influenced possibly by Savage's friendship with James Thomson), and a new interest in the perceptions of science, particularly with regard to light and colour, eschews such coherence. Some of the more conventional episodes from the title character's wanderings show that Savage's poetic identity, though temporarily removed from its usual haunts, still came back to familiar questions, as when (in the poem's third canto) the Hermit offers a critique of the morals of the inhabitants of a distant city:

> What are thy Fruits, O *Lust*? Short Blessings, bought
> With long Remorse, the Seed of bitter thought;
> Perhaps some *Babe* to dire Diseases born,
> Doom'd for *Another's* Crimes, thro' Life, to mourn;
> Or *murder'd*, to preserve a *Mother's Fame*;
> Or cast obscure; the *Child* of *Want* and *Shame*!
> False Pride! What Vices on our Conduct steal,
> From the World's Eye one Frailty to conceal?
> Ye *cruel Mothers*! – Soft! those Words command!
> So near shall *Cruelty* and *Mother* stand?
> (*Poetical Works*, p. 124)

Apart from the familiar ironic apostrophe to Lady Macclesfield, this is a far more effective, though no less melodramatic account of the denial of Savage's rights. Not the least reason for this is his also including scenarios worse than his own – to be 'cast obscure' is to still be alive, and without crippling illnesses, after all. Furthermore, the location of pride and hypocrisy as the engine of concealment at least attempts to diagnose the reasons for such actions, which he has usually in the past condemned simply as unnatural wickedness.

The Wanderer sees a move away from society, with Savage presenting a sense of isolation as necessary to the eponymous title character, and the other protagonist, the Hermit. There is something of an irony in the time of Savage's most secure economic comfort producing a poem about the rejection of the world, and its pomp and vanity. What comes across through the inset stories that the Hermit produces or offers in the bewildering landscape that the two discover is a search for transcendence above and away from the quotidian, epitomised in the strange and sudden transformation of a beggar into a 'Seraph Bard'. The divinely inspired bard is, however, somewhat disgruntled at the 'ostentatious Pride' of his 'sculptur'd Tomb':

> ... Are these the Gifts of State?
> Gifts unreceiv'd! – These? Ye ungen'rous Great!
> How was I treated when in Life forlorn?
> My Claim your Pity; but my Lot your Scorn.
> Why were my studious Hours oppos'd by Need?
> In me did Poverty from Guilt proceed?
> (Canto 5, p. 145)

His complaint appears to be based upon the lack of material recognition of his real merit when it would have been of use. He resembles an idealised version of the noble, unrewarded poet, brought low because of the vanities and corruptions of others:

> ... And yet when Envy sunk my Name,
> Who call'd my shadow'd Merit into Fame?
> When, undeserv'd a Prison's Grate I saw,
> What Hand redeem'd me from the wrested Law?
> Who cloath'd me naked, or when hungry fed?
> Why crush'd the Living? Why extoll'd the Dead? –
> But foreign Languages adopt my Lays,
> And distant Nations shame you into Praise.
> Why should *unrelish'd* Wit these Honours cause?
> Custom, not Knowledge, dictates your Applause:
> Or think you thus a self-Renown to raise,

> And mingle your Vain-Glories with my Bays?
> Be yours the mould'ring Tomb! Be mine the Lay
> Immortal! – Thus he scoffs the Pomp away.
>
> (p. 145)

The moral thus pointed, the Seraph Bard has served his purpose of being an indirect mouthpiece for Savage's grievance against the attacks on real merit back in the world away from his strange landscape. The matter of the Bard's diatribe is familiar – fashion and style win over talent and substance, in the eyes of egotistical critics, and no-one of real merit is appreciated properly. In another poem, the outburst would seem somewhat extraneous, but in the comings and goings of *The Wanderer*, it is merely another spirited but random set piece. Dussinger argued that 'as a "vision," Savage's major poem abides too much in the public domain of eighteenth-century allegory to profile the psychological growth of the writer'.[31] Although it is indeed such an abstracted and symbolic work as to seem to defy biographical insight, the theme of the redemption of the idea of the bard from the ignorant and cruel world can be aligned with Savage's other works, and the resentment that often dominates them. If Savage's fascination with legitimacy and entitlement generally hampered him when writing, the case with *The Wanderer* is slightly different, in that although his best work was submerged and somewhat lost within its whole, it was his attitude towards the poem (which allowed nothing to its detractors) that was the problem: Johnson famously described *The Wanderer* thus:

> It has been generally objected to the *Wanderer*, that the Disposition of the parts is irregular, the Design is obscure, and the Plan perplexed ... and that the whole Performance is not so much a regular Fabric as a Heap of shining Materials thrown together by Accident, which strikes rather with the solemn Magnificence of a stupendous Ruin, than the elegant Grandeur of a finished Pile.

What is less often quoted is the next paragraph:

> This Criticism is universal, and therefore it is reasonable to believe it at least in a Degree just; but Mr. *Savage* was always of a contrary Opinion; he thought his Drift could only be missed by Negligence or Stupidity, and that the whole Plan was regular, and the Parts distinct. (*Life*, p. 53)

It is no surprise to find Savage of a 'contrary Opinion'; misunderstood (in his own mind) as usual, he turns the blame instead on all his stupid or negligent readers. Rather than being mere pride, his refusal to admit of any fault in his design (or to design to explain it) smacks of the displaced aristocrat waiting for his time to come; it is a failure of artistic imagination, showing an inability or unwillingness to contemplate the opinions of others, or to question his own execution, in what was acclaimed as a remarkable, if uneven poem. The quoting here from Savage is one of Johnson's deftest and gentlest pieces of irony in a work riddled with them, and there are few more telling anecdotes about the self-imposed limits of Savage's career.

The poverty of bad authors

In *The Wanderer*, Savage (in Clarence Tracy's words) 'sang the virtues of retirement and contemplation'. The poem was his first publication after he gave up on his public claims to legitimacy in respect of the former Lady Macclesfield. Tracy surmises that he 'abandoned his campaign for recognition', because 'he recognized that he had undertaken more than he had the power to achieve'.[32] Alternately, Tyrconnel had bribed him into silence. Although he had achieved a certain level of patronage from Tyrconnel, by the time that relationship broke down and his level of comfort was reduced to indigence, the momentum of his claim (supported by the sensation of his trial and 'The Bastard') had long dissipated, and the difficulty of regaining such a cohesive body of support evidently proved beyond him. The sufferings of the bleak years after the break from Tyrconnel are prefigured rather eerily in one of the most striking works in Savage's oeuvre, one that is equally notable for a lack of self-awareness that also anticipates his later troubles. This is his prose pamphlet of 1729, *An Author to be Lett*. It is an obvious offshoot of *The Dunciad Variorum* (appearing only six weeks after it), given Savage's informal helping of Pope with regard to the circumstances and histories of various hack writers.[33] It is worth recalling that Savage had strongly criticised the unseemly haste and lack of scruples endemic in hack authorship. In *The Authors of the Town*, a few years before, he described his outrage at how

> IF Ruin rushes o'er a Statesman's Sway,
> Scribblers, like Worms, on tainted Grandeur pre[y.]
> While a poor Felon waits th' impending Stroke,
> Voracious Scribes, like hov'ring Ravens, croak.
> In their dark Quills a dreary Insult lies,
> Th' Offence lives recent, tho' th' Offender dies;
> In his last Words they suck his parting Breath,
> And gorge on his loath'd Memory after Death.
> (*Poetical Works*, p. 70)

It is a memorable portrait of the gothic figures which embody the carrion and appetite of Grub Street. The hacks running into the condemned man's cell to write a quick biography or 'last account' would become more than figurative – whilst in gaol in 1727, Savage was approached by such a biographer. Yet, for the bohemian Savage, there was always a proximity of circumstance to the targets of his satire, making it difficult for him to take the moral high ground, given his own unpredictable future. (Conversely, the financial independence of Pope ensured that he could never be so reduced, strengthening his representation of detachment and disdain in *The Dunciad*.) By 1729, rather than fulminating against Grub Street from a distance, *An Author to be Lett* took the ultimately misguided approach of expressing its evils through a persona. This is not the least of Savage's self-representations, because he chooses to inhabit the character of an utterly amoral failure. Johnson's description of the pamphlet is an excellent example of his criticism of Savage the writer doubling up as a veiled critique of the man:

> Of his exact Observations on human Life he has left a Proof, which would do Honour to the greatest Names, in a small Pamphlet, called, *The Author to be let*, where he introduces *Iscariot Hackney*, a prostitute Scribler, giving an account of his Birth, his Education, his Disposition and Morals, Habits of Life and Maxims of Conduct. In the Introduction are related many secret Histories of the petty Writers of that Time, but sometimes mixed with ungenerous Reflections on their Birth, their Circumstances, or those of their Relations; nor can it be denied that some Passages are such as *Iscariot Hackney* might himself have produced. (*Life*, p. 45)

The praise seems excessively generous (even Savage's kindest critics have not positioned the work in any pantheon of great art) but this does place greater emphasis on Johnson's crucial blow – that 'some Passages' are no different from those that Iscariot Hackney 'might himself have produced'. This shows Johnson's awareness of Savage's supposed self-reflexivity: that he is an author pretending to be a 'prostitute Scribler', and that this knowledge prevents him from being identified with the attributes of his persona. But, of course, as Johnson points out, such self-reflexiveness cannot just be assumed; what seems almost an afterthought is damning indeed in its implications: Savage's satire rebounds on him until, at times, his work cannot be separated from that of the hack authors he is satirising.

The splendidly named Iscariot Hackney, Savage's narrator, is not inclined to express himself ambiguously; the pamphlet's epigraph ties him to a more celebrated dissembler: 'Evil be thou my good', proclaims the title page, and although Milton's Satan is forcing himself away from the guilt of conscience, Iscariot Hackney had long since moved beyond such shame. This lack of embarrassment causes the most obvious conflation of narrator and author. What Johnson called 'ungenerous Reflections' on his fellow writers are potential symptoms of hubris in a first-person narrative. The so-called 'Publisher's Preface' shows Savage oblivious to this:

> I have also laugh'd at the Clamour of the Gentlemen of the Bathos against the Dunciad, for insulting them on their Poverty. I own that a Man's Poverty, when it proceeds not from any Folly, but is owing, (as it often happens) to his Vertue, sets him in an amiable Light. He becomes the Object of Compassion; and, if he bears his Misfortunes like a Man, instead of falling into Contempt, raises our Admiration. But when his Wants are of his own seeking, and prove the Motive of every ill Action, (for the Poverty of bad Authors has always a bad Heart for its companion) is it not a Vice, and properly the Subject of Satire?[34]

As Savage had for his adult life either lived off his wits, the meagre rewards of the pen, or the sporadic flow of patronage, the high-handedness here seems ill chosen. The relative comfort and prosperity offered by Tyrconnel at this time was probably reinforced by the security of Pope's friendship, but even this does not prevent the passage from being horribly prophetic in its misguidedness: in arguing that 'the Poverty of bad Authors has always a bad Heart for its companion' he makes no allowance for the lack of control that most writers exercised over their own fates. The best reply to this deluded and subjective sally was provided by Johnson ten years later, in a poem featuring a figure often seen as a portrait of Savage. The famous line in *London*, 'SLOW RISES WORTH BY POVERTY DEPRESSED', has pathos in its knowledge of how penury destroys both good and bad authors, to the point where any attempt at such dismissive judgement is offensive and dangerous.[35] Or, as Johnson puts it in the *Life of Savage*:

> That Mr. *Savage* was too much elevated by any good Fortune is generally known; and some Passages of his Introduction to *The Author to be let* sufficiently shew, that he did not wholly refrain from such Satire, as he afterwards thought very unjust, when he was exposed to it himself; for when he was afterwards ridiculed in the Character of a distressed Poet, he very easily discovered that Distress was not a proper subject for Merriment, or Topic of Invective. (p. 67)

This needs no explanation as an analysis of Savage's foolhardiness, and its unfortunate results. The result of Johnson's judgement is to make the shrill invective of Savage's 'Preface' wilt into a self-fulfilling prophecy:

> When this Lady, or these Gentlemen are ask'd why they abuse such and such Persons, their Answer is, they are obliged to write for want of Money, and to abuse for want of other Subjects. Is want of Money an Excuse for picking a Pocket? Or what is worse, taking away a Man's good Name? (*An Author to be Lett*, A3^v)

Savage's interest in a 'Man's good Name' was greater than most people's, but the degree to which he could stop his own from becoming synonymous with that of Iscariot Hackney was reduced, proportionately, with every such attempt to look down upon writers whose situation he had so often shared. Clarence Tracy begs to differ: 'In satirizing the literary hack, Savage was aligning himself with a respected body of opinion in his time, and counting heavily on his own widely acknowledged position as a nobleman by right. He may have been compelled by fortune to live by his wits, but by birth and disposition he was above such things.' Yet he also admits that 'by deliberately electing to write in this vein, Savage betrayed a certain insecurity in his mind'.[36] Moreover, even if the dismissiveness of Savage's attitude was vindicated by the contemporary idea of him as a true if frustrated aristocrat, there are other ways to show such gentility of spirit, including a polite reticence to scorn and belittle.

Whether or not the vociferous mockery of his writing showed a neurotic fear of his own origins, Savage would increasingly be attacked by the terms of his own satire. This begins when, in the pamphlet proper, Iscariot Hackney's boastful accounts of his own self-serving, mendacious relationships with his peers become hard to separate from Savage's posturing in the 'Preface':

> Tho' I am so ready to libel others, I am downright frighten'd if I but hear of a Satire where my Name is likely to be inserted. When a Person does me a Favour, I either suspect he has some Design on me; or think it less than my due, and that he is obliged to me, because an *Author*, for accepting it. I am very testy if I am not allow'd *Dictator* of my Company; nor had I ever a Friend, whom I did not in his Absence sacrifice to my Jest. I contemn the Few who admire me, am angry with the Multitude who despise me, and mortally hate all, who have any Ways obliged me. (p. 12)

This reads, unintentionally, like a continuation of Savage's attack on the dunces, in that the pride of both Hackney and Savage has raised them above those with whom they are actually level; this is amplified by another passage from Johnson that appears to be taken from both his knowledge of Savage and the evidence of the pamphlet:

> He was accused likewise of living in an Appearance of Friendship with some whom he satirised, and of making use of the Confidence which he gained by a seeming Kindness to discover Failings and expose them; it must be confessed, that Mr. *Savage's* Esteem was no very certain Possession, and that he would lampoon at one Time those whom he had praised at another. (*Life*, p. 45)

Loyalty is thus a joke for Hackney, and a shifting concept for Savage, whose career is littered with incidents resulting from the perceived ingratitude or betrayal of a large cast of characters. Hal Gladfelder has argued that even before Savage's most severe indigence in the 1730s, the reader of *An Author to be Lett* would be familiar enough with his tumultuous career to make the identification between him and his rascally narrator: 'the details of his own life, largely because of his repeated entanglements with the law, were too well known for any reader not to recognize the author's own lineaments in his scathing portraits of a desperate hack'.[37] Hindsight certainly provides the link explicitly, in Savage's subsequent travails, as Savage in the 1730s loses patronage and pension, and grows ever more penurious. Needless to say, Johnson's initial warning about *An Author to be Lett* is fulfilled, and Savage begins to live like his anti-hero. The tale of Savage's personal and artistic decline in the 1730s is a melancholy one, as he becomes so ravaged by his extravagances and sufferings as to almost destroy any artistic legitimacy. *An Author to be Lett* shows this process in microcosm, as Iscariot Hackney lists expedients to which Savage will in some instances resort:

> I have tried all Means (but what Fools call honest ones) for a Livelihood. I offer'd my Service for a secret Spy to the State; but had not Credit enough even for that. When it was indeed very low with me, I printed Proposals for a Subscription to my works, received Money, and gave Receipts without any intention of delivering the Book. Tho' I have been notoriously prophane, and was never at an University, I once aim'd to be admitted into Orders; but being obliged to abscond lately from the Parish-Officers, on Account of a Bastard Child, and falling besides into an unlucky Salivation, my Character was so scandalous, that I cou'd not prevail even on the lowest of the Fleet-Prison Parsons to sign my Testimonials. (p. 9)

The mention of the bastard child brings back the issue of legitimacy to the foreground, and it is appropriately connected to the theme of finding a livelihood; all the ones that Hackney suggests are shadowy and inauthentic, requiring him to dissemble and falsify in a way that recalls the disputed authenticity of his birth. The trick with the subscriptions is a more accurate prediction of what became a pipe-dream for Savage in the later 1730s, the publication of a collected works. As Johnson relates,

> This Project of printing his Works was frequently revived, and as his Proposals grew obsolete, new ones were printed with fresher Dates. To form Schemes for the Publication was one of his favourite Amusements, nor was he ever more at Ease than when with any Friend who readily fell in with his Schemes, he was adjusting the Print, forming the Advertisements, and

regulating the Dispersion of his new Edition, which he really intended some time to publish, and which, as long Experience had shewn him the impossibility of printing the Volume together, he at last determined to divide into weekly or monthly Numbers, that the Profits of the first might supply the Expences of the next.[38]

The grasping, voracious Hackney is replaced with the softer, more ludicrous and naïve figure of Savage childishly planning out his scheme for a book that can never be published. Like Samuel Boyse selling the very books that he is simultaneously translating, Savage's projection is the nadir of subsistence hack writing, in that the publication of each part of his nebulous *Works* is dependent for its existence on the sales of its companion. It is also a reminder of how the unevenness of much of Savage's work is a result of material vicissitudes, hence his not having the time or money to give it the care required, either in composition or revision. By this point in the 1730s, Savage had truly, like his fictional narrator, tried all means for a livelihood. *An Author to be Lett*, when read against his later experiences, anticipates the extent to which his authority as a writer became replaced by delusion, when he was far less likely to make light of the poverty of authors.

It is hard to avoid reading works such as *An Author to be Lett* retrospectively as part of the larger failure that Savage's career was to become, but the reasons for this failure lie deeper, in his not being able to measure the satiric authority he claims for himself. What was intended as a witty salvo in Pope's larger war against the dunces became a self-incriminating document resonant with the uncertainties of Savage's life as an author, and his wider fixation with legitimacy: in ironically celebrating the least authentic writer possible, Savage's pamphlet became damning evidence for his own artistic and existential failure to validate what he thought was his due.

The Volunteer Laureate

The precise reasons behind Savage's break with Tyrconnel are not known, but it proved a decisive factor in Savage's remaining years: with dry wit Johnson observed that the highfalutin thanks offered to Tyrconnel by Savage in the front matter of *The Wanderer* went the way of so many things in his life, when, after 'being discarded by the Man to whom he had bestowed them', Savage 'then immediately discovered him not to have deserved them' (*Life*, p. 59). Johnson offers Tyrconnel's criticism of Savage's intemperance, and cavalier treatment of his house and valuables; Savage's response was to criticise as 'Censure' Tyrconnel's request that he moderate his life. Johnson recalls that the Savage he knew slightly later declared his 'Resolution, *to spurn that Friend who should presume to dictate to him*'.[39] Like so much of Savage's behaviour, this stance asserts natural dignity but comes across more as absurd bravado, and was to prove more masochistic than self-fulfilling.

With the exception of *The Wanderer*, Savage's writing became more occasional during the time spent under the aegis of Tyrconnel, and not often in the best sense of the term. Time had forced changes upon the choice of subjects of Savage's writings: though much of his work had always been marked by a subliminal plea for patronage, the progressive decline in his fortunes in the 1730s saw an increase in his writing to order, with loyalty almost explicitly for sale. Inevitably, the opinions offered by his verse often directly contradicted his earlier loyalties or values; this stems from what Steven Scherwatzky has described as the paradox of Savage's simultaneous inability to accept his dependent state, and need to be supported by others. As a result, his political views 'could rarely be his own' and 'his citizenship' was

> always compromised by those he needed to please. Having been condemned to a life of dependence, Savage found himself struggling to survive as a writer under a political patronage system that had proscribed Tories from its rewards. As a result, Savage, who had once been a vocal Jacobite, found himself writing a poem in praise of Robert Walpole entitled 'Religion and Liberty' as well as annual 'Volunteer Laureat' verses in honor of the Queen.[40]

Savage's vain attempt at the laureateship won by Colley Cibber in 1730 inadvertently produced the annual poems to his old protector Queen Caroline that are something of an oddity even by Savage's standards. He was presented to her, and received an annuity of £50. The so-called 'Volunteer Laureat' poetry is notable for the eagerness with which Savage proffered exactly the sort of work that he had so often affected to despise as insincere toadying. But his need for money and the lifeline of patronage obviated his earlier principles. It is sufficient to note that these voluntary poems express their gratitude at the Queen's magnificence and kindness through the familiar subject of his misfortunes:

> No Loss I mourn;
> Though both from Riches and from grandeur torn.
> Weep I a *cruel Mother*? No – I've seen,
> From Heaven, a pitying, a *maternal Queen*.
> ('The Volunteer Laureat ... Number IV. For the YEAR 1735',
> *Poetical Works*, p. 206)

It was significant for Savage's fortunes (if not for the glories of English verse), that this source of patronage was cut off with the death of the Queen in 1737, and the removal of Savage's pension precipitated the last phase of his life.

Before this, however, there was to be more sporadic journalism and poetry. The choice of subject of much of the verse seems designed to satisfy a patron, rather than any sense of interest in the ostensible subject *per se*. Such calculation shows through in the finished lines, of course. Whilst usually directing himself to political favour, Savage also chose to shock in 'The Progress of a Divine' (1735), a scurrilous satire that describes the life of a clergyman who is the apogee of cynicism. Meant as a contribution to an argument between the Bishop of London and the Lord Chancellor, the poem (Johnson says) 'drew more Infamy' on Savage 'than any incident of his Life', a large claim for a pardoned murderer.[41] The poem's ill-judged account of the riotous life of the debauched man of God rehearses old grudges and introduces variants on them, as Savage bemoans the nepotism of Oxford and Cambridge, yet another thing lost to him by the denial of his inheritance:

>   Mark how a country Curate once could rise;
>   Tho' neither learn'd, nor witty, good, nor wise!
>   Of *Innkeeper*, or *Butcher*, if begot,
>   At *Cam*, or *Isis* bred, imports it not.
>   (*Poetical Works*, p. 191)

Such opinions are typical of this breezy poem that seems calculated almost to alienate any potential audience. The enthusiastic portrayal of a drunken hypocrite whose loyalty lasts only as long as his income is somewhat close to home:

>   The Man has many, meritorious Ways:
>   He'll *smoke* his *Pipe*, and *London's* prelate praise.
>   His *publick Prayers*, his *Oaths* for *George* declare;
>   Yet mental Reservation may forswear;
>   For, safe with Friends, he now, in loyal Stealth,
>   Hiccups, and, stagg'ring, cries – '*King Jemmy's* Health.'
>   (p. 195)

The attempt to satirise the mendacity of this disloyalty is unconvincing. The unsavoury divine chooses his opinions to please his masters, but although almost all of his behaviour in terms of satisfying his passions is objectionable and repulsive, neither in this passage nor anywhere else does the poem's mundane litany of hypocrisy and treachery seem alien from the compromises and dissembling inherent in the authorship of those who, like Savage, would write the life of a broomstick for money. It is a spirited satire, but an odd, malicious spirit.

In less splenetic style was 'Of Public Spirit in Public Works' (1737), which started out as a birthday poem of 1736 to Frederick, Prince of Wales. It is typical of Savage (and somewhat to his credit, perhaps) that this attempt at patronage and act of allegiance to the 'Patriot' opposition showed his naïveté at political intrigue, potentially alienating Frederick's mother, Savage's adored Queen Caroline (whose relationship with her son was the opposite of adoration), and guaranteeing no support from Walpole.[42] The fate of the revised version was told by Johnson: 'only seventy-two [copies] were sold', but Savage 'easily reconciled himself to Mankind without imputing any Defect to his Work, by observing that his Poem was published two Days after the Prorogation of Parliament', thus finding statesmen too busy for its contents (*Life*, p. 96). The ease with which Savage accounts for this setback shows a worrying sense of self-delusion that even Johnson cannot help but turn into gentle mockery.

The less wry side of such an inability to deal with the actuality of his failure was the gradual removal of Savage's little pockets of financial support, and the reduction of him to utter destitution. Around this period (1737–8) he also met Johnson, who describes Savage's descent towards vagrancy, in a famous description:

> On a Bulk, in a Cellar, or in a Glass-house among Thieves and Beggars, was to be found the Author of the *Wanderer*, the man of exalted Sentiments, extensive Views, and curious Observations, the Man whose Remarks on Life might have assisted the Statesman, whose ideas of Virtue might have enlightened the Moralist, whose Eloquence might have influenced Senates, and whose Delicacy might have polished Courts. (*Life*, p. 97)

This was highly influential in the development of the posthumous mythology of Savage's failure, and though his ill-fated attempts at gaining public influence or funding do not bear out Johnson's very high estimate of his talents, it is another reminder of how Savage's bearing, manners, and eloquence were always persuasive of greater things. That these were not fulfilled, however, is not the least due to the abiding contradiction between the independence he asserted and the requirement that he ought to be supported by the funds of others. What little evidence there is suggests that, even in the midst of dire poverty, Savage carried on with his chosen role as man of letters with his usual insouciance.[43] By 1739, though, there was little obvious relief for Savage. Then came the practical assistance of Alexander Pope, who wrote a letter on Savage's behalf, in an attempt at reconciliation with Tyrconnel. This came to nothing, because, as Johnson says, Savage refused to bend the knee, being offended by the 'abject' and 'supplicatory' tone of the letter, and refusing to 'write the Paragraph in which he was to ask Lord *Tyrconnel's* Pardon; for *he despised his Pardon, and therefore could not heartily, and would not hypocritically ask it*.⁴⁴ There is something tragic about a man who could find a point of punctilio so important in a matter on which his future depended. Such self-defeating pride would also characterise Savage's attitude in Pope's more successful plan, to raise a subscription that would allow Savage to retire to the country, and give him £50 a year.

Pope went to a deal of trouble for Savage, and displayed a lasting loyalty that required some tenacity, given the explicit lack of gratitude he found from Savage in response. In his letter to Ralph Allen formulating the plan, in May 1739, Pope talks of

> the Sending a Man to be Saved, both in this World & in the next (I hope). He is to cost me ten pounds a Year, as long as he thinks fit to live regularly, & if you will let him cost you as much, we shall want few further Aids, & I believe you don't care how long our Benevolence may last, tho' I think it can't many years.⁴⁵

The tone suggests seriousness of purpose – Pope and the subscribers are removing Savage from London and (it has always been assumed) from the heavy drinking that formed part of his increasingly vagrant existence. Implicit in the future dispute concerning this plan was a difference in purpose: Pope and his allies were evidently getting Savage out of the city to save him from his creditors and himself, whereas he went along with this scheme, then shifted his ground once funds ran low: Savage then claimed that he had never had any intention of staying in the country, but saw the subscription scheme only as a pleasant detour which would allow him to fulfil his plan to revise *Sir Thomas Overbury* and the long gestated collected works, before returning to literary London to reap the profits of his labour.⁴⁶ The unlikeliness of the latter scenario apart, Savage thought his retirement temporary, whereas Pope and his friends (paternalistically, but for very good reasons) thought Savage's permanent retirement from London and its temptations was necessary if he was to survive.

The difficulties of helping Savage are illustrated by the subscribers' attempts at clothing him. A tailor 'was sent to measure him', so that his benefactors could buy him some clothes. This 'was not very delicate', as Johnson says, but 'by affecting him in an uncommon Degree', it showed 'the Peculiarity of his Character', filling him 'with the most violent Agonies of Rage' (*Life*, p. 112). Clarence Tracy has offered this episode as evidence of the cultural divide between Savage and the modern reader: 'It is hard for us to understand the distinctions he drew between acceptable and unacceptable charities, for he had no reluctance whatever to living on the bounty of others; in fact he constantly demanded it as a right.' On the other hand, he would not be 'reduced to a state of infancy', and thus 'preferred to order his own clothes, even though he felt no desire to pay the bill himself'.[47] It is true that the apparent absurdity of Savage's overwhelming selfishness and arrogance would have been regarded by contemporaries (to some extent) as the pride of a nobleman in distress. Yet when all allowances are made for changing attitudes towards the (apparent) nobility, there is a point in Savage's case where his outbursts move towards a problem of pathology: even Johnson, for all his affection, is sometimes stunned by his behaviour, as the *Life* moves through Savage's most troubled years.

This can come across as fond amusement: when discussing Savage's own notion of his planned retirement, to Swansea in Wales, his mood, Johnson says, was typical in its optimistic visions of the future:

> As he was ready to entertain himself with future pleasures, he had planned out a scheme of life for the country, of which he had no knowledge but from pastorals and songs. He imagined that he should be transported to scenes of flowery felicity, like those which one poet has reflected to another; and had projected a perpetual round of innocent pleasures, of which he suspected no interruption from pride, or ignorance, or brutality. (p. 103)

This is a genuinely tactful and compassionate way of suggesting the extent of Savage's delusions, but also an acknowledgement of the peculiar innocence of his character: the fantasy is not the usual wish that someone else will support him, so much as a type of pastoral in which the gentility of his nature is free from the coarsening influences of modern life. As the simile implies, it is a poet's view of the country, and Johnson is right to both smile at it, and yet elegise Savage's wish for a less complicated world.

Independence

Such a vision was to prove elusive, of course, in Savage's travels, which created the same problems in different venues, being the usual mixture of high-handedness, supposed misunderstandings over money, and an eventual overstaying of an initially genuine welcome. Claims of an embargo on shipping because of the War of Jenkins' Ear that trapped him for a time in Bristol were convenient, and it seems likely that Savage used this as an excuse to stay (Pope refused to see him whilst in Bristol in 1739, but seems to have persuaded him to go on to Swansea by Christmas). As usual, the charm of his demeanour, conversation, and fascinating life story made him appealing to a new audience, though as ever he overestimated the value of novelty. His eventual time in Swansea, where he seems to have stayed for a year or so (courting in verse a celebrated local beauty, Mrs Bridget Jones), was uneventful, and then quashed by his decision, against the wishes of his subscribers, to return to London. He started the journey back and got to Bristol by 1742, whereupon he ran out of money, mainly due to the progressive decline in his relationship with the subscribers, held together by the good will of Pope. According to Johnson, ominously, 'He was now determined, as he expressed it, to be *no longer kept in Leading-Strings*'. In a familiar pattern of suspicion (overlooking the fact that they were keeping him alive) he complained that the subscribers were controlling him, and keeping him from his chance of prosperity in London.[48]

The refusal to be kept by others bespoke the familiar claims for independence that could not be supported; Pope's good nature in this regard is remarkable, and he continued to aid Savage until 1743.[49] Other income, however, was harder to find, and Savage's stay in Bristol was protracted by extravagance, which evidently wore through a collection of £30 that was made for him on his return to the city from Swansea. Rather than getting back to London when he could, Savage made the fatal error of reclining in the sun of his new welcome, not realising, as Johnson says, 'that this Ardour of Benevolence was, in a great Degree, the Effect of Novelty, and might, probably, be every Day less', and was 'encouraged by one Favour to hope for another', until all favours stopped altogether (*Life*, p. 118). It has also been posited that Savage's bohemian ways were inimical in any lasting degree to the necessarily ordered lifestyle of a mercantile city.

What happened next was predictable enough: as his means became exhausted, so did the generosity of his new friends. Signs of this can be gleaned from the appearance in November 1742 of a curious poem in *The Gentleman's Magazine*, called 'On Richard Savage, Esq., Son of the late Earl Rivers' and signed 'By a Clergyman of the Church of England'. This was one William Saunders, a canon of the cathedral and the only one of Savage's Bristol friends of whom much is known. Saunders's poem is a series of lavish compliments to Savage, delivered with a flighty ineptitude:

> Pleasing associate! still with winning ease
> He studies every method how to please;
> Complies with each proposal – *this* – or *that*;
> With time-beguiling cards, or harmless chat;
> Or moralizes – o'er the sprightly bowl –
> *The feast of reason and the flow of soul.*
> Quells the deep sigh, conceals the present pain,
> Which *less* philosophy could not restrain

It is not perhaps the summit of praise to be acclaimed for your compliance with '*this* – or *that*'. Saunders is so keen to set up Savage as a good man that he overstrains his praise, so that the final couplet proclaims, ''Tis mine *deserted* merit to commend, / Nor blush to *own* that *Savage* is *my* friend.'[50] The adoption of a defensive tone – Saunders's refusal to be embarrassed by his friendship – suggests that Savage was already in trouble around the town, and that Saunders's verse was a gesture of support (much good it did him, judging by his 'friend' Savage's opinion of him, as shall be seen). The feast of reason was evidently being outweighed by the 'sprightly bowl', and Savage was becoming debt-ridden and ostracised, reduced to only entering the city at night to avoid arrest by creditors.[51] This nocturnal existence could not last long, and he was captured by bailiffs in January 1743, and arrested for a debt of £8 at the suit of a Mrs Read, who kept a coffee-house.

Although he could not pay the debt, there was no reason why Savage should stay in prison indefinitely; one 'gentleman' offered to pay the bill but Savage refused.[52] In fact, confinement seems, rather ironically, to have given Savage some sort of structure and stability. Johnson includes a letter that he wrote to Saunders describing his arrest:

> I charge you, if you value my Friendship as truly I do yours, not to utter, or even harbour, the least Resentment against Mrs Read. I believe she has ruin'd me, but I freely forgive her; and (tho' I will never more have any Intimacy with her) I would, at a due distance, rather do her an Act of Good, than of ill Will. (*Life*, p. 122)

Johnson praises Savage's forgiveness here, which indeed supports the claims of his generosity of spirit over the years. His advocates in the 1727 *Life* had told the world that 'He is so far from a litigious Man, that he was always more ready to stifle the Remembrance of an Injury than to resent it' (p. 27). Unfortunately, two later letters from Savage in Newgate Prison were posthumously published, and the tone of these is much less magnanimous.[53] Six months later, he takes a different tack towards Mrs Read:

> As for Madam Wolf Bitch, the African monster, Mr Dagge, unknown to me, offered her, before he went to London, three guineas to release me. She asked time to consider of it; and, at his return to Bristol, sent him word, that she was determined to keep me in confinement a twelvemonth[54]

Savage's forgiveness of Mrs Read has evidently not lasted. If 'Madam Wolf Bitch' was at least insulted for obvious reasons, the earnest canon William Saunders got little reward for his friendship in the same letter:

Is the devil always to possess that worthless fellow Saunders? can he never open his mouth in conversation, but out of it must issue a lie? can he never set to writing a letter, but immediately a lie must drop from his pen upon the paper? ... As for the impudent manner in which he says I wrote to him, those words shall cost him dear, unless he retracts them, and asks me pardon under his own hand-writing. I intend very shortly to expose him in print, as he deserves

The image of the destitute Savage, in prison and with no means of release, spending his time accusing his acquaintances and planning revenge on them in print is typical of this sadly deluded man, who assumed himself to be in command of every situation, and who viewed even the most damaging of personal disasters as something of an irrelevance in his ceaseless battles to show the essential rightness of his conduct and character in every conceivable respect; in actuality what is revealed is only a mixture of defensiveness and paranoia.

The pattern of Savage's earlier life (initial acceptance and celebrity, followed by hardship, recrimination, and abuse) plays itself out in microcosm in Bristol. His final act of folly was frustrated: he had composed parts of a satire, 'London and Bristol Delineated', rumours of which had enraged the merchants of Bristol, and they had threatened to pay for his keep indefinitely in prison as a punishment, a threat that Savage 'looked on as bravado, and treated it with contempt'.[55] Edward Cave endeavoured to stop Savage publishing such an inflammatory and foolish provocation, and met with a response the tone of which (to give a flavour, 'neither, Sir, would I have you suppose that I applied to you for Want of another Press') would have seemed high-handed from a real nobleman, let alone an allegedly disinherited one, penniless and in prison for debt. It brought forth exasperated comments even from Johnson: 'Such was his Imprudence and such his obstinate Adherence to his own Resolutions, however absurd. A Prisoner! Supported by Charity!' For Johnson, it is more evidence of how the effect of any 'Opposition' to Savage was 'to heighten his Ardour and irritate his Vehemence' (*Life*, p. 132). The last of this vehemence was displayed in the poem itself, which shows a very real and pungent bitterness. It attempts to blacken the character of Bristol by contrasting it with the sweetness and light of London, the descriptions of which are a series of commonplaces which are far more favourable to the city than Savage's history there would suggest:

> Thus shine thy manly Sons of lib'ral Mind;
> Thy Change deep-busied, yet as Courts refin'd;
> Councils, like Senates that enforce Debate

With fluent Eloquence, and Reason's Weight.
Whose Patriot Virtue, lawless Pow'r controuls;
Their *British* emulating *Roman* Souls.
Of these the worthiest still selected stand,
Still lead the Senate, and still save the Land:
Social, not selfish, here, O Learning trace
Thy Friends, the Lovers of all human Race!

This liberal and high-minded centre of culture and community has as little credibility as the scorching account of its antitype:

In a dark Bottom sunk, O *Bristol* now,
With native Malice, lift thy low'ring Brow!
Then as some Hell-born Sprite, in mortal Guise,
Borrows the Shape of Goodness and belies,
All fair, all smug to yon proud Hall invite,
To feast all Strangers ape an Air Polite!
From *Cambria* drain'd, or *England's* western Coast,
Not elegant yet costly Banquets boast!
Revere, or seem the Stranger to revere;
Praise, fawn, profess, be all Things but sincere;
Insidious now, our bosom Secrets steal,
And these with sly sarcastic Sneer reveal.
('London and Bristol Delineated', *Poetical Works*, p. 258)

The friendly openness of London is replaced with this superficial, two-faced society of philistines. Savage attacks the Bristolians for their bourgeois parochialism, and their unsuccessful aping of the lifestyles of their more fashionable metropolitan counterparts. He turns Bristol into a caricature, filling it with small-minded yokels, but the tirade is also uncomfortably personal:

Thy courts, that shut when Pity wou'd redress,
Spontaneous open to inflict Distress.
Try Misdemeanours! – all thy Wiles employ,
Not to chastise the Offender but destroy;
Bid the large lawless Fine his Fate fortell;
Bid it beyond his Crime and Fortune swell.
Cut off from Service due to kindred blood
To private Welfare and to public Good,
Pitied by all, but thee, he sentenc'd lies;
Imprison'd languishes, imprison'd dies.
(*Poetical Works*, p. 260)

The figure of the mendicant prisoner, denied aid and instead punished with further cruelty by the unjust bureaucratic machine of the law, is the

Independence

last of Savage's dramatisations of himself. Self-pity disfigures the poem, making it a diatribe of personal grievance, invested with a paranoid fury. Its ending is suitably violent, cursing these 'human Hogs' and 'Upstarts and Mushrooms, proud, relentless Hearts; / Thou Blank of Sciences! Thou Dearth of Arts', and hoping the city will 'be, whate'er Gomorrah was before' (p. 260). This fragmentary poem is more of a comment on the sound judgement of Cave and others in urging Savage to suppress it, than any vindication of his own. As the last piece he wrote, it is indicative of how futile his struggles had become, as even his major artistic subject, himself, had lost any interest beyond the reflexes of anger and self-justification.

Savage died, in Newgate, on 31 July 1743. In a life full of ironies, it is perhaps not surprising that the evidence suggests that his time in prison was both one of contentment and something of a fulfilment of the pastoral fantasy with which he had been captivated on leaving London four years before. Unlikely as this seems, compared with the peripatetic and hand-to-mouth existence of so many previous years, imprisonment offered security from immediate want and some sense of routine and even relaxation. As Johnson says,

> He was treated by Mr *Dagg*, the Keeper of the Prison, with great Humanity; was supported by him at his own Table without any certainty of Recompense, had a Room to himself, to which he could at any time retire from all Disturbance, was allowed to stand at the Door of the Prison, and sometimes taken out into the Fields; so that he suffered fewer Hardships in the Prison, than he had been accustomed to undergo in the greatest Part of his Life. (*Life*, p. 126)

The splendidly named Abel Dagge was indeed kind to this unusual prisoner. Savage's last letters suggest that prison had brought to his wandering spirit some peace and a retreat from the constant rancour of his existence, helped in no small measure by the generosity of the keeper:

> One day last week, Mr Dagge, finding me at the door, asked me to take a walk with him, which I did a mile beyond Baptist Mill in Gloucestershire; where, at a public house, he treated me with ale and toddy. Baptist Mill is the pleasantest walk near this city. I found the smell of the new mown hay very sweet, and every breeze was reviving to my spirits.[56]

It is clear that Savage was adept at talking up even the most adverse circumstances. Yet here, there is less argufying and instead a description of temporary relief and contentment from a man who sounds aged beyond his years. The savour of freshness was as rare in Savage's mostly failed life as in his often angry writing, and seems even more heartfelt for it. For all

Savage's manifest flaws and absurdities, it would be nice to think that, amidst the disasters that his stay in Bristol brought him, in some way such interludes (and the attention and decency towards him that they imply on the part of Dagge) offered his troubled mind some peace before he died.

The tragic bohemian

Considering the litany of failure that comprises Savage's career, his influence was to be profound and unexpected. His story had always steered close to myth, and it became enshrined as a legend of failed authorship following the publication of Johnson's *Life* in 1744. After Johnson, Savage was remembered not merely as a byword for bohemian extravagance, or for the folly of outbursts of pride totally incongruous with his situation, but as a negative example that nonetheless offered more allure than a more mundane life with more achieved works would have done. The searching honesty with which Johnson revealed Savage's manifest faults also made Savage part of a larger pattern – the lost figure searching for more satisfactions than life ultimately has to offer – that could not but have great resonance and some degree of identification for his readers. His chutzpah and follies were still visible, but Savage emerged from Johnson's representations as a figure of no little tragic dignity.

A substantial part of this appeal was the nature of Savage's ceaseless attempts to legitimate himself, first as a nobleman and latterly as a poet. Common to both quests was his overwhelming sense that there was a real, immutable reward due to him, both for his birth and his talent (although it is sometimes hard to separate the two, and he made no effort to do so): if the 'true' nature of his circumstances and value of his writing were recognised, and if the mixture of malicious injustice and misfortunes that compromised and plagued his efforts were removed, then he would redeem his existence and regain his rightful place. A bald moralist such as Sir John Hawkins might reject such imaginings as vanity and delusions of grandeur, but even Johnson sympathised with them, and knew them to be widely held enough for Savage to be representative of a human tendency, a basic need for its unpropitious circumstances to be absolutely changed and improved – a natural enough desire, even if its fulfilment is impossible, and its motives ultimately childish in its abnegation of personal responsibility. There is in Savage's desire a sense of wish fulfilment (crossing often into self-delusion and fantasy) that locates happiness (whether through recognition of his birthright, or of his artistic claims) as a germane possibility that can appear instantaneously. Savage thought that all his problems could be solved at a stroke, and he could awake, and find himself if not famous, then contented with the realisation of his true identity and merits.

This idea of a sudden fulfilment recalls Savage envisaging his move to the country as, in Johnson's words, 'a perpetual round of innocent pleasures'. This dream of pure pastoral is analogous to his idea of personal and poetic success: not only would he be legitimised, made financially secure, and feted for his work, but all the myriad frustrations and difficulties of existence would be removed. The unlikely possibility that success could transform the terms of his life forever was, as will be shown in a later chapter, an influence on the similarly delusive Percival Stockdale, who saw Savage as something of a noble model because (rather than in spite) of his failure. That Savage's often miserable, delusive, and depressed life could stand as a model for the future is a paradox explained partly by the allure of the mythology surrounding him, and the resonance of the images of his outspoken and doomed struggle against a harsh and unjust fate (a struggle shared by many, albeit in a lower key). Moreover, Christine Gerrard's designation of Savage's emotional Jacobitism is very helpful in understanding his posthumous reputation. As he enters into myth, the hard-headed practicalities of Savage's claims to nobility (and the ambiguity surrounding it) are obscured, and the reasons behind his whole search become vague, until what remains most evocative is the symbolism of the 'true' and natural aristocrat wandering in exile, prevented from taking up his real position and rights. The specifics of his claims are thus aestheticised, and his demand for recognition becomes a peculiar inspiration for the unsuccessful being who believes (like Savage) that their life too could and should be transformed if only a series of injustices were not perpetuated, and if only the 'real' facts were known, and not distorted by such forces as malevolent reviewers, unscrupulous enemies, and unfeeling patrons.

The idea of the emotional Jacobite fits the aspirant but failed author precisely because it represents a mixture of vague rewards, the self-justification of futility and resignation in the face of a cruel establishment, and a glimmer of genuine hope which stokes their self-righteousness. It is a myth of reward that draws in adherents, as it can explain away failure, and offer either the allure of future success, or a justification for its absence that entails no responsibility on the part of the writer. Savage was neither the first nor the last poet to believe that the problems and disappointments of reality would all be instantly vanquished by the successful recognition of their real talents, but such attitudes became closely associated with him in the eighteenth century, because of the aura of Grub Street that he helped to create, and which was perpetuated by the success of Johnson's *Life*. His strange, failed, attempted career as both *soi-disant* nobleman and author (and the way he was memorialised) was of great significance as a cultural undercurrent: the future pantheon of doomed bohemian artists, from Thomas Chatterton onwards to more ostensibly Romantic models, down through the *poète maudit* and into the twentieth century, find some of their origin in the story of Savage's efforts to be a contender, thwarted, like so many later adherents to artistic fame, by injustice and unfortunate circumstances, in a manner which only adds to the glamorous pathos of their allure.

Yet for all that his failed ambitions helped make him a celebrated figure in posterity, Savage's need for artistic fulfilment was fatally flawed by his ceaseless and stubborn conviction of his own genius, and the importance he attached to its being recognised. As a way of trying to understand your own artistic merits, a belief in literary fame as a solution to all of the problems of existence is, as subsequent chapters will show, a heady mixture of self-delusion, and one that justifies (and even ensures) artistic failure. On the other hand, as the next chapter details, it was equally possible for writers to have no pretensions at all about the quality of their failed work, and to become (ironically) successful and a celebrity, though only by reaching a more desperate end than Savage.

CHAPTER 2

The exemplary failure of Dr Dodd

In the second edition of his *Life of Samuel Johnson* of 1787, Sir John Hawkins added an incident from near the end of Johnson's terminal illness, when 'an accident happened which went very near to disarrange his mind'. Johnson 'had mislaid' a paper to his executors, and according to Hawkins, 'In our search, I laid my hands on a parchment-covered book, into which I imagined it might have been slipped.' Hawkins supposedly feared that an unspecified individual might come round and steal it: 'having stronger reasons than I need here mention to suspect that this man might find and make an ill use of the book, I put it, and a less of the same kind, into my pocket'.[1] Johnson was made aware of the fact, Hawkins stated his reasons for thus acting, and returned the book to an unhappy Johnson. Hawkins's account of the 'book-borrowing' episode is clumsy, and the justification of his own behaviour peculiar, as noted by Richard Porson, who ironically compared the incident to a more famous recent event:

> Would a writer, confessedly so exact in his choice of words as the Knight, talk in this manner: While he was preparing – an accident happened – ? As if one should say of that unfortunate divine, Dr. Dodd, an accident proved fatal to him; he happened to write another man's name, etc.[2]

The lack of agency in Hawkins's description is compared with the 'unfortunate' Dr William Dodd, executed for forging a bond a decade before in 1777, who remains best known for producing Johnson's remark that 'Depend upon it, Sir, when a man knows he is to be hanged in a fortnight, it concentrates his mind wonderfully.'[3] Porson's words were meant to sting: in the *Life*, Hawkins had been dismissive of the massive campaign to save Dodd, led by the pen of Johnson (and had, by a further irony, been the Justice when the Middlesex Grand Jury had decided that Dodd should stand trial at the Old Bailey in February 1777). The blunt lack of sympathy of Hawkins was at odds with the Dodd campaign, which generated a public outcry at the execution of a clergyman, yet Porson's mocking words are also a reference to the lack of trust in Dodd, the suspicion (shared by Johnson, and many others) that for all the barbarity of hanging him for forgery, there was more to the case than a repentant clergyman and unduly punitive authorities; and that the ways in which the attempts to save him represented his forgery as some sort of 'accident' over which he had no control were a form of misplaced sympathy for a disingenuous man.

As Porson slyly implies, there were two very different opinions of Dodd available in the years following his death. Compare the description of him in a gossip column of 1773 as being 'as complete a Macaroni preacher, as any within the bills of mortality', with the apparently sincere (yet hapless) grief of the Irish poet Henrietta Battier after his execution:

> For did the laws at holy frauds ne'er nod,
> Thousands might die, tho' never preach like Dodd;
> Once more with Dodd, to the throng'd church we'll turn,
> And for awhile forget he's in the urn[4]

The idea and name of the 'Macaroni Parson' stuck to Dodd, because of his aping of foreign fashions, the reported splendour of his appearance, and his charisma as a preacher, which made his London sermons public events. Yet the name also indicates a lack of sincerity, a willingness to play any role for social and material advancement. Conversely, for all the bathos of her final line, Battier's point was widely shared: why should Dodd (even if he was less saintly than his followers pretended) suffer for one small crime, when the inevitably worse sins of his ecclesiastical brethren were covered up?

The sensation of Dodd's disgrace and death recreated his life as a sort of literary fable, with either vanity and greed or the severity of justice as the main theme. The effusion of writings about Dodd after his disgrace turned his story from the mundane reality of the forgery of a financially embarrassed parson into a literary event; as Paul Baines has suggested, 'to a great extent, Dodd's case was argued at and across the border between literature and law'.[5] In many descriptions, Dodd is a folk hero, a 'man of feeling', a creature of sensibility at odds with his time, like Henry Mackenzie's Harley, and this obscures the practical problems of his attempting to forge a bond for £4,200 in the name of the Earl of Chesterfield, to whom he had been a private tutor in the 1760s. Dissenting voices painted a blacker picture, with Dodd as a voluptuous spendthrift, and his ecclesiastical career merely an insincere conduit for his desire for fame and money. To complicate these co-existing representations of his life, Dodd was also a writer – in fact, his literary ambitions predated his ordination in 1751, the year after he first attempted to set himself up in literary London. He was hugely productive, and not particularly inspired, but death changed all that: the success of his works after his execution to the end of the nineteenth century is staggering.[6] Paradoxically, the failure and disgrace of Dodd brought him literary success, creating a market for his writings that was entirely based around his new-found notoriety, whereas the preceding quarter century saw a plethora of productions by him that are almost the embodiment of a specific type of literary failure, where the need for material reward overrides any concerns about quality. Dodd thus offers both a failed literary career, and, in the extraordinary way in which his crime and death were turned into a larger myth, almost a fictional alter ego. This chapter examines Dodd's career, both as an undistinguished writer, and as an example of how the unpredictable response of the public towards celebrity can turn failure into success. John Nichols, who often took pleasure in seeing Dodd preach, described him as 'a voluminous writer' who 'possessed considerable abilities, with but little judgment and much vanity'.[7] Illustrating the truth of this evaluation provides a very illuminating case of literary failure, and shows how easily the public representation of a life can transform it into a sort of fiction, and in so doing overturn critical verdicts on literature, when compared to more widespread and effective forms of media. Dodd, like many a celebrity before or since, becomes part of a narrative that transforms his actual life, until his literary mediocrity is an unnoticed irrelevance.

Early literary attempts

Dodd's formative years showed a keenness for literature. He was born in 1729, the son of a parson in Bourne in Lincolnshire, and the first notable event was his admittance as a sizar to Clare Hall, Cambridge, in 1745, from which he graduated in 1750. A. D. Barker has shown how Dodd was both a precocious and productive student: by 1747 he had translated Thucydides, and contacted Edward Cave at *The Gentleman's Magazine*, sending him a mock-pastoral, 'Diggon Davy's Resolution on the Death of His Last Cow'. Cave would publish, in 1749, two fashionable African eclogues, *The African Prince, Now in England, to Zara* and its sequel, *Zara, at the Court of Annamaboe, to the African Prince*. The poems were based upon the recent case of two African boys rescued from slavery and introduced to society by the Earl of Halifax; Dodd would make his intentions explicit in dedicating them to Halifax when they were republished in 1755.[8] These poems (like so much Dodd wrote) show the engrafting of a different situation and locale onto a familiar model, in this case Pope's *Eloisa to Abelard*, the source of so many monologues by lovelorn exotic figures in the eighteenth century. The African prince in London cannot (unsurprisingly) do justice to his experiences without his beloved:

> The time shall come, O! speed the ling'ring hour!
> When Zara's charms shall lend description power;
> When plac'd beside thee, in the cool alcove,
> Or thro' the green Savannahs as we rove,
> The frequent kiss shall interrupt the tale,
> And looks shall speak my sense, tho' language fail.[9]

Language does not fail in these works, so much as find itself unable to offer any lasting idea or impression; Dodd's poetry usually aspires only to the representation of an established mode. It is therefore not contemptible or bathetic, but neither is it memorable; more than anything it is occasional, being produced for specific reasons. Like almost everything associated with Dodd, it gives the impression of serving the advancement of his career.

Gerald Howson, his modern biographer, has complained that Dodd's poetry is largely 'pretentious bunk'.[10] This is unfair, and oblivious to the conventions within which Dodd wrote. Dodd's poetry has few pretensions; its most egregious side is its transparent desire to merely replicate the trappings of greater artistic precedents, and to assume that its task is thus fulfilled. And this too is hardly unusual, when it is considered how little literature transcends the topical trappings of whatever era motivated its creation. What Dodd did possess, to an almost self-parodic degree, was the ability to hitch his cart to any passing trend. Anyone trying to predict the likely subjects of a writer manqué in the 1750s could do worse than look at his choices.

After graduating, Dodd moved to London, and his first major work in his attempt to set himself up as an author was *A New Book of the Dunciad* (published anonymously in July 1750). This took as its rationale the fashionable ridicule of William Warburton, mainly because of his overbearing and editorially eccentric edition of Shakespeare of 1747.[11] Barker makes the very germane point that Dodd's effort predates Warburton's edition of Pope of 1751, which was to increase the level of mockery towards him. Dodd thus sniffed the wind effectively in his replacement of Colley Cibber with Warburton as King of the Dunces. The poem begins:

> Where long unenvied Cibber slept a king,
> Till, by dread W-r-r-n dethron'd, he run,
> Confess'd the victor, and resign'd his crown.

> Relate, oh Goddess, whose inspiring aid
> Through Shakespear's mangled page thy hero led;
> Relate what work, each former work outdone,
> To such high honour rais'd thy darling son[12]

And related they are, from Warburton's pervasive influence on Pope, to the controversies around his *Divine Legation of Moses Demonstrated*, and the edition of Shakespeare, with the Goddess Dulness urging Warburton to 'Still strenuous employ thy critick skill, / Amend, abuse, and utter what you will' (p. 10), with the great man surrounded and supported by the four forms of 'Impudence', 'Pedantry', 'Scurrility', and 'Vanity' (p. 14). The poem is at its best when ventriloquising some of the more outlandish of Warburton's Shakespearean conjectural emendations into his speeches: 'Myself will trempe the paper the year round, / Jargon confute, and non-sense flat confound', he declares (p. 23), and encourages a poetaster to 'Haste, narrify my worth, my laud relate' (p. 24).[13] Whilst showing the influence of Thomas Edwards's 'Glossary' in his *Canons of Criticism* (1748), the best-known response to Warburton's edition, this is the most winning and witty aspect of Dodd's satire. Dodd's dislike of Warburton's edition would shine through in his later Shakespearean works, and his satire of the eminent divine's editing was evidence of deeply held literary principles, rather than opportunism.

The same cannot be said for Dodd's 'Elegy on the Death of His Royal Highness the Prince of Wales', published a scant month after Frederick's death in March 1751. The exuberance that marks *A New Book of the Dunciad* is not as characteristic of Dodd's poetic oeuvre as this pallid work. Its theme, the familiar inadequacy of language to express the depth of sorrow, is unfortunate, in drawing attention to Dodd's own inadequacies of expression:

> Language is faint true sorrow to express,
>   To speak the passion of a wounded soul:
> The more we suffer we complain the less,
>   The rill flows babbling, deep streams silent roll.
>
> The head with mute expressive pity mov'd,
>   The big tear lab'ring in your people's eye,
> Too speakingly proclaim, how much belov'd,
>   Dear prince, you liv'd, how much lamented die.
>   (*Poems*, p. 63)

The insipidity of this is representative of the reams of verse that Dodd would be compelled to write in order to advance claims for preferment; though his efforts were no worse than that of many writers placed under such a compulsion in the eighteenth century, they were sadly no better.

Dodd's time in London as an apprentice author was prolific: it included two plays, 'The Syracusan' (an imitation of Greek tragedy), and in lighter vein, 'Sir Roger de Coverly', containing presumably the further adventures of Addison and Steele's much-loved quixotic knight. Neither has survived, as neither was produced. The latter play would reappear and be hawked about twenty-six years later, at the time of Dodd's disaster. A subscription had also been arranged in 1750 for Dodd's projected translation of *The Hymns of Callimachus*, which would not appear until 1755. The budding literary man was distracted, in 1751, by his marriage to the sixteen-year-old Mary Perkins; rumour made her a mistress of the Earl of Sandwich, and she was undoubtedly of lower birth than Dodd, and possessed no fortune. The legend is that Dodd's father descended to the metropolis and rescued his son from what he perceived to be a life of dissipation, paying off his debts and wringing the promise that he would swap literature for the clergy. Dodd was dispatched to Cambridge, and ordained in 1751.[14] Henceforth, the literary renown that he had sought would have to be achieved by other means.

Embellishing Shakespeare, and fictional voyeurism

Dodd's self-financed *Poems* of 1767 is one of his few purely secular publications of later years – they understandably became more infrequent as his religious career developed. The volume is dedicated to his parents, 'whose partial fondness encouraged, but whose wise, sollicitous, and ever-valued care enabled their son to far better pursuits, than "this idle trade"' (*Poems*, p. iv). History is silent on the genuine enthusiasm of Dodd's move into the Church. Of course, in joining the ranks of clergymen with literary pretension but little money, Dodd's experience was far from singular. Moreover, his interest in literature still produced the one work that would have guaranteed him some recognition, even without his later notoriety.

The Beauties of Shakespear was first published in two volumes in March 1752. Dodd's love of Shakespeare, present at an angle in his previous attack on Warburton, encouraged him to devise a simple idea which, in a growing culture of anthologies, would prove astonishingly successful. He extracted his favourite Shakespearean speeches, play by play (with some omissions), and added an index of subject headings. The reader could thus be introduced to the most celebrated speeches of Shakespeare, or even extract them using the index, if they needed a suitable sentiment. The result was a work that went through six editions in the eighteenth century, twenty-two in the nineteenth, and even four in the twentieth.[15]

Its influence, in the burgeoning literary market of the United States, in Europe, and the colonies, was to be immense – the young Goethe is supposed to have first encountered Shakespeare through reading the 1759 edition, and the general importance of it in the formation of popular reading of Shakespeare is obvious by the number of its reprints.

Dodd's greatest literary triumph would see him remembered as a handmaiden to the Shakespearean muse, rather than for his own work, but there was a lot of him in the *Beauties* (beyond the principles of selection) which was subsequently airbrushed out. In editions subsequent to 1795, his often voluminous notes which accompanied the passages were excised. Not only has no modern critic ever complained about this, the notes have repeatedly been seen as an unfortunate excrescence: Edwin Willoughby complained in different pieces that Dodd 'padded his volume with an unwieldy amount of notes, textual, critical, and illustrative', and was relieved that such 'sophomoric pedantry' was discarded. Howson is similarly pleased that the work, 'overloaded' with annotation and 'pointless comments', was 'stripped of his useless notes' in later editions.[16] Dodd's annotations, though ultimately irrelevant to the success and actual uses of the anthology, are valuable both in terms of the editing of Shakespeare in the eighteenth century, and as evidence of his literary taste and level of scholarship. In a rather flighty 'Preface', Dodd complains about conjectural emendation, with an obvious smack at Warburton: it is unnecessary except in rare cases, and proceeds from the vanity of editors, who wish to raise themselves above their limited importance: 'False glory prevails no less in the critical than in the great world.'[17] The unfortunate result, says Dodd (in a prefiguring of Johnson's comment in his own Shakespeare edition about the time 'wasted in confutation'), is that the squabbling of editors gets in the way. He thus laments that Shakespeare's 'BEAUTIES should be so obscur'd, and that he himself should be made a kind of stage for bungling critics to show their *clumsy activity* upon' (vol. 1, p. xv).

The result is that Dodd's notes are something of an experiment; the final apology, '*P.S.* I have not time to read over the whole work accurately' and must therefore 'plead for the faults of my printer' (vol. 1, pp. xxii), does not augur well, but Dodd's annotation is not really interested in the accuracy of minute scholarship. Instead he paraphrases and appreciates, chiefly by offering a series of parallels – with other Shakespearean passages, with Classical literature, and with the drama of the sixteenth and seventeenth centuries. Circumscribed by his own complaints about self-aggrandising editors, he is prevented from arguing directly with them about textual choices or meanings (though questionings of Warburton creep in, as does the odd suggested emendation), so he usually confines himself to aesthetic remarks, and the noting of allusions. The *Beauties* is thus a sort of quasi-edition, with half the material usually given in annotation, haphazard glossing, and very occasional textual notes. If Dodd expected the notes to be perused equally with the Shakespearean extracts, he was unsurprisingly disappointed, given that extracted passages do not necessarily require annotation or encourage attention towards it to the same degree as an edition. Moreover, as the utility of the *Beauties* proved to be in its making accessible well-chosen passages, Dodd's scholarship was rendered superfluous. In trying to avoid the excessive parts of the apparatus of an edition, Dodd was caught between two stools, offering extended notes suitable to an edition, but extraneous for an anthology. It is a pity that his original contributions pleased so few, as in offering a corrective to Warburtonian over-interpretation and dogmatic textual scholarship, Dodd was trying to answer a genuine problem, even if his solution was often eccentric.

The *Beauties* was also undeniably enthusiastic and sincere in its appreciation, qualities not always associated with Dodd's writing. Compared with the trite and commonplace affectation of much of his previous and subsequent work, the learning and zest for literature exhibited in the notes to the *Beauties* is a revelation. It is not always, however, applied very directly. In *Julius Caesar*, Cassius' anecdote about saving Caesar from drowning is part of his plan to win over Brutus, by pointing out the human weakness of Caesar, and their relative equality.[18] It brings forth the following response from Dodd:

> It is too well known that swimming was a usual exercise with the hardy and noble *Romans*, to insist upon it here: *Horace* makes it a mark of effeminacy to neglect it: and complains to *Lydia*, that she had enervated *Sybaris*, by making him afraid even *to touch the Yellow Tyber's Stream* ... *Julius Caesar* was remarkable for his excellence in swimming: *Beaumont* and *Fletcher*, in their *False One*, thus nobly describe one of the incidents of his life (*Beauties*, vol. II, p. 93)

And so on, until 'The reader is desired to refer to the 109th page of the 1st volume.' On so doing, they find another reference to swimming from *The Tempest*, another analogy (to *Venice Preserved*), and in the preceding note, a quote from Act 4 of Sir John Suckling's *Goblins*. It would be unfair to view this as fustian, mere smatterings of allusion worn heavily in order to impress; Dodd is genuinely enthused by Shakespeare, and his knowledge of and love for English drama in particular cannot be gainsaid. What is more difficult to accept is his lack of discrimination in throwing in these references at every opportunity. Like for many an editor, what is self-evidently relevant to him can become an encumbrance equal to that of Warburton's voluminous and argumentative notes. Text and annotation are therefore, to some degree, at variance. This habit of intruding his knowledge into his writings through footnotes would mark many of Dodd's works, often in ways that are far less modest and sympathetic than the interjections of the *Beauties*, which are redeemed by their gusto. An interesting adjunct to the scholarship of his time, the notes did not deserve to be later brutally stripped out, leaving only the index and the choice of selection as the legacy of Dodd's great labours on Shakespeare, when his anthology entered fully into its own in the century after his death.

The success of *The Beauties of Shakespear* was to prove the high point of Dodd's literary career. His next work was far less considered. This was a novel, *The Sisters: or, the History of Lucy and Caroline Sanson, Entrusted to a False Friend*, published in 1754. The assumption has usually been that it is a result of Dodd's time in London before ordination, being full of town gossip and veiled real-life accounts of debaucheries. It is most notable for its debt to more considerable talents, and though it never found many readers, the poverty of its invention is very revealing.

The Sisters has always been acknowledged as a voyeuristic work, masquerading as a moral warning. Percy Fitzgerald was the model of Victorian understatement in describing it as 'a strange novel, which coming from a working curate, seems a singular and unbecoming composition'. For Barker, 'A prurient interest in the exploits of libertines is thinly concealed beneath the moral posture.' Similarly, Howson laments that 'lacking the novelist's gift', Dodd 'left us with neither a vivid and informative picture of low life nor a piece of straight pornography'.[19] Dodd, in the pretended guise of the 'Editor' (the first of many obvious nods to Samuel Richardson), offers a preface full of humbug: the following story is meant 'To recommend virtue, and decry one species of vice'. It is planned like 'modern historical romances', but offers more satisfaction, as it is 'founded on real facts, and on characters that once existed'.[20] Such verisimilitude is important: 'Fallen as we are among evil times and evil men, it requires no small caution to guide ourselves aright, and to pass thro' life, our virtue unshaken and our principles uncorrupted' (vol. 1, p. iv). 'How inconsistent is man! pride and vanity constitute his very nature', concludes the 'Editor' (vol. 1, p. vi). Unfortunately there is much inconsistency in the moral message of the novel which follows.

Its plot is not profound: Mr Sanson anticipates Sir Walter Elliott in being obsessed with his true pedigree, and sends his two daughters,

Caroline and Lucy, to make their fortune and revive the family name in the city, under the care of their distant relation Dookalb. (An absurdity of the novel is its occasional spelling of the names of real people backwards: Dookalb was based on an unidentified Blackwood, who, judging by his characterisation, must have offended Dodd severely; a less flattering portrait would be hard to find. 'Lucy Repook', a high-class prostitute, is Lucy Cooper, and 'Beau Leicart' is Robert 'Beau' Tracey, a celebrated libertine of the day.) The unfortunate sisters have been filled with the false glories of the family name – their mother 'instilled into their minds, chimerical notions of grandeur, and coaches, titles, honour, diamonds and brocades' as a right (vol. 1, p. 3). Dodd's intrusive narrator attempts digressions, in the style of Fielding. Dookalb, for example, is a villain, a procurer of mistresses for noblemen.

> Such was the man into whose hands these unhappy girls were destined to fall. Such was the man who made no conscience of ruining the good and virtuous, and spreading confusion and horror, despair and agony, amongst miserable and worthy families. My tears almost prevent my pursuing the fatal story, yet as truths, horrid and shocking as these, may warn the unexperienced, and teach the unwary how cautious they ought to be; I shall with some degree of pleasure make my own heart bleed; nay, I shall do it with transport, if thereby I may be so happy as to save even one young helpless creature from misery and destruction. (vol. 1, p. 15)

Whatever its flaws, *The Sisters* is most definitely a work of strong feeling; the action is punctuated as much by sobbing as by orthography.

The claim that the novel is intended as a moral warning is revealed to be a misrepresentation by the evident glee with which Dodd dwells on the salaciousness of scenes, as when the villainous Dookalb begins to pander the sisters to two noblemen, as soon as they have stepped off the mail coach:

> but when the glass was briskly put round, and the god of wine began to hail the god of love, when the mother's tongue enter'd into the realms of luscious talking, and wanton *Charlotte* threw her snowy arms round the neck of her fond lover, imprinting kisses warm with transport, then it was the two young unexperienced lasses gave a loose to love themselves, and were pleased to find the young noblemen pressing their heaving breasts with glowing hands, and sucking from their unpolluted roseate mouths ten thousand and ten thousand sweets (vol. 1, pp. 25–6)

Unfortunately, the revelling in such a scenario makes it difficult for the fulcrum of the plot to work: one sister, Lucy, becomes a mistress, a prostitute, and is eventually ruined by temptation; Caroline, by contrast, resists the evil Dookalb's wiles and protects her virtue, though Dodd undermines this premise by describing the allure of pleasure for her this early in the novel. This is one of many absurdities that litter the action; the fall of Lucy into temptation is the strangest combination of suggestiveness and Miltonic solemnity:

> with his own glowing fingers he freed her from other incumbrances, and locking the doors, put a stop to all her virgin fears; and, in a luckless hour, for a momentary pleasure, gave up the thoughtless and deluded girl to eternal horror. Dreadful introduction to sin and sorrow! fatal beginning of misery and destruction! Thus fell the unhappy daughter of an unhappy father, from her state of innocence and joy; like our first mother, seduced and betray'd (vol. 1, p. 45)

The allusion to *Paradise Lost* is then (unsurprisingly) spelled out by quotation.

The Sisters represents a London where every inhabitant appears to be a saint or a depraved villain. The one apparent exception is Mr Jaison, one of the gentlemen to whom Dookalb is a pander, who turns out to be an innocent and virtuous young man so overwhelmed by the goodness of Caroline that he falls in love with her, and reneges on his plan of deflowering her with Dookalb's assistance:

> On my soul, dearest Miss, I hate the rascal, and I hate myself: It would be no less ungenerous than unavailing, to conceal from you the real purpose of my visit. Do not despise me wholly, (for you cannot but despise me, and, sincerely, I despise myself) when I frankly confess, that you only was the occasion of my presence here to day – But alas! how can I shock your ears with declaring, it was to possess it, if I approved your person? (vol. 1, p. 142)

The unlikelihood of such a change of heart would only be a problem if Jaison bore any relation to an inhabitant of the sublunary world. Such flimsiness in terms of character and plot is obvious, but it is prurience that makes the novel peculiarly offensive. Lucy, for instance, in the lowest mire of prostitution has to hire herself out to some depraved young noblemen: 'at length demanding the perpetration of something too black to be named, too diabolical to be mentioned, which she, with just aversion utterly refusing, and resolutely denying, determined rather to die, they swore, unless she consented, that they would burn her alive' (vol. 1, p. 196). The model appears to be the sort of suggestiveness with which Fielding presented Blifil's desire for Sophia Western: 'nay, he had some further views, from obtaining the absolute possession of her person, which we detest too much even to mention'.[21] The cunning here is the narrator's exploitation of the desire for the reader to know more, and the mockery of his own supposed prudery. Dodd offers little by comparison: considering the young rakes have just forced Lucy to dance naked by attacking her with red hot pokers, the withholding of the thing 'too black to be named' is titillation rather than outrage, and the whole scene an excuse for Dodd to offer hints of pornography. The pretended outrage is even less convincing than the debauchery, and combines with an increased accent on sensibility.

To support this, the novel thus sees an increase in Richardsonian echoes: much of the plot is taken from *Clarissa*. Caroline ends the first volume in a sponging house, imprisoned by pretended rent arrears from Dookalb, and borrows her defiant virtue from Clarissa Harlowe. The madam, Mrs Searchwell, is described in the very words Richardson used for his brothel-keeper, Mrs Sinclair: 'the Beldame, clapping her arms a-kembo, pronouncing a most emphatical hum, and darting keen firebrands from her little red eyes' (vol. II, p. 12).[22] The two share the same fate – Mrs Searchwell too falls down the stairs, and bellows and curses in pain all night (vol. II, p. 58).

The novel is thus a farrago of borrowed impressions of virtue and depravity, and an equally insincere sensibility. The forces of good in the novel are so asinine in their representation as to almost encourage the opposite: Jenny Stevens, a young girl, is made pregnant by a young fop, her virtue destroyed by 'foolish and idle books of romances and novels', which are 'the destruction of youth, and the pest of the age' (vol. II, p. 81). She cannot understand the fuss, blaming her family for having 'the same motives that the charming *Clarissa's* inhuman and brutish parents prevented her happiness with that most delightful creature sweet Mr. *Lovelace*' (vol. II, p. 84). This misreading is the most subtle of Dodd's attempts at supporting moral reformation, but such small triumphs are undone by the reappearance of Mr Sanson, come to find his wayward daughters, and presented as an unintentionally comic combination of Job and Lear on the heath:

> good God – was there ever in all the creation such a wretch as I! oh who wou'd wish to be a father – or if one, who would not teach their daughters virtue, only virtue! vain old man – horrid destructive pride of heart thou hast ruined me and mine – burst my heart, crack every sinew, weep drops of blood, oh my eyes – cursed be the villains – cursed the day my daughters departed from home (vol. II, p. 114)

Mr Sanson dominates the rest of the novel by accident, his reunions with his children providing yet more liquid: 'The poor old man caught hold of [her hand], fell upon her face, which watering plentifully with his tears, he kiss'd a thousand and a thousand times – crying out – "my child, my poor dear child – my *Caroline*, my daughter – oh my love, my dear, dear child!" There was not a dry eye in the room' (vol. II, p. 137). On almost every page tears mingle (except those of Dookalb, who is to hang, unrepentant). More than one scene is 'enough to melt a heart of stone' (vol. II, p. 199). Some of these scenes are so risible as to call into question whether Dodd was embracing the novel of sensibility, or mocking it. The book ends with the following parting advice to parents:

> kindle not in their hearts the detestable love of pleasure, and the delusive smoak of vanity. Teach them to be humble, and you teach them to be happy ... do not instruct them in the vile arts of gain or fill their bosoms with the insatiable thirst of worldly pomp and glories (vol. II, p. 297)

In the most accurate lifetime memoir of him, Dodd's friend John Duncombe complained that despite 'the specious gawze of morality affectedly thrown over' *The Sisters*, its scenes were 'painted with a warmth of imagination and a luxuriance of colouring, which cannot but be dangerous to the young and susceptible, as tending rather to inflame than correct the passions, and being much more likely to seduce than reform'. The novel therefore 'gave no very favourable idea of the purity of [Dodd's] mind, or the rectitude of his judgement' (*Historical Memoirs*, pp. 10, 9). Indeed, its obvious voyeurism made its moral strictures near ludicrous; such sententiousness was not the most attractive side of Dodd's character, and the impression given by such warnings in this feeble novel is that his supposed interest in moral reformation was at the least insincere, a charge that would follow during his public success as a clergyman, which offset the richly deserved failure of *The Sisters*.

Charismatic preaching, meretricious writing

Although Dodd's production as a writer was prodigious, much of it came to be dominated by works ancillary to his religious occupation, such as sermons, biblical commentary, and his sustained efforts as editor (in all but name) of *The Christian Magazine* from 1760 to 1767. The many pages of Dodd's religious hack-work offer few indications of the reasons for the celebrity achieved by his performances as a preacher in the 1750s and thereafter. With the exception of *The Beauties of Shakespear*, Dodd was a perfunctory writer, satisfied to replicate accepted forms and arguments. His temperament seems to have been more suited to the performative; not even his enemies could deny the charisma of Dodd's sermons.

In 1752, Dodd (then a curate) was appointed as Lecturer in West Ham, on the death of the incumbent, 'having soon obtained great popularity as a preacher, partly owing to his pathetic delivery and composition'. This was merely the first of many such posts, won mainly on the tremendous impression that Dodd made as a speaker: the most celebrated would be his involvement with the Magdalen Hospital for repentant prostitutes, which opened in 1758. Although never the official chaplain, Dodd was for a long time a member of its board, and his weekly winter sermons there would draw the fashionable, and greatly enhance his own status, giving him a stipend of one hundred guineas from 1763 (*Historical Memoirs*, pp. 7, 13). Moreover, he was from 1764 one of the King's chaplains, and from 1767 (using money his wife had won on the lottery), the preacher at the Charlotte Chapel he had built in Pimlico – named after the Queen, who occasionally visited.[23] The splendidly named Charlotte Papendick, who would later be the Assistant Keeper of the Wardrobe to the Queen, recalled Dodd's performances there with admiration: 'Dr Dodd was handsome in the extreme, and possessed every personal attraction that could add to the beauty of the service; an harmonious voice, a heart of passion and the power of showing that he felt his subject deeply.'[24] Horace Walpole, less likely to be won over by Dodd, described the spectacle of the Magdalen Hospital, and 'a young clergyman, one Dodd; who contributed to the Popish idea one had imbibed, by haranguing entirely in the French style, and very eloquently and touchingly. He apostrophized the lost sheep, who sobbed and cried from their souls', as did the society women that accompanied Walpole.[25] Overtly suspicious of the welter of feeling aroused by Dodd, Walpole praises the effect of the performance, but signifies the underlying presence of false sentiment.

The question of sensibility recurs in Dodd's life and writing: the limitations of his literary talents made his attempts at evoking genuine sentiment inchoate or insipid, but his charm as a speaker seems to have created for his audience the very air of sensibility. Yet, just as the rapture of fictional sensibility could be met with derision, many seem to have perceived Dodd's talents in the pulpit as a trick, a sign at best of his superficiality of character, and at worst, of his insincere designs. To invert Johnson's praise of Levet, Dodd offered the show of art without the power. From a modern viewpoint, A. D. Barker has suggested that 'Dodd was always disingenuous and ambitious. He employed his talents, which were not negligible, in self-advertisement, sycophancy and money-making', and claimed elsewhere that Dodd's 'success as a minister was based upon an extravagant preaching technique and a talent for self-advertisement, rather than upon a sense of vocation'. A more contemporary voice, of a so-called

Charismatic preaching, meretricious writing 83

'Citizen of London' (admittedly in a pamphlet written to justify Dodd's execution), found a similar lack of substance:

> There was something in the figure, eloquence, and manner of Dr. Dodd, that gave him always the command of his audience in his preaching. It is however granted by his friends, that his parts were rather shining than solid, and that his success was more owing to a polished exterior, to the amiable and graceful manner in which he uniformly conducted himself, which made a most universal impression in his favour, than to any other uncommon share of intrinsical merit.[26]

In his defence, it is impossible to judge whether or not sincerity co-exists with a 'polished exterior', and it would be odd for Dodd to not take advantage of his natural abilities as a performer. He was (to an extent) preaching for his supper for years; by the time he gained his first living, in 1772, he had accumulated and consolidated various religious positions (as well as occasional jobs, such as his role as tutor to the young Philip Stanhope in the 1760s), but was already living beyond his means. Yet something of the point does hit home, and adds to the criticism of speciousness that never escaped Dodd.

Such a critique can be supported by traces in his writings. Even in an age where many writers fawned after preferment, some of Dodd's actions seem ill judged. His publication of the first of three sermons on the topic *The Wisdom and Goodness of God in the Vegetable Creation* (1760) was not a notable event, but the work won a fulsome review from *The Christian Magazine*: 'this discourse contains the finest instruction', and 'every part of the subject is moralised in the most beautiful manner', therefore 'we recommend it as affording the highest entertainment'. Dodd's 'style is at once elegant and nervous, neither careless, nor yet affected; sufficiently open and diffuse for the pulpit, yet neither tedious nor redundant in the closet'.[27] Unfortunately, as Duncombe notes, 'It was not then known that the author was his own panegyrist.' This sort of self-promotion made the title of the journal somewhat incongruous. It was not the last time that Dodd would write glowing reviews of his own works, and suggests, apart from self-advancement, a level of cynicism towards his published works that has moved far from any genuine concern with their merit.[28]

In the same vein, a dedication to a Miss Talbot in Dodd's edition of the works of Joseph Hall in 1759 contained, according to Duncombe, matter so embarrassing 'to her paternal friend Archbishop Secker, that, after a warm epistolary expostulation, his grace insisted on the sheet being cancelled in all remaining copies'. Thankfully, Duncombe recorded for posterity this example of flattery too grotesque even for the mid-eighteenth century:

> To descant on his writings, or enlarge on his character, would be useless to you, madam, who, I doubt not, are so well acquainted both with the one and the other; and that more especially as you live remarkably blest in having daily before your eyes a lively copy of piety as exalted, sanctity unaffected, and labour as unwearied as shone in the life of good Bishop Hall. (*Historical Memoirs*, p. 15)

The Archbishop's disgust at such toadying showed an humility that is notable for its absence in the author.

It is too easy (in hindsight) to find Dodd something of a caricature of the religious life, but it is undeniable that Dodd showed no hesitation in inviting the moneychangers into the temple, and indeed collaborated with them as much as possible. One work that was to gain an extensive posthumous reception was his *Reflections on Death* (1763), which became known familiarly as 'Dodd on Death'. The adoption of the informal name suggests that its appeal was the unwanted familiarity that Dodd gained with its subject, fourteen years after its publication. The fifth edition of this grim collection of short tales from *The Christian Magazine*, published with so many of Dodd's works in 1777 (that ironic *annus mirabilis* for his writing), claimed that they 'were first written with a Design to be published in a small Volume proper to be given away by well-disposed Persons at *Funerals*, or on any other solemn occasion'. Even an age inured to suffering might find the consolation offered somewhat scanty: *The Monthly Review*, as Barker points out, 'could see no other purpose in the work than "to frighten his Majesty's subjects with dismal ideas of Death, and horrible pictures of Damnation."'[29]

On the other hand, the *Reflections* merely replicates the utility of *The Beauties of Shakespear* in a more solemn tone: instead of the convenient collection of Shakespearean themes, those needing hard comfort could reach into the *Reflections*. The commercial pursuit of such an idea seems morbid and inappropriate, yet the real shock is that it worked, and the contempt of *The Monthly Review* did not seem to dent sales. The homiletic gloom of the *Reflections* provides little narrative drama, and no evident characterisation or literary skill. These comparative fables of exalted virtue and condemned vice are no more deliberate or considered than the hasty compilation of regurgitated sermons. Inevitably, there is dramatic irony, as in the criticism of the vanity of monuments: 'How strong is the desire of pre-eminence in the human breast: we wish to preserve it even in death.'[30] More often, the reader is offered only a mechanical devotion:

> And let us all remember, 'That every day of our life is, in the morning, a blank leaf, whereon, during the course of it, we write, and in characters indelible, all the actions of our life; let us be careful, then, that there be

nothing impure, nothing base in them; that he, before whom they are to be laid, may read them with approbation. Let us live so, that we may never die! Let us instantly set about it with all our might, before that tremendous sound be given, *He expires.*' (p. 200)

The *Reflections* consists of such pallid religious commonplaces. In his memoir, Duncombe prints Dodd's dedication of a sermon, *Of Mutual Knowledge in a Future State* (1766), written to Mrs Squire, the widow of the Bishop of St Davids (who had appointed Dodd as a chaplain), because it is 'a disinterested proof of his gratitude, which here speaks (if ever) to and from the heart' (*Historical Memoirs*, p. 22). Duncombe's parenthetical questioning of this rare evidence of Dodd speaking what he felt, not what he ought to say, suggests why it is not surprising that such disinterested and genuine feeling is conspicuously lacking in *Reflections on Death*.

Rising above mediocrity

With the notable exception of *The Beauties of Shakspear*, Dodd's predominant mode of composition was to borrow heavily from the structure and sentiments of other works. Yet this is true of many authors – the problem was that Dodd's works were read retrospectively, after his disgrace, as part of his newly fashioned public celebrity as man of feeling. The origins of his poetry, in particular, are far more modest and humble, and inevitably unable to bear such scrutiny. Isaac Reed, a sympathetic biographer writing after Dodd's arrest but before his execution, attempted to summarise Dodd's literary abilities:

> From the number and variety of Dr. *Dodd's* publications before-enumerated, it will be clearly perceived, that his industry has been very great, and his abilities not to be contemned. If his genius does not intitle him to rank with the first writers of the age, he is very far from sinking to an equality with the numerous race which daily issue from the press ... To whatever extent his abilities may be allowed to reach, it is certain, without unremitted industry, he could never have executed so many works with any degree of credit; and some must be allowed to rise above mediocrity. Amidst the variety of his engagements, in the several capacities of Preacher, Writer, Tutor, and Man of the World, it is rather to be wondered at that he should have been able to do any thing well, than that all should not be excellent.[31]

Dodd thus occupies a middle station in the literary world, above Grub Street, but obviously below the notable figures of the time. The mitigation that Dodd spread his talents so thin that he could not be expected to excel is less convincing, considering the lack of literary ambition that Dodd admitted quite cheerfully: Reed's argument could be inverted, and Dodd accused of being the very epitome of mediocrity, in caring only that his works were published. This is illustrated by his statements in the self-financed *Poems* of 1767: 'Most of the poems in this volume are juvenile performances; the rest, mere amusement of vacant moments; never suffered to intrude upon more important hours, or to interrupt better and more useful occupations.' Furthermore, he adds in a later note, 'If all the graces and excellencies of poetry are not found in them, let the candid remember, that the author presumes not to affect that high character: – a Poet is a rare production; and amongst the number of rhymers and writers, a genuine son of the Muses is but seldom to be found: a SHAKESPEARE, a SPENSER, a MILTON, are the comets of an age.'[32]

It is impossible to know if there is any false modesty about this. Dodd had some designs upon an audience for his verse (hence his troubling to pay for its appearance in the world). He may seem unique in not expecting fame for his work, but he wanted the comfort of material wealth, and realised that these goals were not likely to be gained from his verse. There seems a refreshing lack of cant in his refusal to claim (like so many unsuccessful authors) that his misunderstood works are the victims of critical injustice, and that posterity will realise their true value. Percy Fitzgerald disagreed with the notion that the lack of pretension of Dodd's poetry excused its failings: 'Allowing some margin for the elaborate gallantries of the day, it is impossible not to feel contempt for this trifling', and Dodd's very act of publishing these third-rate verses 'shows a want of self-respect'.[33]

The poems collected in 1767 are unremarkable; the later refashioning of Dodd at his fall from grace as a magnificent and tortured being would certainly not be believed from his verses alone. Many are concerned with friendship, though few in a disinterested sense, hence Fitzgerald's complaint that 'In the tone of these gallantries there is something almost offensive.' For example, the 'Ode, Occasioned by Lady N—d's Being Prevented by Illness from Coming to the Chapel of the Magdalen-House' was obviously occasioned by the need to maintain Lady Northumberland's patronage.[34] The description, in this pindaric, of the Magdalen service, is Dodd at his unctuous worst:

> When thou shalt hear their solemn prayers,
> Mix'd with deep repentant tears:
>   Grateful songs and tuneful praise,
>   Pious orgies, sacred lays;
>   Finer pleasures which dispense
>   Than the finest joys of sense:
>   And each melting bosom move,

> And each liquid eye o'erflow
> With benevolence and love!
> *(Poems*, p. 150)

The alacrity with which Dodd falls back upon the reflexive tears of sensibility is distasteful, considering the pain and suffering of the prostitutes; there is an air of emotional manipulation of the distresses of these women, in order to improve the fortunes of the establishment and (not incidentally) Dodd himself, by the continual presence at its services of Lady Northumberland.

Such writing demonstrates tactlessness and worldliness, for all its supposed piety, as does 'To the Author of Tristram Shandy, on the Publication of His Third and Fourth Volumes', a piece from 1761 that issues a moral reprimand to Sterne:

> Yes, they will laugh; – but whom, O S——e, enquire?
> The wretched sons of vice and foul desire:
> To these your page immoral may be dear,
> But virtue o'er it sheds the conscious tear
> *(Poems*, p. 62)

It is not only through the glass of hindsight that this seems an incongruous performance, as Dodd's apparently genuine outrage at *Tristram Shandy* is somewhat overstrained:

> Search your own heart, you'll find the debt is large,
> And haste, perform the duties of your charge;
> Leave the vile town, nor wish it in your pow'r,
> To shine the giddy meteor of an hour.
> Ah! you have talents, – do not misapply,
> Ah you have time, – seize, seize it, ere it fly;
> Strait seize it, for too short you needs must own
> Whate'er of life remaineth to atone
> For all the filth diffus'd, and evil you have done.
> *(Poems*, p. 62)

After such humbug, what forgiveness? Fitzgerald's comment on it seeming 'almost incomprehensible how such advice could come from one who was notoriously immersed in all the seductions of the vile town' is all that needs to be said on the pomposity of Dodd's attack.[35]

Dodd's poetry contains more than its fair share of exaggerated anxiety about the depravity of the times. The 'Moral Pastorals', written by 1763 but published in 1767, are full of such warnings: they were intended as a corrective to Salomon Gessner's hugely successful *Idyllen* (1756), which, says Dodd, 'though there are many pleasing moral allusions in them, yet the generality of them, it must be confessed, are puerile' (*Poems*, p. 207). Whilst this is not a charge that can be brought against Dodd's efforts, the idea of an explicitly moral pastoral means that the latent qualities of the form (the juxtaposition of worlds and values, the recourse to a more exalted but also removed type of life as a critique of modernity or the urban) are submerged beneath the didacticism. Dodd's models of errant behaviour or challenged piety are locked into a strange landscape, removed from the present, but intended to charge it with their warnings. The third pastoral, 'The Servant', sees the dutiful and earnest Perigot trying to convince the feckless Lobbin that he should not go and spend his time in alehouses and watching wrestling matches, but should instead pursue duty and religious devotion:

> I too, – thrice happy, – should my master have,
> With all his family, attend my grave;
> Smiting their breasts, and saying, with a tear,
> "A good and faithful servant resteth here."
> This be my praise; and for this praise I'll live:
> Your pastimes, Lobbin, no such joys can give.
>
> LOBBIN.
> Why, Perigot, 'tis truth: – you touch my heart;
> Shepherd, indeed you chuse the better part,
> I'll think to-morrow well of what you say, –
> – But can't forego – the pleasures of to-day!
>
> Thus, with a laugh, the dolt departing cry'd;
> While the good shepherd shook his head, and sigh'd!
> (*Poems*, pp. 230–1)

This clumsy attempt at moral instruction has a priggishness in Perigot's warnings that reflects back onto the author's instruction. Dodd produces strange hybrid works that resemble mock-pastoral unintentionally, with the comic relief (however slight) from the swains and clowns overwhelming the clunky messages of reformation. When Dodd claims that the character of Perigot, 'the Good Shepherd, is drawn from a person in that rank of life in Northamptonshire', whose 'praise is beyond all that the pastoral speaks of him' (*Poems*, p. 209), it is a genuine shock that such a mouthpiece for trite exempla should have had a real person as his model; like all of the characters of the pastorals, he seems to belong to fable, rather than to the harsh rural world of the Midlands.

Scandal and simony

Dodd's unsuccessful and meretricious collection of poems was incidental to his (at this point) successful career. By the 1770s, Dodd's fortunes were superficially at their height: he had obtained the living of Hockliffe in Bedfordshire, described by Duncombe as 'the first cure of souls he ever held' (*Historical Memoirs*, p. 39). As well as his work for the Magdalen and the Charlotte Chapel, he was a royal chaplain, and also a chaplain to the young Earl of Chesterfield, his former pupil, now off on the Grand Tour. Yet all was not as it seemed, and the first major setback of his career was about to occur. 'Memoirs of the Macaroni Parson and Mrs. R—n' appeared as part of 'Histories of the Tête-à-Tête annex'd', the gossip section of *The Town and Country Magazine*, in 1773. The purport of the 'Histories' was to offer an account of the life of a well-known public figure, thinly masking their identity and spelling out their iniquities in such a fashion as to make the reader suspicious of exaggeration.

The column applied the tag which was to stick to him in later years: Dodd is 'as complete a Macaroni preacher, as any within the bills of mortality', with the 'brilliancy of his diamond ring', and 'the odour of his well-dispos'd bouquet'. It also alleged that Dodd was riddled with debt, and had recently been imprisoned in the King's-Bench for it. Whilst there, he had an affair with a woman prisoner – a 'widow lady' – and was conducting another with a 'Mrs R—n' (identified by Fitzgerald as Mrs Robinson), a rich member of the Charlotte Street congregation. In a reminder of the peculiarities of Dodd's world, she 'had been influenced by her relations to give her hand to a merchant of considerable prosperity, though she had urged the incompatibility of twenty-three and seventy-four', and Dodd 'endeavours to afford her all the consolation in his power, in the absence of her husband'. Mrs Dodd 'testifies [not] the least concern upon the occasion'.[36]

Whatever the truth of all this, it is possible that Dodd assumed that such allegations were commonplace for any figure in the public eye. The next problem was of his own making. Despite these scandalous claims, Duncombe finds his friend at this point in his career 'admired as a preacher, and esteemed as a man, by many of the great, the worthy, and the wealthy'. Indeed,

> the Doctor was now in the zenith of his popularity, we will not say prosperity, as nothing surely but distress of circumstances and infatuation of mind could have driven him to the unaccountable step we are now to mention; a step, which first opened the eyes of the public to his real character, and alienated many of his former friends and followers. (*Historical Memoirs*, p. 40)

Horace Walpole found justification for his earlier suspicion of Dodd in January 1774, when he described how 'At the end of the month happened the disgrace of Dr Dodd, a precise, affected, and popular preacher, an enemy, but mimic, to the Methodists, Director of the Magdalens, and chaplain to Court, from his hypocrisy and popularity.'[37] This 'disgrace', though on a much smaller scale than the debacle of the forgery three years later, involved a bribe to the Lord Chancellor's wife, Lady Apsley: an anonymous letter offered her 3,000 guineas for the newly available and lucrative living of St George's, Hanover Square. It was traced to Dodd's wife.[38] By the end of January, Walpole related in a letter how King George 'has ordered the pure precise Dr Dodd to be struck off the list of chaplains, not for gallantry with a Magdalen, as you would expect, but for offering a thumping bribe to my Lord Chancellor for the fat Living of St George's'.[39] The 'precise' Dodd is compared to another famous hypocrite, Angelo in *Measure for Measure*. Dodd offered a denial of any knowledge of the matter, in a letter of 10 February to *St James' Chronicle*, where he claimed 'that time will, ere long, put some circumstances in my power which may lead to an elucidation of this affair, evince to the satisfaction of mankind my integrity, and remove every ill impression with regard to the proceedings, which have justly incensed a most respectable personage, and drawn such misfortunes upon me'. As Duncombe notes, 'It is needless to add, *that time* never came'.[40] The misconceived plot to gain Dodd the living suggested that the 'Histories of the Tête-à-Tête' had been right in claiming that his financial circumstances were far from healthy.

The matter of the bribe became public knowledge with the striking of Dodd from the list of King's chaplains. He became a target for satire: Samuel Foote's play *The Cozeners* was performed in the Haymarket in August 1774, with Dodd making an appearance as 'Dr Simony'; his wife describes him to the eponymous swindlers: 'The Doctor's powers are pretty well known about town; not a more populous preacher within the sound of Bow-bell'; she claims that 'the best people of fashion aren't ashamed to follow my Doctor', a charismatic figure with diamond ring and inimitable eloquence.[41] The play indicates how Dodd had entered into the public consciousness for other, less salutary reasons than his genuinely charitable deeds, and that the saintly image presented at the time of his fall three years later was always commingled with a more cynical impression. In the aftermath of the public exposure of the attempted bribe, Dodd fled to the continent, asking for the aid of Chesterfield, then in Geneva. The Earl was full of kindness and hospitality, compensating Dodd for his losses with the living of Winge in Buckinghamshire, and money to relieve Dodd's heaviest debts. These were not helped by the removal of his £100 annual fee from the board of the Magdalen Hospital, after his being absent without leave for five weeks during his trip to Switzerland. The next time that the continent was mentioned with regard to Dodd was when he was seen dressed 'in the costume of a seventeenth-century musketeer' at the Plaine des Sablons races in Paris, 'staggering from a carriage with a group of drunken rakes to place huge bets on the horses, without the least knowledge of form'.[42] The date of this incongruous appearance is disputed, but whether it took place in 1774 or two years later, it is charged with symbolism: the supposedly devout Dodd shows his love of the high life, and loses his money into the bargain.

At the time of his death, it was claimed that Dodd was in Paris to consult printers about the illustrations of Shakespeare, 'to whom he now again turned his attention, and meditated a new Edition, to be printed in a most pompous manner, and ornamented with the most elegant decorations. It is said, that this scheme, as it never was completed, was highly injurious to his fortune.' Unfortunately for this theory, Barker has argued persuasively that 'even a cursory perusal of Dodd's annotated copy of Hanmer's 1747 nine-volume edition of Shakespeare' reveals 'that Dodd was in no position to bring his own edition of Shakespeare to press'.[43] Dodd's poverty was, one obituary suggested, not caused by paying for his Shakespeare edition; more prosaically, it was his losses at the racetrack: 'it is assured, that a run of ill-luck was the original cause of the unfortunate step he took', as one obituary put it.[44] Apart from obvious financial exigencies, it is impossible to know specifically what led Dodd to his ruinous act, but the search for motives, carried out after his execution, illustrated how he had ceased to be merely a fashionable object of admiration or derision, and had become a celebrity.

Forgery and disgrace

Dodd's disastrous attempt to get money by forging a bond in the name of the Earl of Chesterfield for £4,200 began on 1 February 1777: Dodd approached a stockbroker, Lewis Robertson, and asked him to raise a loan for Chesterfield, who needed the money without any attention, for private matters. It has been estimated that at this time, Dodd's 'income from clerical livings alone was £800'; the signal insufficiency of this, and the desperate steps Dodd took, suggests the degree of luxury that he had developed in his lifestyle.[45] Robertson found a bank, that of Sir Charles Raymond; one of its partners, a Mr Fletcher, agreed to finance the loan. The bond was made out for £8,400, but it was only binding for half that sum – thus, it could raise £4,200. The bank's conditions are described by Howson: 'the bond was to be repaid in the form of a life annuity of £700 plus interest. This meant that Lord Chesterfield was bound to pay Mr. Fletcher £700 a year, in quarterly payments of £175, with the yearly interest on £700 added to the last quarterly payment, for the rest of his life, or until the £4200 was repaid in cash.'[46] Such exorbitant conditions show that Dodd could only have been thinking of the bond as a short-term solution, soon to be covered up or paid back; equally, these iniquitous terms partly explain the ease with which people forgave Dodd's crime, in a climate where financial institutions were capable of such a fleecing.

Dodd took the bond and returned, on Tuesday 4 February, with Chesterfield's supposed signature and a similarly fraudulent letter of authorisation and receipt. Fletcher and another partner, Peach, made Robertson witness the bond (even though he had not seen Chesterfield sign anything), and he reluctantly complied: as Barker suggests, 'his broker's commission' (some £200) 'was too large to be jeopardised by such scruples'.[47] It was to be John Manley, a solicitor, who brought down the house of cards, as the trial account describes:

> After the money had been obtained, and the bond deposited with Mr. Manly, who acted as attorney for Mr. Fletcher, he observed upon the bond a very remarkable blot; there was no particular effect, I think, in this blot, but it was in the letter e in the word seven, which you will observe in the bond: ... there were some strokes both above and below the line of the bond, which had a very singular appearance; though they could not tell for what purpose any thing had been done with a pen, yet there appeared scratches with a pen as if something had been done[48]

The disputed 'seven' was in the promising to pay the annuity, 'seven hundred pounds of lawful money'. It is often assumed (erroneously) that Dodd was caught forging Chesterfield's signature, yet it was the general suspicion of malpractice implied through this blot that caused the trouble.

It is likely that the lawyers were worried that the blot could be used in the future as some form of legal wrangle to nullify the bond, and refuse repayment. To obtain a fresh copy, Manley went to Chesterfield, who of course was completely ignorant of the whole matter. Manley and Fletcher gained warrants for the arrest of Dodd and Robertson from the Lord Mayor: Dodd was confronted, on 7 February, confessed, exonerated Robertson, and returned £3,600, making over the rest in drafts and 'through obtaining sworn judgments on his personal property'.[49] At this point, Dodd's prosecution was far from inevitable, not least because of the financial cost incurred. It seems to have happened for various (disputed) reasons: having instigated the arrests, Manley and Fletcher (along with Chesterfield) were obliged to go to the Guildhall, where Dodd was charged with a capital felony in front of the Lord Mayor, Sir Thomas Hallifax. The newspaper reports suggest that the latter was notably vindictive, and zealous to prosecute a capital crime that attacked a commercial culture. Whether or not the bankers and Chesterfield were bullied by him (or that Hallifax's ire merely expressed their unspoken wishes) is hard to ascertain. The Earl of Chesterfield, only twenty-three years old, apparently showed no remorse in prosecuting his former tutor.[50] As with the original suspicions over the bond, what was at stake were the ways in which a structure (whether of commerce or nobility) depended upon the authority and authenticity of its subjects; as Paul Baines has written, in his excellent account of the implications of Dodd's forgery, 'Each trial for forgery confirmed (in theory) the secure and ineluctable identity of signature and character.'[51] What remains inexplicable is the contrast between the Earl of Chesterfield's role in the prosecution (albeit a passive and silent one), and his earlier kindnesses to Dodd, not three years since. Robert Anderson ascribed to Dodd an unlikely belief: 'He flattered himself that his noble pupil would have generously paid the amount of the bond, in case of the forgery being detected, before he might be able to repay it; but he had the mortification to find that he was mistaken.'[52] Indeed he did, and the result was imprisonment, while he awaited trial at the Old Bailey.

Dodd was tried and convicted on 22 February. His last and best hope was a legal error: Lewis Robertson, as suspected co-forger, as Barker says, 'in the panic following the detection of the forgery, had been peremptorily included in the warrant of arrest, instead of being sworn as a witness having "evidence" against Dodd'. Alas for Dodd, the wily John Manley obtained Robertson's release, despite his being committed for trial, and enabled him to give evidence.[53] The surreptitious removal and use as a prosecution witness of a potential defendant was an obvious problem; unfortunately, the judge, Lord Chief Justice Mansfield, was disinclined to regard it as anything other than an irrelevance. Dodd's defence of his conduct began a claim he would make repeatedly – he questioned the probity in his case of the literal charge of an 'intention to defraud':

> Such an intention, my Lords, and Gentlemen of the Jury, I believe has not been attempted to be proved upon me; and the consequences that have happened, which have appeared before you, sufficiently prove, that a perfect and ample restitution has been made. I leave it, my Lords, to you, and you, Gentlemen of the Jury, to consider, that if an unhappy man of any kind, ever deviates from the law of right, yet, if in the single first moment of recollection, he does all he can to make a full and perfect amends, what, my Lords, and Gentlemen of the Jury, can God and man desire further?[54]

Moreover, he asks for mercy, because 'no injury, intentional or real, has been done to any man upon the face of the earth' by his crime. Ostensibly, Dodd is persuasive: the claim that the crime had been followed by restitution, and had hurt nobody, was to win the sympathy of an enormous number of followers. The larger suggestion, however, that it has not been shown that he intended to defraud, is more difficult, and seems a desperate form of sophistry: Fitzgerald put it well in deciding that 'law has no means of ascertaining the secret *intentions* of delinquents; it can only deal with their acts'.[55] The other part of his defence is the idea that a single moment of rashness led to his downfall, and that he should not incur the most severe punishment for an action that was an aberration. This too is hardly convincing, given that a forgery must be deliberated far more than this notion of a moment's aberration suggests. Dodd's strongest suit was not in questioning the semantics of his guilt, but rather in the unjust severity of the sentence of execution; the latter fact would win the help of far from unqualified admirers such as Samuel Johnson.

The only potential relief was that the question of whether Robertson's evidence was inadmissible was delayed until the tribunal of assize judges could act upon it, at the end of their circuit. This gave Dodd a reprieve until May, which did much to foster the campaign to save him. The tribunal offered no hope, however: it met on 18 April, and on 14 May, they told Dodd more or less what Mansfield had – that the gathering of the evidence and the legality thereof was not their concern, so much as its presence and content.[56] Two days later, Dodd was sentenced to death. There was little doubt that he would be hanged, despite petitions and appeals that culminated in an unsuccessful meeting of the Privy Council and King on 13 June.[57] Concern over forgery had made it a capital offence since 1729, and in the prevailing climate, Dodd's crime was unlikely to attract much leniency. His speech on the occasion of his sentencing was written by Johnson, and contains, in its appeal for mercy, an admission of humility that is earnestly self-critical: 'Being distinguished and elevated by the confidence of mankind, I had too much confidence in myself, and thinking my integrity, what others thought it, established in sincerity, and fortified by religion, I did not consider the danger of vanity, nor suspect the deceitfulness of my own heart.'[58] Johnson's efforts on behalf of Dodd may have been unavailing, but they did present him in a light more favourable than his own pleas and self-justifications.

Public sympathy and celebrity

The quantity of the public response in Dodd's case remains astonishing.[59] The vast majority of writings on the topic were favourable to Dodd. Many of these were repetitious in the extreme, or plagiarised, and most followed the quickly established defence that involved mitigation of the crime, and the failure of the punishment to fit it. Dodd had many friends and enemies, but there is no doubt that he was (even if partly for self-aggrandisement) a considerable worker for charities, and this was immediately reflected in the literature:

> This man, with all his faults, was not without his virtues, he was the promoter of many charities, and the institutor of some of them. The Magdalen hospital, the society for the relief of poor debtors, and that for the recovery of persons apparently drowned, will, we trust, be perpetual monuments to his credit, but it is our duty not to conceal or disguise his faults, the principal of which appear to have been vanity, and a turn for extravagance, which ruined his circumstances[60]

As the campaign to save Dodd gathered apace, he stood higher in estimation than he had ever done during the struggles for advancement of the previous decades. At the same time, such public support was never unequivocal, and the questioning of Dodd's real and abiding piety comes through the interstices of private writings of the time. Horace Walpole, rather typically, spoke out loud and bold in his journals, gossiping of Dodd's having 'married a kept mistress of Lord Sandwich' and 'encouraged her love of drinking, that he might be at liberty to indulge himself in other amours'. Furthermore, Dodd's calling was elaborately bound up with his conceit and self-gratification: 'Still were his pleasures indecently blended with his affected devotion; and in the intervals of his mission, he indulged in the fopperies and extravagances of a young Macaroni'. At least his disgrace had humbled him, so that 'he at once abandoned himself to his confusion, shame, and terror, and had at least the merit of acting no parade of fortitude. He swooned at his trial, avowed his guilt, confessed his fondness for life, and deprecated his fate with agonies of grief'.[61] Dodd's false theatricality, for Walpole, had its limits, and there came a time when the canting had to stop.

Walpole was also fascinated with the way that the Dodd case brought out ambivalent responses, until the 'malevolence of men and their good nature displayed themselves in their different characters against Dodd'. Thomas Newton, Bishop of Bristol (whose Milton scholarship had been praised by Dodd), opined that '"I am sorry for Dr. Dodd." Being asked why, he replied, "Because he is to be hanged for the least crime he ever committed."'[62] Sir John Hawkins was similarly blunt, chairing the Grand Jury for Middlesex that sent Dodd to trial, and being far from contrite in his *Life of Johnson*; the years had, it appeared, only deepened the mystery of why Johnson wasted his time on such a miscreant, being 'induced, by a case of a very extraordinary nature, to the exercise of that indiscriminate humanity, which, in him, was obedient to every call'.[63] The unclubbable Hawkins was sceptical of the fashionable and uncritical nature of the campaign to save Dodd:

> The public were, at first, very little interested in the fate of a man, who, besides the arts he had practised to make himself conspicuous as a man of letters, had rendered himself scandalous, by an offer, to the first law-officer in the kingdom, of a large sum of money, for a presentation to a valuable rectory; but, by various artifices, and particularly, the insertion of his name in the public papers, with such palliatives as he and his friends could invent, never without the epithet of *unfortunate*, they were betrayed into such an enthusiastic commiseration of his case, as would have led a stranger to believe, that himself had been no accessory to his distresses, but that they were the inflictions of Providence. (pp. 312–13)

Hawkins is right about the peculiar manner in which Dodd went from being a guilty figure, evoking compassion, to a celebrity who, by some apparent accident or miscarriage of justice, was to be executed. The very epithet 'unfortunate' is itself significant, suggesting that it was unfair that Dodd would be hanged for a crime that hurt only the reputations of a bank and a wealthy nobleman, and implying that he bore no responsibility for his own sufferings, being, in some unspecified way, an innocent victim. It was no great step for an 'enthusiastic' and unthinking response to move from palliating the degree of Dodd's crime, to assuming that he had committed no crime at all. The question of agency, as so often with Dodd's downfall, recurs, and the prevalent idea is that circumstances beyond his control (such as the rash moment when he forged the bond) are to blame, rather than himself.

Hawkins failed to understand that it was possible to not be hoodwinked by the excessive sensibility in support of Dodd, and yet still find it barbarous to hang a man for dishonestly obtaining money. His own zeal against the chic of Dodd's followers blinded him to such considerations. Instead, he insisted that 'We live in an age in which humanity is the fashion', and the innate conservatism of the magistrate is distrustful of the motives of those who would challenge the law. Hawkins's response was what Fitzgerald had in mind when describing how 'The wretched clergyman was the victim of the old, stupid, mulish British complacency, which has so often fancied itself doing something Spartan and splendid, when it is only cruel and ridiculous.'[64]

Johnson's 'indiscriminate' humanity was something Hawkins neither accepted nor fully understood. In the early twentieth century, when editing Johnson's writings on Dodd, R. W. Chapman showed such understanding, even if he was almost as outspoken: 'Nothing in Johnson's history is more characteristic than his efforts to save the life of a canting swindler, to whose true character he was never blind.'[65] And Johnson's attitude towards Dodd is far from simple. When asked by Dodd's supporters, Boswell tells us, Johnson 'seemed much agitated, after which he said, "I will do what I can;" – and certainly he did make extraordinary exertions'.[66] Johnson went to every effort to save Dodd, writing various letters, helping to draft petitions, and writing for Dodd, including his own speech at his sentence, and a sermon which he preached in Newgate Prison. Yet this work was not unconditional. As Robert Anderson put it, 'Johnson thought [Dodd's] sentence just; yet, perhaps, fearing that religion might suffer from the errors of one of its ministers, he endeavoured to prevent the last ignominious spectacle.'[67] Johnson's fear was that to hang a well-known religious figure, for whatever reason, could not be good for the security and authority of the Church, combined with a practical sense that the public may be misled sometimes, but they cannot all be wrong, if their concerted voice is heard: 'The supreme power has, in all ages, paid some attention to the voice of the people; and that voice does not least deserve to be heard, when it calls out for mercy', he wrote to Charles Jenkinson, Secretary-at-War and a man reputed to have the ear of George III. And the people's voice matters, because Dodd's punishment should be a response to their judgement, rather than the concerns of commercial houses. This is made plain in his plea to Lady Harrington: 'Dodd must die at last unless your Ladyship shall be pleased to represent to his Majesty how properly the Life of a Delinquent may be granted to the Petitions of that Society for the sake of which he is to be punished.'[68] The clearest expression of public judgement was the 'Petition of the City of London' for mercy; drawn up by one 'Tomkins of Sermon-Lane', a famous calligrapher, it was thirty-seven and a half yards in length, with 23,000 signatures, making it then the largest petition in British history. In the draft of it, Johnson states of the public 'That when they consider [Dodd's] past life, they are willing to suppose his late crime to have been not the consequence of habitual depravity, but the suggestion of some sudden and violent temptation.'[69] Johnson represents a value system at odds with the merely commercial;

the night before his execution, Johnson wrote to Dodd, telling him to 'Be comforted: your crime, morally or religiously considered, has no very deep dye of turpitude. It corrupted no man's principles; it attacked no man's life. It involved only a temporary and reparable injury.'[70]

Johnson's forgiveness of Dodd was practical and considered, weighing up his crime against a religious standard, and finding that justice and public opinion was best served by mercy (such as transportation), rather than execution, which only exposed the draconian needs of the law. The measured way in which Johnson attacked the injustice of Dodd's sentence, yet made it clear that he was under no illusions about the inconsistencies of his conduct, shows up other giddy and less thoughtful responses that may have done Dodd's cause more harm than good, by offering a mixture of absurd sanctification and voyeurism. Johnson was aware of the discrepancy between Dodd's present martyrdom and his questionable past, hence his writing (in a letter to Boswell the day after Dodd's execution), that 'His moral character is very bad: I hope all is not true that is charged upon him.'[71] Moreover, whilst Johnson did what he could to save Dodd's life, he refused to accept the canonisation of him that followed:

> He talked of Dr. Dodd. 'A friend of mine, (said he,) came to me and told me, that a lady wished to have Dr. Dodd's picture in a bracelet, and asked me for a motto. I said, I could think of no better than *Currat Lex* [let the law take its course]. I was very willing to have him pardoned, that is, to have the sentence changed to transportation: but, when he was once hanged, I did not wish he should be made a saint.'[72]

Johnson resents the impiety of turning Dodd into something he was not, but this gaudy bracelet also shows us another version of Dr Dodd, turned into a different commodity to release the sentiments of the wealthy. It was not a spectacle that delighted Johnson, as it contradicted the whole moral behind his support of the campaign for clemency.

Although he was in many ways its figurehead, Johnson's sincere distrust of the circus surrounding Dodd before and after his death allies him to an extent with those sceptical voices, such as Hawkins, that saw the excess of sensibility as self-indulgent, misleading, and potentially dangerous. The anonymous author of *Thoughts of a Citizen of London on the Conduct of Dr. Dodd* (published in 1777 after Dodd's execution) produced a turgid pamphlet with an unforgiving scriptural vehemence, but the point is made that the quality of mercy that summer seemed to be class-specific:

> There was, about the time of Dr. Dodd's condemnation, a man condemned to be hanged, and a woman to be burnt, for washing a halfpenny to make it

pass for a shilling. No humanity acted here to prevent the sentence taking place, nor no commiseration was shed upon them. But they were poor; and they were also, perhaps, ignorant of the penalty of the law in the case; and they had, perhaps, never once been led into the paths of goodness. So partial is our boasted humanity![73]

For all that the pamphlet replaces one extreme with another, opposing defences of Dodd's innocence by painting him absolutely as a dissembling villain, it is of course true that Dodd's social position engineered much of the sympathy that came his way. As Baines puts it, 'the peculiar status of the crime and the gentility of its perpetrator lent a special poignancy and interest to the suffering criminal'.[74] Such gentility made Dodd seem removed from the grubby responsibility of the crime, as did the raptures of his followers. Dodd's goodness was, many believed, merely a 'shew', but the *cause célèbre* of his downfall and the efforts to save him made him into a fantasy figure of innocence or a vehicle for schadenfreude; above all, the dominant note was not legal rigour but sensibility.

In a letter to Elizabeth Montagu just before the execution, Elizabeth Carter shows a wariness of the cult of Dodd. She comments on a letter to Dodd from Lady Huntington, which was a somewhat convoluted homily:

> nothing but that voice of Almighty power, that spoke from the Cross to your suffering companion here, can be your point now: And we all, like him, must pass sentence upon ourselves, and say, *We indeed receive the due reward of our deeds*. How soon the welcome request, *Lord remember me, &c.* reached the heart of our divine Substitute; how speedy the relief; how lasting and complete the comfort. The meaning of my prayers and tears for your grief, would have no other language but *Go and do thou likewise*.

Carter found this rather purple: 'I heard Lady Huntingdon's letter to Dr Dodd read, and as far as we could disentangle the sense from a strange perplexity of language, the meaning seemed to be, an exhortation to a quiet submission to his punishment, which would be a more excellent sermon than he had ever preached.' There is little pretence that the unfortunate Dodd has lived an unblemished life. She asks, 'Have you read his last paper', in order to note that 'There was nothing ostentatious or affected in it', and she decries the 'madness of petitioning', which sacrifices deeply felt beliefs to spontaneity, with people 'instead of acting upon general principles, to be moved only, as Lord Bacon expresses it, "by the spur of the occasion"'.[75] Just as Dodd's sincerity had so often been questioned, the excessive sentiment of his supporters appeared to some to cover up the questionable substance of its object. Yet in terms of publicity and book sales, Dodd was (ironically) at his height; he had never been more in demand as an author, and his new celebrity renegotiated the perception of success and failure. Even *The Sisters* was reprinted, to cash in. This less qualified support for Dodd saw him as akin to a sentimental hero in a fiction; appropriately, he was busy in Newgate producing his own attempted masterpiece of sensibility.

Prison sensibility

Dodd's time in prison offers abiding evidence of why his career ended up as a failure, even as his new status in the public eye gave his writings an unlikely success. From the accounts of his time from arrest until execution, the convict Dodd can be presented as a pious, devotional saint and sentimental martyr, or a cynical hypocrite so used to surviving pitfalls that even the threat of death was less important than a new scheme for reviving his finances. He was far from idle, both as writer and self-promoter. A telling anecdote concerns 'Sir Roger de Coverly', the manuscript play that Dodd had written during his thwarted attempt to enter literary life, in 1750. He resuscitated it, and sent it to Arthur Murphy at Drury Lane, and then to Thomas Harris at Covent Garden. William Woodfall, the editor of *The Morning Chronicle*, paid a visit to Dodd in June, after the execution date had been set, and after Harris had sent back the manuscript. Howson paraphrases the scene:

> When he entered Dodd's cell he naturally began to condole with him, but the doctor interrupted him, saying he wished to see him about a different subject. 'Knowing Mr. Woodfall's judgment on dramatic matters, he was anxious to have his opinion of a comedy which he had written, and if he approved of it, to request his interest with the managers to bring it on the stage.' Mr. Woodfall was not only surprised, but shocked to find the Doctor so insensible of his position, for whenever he tried to console the Doctor, he replied, 'O, they will never hang me!'[76]

Such insouciance and odd priorities suggest why Dodd offended as many as he charmed. It recalls the monomania of Richard Savage, in prison indefinitely for debt, but oblivious to anything beyond the supposed attempts to cheat him of the inevitable success of the revived *Sir Thomas Overbury*. Like Savage, Dodd's sense of his own importance seems to have survived the worst privations.

This glimpse of Dodd at his least appealing casts a different light on his last and most successful poetic work, *Thoughts in Prison*, composed between February and April 1777. It was published in September, and edited by Weedon Butler, Dodd's long-time friend, editorial assistant on

The Christian Magazine, and general aid in Dodd's anthologised *Commentary on the Bible*.[77] *Thoughts in Prison* was the capstone to the narrative of Dodd as sentimental hero, an innocent betrayed by an uncaring world. It would eventually run to twenty-nine editions, until the aura of Dodd at last vanished almost completely, by the end of the nineteenth century. Such longevity is a testament to Dodd's sensational decline and fall. A major contemporary selling point of the poem was its tragic immediacy: it was, we are told, 'begun by its unhappy Author in his Apartments at Newgate, on the evening of the day subsequent to his Trial and Conviction at Justice-hall; and was finished, amidst various necessary interruptions, in little more than the space of two months'.[78]

Thoughts in Prison is the very height of a certain type of writing, the epitome of the unqualified exhibition of sensibility. It is not an easy read, as its very raptures ensure it has only one register, that of beseeching address, and it is not a matter of decorum so much as the inability of any reader to follow the peak of Dodd's feeling for very long that makes the poem so unyielding. It is supposedly a poetic journal, divided into the melancholy weeks of Dodd's internment. Its content is unsurprisingly repetitive: Dodd wants mercy, he looks at the greater sins of others, then checks himself, as a contrite, lowly worm in God's eye. He muses on his sentence – capital punishment is unjust, and degrading; prison doesn't work, save as a finishing school for criminals. Christianity, in its Protestant sense, is best, with its true mercy and reward of eternity (unlike the falsehoods of Islam and the materialism of Catholicism), though Anglicanism is better still, as it removes the excessive enthusiasm of the Methodists, and non-conformists generally. The poem thus offers the typical opinions of a vaguely liberal clergyman of Dodd's day (moderate, apparently sincere in religious outlook but somewhat intolerant, hating the conditions of prisoners but accepting the general necessity for some sort of punishment) broken down into unrhyming ten-syllable lines.

For all its commercial success, *Thoughts in Prison* has never found a favourable critical view since the time of Dodd's demise. Howson describes reading it as 'a depressing experience, for as one turns over the seemingly endless pages, it becomes increasingly difficult to remember that this is an authentic human document, the actual thoughts of a man condemned to death'. Barker agrees, being surprised that Dodd's 'contemporaries were impressed by the composure and pious resignation' of it, as a 'modern reader will find very little sincerity or contrition in it; its primary aim is self-exculpation'. Years before, Percy Fitzgerald exhibited incredulity at this 'absurd piece of bombast', which 'in its style, matter, length, and quality, makes up one of the most extraordinary performances of the world. It is absolutely unique', but not in any good way: 'every verse furnishes a peg on which to hang some personal reference to [Dodd's] private glories', there are 'notes that show off his erudition', along with 'whining Jeremiads over his fate, and the exaggerated self-laudation of ostentatious penitence and complacent conversion'.[79]

The extravagant performance of *Thoughts in Prison* is misconceived: the context would suggest that a more austere approach would be appropriate. That would reckon against Dodd's genius for theatrical self-presentation, as in the following apostrophe: 'Ah what a wretch thou art! how sunk, how fall'n, / *From what high state of bliss, into what woe!' While it is surely not unusual for a man to self-aggrandise when in extremes, only Dodd could have followed this comparison of himself with the fallen angels of *Paradise Lost* with the footnote, '*Milton. Par. L. B. 5. 540.' Such displays of learning seem perverse under the circumstances, and as Fitzgerald fulminated, suggest that Dodd 'was scarcely in the overwhelmed and repentant condition he professed himself' to inhabit.[80]

Diffidence was evidently not part of Dodd's nature, but undoubtedly the experience of prison must have been singularly shocking for a man accustomed to a high level of comfort and status, and the poem works best in small doses, as in this description of his impressions:

>   – I only hear around
> The dismal clang of chains; the hoarse rough shout
> Of dissonant imprecation; and the cry
> Of misery and vice, in fearful din
> Impetuous mingled; while my frighted mind
> Shrinks back in horror! while the scalding tears
> Involuntary starting, furrow down
> My sickly cheeks; and whirling thought confus'd
> For giddy moments, scarce allows to know
> Or where, or who, or what a wretch I am!
>
>   (p. 38)

For once, it is not the sentiment which lacks sincerity, but rather the degree to which it is extended, with his tears 'scalding' amidst the 'fearful din'. These descriptive excesses remove the scene from specific earthly despair, and make it redolent instead of a generalised sort of Miltonic Hell. This seems to reflect a need in Dodd to make his suffering fit into a sort of literary pedigree. The worst fault of *Thoughts in Prison* is that it takes material of genuine suffering, and negates it by exaggeration.

Sympathy is also vexed by Dodd's contrition. The repeated examination of himself and his sins is unconvincing because perfunctory. It follows a

Prison sensibility 103

pattern whereby Dodd will ask some question of himself or others, only to halt the narrative in a burst of overwhelmed feeling. Early on, he praises the greatness of providence, but (somewhat contradictorily) wonders why its workings will result in his execution:

> Why then, mysterious Providence! pursued
> With such unfeeling ardour? why pursued
> To death's dread bourn, by men to me unknown!
> Why – Stop the deep question; it o'erwhelms my soul;
> It reels, it staggers! – Earth turns round! – my brain
> Whirls in confusion! my impetuous heart
> Throbs with pulsations not to be restrain'd:
> Why? – where? – Oh Chesterfield! my son, my son!
> (pp. 41–2)

An uncharitable, but pragmatic answer to this 'Why' would involve the fact of his crime. Rather than answer the question, Dodd apportions blame: it is the fault of 'men to me unknown', then, as his breakdown develops, of Philip Stanhope, Earl of Chesterfield.

This pattern is repeated, as the poem opens up what appear superficially to be moments of confession, only for the waters to be muddied and responsibility left in abeyance. Dodd's main version of himself is a naïve and credulous figure who is taken in by the wickedness of the world and its inhabitants, 'led to place / Ingenuous all thy confidence of life / In men, assuming gentle pity's guise' (p. 47). This unconvincing façade is developed by accumulation; at many of the points where Dodd supposedly examines himself, what is striking is how often accountability for his ruin is sidestepped. He compares himself, for instance, to famous prisoners, being

> Like thee, oh gallant Raleigh! – or like thee,
> My hapless ancestor, fam'd Overbury! –
> But oh, in this how different is our fate!
> Thou, to a vengeful woman's subtle wiles
> A hapless victim fall'st; while my deep gloom,
> Brighten'd by female virtue and the light
> Of conjugal affection – leads me oft,
> Like the poor prison'd linnet, to forget
> Freedom, and tuneful friends, and russet heath
> (p. 73)

Even Dodd's supporters would presumably have hesitated to bracket him with Sir Walter Raleigh and Sir Thomas Overbury, both imprisoned for vindictive reasons by the machinations (respectively) of an arbitrary monarch and at least one half of an aristocratic couple. If Dodd's appeals for mercy deserved to be heeded, his comparison of himself with these two innocent victims of political power suggests again how he implies that the blame for his downfall lies elsewhere.

Yet, for all his exaggeration, blurring of facts, and insincerity, Dodd does have to attempt to explain the past, in particular the role that finances have played in his present suffering. He does so whilst apologising for the incongruity of his lavish lifestyle with the acceptable morals of the clergy: 'what my heart condemn'd / Unwise it practis'd; never without pang'; he was 'too much influenc'd by the pleasing force / Of native generosity, uncurb'd / And unchastis'd (as reason, duty taught)' and ignored 'Prudent œconomy' and its 'sober school' (p. 111). This is as near to an apology as Dodd gets. Ultimately, his position is that of victim – of passions, of the social aspiration towards luxury, and of men less innocent than himself:

> Deluded, from frugality's just care,
> And parsimony needful! One who scorn'd
> Mean love of gold, yet to that power, – his scorn
> Retorting vengeful, – a mark'd victim fell!
> Of one, who, unsuspecting, and ill-form'd
> For the world's subtleties, his bare breast bore
> Unguarded, open; and ingenuous, thought
> All men ingenuous, frank and open too!
> (p. 170)

This attempt to show how he was a slave to desires and the wicked wiles of others misfires, like most of Dodd's explanations of his life and disaster, because of the alacrity with which it escapes questions of blame.

The contradictions in *Thoughts in Prison* are so obvious, and the repeated attempts at self-exculpation so tangled and unconvincing, that its success remains a mystery, being a triumph of publicity over art. The volume in which it was published concluded with Dodd's 'Last Prayer', supposedly written the night before his execution, which sees Dodd praying for George III (who had signally failed to pardon him). It brought forth Johnson's famous retort: 'A man who has been canting all his life may cant to the last', which remains the best criticism of the fervent apologia of *Thoughts in Prison* itself.[81]

A literary death

The success of *Thoughts in Prison*, published two months after Dodd's execution, showed the degree to which his celebrity guaranteed him a useless popular acclaim, after years of producing hack writing. His work had not changed – it was simply that Dodd the sentimental martyr had become a selling point. It remains the case that his works have never been discussed (except with opprobrium) by literary critics since his death, and that for all his posthumous material success, Dodd's works were devoid of influence, and he left nothing to posterity, save the notoriety of his crime and punishment. Even his part in the huge effects of *The Beauties of Shakespear* was diluted by the removal of all his annotation.

Dodd, then, is a failed author turned into a celebrity by personal disaster, and made successful in such a manner as to render the literary content or qualities of his work irrelevant. It has been a leading argument of this chapter that from the beginning of his career, there were always two co-existent views of Dodd – either he was a charismatic and charming worker of good deeds, or a superficial and insincere materialist. These two views of Dodd continued to be held both during the period around his execution, and in his literary afterlife.

If his many supporters thought that Dodd's new celebrity would prevent him from being hanged, they were proved wrong, but an interesting side to the support for Dodd is the assumption that a man of such sensibility would be punished enough by his disgrace. In a popular contemporary 'it' narrative, *The Adventures of a Hackney Coach*, two passengers pass by Tyburn on 27 June, the day of Dodd's execution. One is in sympathy: 'From the gloomy confines of self-reproach, and never-ceasing anguish, to cast a retrospective look at his former elevated situation in life, – his boundless popularity! – admired genius! – and powerful influence, will be punishment enough, Heaven knows! to a mind formed like his.'[82] This idea of Dodd's intellect and former position places him far away from a messy reality where people accumulate debts and commit crimes, and makes him sound instead like a character in a novel, a hero of sensibility who will be punished forever by his ruined reputation. Dodd's friend Philip Thicknesse described him as 'a man of strong passions, expensive to an high degree, void of all prudence, possessed of extreme sensibility, and went through (long before he suffered death) a torture of mind, between hope and fear, which was worse than a thousand deaths. If therefore he had been pardoned, he would not have escaped without an adequate punishment for his manifold sins.'[83] This more practical view sees Dodd as one who has suffered enough for his numerous excesses, a result of strong, almost uncontrolled feelings and passions – a less high-minded sort of sensibility.

It is not hard to invert Thicknesse's argument and argue that Dodd was not a victim of passion and sensibility so much as a manipulator of them. This was Horace Walpole's opinion: 'He was undoubtedly a bad man, who employed religion to promote his ambition, – humanity to establish a character and, it is to be hoped, to indulge his good-natured suggestions, – and any means to gratify his passions or vanity, and to extricate himself out of their distressing consequences.'[84] These two readings of Dodd's conduct – a sincere, if misguided penitent and vessel of sentiment, or a dissembling, manipulative hypocrite – directed responses to Dodd after his death: the former bought his books, and the latter viewed his sanctification as another example of the absurdity of public taste. Similarly, of the many accounts of Dodd's final day, there are contrasting depictions of him as an emblem of sensibility or a rather nondescript man.

John Villette, the Ordinary of Newgate, published his *Genuine Account* as soon as possible. His Dodd is a high-minded figure, helping particularly with the consolation of one Harris, a young man who was to hang with him. In the yard, before boarding the cart, Dodd 'exhorted his fellow-sufferer, who had attempted to destroy himself, but had been prevented by the vigilance of the keeper. He spoke to him with great tenderness and emotion of heart.' Moreover, 'His conversation to this poor youth was so moving, that tears flowed from the eyes of all present.' Dodd's ministrations continued: 'he again addressed himself to Harris in the most moving and persuasive manner, and not without effect; for he declared that he was glad he had not made away with himself, and said he was easier, and hoped he should now go to heaven'.[85] This description of Dodd is not unlike a novel of sensibility, with the broad noble outlines of Dodd's character and the melting into tears through shared emotion by all present. Villette continues in this strain when the cart reaches Tyburn:

> When he arrived at the gallows, he ascended the cart, and spoke to his fellow-sufferer. He then prayed, not only for himself, but also for his wife, and the unfortunate youth that suffered with him; and declaring that he died in the true faith of the gospel of Christ, in perfect love and charity with all mankind, and with thankfulness to his friend, he was launched into eternity, imploring mercy for his soul for the sake of his blessed Redeemer. (p. 21)

It is the death of a sincere Christian, at peace with himself. Whilst it would be offensive to doubt its veracity, there is something in Villette's writing that presents the Dodd which his many supporters wanted to see – a resigned penitent who represents the full humility of his faith.

Other bystanders saw the event somewhat differently. The nobleman George Selwyn's morbid interest in executions led him to request his friend Anthony Morris Storer to make notes and send him an account of Dodd's death. In Storer's account, nothing happens:

A literary death

Upon the whole, the piece was not full of events. The Doctor, to all appearance, was rendered perfectly stupid from despair. His hat was flapped all around, and pulled over his eyes, which were never directed to any object around, nor even raised, except now and then lifted up in the course of his prayers ... He was a considerable time praying, which some people standing about seemed rather tired with: they rather wished for some more interesting part of the tragedy. The wind, which was high, blew off his hat, which rather embarrassed him ... He never moved from the place he first took in the cart; seemed absorbed in despair, and utterly dejected, without any other signs of animation but in praying.[86]

Perhaps the most telling factor is that some were disappointed by such a nondescript scene. Villette's outwardly reconciled Dodd is replaced by an introverted figure who loses his hat in the wind. 'I really do not conceive an execution with so few incidents could possibly happen', Storer concludes without apparent irony, a terrible reflection both on his own expectations, and on the ease with which a tragic event is entertainment for others (pp. 198–9). Horace Walpole, unsurprisingly, had his say on the event, where Dodd's performance again seems flat:

> The signal criminal suffered decently; but the expected commiseration was much drawn aside by the spectacle of an aged father, who accompanied his son, one Harris, who was executed for a robbery at the same time. The streaming tears, grey hairs, agony, and at last the appearance of a deadly swoon in the poor old man, who supported his son in his lap, deepened the tragedy, but rendered Dr. Dodd's share in it less affecting.[87]

With his own form of irony, Walpole reports on how one spectacle had replaced another: the expected outpouring of support for Dodd was transferred by the appearance of Harris's father, described as if it was a scene from *The Man of Feeling*. Walpole's description shows how the phenomenon of Dodd ensured that the man himself had become a cipher for the expectations or desires of others, and would soon be replaced by whatever fashionable cause became more of a sensation, just as Harris's father gained more attention at the execution.

The immediate posthumous success of his works notwithstanding, these descriptions of his end offer clues to the larger failure of Dodd as a literary figure. Notoriety may have kept him in the public eye for years (a melodrama based on his life ran in Surrey in the 1830s), but his works are as mundane as Storer's account of his death, and their appeal based entirely around his unhappy celebrity.[88] Dodd's fall from grace created his appeal as a writer, but also made him into a stock figure from sensibility (like that drawn by Villette), rather than an achieved author whose works were read for their own value. Refreshingly, Dodd seems to have had little pretensions about his work; that its success was a result of an act of official barbarity that ended his life is significant for what it shows about a culture's ability to consume sensations and scandals: that the cumulative aesthetic failure of Dodd's writing was transformed materially into huge sales suggests how little quality or critical reception matters in terms of literary success, and how arbitrary the rewards granted to authors. The central contribution of the mass media of the day – newspapers, pamphlets, petitions – to publicising Dodd's case shows how relatively rarefied literary production remained: other than his religious compilations, none of Dodd's works seem intended for a large audience, and his writings only found one after his celebrity made him widely known beyond society gossip and journals looking for discreet and well-connected scandal.

Apart from the turgid melodrama of *Thoughts in Prison*, nothing that Dodd wrote (or most of what he edited) can be called original at all. He was happy to sacrifice the mediocrity of his literary career for a life that was more directly acquisitive and played to his charms as a performer. It was only the unfortunate celebrity of his disastrous fall that represented him as an author again, albeit one that represented a sentimental ideal of suffering. Dodd's case is in many ways eerily predictive of modern movements which see the artist as a spectacle, with the narrative performance of their life providing a substitute for any substantial canon of works. Nor is it a coincidence that Dodd's life is contemporary with the emergence of widespread literary and artistic celebrity, with cases such as Johnson and Garrick. Yet ultimately, Dodd's failure offers a sense of perspective, whereby the question of literature seems ultimately of little relevance, given his fate. Like many a celebrity since, whose career his example superficially anticipates, Dodd was made famous not by hard work, artistic skill, or inspiration, but by publicity; unlike most, he paid a rather higher price.

In consideration of his eventual fate, literary fame was a trivial matter for Dodd. For the subjects of the next two chapters, failure to achieve such fame was a defining part of their lives.

CHAPTER 3

Anna Seward's cruel times

The literary criticism of Anna Seward (1742–1809) was rarely dull or disinterested, not least in her writings about her fellow Lichfieldian Samuel Johnson, the former pupil of her grandfather, and an abiding presence in the six volumes of her letters (published posthumously in 1811), though her anecdotes of him are far from Boswellian bonhomie. In 1785, she wrote to the novelist Frances Brooke, praising Thomas Warton's newly published edition of Milton's shorter poems:

> Its critical notes have all the eloquence and strength of Johnson, without his envy. Johnson told me once, 'he would hang a dog that read the Lycidas twice.' 'What then,' replied I, 'must become of me, who can say it by heart; and who often repeat it to myself, with a delight "which grows by what it feeds upon?"' 'Die,' returned the growler, 'in a surfeit of bad taste.'[1]

Seward would later claim that *Lycidas* was a 'test', as to read it without pleasure 'argues a morbid deficiency in the judgment and in the affections' (*Letters*, vol. 1, p. 191). It is a test that the churlish Johnson fails. The anecdote presents many of the key elements that make Seward such an odd literary figure: even the reader disgusted at his rudeness will note that the opposing dichotomy – blunt, dismissive Johnson, and open, generous Seward – is somewhat artificial, and affected in manner. The juxtaposition of an apparently self-evident premise (the greatness of *Lycidas*) with the folly of those who oppose it is typical of Seward, dramatising the huge importance of poetry to her in a way that also leaves her vulnerable; it is a pattern that is repeated in the many literary controversies in which she engaged. 'I am impetuous, resentful, and without an atom of what the world calls discretion', she remarked in 1781, and such qualities were to lead her into many strange waters.[2] It is the purpose of this chapter to open up intriguing aspects of Seward's aesthetic, and to suggest why her work has always gained attention, and yet never gives the impression of satisfaction, enacting instead a peculiar set of (partly) self-imposed limitations.

To speak of Seward as a failure is in one sense unjust: her poems were often successful with the public, and her importance as a woman writer in the provinces who nevertheless developed an influential literary circle, and knew Johnson and Erasmus Darwin, and later Scott and Southey, has ensured her posthumous attention. Yet such success as she had was often compromised, in her lifetime and posthumously: her life and writings are, in a sense, about failure, both overtly in the reflection of her own difficulties and the boundaries placed upon her literary life, and also as a subtext to the intellectual problems that blighted her. For all her outward enthusiasm, Seward often seems to fetishise failure, and her writing is implicitly concerned with regret, loss, and the injustice of a world which does not encourage or support her. This chapter will look at Seward's work more closely than has often been the case, in order to present her as a notable example of the unfulfilled literary life, one that raises substantial questions concerning taste, literary judgement, and the possibilities open to a non-metropolitan woman writer in the later eighteenth century. Moreover, her attempt to fashion her career through posterity, using the medium of collected works and correspondence, is a flawed but revealing enterprise. Seward's career epitomises a certain absence of fulfilment that is as telling, in its own way, as cases of more abject and obvious failure.

In the past, criticism refused to take Seward's poetry or criticism at all seriously; more recently, she has been applauded for the integrity and independence of what she represents – a provincial woman speaking out against a male establishment – yet this generalised approach tends to appreciate the idea of her as an author, rather than its more complicated details. Norma Clarke, for example, in separate accounts of Seward, argues that she 'took a resolute stand for scholarship and impartiality over the burgeoning world of professional literary journalism', and 'constructed an authoritative role for herself, espousing the absolute value of a literary canon based on correct critical principles'.[3] These are large claims, and the evidence both supports and conflicts with Clarke's assertions, as Seward's scholarship and critical principles are not as consistent as she suggests. A thorough examination of her criticism and poetry is useful in showing the rounded literary career of Seward, even with its failures.

The contention of this chapter is that the unevenness of Seward's writing and the eccentricity of some of her views make her a valuable witness indeed: she consistently overturns the conventional wisdom of literary history, praising to the skies figures now all but forgotten, and damning writers assumed to have been secure in their reputation. She also had an inconsistent but sure poetic talent. Not the least of her attractions is that she is too outspoken to be a representative figure. It is often the case that even Seward's more peculiar opinions lead to obscure, but pertinent areas of attention, just as her own lack of fulfilment suggests much about both the ambitions and frustrations of authorship.

Bardolatry and self-editing

The older view of Seward, widely held until relatively recently, was of a literary eccentric who covered up her small talent by the asperity of her opinions. The success of poems such as her *Elegy on Captain Cook* (1780), and verse-novel *Louisa* of 1784 (which went into five editions), as well as her near ubiquitous presence in *The Gentleman's Magazine* in the last two decades of the century ensured Seward's status as perhaps the most publicly recognised British female writer of the time, yet it has usually been seen as a triumph of publicity. Egerton Brydges, a writer not known for understatement, summarised this reading of her, in his *Memoirs*: 'She both gave offence and provoked ridicule by her affectation, and bad taste, and pompous pretensions. It cannot be denied that she sometimes showed flashes of genius; but never in continuity.'[4] More critical examinations of Seward came to similar conclusions. An essay in 1939 by Samuel Holt Monk claimed that her enthusiastic amateurism revealed her limitations: Seward's 'literary vanity' and connections 'have earned for her name a memory that is denied to her works'. She 'took pleasure in literature; in fact, it may be said that she lived it', hence her 'naively frank and sometimes self-damaging utterances'. She was 'by nature a sentimentalist and an enthusiast', and 'bardolatry was her forte', but she was 'endowed with no remarkable critical perceptions'. This led her to make incongruous judgements, illuminating a contemporary by placing them indiscriminately at the same estimation as Milton or Shakespeare. Her 'weakness as a critic' is that she 'almost abandoned thought and objectivity for feeling'. Furthermore, she was 'forever dramatizing the literary scene' as 'a milieu in which geniuses (received with laurel crowns by herself) were destroyed by reviewers'.[5]

Monk makes some telling points, but his blanket dismissal of Seward as an empty enthusiast is unforgiving. Seward indeed rejected contemporary critical standards (to the detriment of her own criticism), but for significant reasons. Whereas Monk regards her as an isolated case of literary vanity, more recent criticism stresses the historical importance of Seward (who occupied rooms in the Bishop's Palace at Lichfield for the last fifty-four years of her life) as a provincial woman writer. Norma Clarke's readings take Seward far more seriously, claiming that she 'set herself up as an arbiter of taste', had a 'strength of belief in her own genius that never wavered', and 'believed her genius and application had earned her a place in English literary history'. Clarke sees 'her strongly expressed literary and political opinions which some considered malignant as well as vain and egotistical' as offering a refreshingly 'passionate engagement', at a time just before criticism became gendered through increasingly professionalised literary journalism. There is also the matter of geography: in his survey of eighteenth-century British culture, John Brewer uses Seward the provincial writer as an example of literary culture that is not exclusive to London, but 'a broadly based critical heritage in which poetry was a sign of higher sensibility and not a professional property'.[6] More recently, Teresa Barnard has produced a sympathetic biography, looking in particular at the large amount of material unpublished by Seward's executors. Her argument is that Seward's collected writings were mutilated, before they ever got to be seen by posterity, destroying the carefully constructed image of 'the independent, self-sufficient writer, an intellectual who constantly searches and challenges, exploring numerous and varied aspects of culture and society'.[7] A similar approach is taken by Claudia Thomas Kairoff in a monograph dedicated to Seward's poetry, which finds her 'difficult to place' as an eighteenth-century poet amidst the beginnings of Romanticism, but still 'a major writer', and 'invaluable guide to the trajectory of British poetry in her century'.[8]

One thing these divergent views have in common is that the source of the majority of their judgements is Seward's correspondence. She deliberately set up the posthumous publication in 1811 of these letters as an historical document for posterity. In Clarke's words, the letters were an attempt 'to put in place something magisterial and permanent' which 'displayed her critical acumen and critical authority in a form which incorporated other people's acknowledgment of the significance of her views'. Moreover, the 'degree of control she sought to exercise over posthumous publication' and 'her unembarrassed self regard' expected her 'considered thoughts to be received as something akin to laws'. They were 'designed as a monument to her genius', and fashioned in such a way as to make them a literary work in their own right, a 'formal invention' of 'cultural history, literary criticism, and autobiography'.[9]

Yet this 'formal invention' extends to the process by which Seward collected her letters (beginning in 1784), and revised them for publication. This has been controversial. James Clifford waxed indignant over Seward's changes, after noticing that her manuscript copies of letters to Hester

Lynch Piozzi bore significant differences from the published results. He fumed that 'these rather pretentious epistles have been used ... as genuine contemporary evidence concerning the social and literary life of the late eighteenth century', but 'it seems certain that they do not represent what Anna Seward originally wrote but rather what she decided in late life would better enhance her reputation'. He concluded that these 'late revisions ... cannot be trusted as evidence in controversial matters'.[10] Clifford's chief exhibit is a letter congratulating Piozzi on her publication of Johnson's letters. The manuscript is dated 14 March 1788, and suggests that the correspondence 'shews the great man in an infinitely more *benign*, tho' less *resplendent* point of view than any other of his writings, or than any veritable record of his conversation could possibly place him'. In the 1811 published version this is dated 7 March, and becomes 'They shew him in a more benign, tho' less resplendent point of view, than, perhaps, any other of his writings, or than he could appear from any veritable record of his conversation, since you have, doubtless, expunged the malignant passages, from your benevolent attention to the feelings of many.' Of this important addition, Clifford surmises that initially, Seward 'did not show her true feelings', and that the revision 'was to be her revenge for real or fancied slights received at Johnson's hands. But it certainly does not represent what she was willing to write to Mrs Piozzi in 1788.'[11]

Indeed it does not, though Seward's rewriting is not as important as this denunciation suggests. The letters have rarely been used as authoritative 'genuine contemporary evidence', given that they are extraordinarily subjective (hence, in part, their decidedly mixed reception and reputation); the eccentric spirit of Seward's writing has ensured that few have seen her as a disinterested literary historian. The letters present an obviously partial picture of late eighteenth-century life. Moreover, such lack of objectivity often works against her: if the motive in revising the letters was to 'enhance her reputation', she arguably diminished it by her changes. The Piozzi letter is a case in point. Seward's dislike of Johnson's criticism is central to the correspondence, with his appearances in its six volumes usually an example of critical jealousy and misanthropy. The claim added in Seward's revision of the letter – that Johnson appears 'benign' in his correspondence because Piozzi has expunged passages relating to his envy or rudeness – makes little logical sense: why would Piozzi need to expunge such materials, given the unlikelihood of them appearing in Johnson's correspondence, where formality militates against the possibility of their presence? The accusation of malignance shows how Seward's view of Johnson had become an *idée fixe*, so frequent are her animadversions against him.[12]

When revising her correspondence for publication, Seward may well have exaggerated her earlier opinions, but the letters are very much a manufactured portrait of a literary career, and hardly plain matters of historical fact. John Brewer makes the valid point that the 'artifice and contrivance' of the letters is 'revealing, for it represents the idealized version of a literary community she wishes posterity to imagine, a body of men and women united by their good taste, at the centre of which Seward herself is to be found'. The correspondence is thus an obviously constructed narrative. Clarke's implied response to Clifford is that 'when [Seward] rewrote, it was not in the spirit of a letter-writer falsifying documents, but as a professional writer revising her manuscripts'.[13] Whilst agreeing that the picture of the dissembling Seward forging her own past is not entirely helpful, this alternative does not allow for the odd way in which Seward's revisions seem to work against her own interests. This is equally true of the manner in which Seward instructed Walter Scott to print the youthful letters (which date from 1762 to 1768) that she left him, along with manuscript and print copies of her poems, for posthumous publication. Of her poetry, she requested, 'I wish the juvenile letters may be added, succeeding the poetic volumes as in Warburton's edition of Pope's works.'[14] This modelling of her legacy on that of Pope is self-conscious vanity, and it is not Seward's best side.

A larger problem in the 1811 *Letters* was Seward's prose style, which seems (as is often the case) to have become more florid with the years and with revision. Contemporary readers found it unusual: Jane West told Bishop Percy that 'I know not what to call it; I agree with you it is not English'; Egerton Brydges thundered that 'I am not acquainted with any literary letters which exhibit such corrupt judgment, and so many false beauties as her's. Her sentiments are palpably studied, and disguised, and dressed up. Nothing seems to come from the heart, but all to be put on.' Even for a sympathetic reader such as Clarke it is 'orotund and over-embellished'. The editor of the letters murmured an apology: 'it is to be feared, that even in these familiar epistles, several affectations of style, arising from too free an use of poetic imagery, may tend to obscure their real merit'.[15] Seward's stylistic excesses now seem a part of her attempt to write herself into literary history, being (like her judgements) sometimes hyperbolic and overblown. Like her enthusiasm, it signifies a larger absence of moderation – a telling factor in the generally unfulfilled tone that the correspondence, like Seward's writings in general, evokes.

The workings of envy

Seward's letters display the ideas that would dominate her literary career. They are dominated by passion – from her eulogies to various types of genius that make up her literary canon, to her often heated responses to criticism of these favourites. Her criticism is usually reactive, responding to an adverse judgement, often with great indignation, which prevents her from making a considered reply.

The mixed critical reception of Seward is partly due to this vehemence. She justified her reactions by stressing the fundamental importance of literature: 'Not even unjust reflections upon myself can excite my disdain more insuppressively than the injustice of criticism upon the talents of those great writers, from whom I have derived instruction and delight' (*Letters*, vol. 1, p. 149). 'Injustice' is a constant in her critical vocabulary. For Seward, the ways in which writers were treated by critics were part of the keystone of her literary theory, the workings of envy in human psychology: the genius of a Milton or a Gray was so obvious that those who deigned to criticise them must be motivated by jealousy. Like many of Seward's ideas, this one had a germ of truth in it, but was produced too readily. The opening letter of the correspondence summarises it: 'Every being of distinguished genius will, from the prevalence of envy, have a number of foes' (*Letters*, vol. 1, p. 3). Clarke's description of Seward as 'highly attuned to the workings of envy' is something of an understatement.[16]

Seward's accusations of jealousy are most strange when she defends a highly valued contemporary who has now been all but forgotten. One of her more admirable qualities was the refusal to accept that all great cultural works were in the past. Seward fought a battle on behalf of the moderns as being equal to the ancients, if not in some respects superior, and thus avoided the all too easy path of critical dismissal of the contemporary; yet, in repudiating this intellectual laziness, she often over-compensated. Of course, Seward's rapturous praise of now very obscure contemporaries had a context: some of these figures had considerable success in her time, making her judgements somewhat less eccentric. Take, for instance, her poetic enthusiasm for the tragedies of Robert Jephson:

> Poetic Spirits, bend your ardent gaze
> On this rich effluence of dramatic rays!
> Than those alone less eminently bright,
> That dart from Shakespear's orb their solar light,
> Fastidious Spleen, and canker'd Envy fly,

> Nor thou! O mole-eyed Prejudice, be nigh!
> Then, nervous Jephson, shall thy muse obtain
> Applause, that opes the gate of Glory's fane.[17]

Placing Jephson (1736/7–1803) on a pedestal just below Shakespeare now seems incongruous, but it should not be assumed that Seward was utterly at odds with public taste: although now almost totally neglected, Jephson was a lifelong friend of Malone, and the subject of a monograph as recently as the 1930s; several of his plays had some success, being reprinted in collections in the nineteenth century, though not acted.[18] The problem with Seward's over-praise of Jephson will recur: having gone too far in her estimation, she accuses those who do not share her taste of prejudice. Opinion can be divided, surely, on a contemporary dramatist without accusations of jealousy and malice. In cases such as Jephson, Seward's support is so fervid as to appear curiously insincere (one thing it most certainly is not), and the lines written into the book read like an explicit gesture to posterity rather than an ingenuous act of appreciation.

Seward places blame onto supposedly envious critics whenever there is a divergence between her literary judgement and that of the wider public or the critical establishment. In 1786, she was involved in a running argument with George Hardinge, friend of Walpole and another enthusiast, though unlike Seward, he dismissed most modern poetry. At one point, disarmed by Hardinge's kindness, Seward puts forth a hypothetical response to his strictures that is very revealing of her opinion of the literary world: 'We will remember how the genius of Collins was, while he lived, neglected and despised, till the poverty and disappointment, produced by that neglect and scorn, made a chaos of his brain, and an ice-stone of his heart.' The myth of poor William Collins the martyr to critical ignorance was pervasive, but it leads her to claim that such examples fortify the true artist: 'In the shelter of independence, we can smile at literary injustice, and commit our pretensions to posterity. If they are cogent they will prevail, and we shall be remembered when those who despise us shall be forgotten; – if they are not cogent, the dismission of them into the limbo of vanity will be nothing to us.'[19] As philosophy, this is worthy of Epictetus (if in somewhat peculiar prose), but in practice, it was as much use to Seward as the lecturer's ideal of Stoicism in *Rasselas*: Seward's early twentieth-century biographer described how she 'suffered agonies of mortification when her own published works were assailed', and there is little to suggest effective resignation in Seward's writings about the reception of literature, whether her own or that of her pantheon.[20]

The question of posterity brought out Seward's vulnerability, which she disguised by an unconvincing air of disinterestedness. In 1787, she writes to her great friend Thomas Whalley, who has been encouraging her to publish more poetry:

> After poetic fame, I confess I often feel very ardent aspirations; yet are they but a short-lived blaze, and fade away into embers, that scarcely gleam. No fuel more potent can be given them, than your seeming interested that I should publish what I have written. It is needful enough to prevent the very embers from being extinguished by the stupidity or venality, the malice or ignorance of the public critics (*Letters*, vol. I, p. 386)

The desire for fame is thus combined with a fear of failure. A couple of months later, she replies to Josiah Wedgwood, who wants her to write a poem on the iniquities of the slave trade. Her reasons for declining include her suspicion that such a poem would be the target of premeditated scorn, because 'the public hireling critics are not my friends; and I have personal enemies in some of them, rendered such by my sincerity, and because I could not stoop to flatter with praise the miserable rhymes they presented to me' (*Letters*, vol. II, pp. 30, 32). Seward seems convinced that nothing could ever be read impartially, in a literary world where personal prejudice eroded sincerity of judgement.

The evidence suggests some truth in the charge that criticism of her works was sometimes premeditated, and based on a dismissive estimation of her gender. Seward gave as good as she got in controversies, but the patronising view of her as merely an eccentric woman shines clearly from some of her adversaries. Yet Seward's paranoia about critical prejudice made it a self-fulfilling prophecy, turning perfectly constructive criticism into the malice of establishment toadies. This makes it hard to take seriously her assertion that she is sure posterity will bring her justice, whether this is immortality or oblivion: 'That my writings should ever experience this regeneration, I am far from depending; but I believe they will, if they deserve it. It has long been my wish to "leave my name in life's visit." Should the ink in which it was written prove of a fading and perishable quality, there is no help for that, you know' (*Letters*, vol. II, p. 37).

Seward seems to have viewed literary fame as eminently desirable because it removed the author from the slings and arrows of unjust criticism. This ignored the counter-argument: that even the famous continue to suffer critical attacks and declines in reputation in the future (in spite of her writing so many words defending dead idols against modern calumniators). This idea of fame comes across well in a sonnet on Pope's Twickenham; to have sat there 'is the Poet's triumph':

>   and it towers
> O'er Life's pale ills, his consciousness of powers
> That lift his memory from oblivion's gloom,
> Secure a train of these heart-thrilling hours
> By his idea deck'd in rapture's bloom,
> For spirits rightly touch'd thro' ages yet to come.
>   (Sonnet xx, 'On Reading a Description of Pope's Gardens at
>   Twickenham', *Poetical Works*, vol. III, p. 141)

Literary fame is thus an escape from a predominantly negative view of life, and it allows you to anticipate a communion with other like-minded souls. Seward speculated further that we may even notice the effects of our fame in the afterlife: 'if we retain any consciousness of what passed, and yet passes on earth, when ourselves have soared above it, the consciousness of being remembered with esteem and honour by our fellow-creatures on the score of virtuous compositions, will probably prove a source of delight, worthy to be admitted into the number of angelic gratifications' (*Letters*, vol. I, p. 59). This odd speculation suggests the central significance of literary success and failure to her, but such a strain also indicates vulnerability: when Walter Scott met Seward, in 1807, he was impressed that the enthusiasms of her younger days had been sustained, despite age and considerable physical infirmity: she 'entered into every topic with the keenness and vivacity of youth'. Yet he saw how such sensitivity caused problems, which he described as 'a sensibility to coldness, or to injuries real or supposed, which she permitted to disturb her more than was consistent with prudence or with happiness'.[21]

Seward hoped that she would find a place among the literary immortals: many declarations of her own limitations read like false modesty, though she did tend (with generosity) to spend more time exalting the genius of others. Margaret Ashmun concluded from the evidence that Seward's sense of self-worth was heartfelt: 'She died in the full assurance that she could never be forgotten, and that her verses would live on as inevitably as Spenser's or Milton's.'[22] If this was so, it acted as confirmation of what she believed about the reception of those she admired – that criticism was often unjust and worth would slowly be recognised by the truly perceptive.

Thus, for Seward, the neglect of Milton's shorter poems in the later seventeenth century proves the 'absolute incompetence of the public to discern and estimate the claims of genius, till, by the slow accumulation of the suffrage of kindred talents, it is taught their value' (*Letters*, vol. I, p. 64). The circular logic (and evidence of the heterogeneity of reception) contradicts this: many works were always successful, some had a brief fame then disappeared for ever (such as Jephson's tragedies); more were immediately dismissed. Seward thought that Gray's two Pindaric odes of 1757, *The Progress of Poesy* and *The Bard*, were the greatest examples of lyric poetry in the history of the world, and seems to have felt personally wounded by Johnson's criticism of them.[23] Yet these poems, despite being lampooned as a byword for obscurity, were not remotely unsuccessful, and never disappeared out of print to be rescued by future generations. Many found these complex poems impossible, but a substantial readership always appreciated them. What Seward seems to mean by 'public incompetence' is the absence of universal affirmation of her literary idols. This points to the central flaw in her critical aesthetic: to put it bluntly, the taste of some people may well differ from your own. Equally, her idea of taste was that it was universal, and the idea that some works of art (such as Gray's odes) appealed to a more limited audience would have been anathema to her.

Seward refused to accept alternative possibilities to her own critical judgement, and relied instead upon those trusted explanations of unfavourable criticism – bias or lack of discernment. In 1789, she told Hester Piozzi of her 'long conviction concerning the total incompetence of our modern public critics to estimate the genuine value of poetic compositions; my nausea of their false rules and blundering analizations, their venal praise and malicious abuse' (*Letters*, vol. II, p. 242). Such a conviction negated the need to read criticism at all, and by 1796, she responded to a query about a review of her poem 'Llangollen Vale' with a regal dismissal: 'there is no good in ruminating, or ever once looking at the injustice or stupidity of spiteful or incompetent critics. I have, therefore, constantly desired my friends not to obtrude any such upon my attention' (*Letters*, vol. IV, p. 203). The exception was *The Gentleman's Magazine*, where she continued to publish, and found congenial, if occasionally fractious spirits; as John Brewer points out, the eclecticism and catholicity of contributors meant it was not full of the professional critics she despised. But it is hard to think that she did not read them, for all her defiance. The insoluble problem was that her literary reputation meant too much for her to ignore criticism. As Ashmun says, she 'made herself miserable by paying both too much and too little attention to her critics'. If she had taken less notice, she 'might have been less harrowed' by them; if she had considered some of the criticism as constructive, she might have curbed some of the excesses of her writing.[24]

In his account of the importance of Seward to provincial culture, Brewer claims that she was 'representing a view of poetry as woven into the fabric of genteel social life, best sustained in provincial tranquillity and enhanced by friendship, especially friendship among women'.[25] This is supported by the letters which – no matter how reworked – record the manner in which Seward fostered a regional cultural life that was self-sufficient, and not dependent upon London for its impetus. On the other hand, the letters are far from tranquil or friendly (and there are arguably more important male literary correspondents – Thomas Whalley, William Hayley – than female). The Swan of Lichfield's literary circle was repeatedly oppositional, and the tone of its leader's pronouncements frequently embattled. This is as much a description as a criticism.

This air of reaction is clearest in the extraordinary centrality of literary jealousy to Seward's critical oeuvre. Her descriptions of artistic workings are full of mentions of envy; Dryden was 'known to have some jealousy of the fame of Milton' (*Letters*, vol. v, p. 314). Of Lady Mary Wortley Montagu's argument with Pope, it is the 'contempt with which she spoke of his immortal poetry' that concerns Seward: 'Thus it is to envy what we ought to admire' (*Letters*, vol. vi, p. 146). Charles Churchill was rude about almost every writer that Seward admired; unsurprisingly she finds him 'an envious detractor from the literary reputation of others' (*Letters*, vol. vi, pp. 166–7), which is unfair and inaccurate – the sheer cynical disdain of Churchill's satires hardly suggests a writer consumed with jealousy. Towards the end of her life, Seward was told by Scott that her great new hope, Robert Southey, was 'above that jealousy of his poetic rivals'; a relieved Seward remarks, 'in how many highly-gifted minds has it lurked!' (*Letters*, vol. vi, p. 280).

Seward's belief in literary jealousy as a ruling passion amounted to an obsession, and became an all-purpose rationale. Time and again, criticism of a work she admires is dismissed as envy on the part of the author. In the last major work published in her lifetime, the *Memoirs of Erasmus Darwin* (1804), the acerbic scientist and poet is rude about Cowper's *Task* because, explains Seward, after starting to write poetry, 'the jealous spirit of authorism darkened his candor'.[26] William Crowe, the author of *Lewesdon Hill* (1788), a topographical poem much admired by Seward, is equally castigated for his dislike of Darwin's *Botanic Garden*: on his part, this is a 'selfish desire, a weak, because an impossible, attempt to confine all claims to poetic excellence, within the pale of that style and manner in which themselves excel' (*Letters*, vol. iii, p. 186). There are numerous other examples.

Yet this predilection for finding writers jealous did not mean that Seward herself was a victim of it. Many testified to the generosity with which she promoted the contemporary writers that she admired (a peculiar exception might be her criticism of Charlotte Smith, and accusations of her plagiarism).[27] She proclaimed that 'I always alike divest myself of personal partiality, and of personal dislike, to authors, when I comment upon their works' (*Letters*, vol. III, p. 8), a comment lacking in self-awareness, given some of her outbursts against supporters of Johnson, or detractors of her canon. She did possess an ingenuous but excessive sense of praise or blame. Such passions co-existed in a nature which Scott saw as 'an active stranger to that paltry jealousy which too often disturbs the harmony of the literary world'.[28] There were of course exceptions: her claim that 'If there is ought of estimable in my composition, it consists in an utter exemption from envy' would be more credible did it not follow on from a complaint against Joseph Banks and the Royal Society for not including her in the recipients of medals cast in honour of Captain Cook, preferring 'those who direct their attention to the moths, butterflies, and curry combs of that voyage, to her who attempted to sing the purposes, the exploits, and the virtues of its commander'.[29] Her claim not to be the least concerned is a wonderful exhibition of false modesty. The greater problem was the perceived fashion in which envious literary reviewers were deliberately unfair to her work.

One of the few times that Seward unequivocally agreed with Johnson is her quoting an anecdote, where Lucy Porter asked him if she may trust literary reviews: '"Infallibly, dear Lucy," he replied, "provided you buy what they abuse, and never any thing they praise"' (*Letters*, vol. VI, pp. 299–300). For Seward, reviewers are worse than jealous authors, who at least have their own genius. This is spelt out in 'Epistle to Nathaniel Lister', written in 1786. Lister was a Lichfield schoolboy who had sent Seward some verses; her reply is a cautionary tale of the dark arts of the literary world to an unsuspecting soul entering

> In authorism's dangerous ways,
> Where Envy's restless ills betide,
> Her thorns infest, her serpents glide,
> Those rhyming snakes, whose malice long
> Pursues the Bard of higher song.
> And mark the scribbling Serpent's station,
> Artificer of defamation!
> Who, sore beneath the general sense
> Of his vain Muse's impotence,
>
> Turns public Critic, to supply
> His spleen, and gaunt necessity;
> Breathes purchas'd praise, in servile tone,
> On lays as meagre as his own
> (*Poetical Works*, vol. II, pp. 334–5)

Thus great talents are defamed and feeble ones exalted, in the conspiracy that Seward found in the world of letters (what Lister, then only thirteen, would have made of it can only be imagined). Seward's conception of literary justice was of adamantine simplicity, unlike the supposed duplicity of book reviews, puffs, and critiques. Unfortunately, her notion of the pre-ordained malicious jealousy of literary criticism led her to respond with indignation, which often vitiated the coherence of her critical writing. The effect is of a writer reacting against a system she is convinced she cannot beat; the origins of such a mindset can be traced to her beginnings as a poet.

Poetic enthusiasm

Seward was not fated to float down to posterity as one of the poetic elect; her best poems are sometimes anthologised, but not widely available in print. Margaret Ashmun admits that her biographical subject 'may not have been a poet of permanent value'; the three-volume *Poetical Works* edited by Scott in 1810 did not sell well, and his son-in-law Lockhart called it 'a formidable monument of mediocrity'. Scott himself described much of her poetry as 'execrable'.[30] Neither judgement is fair, though the *Poetical Works* is undeniably uneven. One reason for this is that Seward complicated Scott's posthumous editorial task by augmenting her published works (what Scott thought he was editing) with manuscripts of all her occasional poetry. The intention was the presentation of a comprehensive body of work, but the impression is of excess. Seward's talent was for lyric description and reflection, and the best of her shorter, pensive poems and Miltonic sonnets are buried beneath the repetitive accumulation of her every occasional attempt.

Seward's poetry is distinctly of a time when sensibility was a watchword, and ornate and florid epithets were encouraged. Her first poetic success, *Elegy on Captain Cook* (1780), was inspired by the competitions carried out by Lady Miller at Batheaston in the 1770s, where poems were written on a pre-ordained subject, and placed in Lady Miller's vase, to be judged afterwards. Seward's offerings were successful, and the events also introduced her to an important friend and literary ally, William Hayley.[31] The elegy on Cook shows Seward's characteristic style, not least in the description of the murder of the great man:

> On a far distant, and remorseless shore,
> Where human fiends their dire libations pour;
> Where treachery, hov'ring o'er the blasted heath,

> Poises with ghastly smile the darts of death,
> Pierc'd by their venom'd points, your favorite bleeds,
> And on his limbs the lust of hunger feeds!
> (*Poetical Works*, vol. II, p. 44)

This is somewhat unrestrained in its feeling. A few lines on, Cook is compared to Orpheus: 'Round the bold bard th' inebriate maniacs crowd – / Red on the ungrateful soil his life-blood swims, / And Fiends and Furies tear his quiv'ring limbs!' This is suggestive of the character of Seward's longer poetry, with its piling up of intense descriptive superlatives. Claudia Kairoff describes how the poem's 'mixture of sentiment, classical allusion, and dramatic harangue appeared seamless to most British readers', yet such an impression might well, as with many works of sensibility, lead to the appeal of such poetry being short-lived, and soon appearing dated.[32]

Seward's use of a heightened poetic strain is usually blamed on her near-neighbour Erasmus Darwin, a poet not marked by descriptive austerity, who took an early interest in Seward's poetry. According to Scott, Darwin 'encouraged the first notes of her lyre', and it was from him 'perhaps, it had borrowed some of its peculiar intonations'.[33] More important is the role of her father, in Seward's own recollection of her nascent poetry: 'at first my father encouraged it, but my mother threw cold water on the rising fires; and even my father ceased to smile encouragement upon these attempts after my 16th year, in which Dr. Darwin unluckily told him, that his daughter's verses were better than his; a piece of arch injustice to my father's muse, which disgusted him with mine' (*Poetical Works*, vol. I, p. lxviii). Her father placed an injunction on her writing verse, and henceforth, she took up embroidery. Thomas Seward's very minor literary career had included a poem in Dodsley's first *Miscellany* of 1748, but his arbitrary act of parental censorship is significant in its prefiguring Seward's later battles with the male literary establishment. Ashmun speculates on Seward's parents' fear of her becoming 'a literary spinster', and that the poetic ban reflects the contemporary problem of the superfluity of the 'over-educated woman'. The acquiescence of Seward combined with her refusal to bear a grudge: she 'readily forgave the sinister motive in the repression of her talents'. This is as admirable as her care of her father during the increasing mental frailties of his last decade, until his death in 1790 (her mother having passed away in 1780), but the injustice is striking, and the egotism of Thomas Seward discreditable. It marks the formation of the literary side of the 'thwarted affections and suppressed energies' that Ashmun finds in Seward's life.[34]

The twenty-two-year-old Seward's affections were very severely thwarted in 1764, by two events. The most significant was the death from a fever of her sister Sarah, in June, after she had been betrothed to Joseph Porter, Johnson's stepson. Seward paints no happy picture of this arranged marriage between a middle-aged merchant who had spent his adult life trading in Italy and a sensitive young girl; its arrangement appears to have been very much at the volition of her father.[35] Furthermore, we know that Seward had contracted unofficial engagements with a Major John Wright (which was broken off by her father) and also a Captain Temple (confusingly called Taylor in the *Letters*), later to reappear in her life in strange circumstances.[36] Temple had been warned, however, by his guardians, that his inheritance at the time of majority was likely to be significantly less than had been thought, and the couple accordingly agreed to break the engagement if this proved to be the case. Then, Seward wrote, in a letter, 'My hopes for Mr T—'s happiness and my own are vanished as a dream' (*Poetical Works*, vol. 1, p. clxxxiii). Thomas Seward had found out about the relationship, due to 'the officiousness of mistaken friends', whose 'information caused my father to question me upon this subject – to be angry at the correspondence which I acknowledged – to write an ill-judged letter to Mr T—, and violently to insist on the dissolution of an engagement which we had mutually agreed to renounce'.[37]

The reason for her father's insistence was purely financial. Considering Thomas Seward's marriage dealings with his daughters – refusing two suitors and arranging a completely unsuitable one, both for questions of money – Ashmun finds him 'conventional and mercenary, if no worse'.[38] Given that Seward seems to have enjoyed the freedoms that an unmarried state gave her (not least intellectually), it is hard to see the end of the Temple engagement as a life-changing disaster, but it does illustrate once again the degree to which Seward's fate was controlled, and this naturally plays a part in the predominant themes of her writing – regret, loss, and injustice – and in its sometimes combative tone. Her father's actions played an indirect part in shaping her poetry, especially when it is considered how much of it concerns the unattainable and the forbidden. Norma Clarke links this topos to objects of Seward's desire that were taken away from her or denied, particularly her extraordinary affection for Honora Sneyd, adopted by the Sewards in 1756, and to whom she addressed some of her most heartfelt poems following Sneyd's marriage in 1773 and early death in 1780. There is also the other great platonic love of Seward's life, John Saville, the Vicar-Choral at Lichfield Cathedral.

Saville was married and relatively poor: his friendship with Seward, based on shared literary and musical enthusiasms, raised questions, and in 1771, his wife refused to receive her. Saville left his wife, but refused to leave Lichfield, and continued to live in a cottage near Seward and the Bishop's Palace. As Teresa Barnard explains, 'According to unpublished letters, the musician could not afford to divorce his bitter, angry wife, and his conscience would not allow him to live openly with Seward, so they chose an ostensibly companionable but intense relationship.'[39] Their relationship was the closest and most important of Seward's life, and when Saville died in 1803, her loss was so great that she did not leave the Palace for four months. It is obvious that in the prevailing moral climate, Seward must have been the target for a great deal of gossip, not to say more direct pressure to desist from her scandalous friendship. Her response was commendable and courageous: 'No prospect of worldly disadvantage – and I was threatened with the highest – could induce me to renounce the blessing of a tried and faithful friend', she wrote, 'but by ill-advised and mistaken authority, most of its sweetest comforts were mercilessly lopt away.' As for Saville, 'His truth is sacred. His honour was never doubted, even by those who abuse him for not living with an ignorant and shrewish wife.'[40] The dignity of her response to criticism of her and Saville is admirable, especially as she would have to hold her head up for more than three decades. The tendency to dismiss Seward as an outspoken eccentric fails to realise the emotional and intellectual privations she suffered, and the robust manner in which she challenged these impositions.

The tribulations of Seward's relationships provide an obvious context for her poetry; the section of the *Poetical Works* called 'Love Elegies and Epistles', for instance, is introduced as 'written in the early youth of the author. They describe an attachment between a lady of birth, rank, beauty, and talents, the daughter of wealthy parents, and a gentleman, much her inferior in family and station, without fortune, and her equal only in intellect, merit, and affection' (*Poetical Works*, vol. 1, p. 25). Such a scenario reflects the enforced antinomies in Seward's life between love and money and social circumstance. These poems trace the verse-correspondence of the frustrated lovers Evander and Emillia, whom Clarke identifies as heightened versions of Saville and Seward, though the situation replicates in part Seward's failed engagement with Temple.[41] These unremarkable poems serve as apprentice pieces for the topic of frustrated love, which Seward would explore repeatedly.

It was frustrated platonic love that generated Seward's most important early poetry. The marriage of her beloved friend Honora Sneyd to Richard Lovell Edgeworth in July 1773 was marked by Seward with sonnets that are nothing less than elegies for her beloved companion. The relationship between Sneyd (adopted by the Sewards at the age of six, after her mother's death) and Seward remains mysterious, inasmuch as the strength of her feeling is obvious, but the details (and level of reciprocity) more ambivalent.

Seward's previous poems about Honora had a fervent quality, being raptures on the wonder of her character, but also almost morbidly afraid of their parting. Sneyd (1751–80) had been a ward in the Seward house from 1756 until 1771; Seward's writings on her (and particularly her absence) represent an extremity of pain that Ashmun calls 'a sense of total estrangement and loss'. She also suggests that the obvious jealousy that Seward felt towards Edgeworth forced Honora into escaping into marriage. It seems that Seward and Honora fell out after the marriage of the latter, though for reasons unknown (though thought to be related to Sneyd's father), and the assumption that Seward felt rejected by her from the date of her marriage is erroneous. Ultimately, as Kairoff summarises, the 'cause of Seward's estrangement from Honora remains mysterious', and moreover, the 'depth of Seward's response to these events has perplexed everyone who has written about them'.[42]

Norma Clarke offers the intriguing suggestion that the idea of the loss of Sneyd became something of a trope for Seward, where 'loss of the loved one offered the poetic subject of unattainability'. The related idea, by Kairoff, is that she represented 'Seward's adopted child', who was 'given in recompense for her failed courtships'.[43] The level of anxiety expressed in the Sneyd poems is extraordinary, even if it was at points exaggerated to suit Seward's muse. Indeed, the strangest factor about these poems is the distance between the melancholy of their address, and the apparent banality that motivates them. The title alone of 'Honora, an Elegy' suggests doom and foreboding, yet we are informed that it was 'Written on the terrace walk in the palace garden, Lichfield, the day on which Miss Honora Sneyd left that place for a month's residence in Shropshire, May 1769' (*Poetical Works*, vol. 1, p. 65). Such a gap between the poem's occasion and its level of gloom is heightened by the description of how 'Honora fled, I seek her favourite scene', the 'bowery terrace' referred to in the note:

> I seize the loved resemblance it displays,
> With mixture strange of anguish and delight;
> I bend on vacancy an earnest gaze,
> Where strong illusion cheats my straining sight.
>
> But ah, it fades! – and no relief I find,
> Save that which silence, memory, hope confer;
> Too soon the local semblance leaves my mind,
> E'en where each object seem'd so full of her.

> And Memory, only Memory, can impart
> The dear enduring image to my view;
> Has she not drawn thee, loveliest, on my heart
> In faithful tints, and permanent as true?
> (*Poetical Works*, vol. 1, p. 66)

The strangeness of this is that it would seem appropriate if Honora Sneyd's tragically young death had happened in 1769, rather than her merely being away in Shropshire. Indeed, the imbalance between Seward's grief and the mundane events which provoke it means that the emotion seems manufactured for the occasion, and Honora a vehicle for an ideal, in the manner of an Elizabethan sonnet sequence. In this vein, the theme and language of 'Elegy, Written at the Sea-Side' almost echo Shakespeare's Sonnet 54, and its war with time, with a nod to Gray's *Elegy*:

> But Time's stern tide, with cold Oblivion's wave,
> Shall soon dissolve each fair, each fading charm;
> E'en Nature's self, so powerful, cannot save
> Her own rich gifts from this o'erwhelming harm.
> Love and the Muse can boast superior power,
> Indelible the letters they shall frame;
> They yield to no inevitable hour,
> But will on lasting tablets write thy name.
> (*Poetical Works*, vol. 1, pp. 82–3)

Seward thus immortalises her beloved companion and asserts her own place in posterity, a more confident pose than usually adopted in the Sneyd poems. More typical is the first sonnet that Seward wrote to Sneyd in April 1773. Eventually, this would be published in Seward's *Original Sonnets* of 1799. Seward's opinion of 'the murderous Edgeworth, who cankered first and then crushed to earth, the finest of human flowers' was partly a reflection of her fury over Edgeworth's absence from Sneyd when she was initially ill with the consumption that led to her death, in May 1780.[44] In 1773, before the impending wedding, Seward offers a potential olive-branch:

> Honora, should that cruel time arrive
>   When 'gainst my truth thou should'st my errors poize,
>   Scorning remembrance of our vanish'd joys;
> When for the love-warm looks, in which I live,
> But cold respect must greet me, that shall give
>   No tender glance, no kind regretful sighs;
> When thou shalt pass me with averted eyes,
>   Feigning thou see'st me not, to sting, and grieve,
> And sicken my sad heart, I could not bear
>   Such dire eclipse of thy soul-cheering rays;
> I could not learn my struggling heart to tear

> From thy loved form, that thro' my memory strays;
> Nor in the pale horizon of despair
> Endure the wintry and the darken'd days.
> *(Poetical Works*, vol. 11, p. 131)

This is one of Seward's most memorable poems, turning emotions that could easily be self-pitying into something more profound: it conveys the loss of her friend as an event of great moment to her, without any excess of ornament. Instead it defines potential feelings and scenarios by negatives. The assumption of former intimacy is heightened by these fears of what will follow from its imminent removal; the final negative calls attention to what Seward says she will not be able to endure, whilst showing her belief in its inevitability. The finale evokes the inability of lost love to comprehend, let alone deal competently with, the nature of its pain. It is a plea for understanding, and an account of the importance of their relationship; whereas elsewhere, the extent of Seward's grief over Sneyd seems unreal, here the level of her feeling is clear: to lose their closeness would be like death to her. Similarly, 'Invocation to the Genius of Slumber' of October 1787 sees her beseeching the power of dreams to show her Honora, as 'when thou giv'st it, then, and only then, / Lost to my woes, I live with her again' (*Poetical Works*, vol. I, p. 101). Honora Sneyd becomes for Seward a symbol of the true happiness that life denies; an elegiac sonnet written in June 1780 uses Seward's favourite Miltonic form, and the subject matter of 'Methought I saw my late espoused Saint':

> Nightly I cry, – how oft, alas! in vain, –
> Give, by thy powers, that airy shapes controul,
> Honora to my visions! – ah! ordain
> Her beauteous lip may wear the smile that stole,
> In years long fled, the sting from every pain!
> Show her sweet face, ah show it to my soul!
> *(Poetical Works*, vol. 11, p. 154)

The sharpness of the overwrought ending refuses to conceal its pain. The deliberate defencelessness of Seward's best poems about Sneyd expresses an affecting sense of suffering, so that the rhetorical effects and exclamations interfere but do not overwhelm the subject. The loss of Sneyd is a metonym for larger limitations and deprivations, and writings about her would continue to be a symbol of Seward's ultimate lack of fulfilment.

The theme of frustrated relationships was also to produce a work which now seems far less substantial than the Sneyd poems, though it was one of Seward's most notable contemporary successes. *Louisa, a Poetical Novel, in Four Epistles* was published in 1784, and went through four editions in the year; a fifth followed in 1792. Distance from the vogue for literature of sentiment has made this success hard to reconcile with a reading of what Ashmun calls an 'artificial, far-fetched piece of bathos'. Claudia Kairoff has recently defended it as a work of generic experiment, 'stretching the boundaries of available poetic kinds, techniques, and values, as the best writing always does', noting its debts to Rousseau, Pope, and Prior, and its identity as part of the cult of sensibility, so that 'we have almost lost the keys that once enabled readers to engage the poem with rapture'.[45] Yet such rapture also suggests the poem's limited appeal to its own time and literary fashions.

Though a novel in verse, *Louisa* is far from epistolary fiction in the Richardsonian sense, with multiple perspectives of characters complicated by interactions. Seward uses two letter writers, recounting their history through numerous flashbacks, but the verse-letters are in no real way dialogic. The plot concerns a young man who accidentally leaves his betrothed and is forced to marry a rich, brazen damsel in distress he has rescued because of the financial ruin of his father. The world of *Louisa* is a strange fantasy, whereby modern England co-exists with a medieval chivalric setting. It is, in many ways, a prose romance in heroic couplets, and its affectations would have seemed entirely appropriate to the genre. Louisa's opening despair, for instance, seems to take place in a heightened emotional world:

> O ye known objects! – how ye strike my heart!
> And vain regrets, with keener force, impart!
> Slow, through the faded grove, past pleasures glide,
> Or sadly linger by the fountain's side.
> Dear, awful witness of a broken vow,
> Steep rock, how sternly frowns thy rugged brow!
> (*Louisa, a Poetical Novel, in Four Epistles, Poetical Works*, vol. II, p. 224)

Such outbursts and personifications are indicative of an endless excess of feeling (their model, as so often in the century, being Pope's *Eloisa to Abelard*). The strange vocabulary is often twisted out of shape – it seems a back-handed compliment to describe how in one character 'Grace, grandeur, truth, and tenderness combin'd, / The liberal effluence of the polish'd mind' (*Poetical Works*, vol. II, p. 293). It often seems that more austere diction would have served better; affected vocabulary is often the subject of surface ridicule, but its real difficulty is that it diffuses meaning, creating needless obscurity.

The problems of its language make the failure of the poem to gain any sort of readership since the end of the eighteenth century perfectly understandable: its place is among the ranks of once-popular works that now seem marooned in the style of their time. Its success was accompanied by a strange event in its reception. In November 1784, Seward told Thomas Whalley that she had 'received the highest encomiums' from 'the first literary characters of the age' for *Louisa* (*Letters*, vol. 1, p. 11). Contemporaneously, *The Monthly Review* criticised the superficial glitter and vagaries of the poem. An indignant reply came in an anonymous thirty-four-page pamphlet, called *Hyper-Criticism on Miss Seward's Louisa*, of 1785. A pamphlet response to a bad review is unusual, but not unprecedented; what makes this even odder is that there can be little doubt that its author was Seward herself, given its approach and materials.

The pamphlet endeavours to expose the 'false principles' of the writer in *The Monthly Review*, who thinks that *Louisa* 'approaches not to that degree of excellence which might have been expected from her talents', and objects to its 'glaring metaphors' and its 'aiming to dazzle by superfluity of ornament'. As 'repeated perusal' has convinced the present writer otherwise, they 'resumed the poem, to re-examine it with impartial attention'.[46] If the writer is indeed Seward, this shows no little chutzpah. It goes on to argue for the normalcy of the poem's metaphors by repeatedly casting them into prose. One instance can serve, where the father of Eugenio, the hero, beseeches his son to save him from impending ruin:

> These hovering woes, that o'er our house impend,
> Thou, my dear Son, e'er their dread weight descend,
> Thou canst avert! – but oh! at what a price!
> Persuasion shall not urge – nor prayers entice.
> Two hours ere thy return, Emira found
> Thy Sisters' eyes in streaming torrents drowned;
> Learn'd, from their trembling lips, the cruel cause,
> Which the dark cloud of consternation draws
> Wide o'er my roof – that yesterday survey'd,
> Domestic comfort's fair, and favourite shade.
> (*Poetical Works*, vol. 11, p. 255)

This is transposed thus:

> These woes that hover over our house, ere their dread weight descends to crush us, thou, O my dear son! *Thou* canst avert – but, alas! at what a price! – My persuasions shall not urge, neither shall my prayers intice thee.
>
> Two hours ere 'thy return, Emira found thy sisters drowned in tears; and learnt from their trembling lips the dire event that spreads the dark cloud of consternation so wide over my roof, which yesterday beheld the fair and favourite asylum of domestic commerce. (p. 9)

The argument is not convincing, as the peculiarity of the original is merely diluted when taken out of verse: Eugenio's sisters may not be covered in 'streaming torrents', but they are still 'drowned' by tears, and the metaphors still as removed from spoken language as in the original.

To show the grave injustice that the reviewer has done to Seward, the pamphlet claims that all great writing uses such rich metaphors, and cites *King Lear*, *Romeo and Juliet*, and *Macbeth* in its defence. Intriguingly, it quotes a passage from the latter for which Seward would later suggest an emendation.[47] Given her love of Milton, it is then telling that a scene in *Comus* is also brought up. Most relevant of all is the canon which is introduced, when the pamphlet's author thinks that the 'censure in question has doubtless proceeded from the want of strict attention to the varied operation of the passions; which on minds, differently constructed, produce effects so different; and still more, perhaps, to that want of intimacy with the best *English* poets' (p. 29). Turning the argument on subjectivity is hardly a strong point (it is hard to see how the reviewer can be punished for reflecting this 'varied operation' in not liking Seward's metaphors), but the remark on the lack of knowledge of the greatest national poets is telling: Seward had a firm belief in the absolute centrality of English poetry. The following passage could be written by no one else:

> To criticise English verse justly, it is not sufficient that a man is a good classic in the learned languages, and conversant with the Italian and French poets. He ought to be perfectly acquainted with the works of Spenser, Shakespeare, Milton, Dryden, Pope, Prior, Thomson, Young, Collins, Gray, and Shenstone (who was the most beautiful pastoral writer that our nation, or perhaps any other, has produced; as Gray was the most perfect master of the sublimer lyric style); together with the brilliant, and in point of number, matchless collection of male and female writers, which forms the poetic galaxy of our modern hemisphere; and whose laurels have not yet taken root on their graves, the only soil in which they have a chance to flourish unmolested. There they may perhaps flourish now *he* is gone, whose too potent hand, impelled by rival-hatred, and thirst of exclusive fame, tore, even from *that* sanctuary, those laurels which the just admiration of many generations had reared to maturity.[48]

The taste expressed here would remain consistent throughout Seward's life, with the exception of the high places of Dryden and Spenser, who would be downgraded. More specifically, the inflated praise of William Shenstone and the rapture over Gray are as characteristic as the defence of modern poets as being superior in quantity to the ancients. The point which virtually confirms this as Seward's writing is the reference to the baleful influence of the recently deceased '*he*', motivated by envy. This is

Samuel Johnson, who had died only in December 1784, and this is one of Seward's many comments on his jealousy.

The act of anonymously writing a pamphlet defending your own poem undermines Seward's erstwhile claims of critical impartiality, apparent especially in its conclusion: 'Those who are concerned in reputable publications, should take especial care of pronouncing rashly upon the works of established poetical writers, who must sedulously have studied the principles of their science' (p. 34). Whilst such self-righteousness does Seward no credit, it should be considered why she would go to the trouble of writing a disguised apologia at all, given that the public success of *Louisa* should have negated any lukewarm reviews. It suggests a deep insecurity about criticism; Seward's need for something approaching absolute literary acceptance would continue to imbue (and undermine) both her criticism and poetry.

Luminous intellect and prejudiced darkness

It has been considered, since the publication of Seward's *Letters*, that her constant attempts to contest the legacy of Samuel Johnson's criticism are something of a mania (she maintained that as a moralist and essayist he was of the first order). Ashmun describes Seward's 'passionate (almost hysterical) dislike' of Johnson's criticism and how 'her desire to emphasise the flaws in the character of Johnson seems to amount almost to an obsession'.[49] Seward locates these flaws as motivations behind any of Johnson's literary criticism that she dislikes, particularly the *Lives of the Poets*. Amongst his other sins, Johnson had (in her opinion) been lukewarm about Milton, rude about Gray, and ignored Chatterton. In her universe, he becomes a critical Nobodaddy, inspiring the slighting of her favourites for malicious reasons. The negative influence of Johnson on Seward is so important as to require some examination.

Explanations for the reasons behind the vehemence of Seward's writings on Johnson's criticism usually begin with the difference in temperament between the two; as Brewer says, 'She was a person of passionate and sometimes misplaced enthusiasms; he personified tough-minded, sceptical criticism. She believed in progress and enlightened Christianity; his views of man and his religion were altogether darker.' Brewer also speculates on her animosity as an amateur writer in the provinces towards the London professional who has little love for his birthplace (she would accuse him of slights against Lichfield). It is hard to concur with Brewer's conclusion that 'Her view of Johnson ... was more balanced than might at first appear', or with Kairoff's similar argument that 'Seward's persistence was neither obsessive nor unfair from certain perspectives.'[50] In her numerous mentions of Johnson, the degree of Seward's disdain suggests instead that the effect on her of Johnson's supposed critical crimes was unbalancing, and harmful to her writing.

Seward's suspicion of Johnson went beyond her disputes with his criticism; it has been speculated that he looked down upon the Lichfield cultural world that she represented, partly from fear of their acquaintance with his more humble days. He never seems to have taken a great deal of notice of Seward, except for once praising the *Elegy on Cook* to her, a departure from what she saw as his absolute misogyny towards women writers (*Letters*, vol. II, p. 45). It is impossible to know how much the letters that Seward wrote describing the gravely ill Johnson in Lichfield in 1784 were later revised, but they set the tone, describing why the two would never be in much agreement, as on 29 October:

> The great Johnson is here, labouring under the paroxysm of a disease, which must speedily be fatal ... It is by his repeatedly expressed desire that I visit him often: yet I am sure he neither does, nor ever did feel much regard for me; but he would fain escape, for a time, in any society, from the terrible idea of his approaching dissolution. I never would be awed by his sarcasms, or his frowns, into acquiescence with his general injustice to the merits of *other* writers; with his national, or party aversions, but I feel the truest compassion for his present sufferings, and fervently wish I had power to relieve them. (*Letters*, vol. I, pp. 7–8)

Seward's feelings for the dying man are evident, even if she confirms how little the two have in common. Or should this be how much? After all, Seward claims that she stood up to Johnson, rather than meekly agreeing with his rude assaults; they are both strong-minded and outspoken people, with a conviction of the validity of their own judgements. Seen in this light, it becomes easier to envisage that Johnson for Seward was a powerful presence precisely because he embodied so many of her own characteristics. The difference is that he was successful, and his critical judgements treated as gospel by the many, whereas her views were only accepted by a few sympathetic souls. Johnson was an abiding reminder of the literary success and critical acceptance after which she yearned; the fact that his views of poets whom she worships have thus become enshrined makes him the lasting symbol of literary injustice, and her attacks upon his legacy a struggle with her own perceived lack of fulfilment.[51]

This goes some way to explain her repeated argument with his legacy, as his influence reminds her of the low estate into which literary criticism has fallen, and of the alternative ideal poetic consensus that could be universally accepted, if the true taste of her and her friends replaced Johnson's embittered critiques. Such seems to have been Seward's motive for engaging with the shade of Johnson. The content of her criticisms is not particularly varied. Her more forgiving reading is illustrated by a letter about Johnson's death of December 1784, to her most important poetic ally, William Hayley:

> At last, my dear bard, extinct is that mighty spirit, in which so much good and evil, so much large expansion and illiberal narrowness of mind, were blended; – that enlightened the whole literary world with the splendours of his imagination, and, at times, with the steadiest fires of judgment; and, yet more frequently, darkened it with spleen and envy. (*Letters*, vol. 1, p. 13)

Literary jealousy is again Seward's *ignis fatuus*, an unconvincing way of displacing and explaining away conflicting opinion. The weakness of such an *a priori* argument is that Seward has to posit a vicious literary world of resentment to support her case: 'Truth, from Dr. Johnson's lip, yielded to misrepresentation in his rage of casting rival-excellence into shade ... he has industriously laboured to expose the defects, and defame the virtues and talents of his brethren in the race of literary glory' (*Letters*, vol. 1, pp. 36–7). There can be little doubt that this is an exaggeration and a simplification. The most constructive light that can be shed on this claim of envy is Kairoff's suggestion that Seward 'assumed Johnson resented his many years of obscurity before achieving recognition and financial security', yet it is not clear why he would envy the disparate poets that he attacked in the *Lives* for this; nor is it possible to equate such jealousy with his different degrees of criticism of Milton, Gray, Collins, and Akenside, amongst others, except in a sense so generalised as to be misleading.[52]

One of those most likely to disagree with Seward's analysis was James Boswell, who visited Seward in 1785. Seward had written to him in March, just before his visit, warning him not 'to invest [Johnson] with unreal perfection, injurious, from the severity of his censures, to the rights of others', so he knew what to expect (*Letters*, vol. 1, p. 43). After the visit, Seward told Hayley of their lack of agreement on the question of jealousy. To Seward's argument Boswell 'urged the unlikelihood that he, who had established his own fame on other ground than that of poetry, should envy poetic reputation, especially where it was posthumous; and seemed to believe that his injustice to Milton, Prior, Gray, Collins, &c. proceeded from real want of taste to the higher orders of verse, his judgment being too rigidly severe to relish the enthusiasms of imagination' (*Letters*, vol. I, p. 62). Seward refused to accept this, but Boswell's alternative, that Johnson simply did not like much modern poetry, is more credible, allowing (as Seward's thesis of envy does not) for the different level of Johnson's 'injustice' to these writers. The style of much of Gray and Collins, for instance, was not to his taste, but for all the controversy surrounding the 'Life of Milton', some found it just, and some grudging and lukewarm; it was fervent worshippers of Milton such as William Cowper who met it with outrage. Seward went one step further, and saw it as blasphemy.[53]

The conversation between the two was no real dialogue, as Boswell suggested that taste is subjective and the result of many factors, whilst Seward asserted its uniformity, in the case of what she considered greatness. In July 1788, whilst telling off Henry Cary for questioning William Mason's taste in attacking the deceased Johnson, she puts the matter quite clearly: 'To me there appears no middle path to be adopted with any rationality, after having read the Lives of the Poets, but either we must perceive and despise the envy and injustice of their author, or believe that there is little or no English poetry worth reading' (*Letters*, vol. II, p. 145). She told Boswell that Johnson was 'the most wonderful composition of great and absurd, of misanthropy and benevolence, of luminous intellect and prejudiced darkness, that was ever produced in the human breast', but she never tried to understand his criticism as the product of these mixed qualities, insisting instead that it was univocal and pernicious in intent (*Letters*, vol. I, p. 131). It is this inability to consider the complexities of the argument that makes her writings on Johnson so peculiarly self-defeating.

Seward would bang the same drum about Johnson, the *Lives of the Poets*, and the 'poison they have given to public taste' for the rest of her life (*Letters*, vol. III, p. 43), sometimes accompanied by William Hayley, in letters, poems, and *The Gentleman's Magazine*. Occasionally, she would add a speculation, musing that it was probable that the failure of Johnson's *Irene* 'whetted the fangs of his envy against the whole poetic race' (*Letters*, vol. I, p. 304). She also maintained the distinction between Johnson as critic and essayist, telling George Hardinge that his 'criticisms are monsters of sophistry, prejudice, and envy', but 'his language, his best prose language' is excelled 'by none' of his contemporaries (*Letters*, vol. II, p. 36), yet she did not see the problems of upholding such a strict dichotomy. Even when asked, she denied that her idea of the jealous and malign Johnson was motivated by her anger at his criticism: Joseph Weston, with whom she debated the merits of Pope over Dryden in *The Gentleman's*

Magazine, must have questioned her on these lines, given her response: 'Why do you fancy it was Dr Johnson's blindness to the merits of some of my favourite writers, that produced my conviction concerning the rancour of his spirit?'[54] The air of surprise in the question would not be felt by the reader of the many words that Seward wrote on Johnson – indeed, it seems a more than reasonable surmise. When asked elsewhere for evidence of Johnson's jealousy, she claimed that he envied 'at times, every celebrated author, living or dead' (*Letters*, vol. IV, p. 158), and that Johnson could not bear to read or have mentioned any attack upon him (*Letters*, vol. IV, p. 162). This flies in the face of much evidence, which suggests that Johnson's far less exalted view of human nature left him less vulnerable to criticism than Seward herself; his relative carelessness about such matters is a contrast to Seward's hypersensitivity.

Her indignation at Johnson's criticism also found its way into much of her verse, including an angry poem to William Mason, 'On His Silence Respecting Dr Johnson's Unjust Criticisms upon Mr Gray's Works', ordering him ('Blush, Loiterer, blush') to take up arms against the 'Philistine critic'; there were also poems sent with copies of Warton's edition of Milton's shorter poems, and Hayley's *Life of Milton*, celebrating these authors for refuting Johnson's heresies.[55] A sonnet, 'On Doctor Johnson's Unjust Criticisms in His Lives of the Poets', lays out her critical theory:

> Could aweful Johnson want poetic ear,
>   Fancy, or judgment? – no! his splendid strain,
>   In prose, or rhyme, confutes that plea. – The pain
>   Which writh'd o'er Garrick's fortunes, shows us clear
> Whence all his spleen to Genius. – Ill to bear
>   A friend's renown, that to his own must reign,
>   Compared, a meteor's evanescent train,
>   To Jupiter's fix'd orb, proves that each sneer,
> Subtle and fatal to poetic sense,
>   Did from insidious Envy meanly flow,
>   Illumed with dazzling hues of eloquence,
> And sophist-wit, that labour to o'er-throw
>   Th' awards of Ages, and new laws dispense
>   That lift the Mean, and lay the Mighty low.
>   (*Poetical Works*, vol. II, p. 189)

Johnson's own writings show his ability to judge poetry, so the *Lives* must be the product of the sort of envy he displayed towards the success of his former pupil Garrick; thus runs the argument, through the Miltonic sonnet.

Over the years, few seem to have been convinced by it: as well as Hayley, who wrote accompanying pieces decrying Johnson's *Lives*, Anna

Rogers Stokes apparently urged Seward to publish a comprehensive response to Johnson in a form that is unspecified, but which presumably would be of book-length. In a letter of 1794, Seward refused, because of ill health, and the futility of 'attempting to stem that overwhelming tide of injustice and malignity', a 'surely hopeless task', not least because it is 'more acceptable to the mass of mankind to see excellence degraded than exalted'. She also doubted the reception of 'An unlearned female entering the lists of criticism against the mighty Johnson' (*Letters*, vol. III, pp. 351, 352). The last point is more accurate than Seward's outbursts against Johnson's critical malice, in its knowledge of how she was likely to be patronised by the literary establishment. Johnson's remarks against her favourites may have led her to travesty his criticism, but the male literary world that had made him a critical benchmark was indeed condescending towards her.

The clearest example of this was Boswell. Seward's relationship with him ended with her descriptions of the 'unprovoked and malicious insolence' of this 'ungrateful and impudent' man (*Letters*, vol. III, pp. 346, 353), after an extended argument in *The Gentleman's Magazine* (from October 1793 to January 1794) which had concluded with Boswell's sarcastic portrait of her as an amateur who would be better off leaving such things as literary criticism to those who understood them. It was a thinly veiled attack on her gender, but was also skilfully wounding.[56] Their acquaintance seems to have begun in letters of 1784, and included Boswell (with his usual tact) making a pass at Seward.[57] Their dramatically different perceptions of Johnson were aired publicly in 1787, when Seward commented on Boswell's *Journal of a Tour to the Hebrides*; later, Seward initially found the *Life of Johnson* 'infinitely entertaining', but inevitably saw it as something of a whitewash, and doubted Boswell's veracity: 'in this work, almost every thing is kept back which could give umbrage to Johnson's idolaters, by just displaying the darker, as well as fairer sides of the medal' (*Letters*, vol. III, pp. 75, 86). One such thing that had definitely been 'kept back' was a transcription made by Seward of a conversation from 1778. It featured Johnson arguing with the Quaker Mary Knowles about the recent young convert Jenny Harry, to whom Johnson had formerly been friendly. Johnson views Quakers as 'fools'. Knowles begs him to reconcile himself to the girl. Johnson is adamant: 'Madam, I hate the odious wench, and desire you will not talk to me about her.'[58] There is much more of the same, and the tone is far from the outspoken but winning Johnson of Boswell's writings. Seward gave Boswell a copy, and was dismayed to see it elided to a one-sentence summary of Johnson and Knowles's disagreement. The likely reason for Boswell's omission is summed up by James Woolley – the uncouth vision of Johnson is so incongruous with the more jovial combative figure that his Flemish picture draws as to disfigure his canvas: 'For the deepest rhetorical reasons, her account was unusable.'[59]

Boswell finished the public argument in 1794, but Seward's revelation of his withholding of the account, and her depiction of Johnson's 'ruffian asperity' in this case (*Letters*, vol. I, p. 111), is one place where she effectively shone a light on Johnson's sporadic social rudeness and brutality, and offers a corrective to the cosier sides of him emphasised by some admirers. More generally, she never managed to argue convincingly her claim that this same brutality disfigured and invalidated his literary criticism. Ashmun suggests that Seward pursued the point to her own detriment, being 'too persistent and vehement, even though there may have been some truth in what she said'. Jane West's judgement seems to be representative in admiring the 'ardour with which she supports the cause of genius', but that with her abuse of Johnson, 'in her vindictive enmity she out-Herods Herod'.[60] Seward never seems to have realised how distorting her critical ire towards him had become. In 1804, apropos of Hayley's *Life of Cowper*, she tells him that 'I yet have never admitted' the *Lives of the Poets* 'to a place on my book-shelves, since the specious injustice of those volumes is a caustic on my feelings whenever I open the leaves' (*Letters*, vol. VI, p. 172). This almost childlike ingenuousness contributed to the unfortunate process by which her writings on Johnson became a caricature, undermining the rest of her literary judgement.[61]

An age of wit and genius

Seward's long argument with Johnson's criticism was part of her wider campaign to assert the true genius of contemporary poetry; in doing so, she revealed an individual, somewhat flawed aesthetic that contributed significantly to her own relative lack of happiness and fulfilment, in terms of public letters, as can be seen in the following survey of her critical judgements.

Seward's aesthetic is enthusiastic in fervour and depreciation, perfectly happy to contradict itself, and based fundamentally upon analysis of character and temperament. Here, optimism plays its part. For Seward, Johnson's scepticism about the sincerity of human motives, combined with his public rudeness, were expressions of a profound misanthropy. Seward, a woman of feeling, preferred open-hearted benevolence; more cynical souls were tarred with the misanthropic brush. Thomas Day, whose quixotic adventures in importing the doctrines of Rousseau into the Midlands formed one of the most enjoyable parts of Seward's *Memoirs of Darwin*, had a 'tincture of misanthropic gloom and proud contempt of common-life society', and 'resembled [Johnson] in want of sympathy with such miseries as spring from refinement and the softer affections; resembled him also, in true compassion for the suffering of cold and hunger'.[62] It is this lack of a certain type of sensitivity that alienates Johnson from her, even as she recognises his pragmatic Christianity.

Against the Johnsonian dismissal of Gray, Milton, and others, Seward promoted her own literary canon, in which the contemporary combined with an absolute veneration of the past. A problem for this pantheon was William Cowper, as Seward had admired *The Task*, but with important qualifications, summarised in 1786: 'The Task ... has many and great poetic beauties, both as to imagery, landscape, and sentiment; yet the author perpetually shews himself to be a sarcastic misanthropist' (*Letters*, vol. I, p. 121). In the following years, this view is reiterated with a peculiar lack of patience for Cowper's mental sufferings, and contempt for the doctrines of Calvinism that produced them.[63] She counters Miss Scott in 1787: 'You plead Cowper's constitutional melancholy in excuse for his misanthropy. That plea is often made for Johnson also; but if it is possible that Melancholy can so narrow the mind ... it then becomes a vice, against which every generous reader will bear the most renouncing testimony' (*Letters*, vol. I, p. 297). This refusal to see that an inherent melancholia should deserve sympathy is odd, in such an otherwise warm writer.

A melancholy constitution narrows the mind in the same way as an over-enthusiastic one. Cowper, in Seward's eyes, was also guilty of the Johnsonian sin of ignoring the genius of the present.[64] Her taste would always value the absolutely modern as being potentially equal to the past. As she argued, 'What an age of wit and genius is the present! But the world will never be cured of its cant about "weakened nature and exhausted art." Shaftesbury and Addison so canted in *their* period, now called the Augustan: Envy of contemporary claims produces, and will ever produce it.'[65] The final return to jealousy as motive somewhat compromises what is otherwise the most commendable side of Seward's criticism – her rejection of reflex condemnations of contemporary writing. Her extended argument with George Hardinge was a result of his 'prejudice against the moderns', which she aligns with Johnson's attitudes in the *Lives*.[66]

Her promotion of the contemporary centred originally around her friendship with William Hayley. Now noticed mainly for his dealings with

Blake, his biographies of Milton and Cowper, and his friendship with the latter, Hayley was a prolific writer whose 'name was literally a household word' at the end of the eighteenth century, as Ashmun claims; he refused the laureateship in 1790.[67] It may now seem a typical piece of Sewardian exaggeration to suggest as she does that 'Neither [Dryden] nor Pope have one original poem so rich in poetic invention, that first gift of the muses, as Hayley's Triumphs of Temper' (*Letters*, vol. II, p. 211), but this mock-epic instruction manual for young ladies went through ten editions by the end of the century after its publication in 1781, even if it now seems irredeemably mannered. Hayley's renown was valuable for Seward's battle for contemporary poetry, as shown in her many glowing mentions of the 'brilliant bard of Sussex', the 'transcendent English bard of the present æra'; writing an inscription in his works in 1793, she referred to the 'Sun of Genius' which 'pours a flood of radiance' through his poetry; a decade before, she had compared critics of Hayley to Pope's dunces, and suggested it would be their only memorable act: 'And Hayley bear you through the walks of time, / Rendering your worthless names immortal as his rhyme!'[68]

In a letter of 1788, arguing that contemporary literature was superior in variety to the time of Queen Anne, Seward suggested that 'Surely Mr Hayley's verse breathes a more creative and original genius, than even the brilliant Pope, who excels him in nothing but in the high and laboured polish of his enchanting numbers.'[69] She also helped with the practical difficulties of Hayley's wife, described (tactfully) by Ashmun as 'eccentric to the point of being unbalanced'; they separated, and he moved her to Derby, where Seward occasionally visited her until her death in 1797.[70] Yet there is suggestion of neglect of Seward on Hayley's part, and their correspondence becomes more sporadic from the end of the 1780s. Seward also made criticisms unknown in the halcyon days of their relationship, attacking Hayley's duplicity in publishing different editions of his *Life of Milton*, one of which had additional notes full of the 'pernicious infatuation' of 'democratic principles'.[71] She was pleased that the same work refuted the 'malignant slanders' of Johnson, but disliked Hayley's claims for the 'supposed goodness and greatness of mind' of the latter (*Letters*, vol. IV, p. 154). Of Hayley's *Triumph of Music* (1804), she wrote that 'This strange composition is a chaos of ludicrous absurdities, on which scarce one ray of genius gleams' (*Letters*, vol. VI, p. 217).

Yet Hayley had by then played his part in giving Seward a contemporary who could be an equal to the ancients, and as the workings of her canon resembled T. S. Eliot's idea of a tradition in one cogent way, an author had to be removed from the shelf to allow Hayley in. This might explain the progressive degradation of John Dryden in Seward's writings. At first, he plays a central part in her list of the English immortals (*Poetical Works*, vol. 1, p. lxxxiii), but then she finds that Hayley is his equal, 'as to the luxuriance of poetic creation, and the happiness of allusion, avoiding the slovenly coarseness of his style', and that he 'has the fire and the invention of Dryden, without any of his absurdity'.[72]

This seems an odd judgement, like Seward's lobbying for the genius of Hayley's friend John Sargent's distinctly strange though not unsuccessful *The Mine* (1785), a verse drama set underground that anticipates some of the grandiose excesses of *Das Rheingold* in content, if not in skill. Of this long campaign, Seward's remark that 'The first speech in blank verse of the Gnome is perfectly Miltonic' gives an accurate flavour.[73] Her belief in the importance of modern poetry made her exaggeratedly condemn some past writers, and over-praise her contemporary favourites. The result is that Seward's modern pantheon is made up of figures such as Hayley, and poets of reputation whom she endeavoured to make greater. Gray is the exemplum of this, being rarely introduced other than as 'our English Pindar' and 'the first poetic name of this century'.[74] The level of her rapture might be contentious, but nobody argued with Gray's centrality. With his executor William Mason it was rather different, and for all Seward's resounding confidence that he 'stands second to Gray as a lyric Poet', there would always be a George Hardinge, who had the temerity to suggest, as Seward paraphrases incredulously, that 'Mason, the sweet Claude of our science, is no poet. No poet! What is it then that thrills my veins, and fills my eyes with the tears of delight, whenever I open his volumes?'[75] As usual, the discussion reached an impasse because the degree of Seward's enthusiasm could not possibly be matched by her correspondent, and precluded any common ground, once he had denied Mason's inherent genius.

In the case of Erasmus Darwin, Seward's enthusiasm for *The Loves of the Plants* in 1789, and of the larger work of which it became a part in *The Botanic Garden* (1791), was moderated by other factors. In 1790, she told Hester Piozzi that *The Loves of the Plants* was a 'masterly result of a creative, elevated and brilliant imagination' which will 'entitle their master to a very high place in the temple of the British muses'. This is later reiterated: the poem 'will shine to future ages, largely contributing to the lyric glories' of the period. But there is a problem – Darwin has inserted her commendatory poem as the exordium to *The Botanic Garden*, with neither permission nor acknowledgement (despite its already having been published under her name in *The Gentleman's Magazine* in 1783), an affront to which she would draw further attention over the years.[76] Her later references to Darwin's poetry check her praise: a reference to the well-known parody *The Loves of the Triangles* in 1798 calls the original 'very affected', and she claims to have been 'always aware' of the 'absurdities and affectations' of his verse (*Letters*, vol. v, pp. 113, 136). Her criticism of his character is unsurprising – 'poetic authorism, commencing with him after middle-life, engrafted all its irritability, disingenuous arts, and grudging jealousy of others' reputation' (*Letters*, vol. vi, pp. 24–5) – but there is also a genuine acceptance that time has taken some of the shine from what had seemed to be genius.

That her admiration remained is testified by the rambling extended analysis of *The Botanic Garden* that would make up the majority of her *Memoirs* of Darwin in 1804, and where she defended 'his poetic style': that he 'was a mannerist cannot be denied', but so was Milton in *Paradise Lost*, Young in *Night Thoughts*, and Akenside in *The Pleasures of Imagination*.[77] Darwin's poem is 'one of the richest effusions of the poetic mind, that has shed lustre over Europe in the eighteenth century'. Posterity will see its value, and 'the querulous and disdainful tones of peevish prejudice will not venture to assail the ear of an admiring Nation' (*Memoirs*, pp. 378–9, 381). Yet this co-exists, somewhat uneasily, with a biography that Seward admits may 'displease' the 'dazzled idolaters of the late Dr. Darwin, who will not allow that there were any spots in his sun' (*Memoirs*, p. 429). It certainly displeased Darwin's family: they objected to the presentation of the suicide of Darwin's eldest son Charles, who in December 1799 had drowned himself in the river Derwent, because of debt and mental breakdown. Most controversial was her description of Darwin's response: 'When the Doctor received information that [the body] was found, he exclaimed in a low voice, "Poor insane coward!" and it is said never afterwards mentioned the subject.' She was forced to retract this, but the damage was done, and was compounded by her noting the 'universal surprise to see [Darwin] walking along the streets of Derby the day after the funeral of his son, with a serene countenance and his usual cheerfulness of address'.[78] Seward continued to admire Darwin's poetry, but without unqualified enthusiasm.

Such a quality was saved for James Macpherson and the Ossian poems; Seward was not especially interested in arguments over their provenance (other than to note that Johnson's envy was his motive in the controversy), but had 'wept for joy' on first reading him at the age of sixteen: an early letter of November 1762 finds 'a daring spirit in this work, resembling that of the sacred writings' with 'a great blaze of imagination'. Seward reprimanded Sophia Weston in 1786: 'And so you fancy you do not like Ossian. You, who are so alive to the sweet, the majestic, and the terrible graces in actual prospect, to be insensible when they are finely presented by the old Bard to your internal sight!!! Surely it is whimsical.' Weston, a relation of the wife of Seward's great friend Thomas Sedgwick Whalley and future houseguest of Hester Lynch Piozzi, responded that she finds it bombastic, whereupon Seward counters that 'I always conclude the bombast to be his own, the sublime to be Ossian', an opinion she repeated in 1792: 'I impute the fustian passages, of which it must be allowed there are several, to Macpherson; and it is almost all I can allow him as to the images and ideas.' With great ingenuity (or amnesia), she was delighted when Walter Scott told her of the finds of Mackenzie's commission of 1805: Macpherson's authorship of most of the Ossian canon means that 'Henceforth, therefore, I shall consider him as one of the greatest poets which the late century, so rich in great poets, has produced.'[79]

Seward's modern canon is a mixture of the eminent and the mediocre, and has not worn well with time (though such polemic efforts at canon formation rarely do). In constructing it, her absolute conviction of the genius of these writers energised her efforts, but the persuasiveness of a critic who repeatedly exhausts superlatives is inevitably compromised. Conversely, one of the most winning sides of Seward is her capacity to continue to enthuse, even in cases where it would be easy for her to adopt a reactionary position. Her passion for William Godwin is a good case in point. She was a huge admirer of *Caleb Williams* (despite her abhorrence of its politics); she also recommended his second novel *St Leon* to every correspondent.[80] If this speaks well of her sometime ability to notice works of lasting effect, the same cannot be said of Seward's last poetic idol, Robert Southey.

Seward hugely admired Southey's *Joan of Arc* (1798), opining that she had read 'nothing of such manly greatness, except from Chatterton', by such a youthful author, but had disliked its political intentions, the praise of 'that hellish revolution' which was its aim.[81] It was to be his *Madoc* (1805), 'by far the most captivating work of its genuinely inspired author', that was the glory of her twilight years: the poem 'has more for the understanding and the heart than any composition without the pale of Shakespeare and Richardson' (*Letters*, vol. VI, pp. 223, 228). When speculating on the possibility, she thought that meeting its author 'would have sensations similar to those which Milton allots to Adam in his conversation with the angel Raphael'. Such hyperbole is accompanied by Seward's failure to give much corresponding attention to Southey's contemporaries;

a few lines on from her rhapsody, she adds a comment on Wordsworth: 'on the whole, it is not first rate; often meanly familiar, and almost as often turgid and obscure' (*Letters*, vol. VI, p. 258).

In lines to be 'Inscribed on the blank leaves of the Poem Madoc', Seward saluted 'this noblest effort of the Nine', thought (through a familiarly odd metaphor that offers a carcinogenic defence against the old bugbear, jealousy) that 'The asbestos robe which the chaste style arrays' was an 'Impassive shield from Envy's lurid blaze', and encouraged 'Such minds, where never Envy's cloud appears' to 'View Madoc buoyant on the tide of years' (*Poetical Works*, vol. III, pp. 391, 392, 393). Scott noted that she mentioned the 'inadequate success' of *Madoc* as the 'most decided symptom of degenerate taste' in contemporary literature (*Poetical Works*, vol. I, p. xxii). She told Southey that it was 'amongst the first poetry the world has produced', and that her conviction of its genius was an 'ark of my covenant with future generations' (*Letters*, vol. VI, pp. 359, 360). She was still less than positive about Wordsworth, who 'has genius – but his poetry is harsh, turgid, and obscure. He is chiefly a poetic landscape painter – but his pictures want directness' (*Letters*, vol. V, p. 61). Nor would the *Poems* of 1807 win her over – they 'have excited, by turns, my tenderness and warm admiration, my contemptuous astonishment and disgust. The two latter rose to their utmost height while I read about his dancing daffodils.' Elsewhere she concludes of the volume that 'Many of their contents lie fairly open to the reprehensive disdain of even a just critic' (*Letters*, vol. VI, pp. 366, 389).

Seward's critique of Wordsworth, allied with her inflated opinion of Southey, has undermined her critical credibility, yet it should be considered why she failed to find much in the former, and grossly misjudged the longevity of the works of the latter. Samuel Holt Monk argued that she was not alone in being incapable of understanding the sort of subjectivity so central to Wordsworth's poetics, and that, equally, what she was drawn to in the supposed fresh genius of Southey was really the palatable old wine of eighteenth-century Miltonic blank verse in a new bottle.[82] He also makes an important related point. Seward's repeated comments on the need to free criticism of English poetry from adherence to Classical or foreign literatures have been interpreted positively – Brewer finds that 'her desire to find the sources of modern English poetry in a native tradition, and not in the influence of the ancient classics or French and Italian verse, stimulated her enthusiasm for patriotic medievalism'. Yet as Monk points out, when Seward was presented with such a tradition, she disliked it.[83] When Henry J. Todd sent her his annotations and variants of Spenser, for instance, she found herself bored, and complained that

'To me there is little genius in the fabrication of such hobgoblin tales. I am wholly at a loss to guess what has procured for Spencer the high place he holds amongst our classics' (*Letters*, vol. VI, p. 229). Chaucer fared just as badly. She told Henry Cary that 'Chaucer had certainly genius; but beneath the rust of his obsolete, coarse and inharmonious diction, there is no ascertaining its degree' (*Letters*, vol. III, p. 140). She was interested in the (highly dubious) history presented in Godwin's *Life of Chaucer*, and annoyed when the poet got in the way: Godwin is 'insanely partial to the poetic powers of Chaucer, whose compositions, allowing for the disadvantage of obsolete language, have so little good which is not translation, and so much that is tedious, unnatural, conceited, and obscure' (*Letters*, vol. VI, pp. 269–70). In 1807 she told Scott that Dryden, 'Spencer, and Chaucer, have, in my opinion, been over-praised. On a balance of their beauty and deformity, not one of them equals yourself or Southey' (*Letters*, vol. VI, pp. 330–1).

Given such reflections, it would seem that Seward's interest was not in the linguistic base of a native English poetic tradition (as she was far more sympathetic to the ersatz authenticity of an Ossian or Chatterton), but in a manufactured canon that confirmed her predominant interest in the contemporary, and which would be a lasting reproach to the injustices of the Johnsonian critical establishment. In other words, Seward constructed a Whiggish narrative of literary history that depended upon her own taste, rather than any compromise towards an historical consensus. This made her place her trust in the genius of William Hayley and Robert Southey. It is hard, however, to see much satisfaction in such vehement reiterations of her poetic beliefs and creed; they are more indicative of a passionate but anxious need to challenge the status quo of a literary world which she is convinced is prejudiced against her, and would never acknowledge her real merit and genius.

Bitter is my tear

Seward's critical enterprise never lost momentum; that her views were repeatedly shown to be at variance with the majority of readers was a spur to present again her anger at Johnson's calumnies, and her support for unfairly maligned talents. By contrast with this confidence, much of the poetry she published after the 1780s shows a greater diffidence, and a growing sense of introspection. When compared to the successful superficial melodrama of *Louisa*, the poems and sonnets of the 1790s have much greater depth, and less of the affected trappings of sensibility.

If Seward's poetry in this decade was more pensive and reflective, one reason for its gravity was an increasing sense of loss and nostalgia, embodied in the death of her father in 1790. He had suffered a progressive mental decline: he suffered his first stroke in 1780, and Scott refers to his being afterwards 'embittered by a frequent recurrence of paralytic and apoplectic afflictions, which broke Mr Seward's health, and gradually impaired the tone of his mind'.[84] Seward bore the brunt of these as his nurse (which makes her prolific output as poet, critic, and controversialist more remarkable), and his mental problems entered her poetry; a sonnet first published in 1799 records how

> Dim grows the vital flame in his dear breast
> From whom my life I drew; – and thrice has Spring
> Bloom'd; and fierce Winter thrice, on darken'd wing,
> Howl'd o'er the gray, waste fields, since he possess'd
> Or strength of frame, or intellect.
> (Sonnet LXII, *Poetical Works*, vol. II, p. 183)

Her greatest tribute to him, and perhaps her greatest poem, was published in 1792. The subject of *Eyam* is a visit of August 1788 to Seward's eponymous birthplace in Derbyshire (where her father had remained official rector) and it turns the conventional exploration of the pastoral of childhood into a meditation on memory and loss. Eyam is mentioned throughout Seward's works – an early letter has an extended description of it and correspondence from an ancestor of her great friend Mrs Mompesson, detailing the sufferings of the village during the plague in 1666.[85] In 1793, Seward returned to Eyam for the first time since her father's death, phrasing her wish to revisit the past in an odd way: 'I cannot resist the desire of indulging this mournful luxury, in a scene which bears such striking traces of the dear and for ever lost.' Any trace of an affected indulgence was far from the reality of what she felt when she arrived:

> I could not restrain the gushing tears, through almost the whole of the five hours I passed in that dear village ... every face, every voice recalled, with redoubled force, my lost father. – And the sight of the desolate rectory! – I did not enter it, – I could not, but I lingered in the churchyard, weeping bitterly, as I gazed on the walls, the windows, the neglected garden, which, in despite of their altered appearance, yet strongly bear the stamp and magic of their vanished possessor. (*Letters*, vol. III, pp. 258, 268)

This letter is akin to a prose version of the earlier poem, where the initial urge to rediscover the past leads similarly to a heightened sense of grief. There is a conventional apostrophe – 'Not two short miles from thee, can I refrain / Thy haunts, my native Eyam, long unseen?' – but it is accompanied by a sense of spontaneous feeling, as the welcoming of villagers encourages a level of emotion that is greater than expected, and hard to control: 'But, while on me the eyes of Friendship glow, / Swell my pain'd sighs, my tears spontaneous flow' (*Poetical Works*, vol. III, p. 2). The bald reason for this is that the scenes in Eyam are a reminder of how far her father has fallen from his former eminence:

> In scenes paternal, not beheld through years,
> Nor view'd, till now, but by a Father's side,
> Well might the tender, tributary tears,
> From keen regrets of duteous fondness glide!
> Its pastor, to this human-flock no more
> Shall the long flight of future days restore!
> Distant he droops, – and that once gladdening eye
> Now languid gleams, e'en when his friends are nigh.
> (*Poetical Works*, vol. III, pp. 2–3)

The poem's achievement is to make this sense of present loss co-existent with the Edenic past that the village represents; Eyam is Seward's Auburn, and its pastoral is rooted in the centrality of her father to its past, and to her own life. Her nostalgia is tinged with a bittersweet sense of the likelihood of pain, as her vision is both of the desolate emptiness of the present, and the dominating paternal presence that exacerbates this. Eyam is both past and present for Seward, as she cannot escape the spectre of the memories of her father, and the contrast with his current decay:

> But O! thou blank, and silent pulpit! – thou,
> That with a Father's precepts, just, and bland,
> Did'st win my ear, as reason's strength'ning glow
> Show'd their full value, now thou seem'st to stand
> Before my sad, suffus'd, and trembling gaze,
> The dreariest relic of departed days.
> Of eloquence paternal, nervous, clear,
> Dim Apparition thou – and bitter is my tear!
> (*Poetical Works*, vol. III, p. 4)

A poetic meditation on the ways that those you admire are assailed by mortality, and the impossibility of reconciling yourself to the way that memory inevitably links to loss, *Eyam* is a stirring and powerful corrective to the charges of affectation often brought against Seward as a poet. Moreover, it indicates a poignant realism, a sense of being cast out from the pastoral refuge that Eyam represented. The poem is concerned with the removal of those consolations – symbolised by her father's authority and role as shepherd of the flock – that are a mainstay of life, until their removal necessitates standing alone. The result is affecting precisely because Seward seems to view a tableau of the past, with no-one to console her, or to reconcile her losses with present or future happiness.

The most popular poem of her later years was 'Llangollen Vale' (1796), a garland for the so-called 'Ladies of Llangollen', Lady Eleanor Butler and Sarah Ponsonby.[86] Yet Seward's arguably most distinctive work came in the collection of *Original Sonnets* of 1799, which was published with her versions of Horace. Seward's Miltonic sonnets were written over a twenty-year period, and many of their subjects (Johnson's *Lives*, Honora Sneyd, the genius of contemporary poets) are familiar. The result is not a sequence, as its themes are too disparate to follow a narrative; a significant topic, however, is the conflict between the prospects of hope and imagination and the prosaic dullness of reality, and the concomitant argument that hopes are themselves necessary delusions. The opening sonnet is an appreciation of the powers of reading:

> When life's realities the soul perceives
>   Vain, dull, perchance corrosive, if she glow
>   With rising energy, and open throw
> The golden gates of Genius, she achieves
> His fairy clime delighted, and receives
>   In those gay paths, where thornless roses blow,
>   Full compensation. – Lo, with alter'd brow
> Lours the false world, and the fine spirit grieves!
> No more young Hope tints with her light and bloom
>   The darkening scene. – Then to ourselves we say,
>   Come, bright Imagination, come! relume
> Thy orient lamp; with recompensing ray
>   Shine on the mind, and pierce its gathering gloom
>   With all the fires of intellectual day!
>   (Sonnet 1, *Poetical Works*, vol. II, p. 122)

The danger of being dragged down by the dour and unrelenting nature of life can be escaped by the consolation of books and the imaginative freedom they offer; this is seen as a compensation, a way of warding off the 'gathering gloom'; it cannot dispel it completely.

Accordingly, the next sonnet counters such escapism by suggesting that the idea of future happiness is both necessarily inherent and doomed to disappointment:

> The future, and its gifts alone we prize,
>   Few joys the present brings, and those alloy'd;
>   Th' expected fulness leaves an aching void;
> But Hope stands by, and lifts her sunny eyes
> That gild the days to come. – She still relies

> The phantom Happiness not thus shall glide
> Always from life. – Alas! – yet ill betide
> Austere Experience, when she coldly tries
> In distant roses to discern the thorn!
> (Sonnet 11, *Poetical Works*, vol. 11, p. 123)

Since sorrow never comes too late, we should not go looking for it; the distance between hope and expectation is made more central in these sonnets than in Seward's prose, where the hope for the future fame of herself and other poets is more strident and confident that justice will be done. Many of the sonnets instead illustrate a vulnerable sense that the possibilities of the future redressing the unhappiness of the past will always be a chimera. The idea is applied directly to her literary career in a very Shakespearean sonnet:

> Ah! why have I indulged my dazzled sight
>   With scenes in Hope's delusive mirror shewn?
>   Scenes, that too seldom human life hath known
> In more than vision rise; – but O! how bright
> The Mind's soft sorceress pour'd her rosy light
>   On every promis'd good; – oft on the boon
>   Which might at Fame's resounding shrine be won,
>   Then lanc'd its beams where all the Loves invite!
> Now, with stern hand, Fate draws the sable veil
>   O'er the frail glass! – Hope, as she turns away,
>   The darken'd crystal drops. – Heavy and pale,
> Rain-drizzling clouds quench all the darts of day:
>   Low mourns the wind along the gloomy dale,
>   And tolls the death-bell in the pausing gale.
> (Sonnet XVII, *Poetical Works*, vol. 11, p. 138)

This is partly a valediction to Seward's hopes of literary fame as a distinct way of life, free from existential troubles: the delusive 'scenes' of imagined happiness have 'seldom' proved to be anything more than a fantasy, rather than a coherent answer to problems, whether concerned with love or fame. Then again, the lure of what can be imagined will soon lead to the dialectic between hope and experience being explored again, with little sign of any resolution to the struggle. The gothic ending of this dour poem may overstate the case, but Seward's struggles between the hopes of the imagination and the disappointing world of the quotidian make this very personal poetry a more realistic counterpoint to the over-egged claims of her criticism. Like so many prolific poets, her work is uneven; her more reflective and personal poetry is more substantial and more effective than her publicly successful but somewhat superficial works of sensibility, which follow the reflexes of fashion or mark an occasion with little of the rigorous self-examination and intense elegiac sense of poems such as *Eyam*. Seward's long poetic career cannot be called a failure, though neither was it the success that she wanted (and apparently needed) for self-validation. Sadly, as with her critical views, even partial rejection seems to have given her a pain which she could as little alleviate or moderate as her enthusiasm.

Unfeeling critics

Seward's literary legacy has been as mixed as the reviews of her poetry in her lifetime. Her importance, as the creator of a provincial literary salon, and as a woman writer who fearlessly spoke her mind, even in the face of ridicule and opprobrium, has been overshadowed by the criticism of her excesses, both of style and content. This began with the posthumous publication of the *Letters* in 1811. Constable, the publisher, ignored Seward's request that twelve volumes be published at intervals, with two volumes arriving annually. A possible reason for this wish was that it lessened the risk of impugning some of the persons mentioned (as there was a greater chance of their passing away during the intervals). Constable seems to have seen the request as authorial vanity, and was also motivated by financial concerns (if the initial volumes did not take, he would be left with an obligation to publish writings guaranteed little sale).[87] Seward seems to have designed her correspondence to be a central document in her posthumous self-fashioning: it would secure her literary fame, and give a suitable riposte and last word to her many arguments over the years with Johnsonian critics. Teresa Barnard argues that by thwarting Seward's preferred plan of publication, Constable fatally compromised them: 'Had the letters been published over the course of several years as she requested and had they been left uncensored, they would have opened up a new conception of Anna Seward.' The counter to this is the reaction to the selection of Seward's compendious correspondence, which suggests that Constable gauged how much of Seward to publish quite well, for his commercial purposes. Barnard points out the censoring of certain areas of the *Letters* (especially remarks by Scott about Francis Jeffrey that he wanted to conceal), which does nobody any credit. Her larger claim, though, that this, together with the publication of only half of the *Letters*, meant that Seward's 'plans for a self-constructed literary image were seriously impaired' is more contentious; given the response to the matter and style of what was published, it is hard to see how the elided and suppressed letters could have ameliorated such an impression.[88]

For it is undeniable that the publication of the *Letters* brought forth a great deal of abuse. Ashmun records 'numerous references' to them, 'many of them spiteful, some of them sympathetic, and most of them censorious of the affectations of style'. It would seem that the peculiarities of the writing enhanced objections to their contents: Robert Anderson was put off by this 'disgusting affectation of verbal ornament', but seemed equally shocked that the letters were 'everywhere tinctured with personal, political, and poetical prejudices'. Barnard describes how the 'general reaction from the literary world was one of incredulity at her apparent egotism', and this has been seen as gender-specific: Ashmun argues that for all their 'curiously pompous style' the level of abuse towards Seward's correspondence was due to 'a woman usurping the prerogatives of men'.[89] But whatever the motives behind the attacks, the fact remains that the *Letters* did not help Seward's case for posterity; however much they were revised, the final portrait that emerged was not received as its author intended, and Thomas Percy was not alone in finding them 'a display of vanity, egotism, and, it grieves me to add, malignancy'. Hill Wickham, the editor of Thomas Whalley's *Correspondence*, noted Whalley's recollection of the 'indignation at Lichfield excited by the publicity given by her to the private interchange of thought amongst friends'. William Hayley was also angered by her free descriptions of his marital problems.[90] Her former correspondent George Hardinge had less excuse to combine criticism of her purple prose with markedly ungracious comments about Seward after her death.[91] Questions about Seward's revision of the correspondence would include why she did not exclude (or at least tone down) some of the examples of her outspoken ire, though it is equally possible that she augmented their number; if so, her fashioning of her posthumous image was, like so many of her critical efforts, self-defeating.

Writing in the 1930s, Ashmun complained (with some justification) that most of the modern commentary on Seward was 'too mocking' and 'too much tinged with satire', but even allowing for undoubted casual misogyny, the attitude of posterity towards Seward was in part a fundamental disagreement with what she thought would be vindicated – her taste and literary judgement.[92] Moreover, attacks on her were inevitable, given that she repeatedly promoted arguments that were not accepted by most readers, then and since. We should decry the extent to which Seward has been vilified because of her gender, but that should not lead to the conclusion that the critical premises of these dismissals were always faulty. It remains the case that Seward has been proven wrong in most of her judgements on who were to prove consequential English poets and writers.

It is equally possible that the hyperbole of Seward in favour of such writers was to some extent an act of wish fulfilment, an attempt to influence critical justice away from the Johnsonian prejudices which she found in so many critics and authors. Scott apologised for it in introducing her poetry, seeing it as a part of her nature: 'if she sometimes errs in praising her favourite authors with too little discrimination, the error is of that generous kind which marks the warmth of her character, and can proceed only from an enthusiastic admiration of every thing which seemed to her to bear the stamp of genius' (*Poetical Works*, vol. 1, p. viii). There was equal warmth in her attacks on those whom she thought to be over-rated, or to be yet another instance of the disfiguring effects of jealousy.

Seward's poetic and critical achievement remains as partial as her character, in its mixture of ingenuous warmth and kindness, furious indignation and pain at contradiction, and damaging obsessions. Norma Clarke finds Seward 'a born literary academic, never happier than when doing close reading, textual criticism of the most precise and laboured kind', claiming that many of her letters are 'extended literary essays' offering 'an alternative model of criticism'; this meant that Seward 'dramatised herself as a sedulous and discriminating reader of English literature'. Such a summary is not incorrect – Seward did indeed write many such letters – but it is only a part of the story.[93] Such 'pedantic' close readings are often combined with generalised assertions, and reiterations of the obvious rightness of her taste, which are far from scholarly in refusing to investigate their own premises. For every detailed criticism, there is another example where argument is stopped (with very Johnsonian brusqueness) because of her dislike of its terms, which she then blames on the pedantry of analysis, or explains away by the charge of envy; these make Seward's presentation of herself as a 'discriminating reader' unsuccessful. Seward's criticism oscillates between examination of minutiae and expression of the most unsupportable generalities; the strength of her delight in poetry means that close reading is always tempered (and often replaced) by feeling. The latter often dominated: 'But O! While I thus transform myself into one of those unfeeling critics, of whom my spirit is so impatient, how sincerely do I abjure such sickly accuracy' (*Letters*, vol. 1, p. 208). This is not a contradiction of Clarke, so much as a different side of Seward's very partial critical nature.

Seward's writings offer enthusiasm, often in the form of subjective and emotive claims that suggest a need to exaggerate her position, which is in turn indicative of a greater absence of fulfilment. Her imputation of jealousy to so many writers is peculiarly disabling to her criticism. But it

Unfeeling critics 153

is also explained by the fervour of her response to literature, and the absolute centrality of it to her life. Criticism for Seward is ultimately an expression of feeling, and a personal matter: Johnson's critical injustices must be motivated by jealousy. Nothing else could assuage her feelings, deeply and sincerely wounded by the *Lives of the Poets*. But Seward failed to acknowledge that feelings, like taste and judgement, could differ, and (most importantly) how the 'truth' and 'justice' that she sought to vindicate was a compromise, a result partly of the arbitrary workings of time and future critical argument, rather than an absolute.

There is pathos in Seward's writing (intended or otherwise) because literature did mean almost everything to her. Yet this is also why her literary career was, and remains by her own standards, unfulfilled. A prolific and successful writer central to the British literary world of the time, Seward's writing is nevertheless full of a yearning for acceptance and acknowledgement that could never come, because the nature and degree of what she required was impossible. No level of personal acclaim, or vindication of the many talents in whom she had vested her interest, would be sufficient to satisfy her. In asking everything as a reward for her literary enthusiasms, Seward was bound to be disappointed. It is her remarkable unwillingness to accept that taste is not universal that makes Seward such a peculiar guide to her literary times. After directing a fearful blast at William Hayley over the supposedly jealous Cowper's wilful ignorance of contemporary genius, she ends the letter, 'Adieu! forgive my ingenuousness' (*Letters*, vol. VI, p. 173). It is this open response to literature that ensured that Seward could not find the degree of acceptance and fulfilment that her critical and creative work required; conversely, she was always somewhat consoled by her enthusiasms, eventually. In contrast, for the subject of the next chapter, literary fame mattered so absolutely that the result was not the qualified disappointments of Seward, but a far more complete sense of failure.

CHAPTER 4

Percival Stockdale's alternative literary history

In 1799, the clergyman, poet, and literary critic Percival Stockdale was the subject of a contemptuous pamphlet. Written by the pseudonymous 'Veritas', it was a rebuttal of Stockdale's public criticisms of the Bishop of Durham, Shute Barrington, the target of a series of attacks that had commenced in 1792. Most recently, Stockdale had berated the Bishop for not using his sermon to denounce the iniquities of slavery.[1] After pointing out the folly of his aggressive publications, 'Veritas' leaves Stockdale in no doubt whatsoever about his marginal place in the world of letters:

> Your talents, Sir, are not so peculiarly eminent, (however vanity and self-conceit may have led you to form a false estimate of them) that the world would be any loser if you were never again to commit a single work to the Press; or, even, if you never had committed one. You are, really, thought very little of, as an Authour. Your station, on the parnassian mount, is a very humble one. It is not the number, but the merit, of Works, which gives celebrity. The Reviewers, whom you have so violently and illiberally attacked, only proclaimed to you, beforehand, what would be the sentiments of the public. Facts speak for themselves. The crowded shelves of your booksellers, and your own very moderate gains, are but slight encouragement for you to continue your Authority. Not even the names of many of your Works are known to the public, except by the catalogue which you so assiduously affix to every performance.[2]

It is a series of melancholy, irrefutable truths, as 'Veritas' points out what everyone, save Stockdale, has long realised: that his claims of poetic and critical authority are written on sand; that his intemperate attacks upon his critics are merely another reflection of his self-delusions; that it would be irrelevant to the present and posterity if he had never written; and that it is only Stockdale's own ceaseless self-promotion which has kept him in the public eye at all. It is a devastating indictment of a conceited, failed writer, striving to catch the attention of a world which has long since forgotten to pay him any. The acid disdain of 'Veritas' is a reaction against Stockdale's often haughty and ill-advised claims of grandiose literary status. Hence the judgement of Howard Weinbrot, who finds Stockdale 'a man of uncommon intellectual diligence and modest but genuine literary talent; but he also combined John Dennis's destructive hostility to others with Richard Savage's destructive hostility to himself'.[3] The presence of this small but genuine talent is often overshadowed by Stockdale's endless intemperate attacks on anyone who criticised him, and generally disastrous lack of self-awareness. The results were brutal criticisms like that of 'Veritas'.

Such attacks were not unusual throughout Stockdale's literary career. In many ways, Stockdale was hardened to such criticism, yet he refused to accept its verdict. This makes his life and work an exceptionally valuable example of literary failure: whereas many aspirant writers were understandably deflated by the repeated derision of their contemporaries, Stockdale never stopped believing that posterity would judge him differently. Rather than retreating quietly into obscurity, Stockdale consistently reminded the world of the unjust treatment of his works, and the misfortunes of his life. Few writers have left such a large record of their failures: in the decade before his death in 1811, the aged Stockdale finished two long final works of self-justification, his *Lectures on the Truly Eminent English Poets* (1807), and his *Memoirs* (1809). Both works garnered reviews that were at best lukewarm. But, along with Stockdale's many other publications, including poems (of which those on Samuel Johnson's cat and on the evils of slavery have garnered a slight amount of critical attention), translations, sermons, essays, and a play, these histories of his own resentments and arguments give a remarkably full anatomy of an unsuccessful eighteenth-century writer.

It is the purpose of this chapter to show how Stockdale's well-documented example illustrates particularly the idea of failure in the eighteenth century. By examining the litany of non-events that make up Stockdale's public career, it is possible to show how the desire for literary fame develops, and in many ways destroys the possibilities of the aspirant author; how a supposedly burgeoning literary marketplace offered an endless chance of celebrity (and an equal opportunity for self-delusion), and how the worship of famous authors could blight a literary career, and colour every production with bitterness and recrimination. Through his writings, Stockdale offers an alternative literary history of his own times, contrary to both his contemporaries and posterity. It is a history in which failure accidentally becomes the dominant subject.

A great sensibility

An understanding of Stockdale's troubled life on the edge of literature is greatly aided by the account of his childhood in his *Memoirs*. Stockdale was born in Northumberland in 1736, and his attitude towards his home county was not one of great affection: on the many occasions in the future when he failed to conquer literary London, he would retreat grudgingly to the North-East; his writings exhibit a low-level resentment towards the provincial. Here, as throughout his life, there is a parallel with the circumstances of his sometime friend and future neighbour, Samuel Johnson. Stockdale's childhood was not unhappy, and was marked by a bookish sensibility. Indeed, the somewhat bitter evidence of Stockdale's *Memoirs* suggests that he already saw in literature an escape from a hard and unfeeling world: he preferred books to people because 'They never envied, nor aspersed; nor insulted me; they never maliciously, and industriously, aggravated my faults', and instead 'they fortified me against the malevolence of the world; and against my own passions'.[4] The nature of these 'passions' is something of a mystery, though an important one: his clergyman father 'already saw that I had natural advantages, above those of common men', but was also aware of the dangers of his 'exquisite sensibility, and strong passions' (*Memoirs*, vol. 1, p. 18). Already there is the suggestion of a recurrent excess of nervous sensitivity that will plague him from time to time, as when he tells us that 'My great sensibility, however, still frequently made my parents, and myself uneasy'; they send him back to school, since their 'happiness' is 'best promoted, if I was out at a distance from them' (*Memoirs*, vol. 1, p. 83). This extreme sensitivity would never entirely leave Stockdale; whatever its medical origins, it seems to have produced periods of great elation and despair, leading him, for instance, to burn his works at times of extreme dejection. The frequent letters that Stockdale wrote to the novelist Jane Porter from 1793 onwards feature many references to his ill health, and 'my awfully, and dreadfully permanent nervous malady', which causes repeated enervation of his spirits.[5] It also affected his writing. In terms of literary style, Stockdale, a man of feeling, produced a rapturous prose that (like Anna Seward's) veers off towards extremes of passion, but is often devoid of a controlling register. For all that his critics were often justified in their contempt for his wildly imbalanced writings, Stockdale's learning and critical acumen were considerable; what he lacked was the ability to express these qualities within a measured, structured critical argument, given his dependence upon his passions.

Stockdale's father was far from wealthy, but some of their relations had financial resources. He claims that his father was cheated out of his inheritance, and was affected by 'the unmerciful defalcations which were struck off his legal rights by rude, and unprincipled villainy' (*Memoirs*, vol. I, p. 24). Even at this early stage, Stockdale's memories are coloured by the shadow of various persecutions. Thus, the meanness of his relations, and their mendacity towards his father leads, in a characteristic link, to the first big disappointment of Stockdale's life: lack of money meant that he could not go to Oxford or Cambridge, and his university career was spent at St Andrews.[6] The retrospective form of the *Memoirs* may account for the importance of this; denial of an Oxbridge education seems to be Stockdale's first significant failure. It is the loss of possibilities of influence and status that Stockdale most bemoans. In 1794, he suffered an accident in a chaise near Oxford, and whilst recuperating nearby, wrote 'Verses Addressed to Oxford', a paean to what might have been:

> Oh! had my ardent, and aspiring youth
> Felt in *thy* hallowed groves, important truth;
> Inhaled, in *them*, the God's inspiring ray;
> Caught the strong thought, and waked the glowing lay;
> Then, reason, fancy, happily combined,
> And tuneful diction, had my verse refined:
> Then would thy liberal sons have raised my fame;
> And high above my merit, fixed my name.[7]

If only, the poem claims, the attractive air of Oxford had encouraged his latent powers, he might have become famous. Already, in this occasional poem, can be seen the defining quality and weakness of Stockdale's verse – its aspiration towards monumentality. Stockdale's critical powers were individual, for better and worse. His poetic abilities were enchained to the past, and to the obsessive need to be recognised (not least by himself) as a significant poet. Stockdale's poetry is often rendered lifeless by its endless debating of its own potential afterlife. And, inevitably, such debate is either wistful or resentful. Few writers can have spent more time detailing how their rightful place in literature has been impeded.

At St Andrews, Stockdale cultivated his love of reading, and a rather feeble Jacobitism. He was attracted by the example of Charles XII, 'Swedish Charles', that European conqueror with a tremendous magnetism in the eighteenth century, now best known for standing to 'point a moral, or adorn a tale', in Johnson's *Vanity of Human Wishes*. With some perversity, Stockdale spends some pages of his *Memoirs* comparing his own career with that of 'Swedish Charles', where the salient point of comparison is that both end in failure.[8] The instance shows Stockdale's inherent attraction towards the famous. Repeatedly, his writing loses discrimination when faced with an object of adulation, and this pattern of hero worship would be a defining feature of his literary career, producing his fiercest quarrels.

After Stockdale's father died, there was little money available for him: 'alas! it is the fortune of a man; not his genius, and exertions, which determines his merit (in the eyes of a prejudiced, and stupid world)', he complains (*Memoirs*, vol. I, p. 242). After leaving St Andrews in 1756, the need for employment and a somewhat unlikely zeal to contribute to the Seven Years' War saw him join the army. This was the beginning of the peripatetic life that would see him live all over England, as well as stints in Gibraltar (twice), Algiers, and the south of France. He sailed to Gibraltar with Admiral John Byng's fleet in 1756. After returning to England, and an unhappy period as a recruiting officer, he changed direction and entered the ministry in 1759. Stockdale's position in the clergy would form the basis of his future. Following his ordination, Stockdale's next decade was one of considerable confusion and depression. Leaving the apparent dissipations of London in 1762, he retreated to Berwick-upon-Tweed and a curacy; he describes this period summarily: 'I passed five years; in which time I waged a determined war against my credit and my happiness' (*Memoirs*, vol. II, p. 22). His next move was to Villefranche-sur-Mer, near Nice (more famous as the haven of later and somewhat different British exiles the Rolling Stones, in the 1970s), where Stockdale's personal tumult continued until 1769. As Howard Weinbrot has shown, using the extensive, scattered correspondence both by and about Stockdale, this 'determined war' waged against himself concerned an unsuitable marriage. In the words of William Johnson Temple, Stockdale was 'engaged to a young Lady, married an old one – the young one prosecuted & recovered damages, which he paid. They then ran away together – to Nice, leaving the woman behind, who went mad and died. The lovers then returned & married & then separated.'[9] In 1769, Stockdale returned to London, and the allure of literary celebrity.

From his exile in Berwick, Stockdale had published poems that do little other than show him adopting a fashionable muse: *Churchill Defended. A Poem Addressed to the Minority* (1764) and *The Constituents* (1765) are both hearty, 'Patriot' poems that lend their support to the 'Wilkes and Liberty' campaign of John Wilkes and his friend, the satirist Charles Churchill (who died in November 1764); Stockdale was acquainted with Wilkes in later years, and both poems adopt a bluff Churchillian mode of raillery, making them a small offshoot of that poet's short, but for a time pervasive influence on English verse. These productions indicate Stockdale's literary ambition, which gathered momentum after his return to London. In 1770, he met Samuel Johnson, John Hawkesworth, and Tom Davies, the bookseller (*Memoirs*, vol. II, p. 40); he would also know Garrick, Burke, Goldsmith, Gibbon, and others, giving him an inside view of the artistic milieu after which he hankered. Also in 1770, he published his translation of Tasso's *Amyntas*, which, he informs us, 'gave me considerable reputation as an authour', being admired by Johnson and Hawkesworth.[10] The same year sees him writing for *The Critical Review*, only for his request for a pay rise, in April 1771, to be denied. The occasion brought forth what was to become a typical reaction of bravado: 'My narrow purse was a little more contracted by this rupture; but my heart was enlarged, and played more vigorously' (*Memoirs*, vol. II, p. 58). The language of his heart was doubtless encouraged by the chance to make literary pilgrimages, showing a very rhapsodic reverence for his idols that is similar to the manner in which Anna Seward would salute Pope, Milton, and Gray. Earlier in his *Memoirs*, Stockdale had remembered that, in London, 'I was eager to examine the house; and to worship in the grotto of POPE; and I have often surveyed, with a religious awe, the spot in RUSSELL street, COVENT garden, where DRYDEN was the poetical and ATHENIAN oracle.' Rather forlornly, he follows this by hoping that 'something like this enthusiastic devotion; that a sincere, and heartfelt, though inferiour intellectual homage, may, hereafter be paid to *me*' (*Memoirs*, vol. I, p. 103). London, for Stockdale, was filled with the beatified air of the glorious poetic past. Yet the more sullied present could not be wholly escaped: in 1771, he edited *The Universal Magazine* for a few months, before falling out with Hinton, the bookseller, 'a sordid, and suspicious creature'. More importantly, in the same year Stockdale wrote his 'Life' of Edmund Waller (*Memoirs*, vol. II, pp. 74, 69), which was published in 1772 as part of a new edition of the poet.

Early success

Notwithstanding his burgeoning publications, Stockdale claimed that this period proved that 'My literary destiny has been often not only peculiarly, but capriciously hostile to my fortune, and to my fame' (*Memoirs*, vol. II, p. 65). The Waller edition failed to bring him the sort of desserts he thought he merited, yet, not for the first or last time, it is far from clear how exactly Stockdale expected his talents to be so rewarded. Stockdale's friend Tom Davies had bought the copyright to Elijah Fenton's edition of Waller of 1729, and the original intention was for Stockdale 'to add notes to these material passages, where Fenton had omitted them'. But Davies could not afford to publish the expanded work that this would produce, so 'WALLER was published without FENTON's notes, and mine, in a contracted, and mean form' (*Memoirs*, vol. II, p. 65). Yet the book is 'mean' only by Stockdale's hyperbolic notions. It is an entirely respectable edition, helped by Stockdale's introductory 'Life'. Stockdale's criticism is often rhapsodic, with all the strengths and manifold weaknesses that this suggests: it venerates, it burns, and it often fails to discriminate. None of these traits are present in the 'Life' of Waller, however. Instead, there is a measured and balancing tone in the prose that may well suggest the influence of Johnson, his then neighbour in Bolt Court. Stockdale shows an evenness of temper that is remarkable to a reader familiar with his later works. The 'Life' also indicates the importance, for Stockdale, of the poetic role, and the inevitable miseries concomitant upon it:

> It must be owned that the poet's journey through life is often difficult to be traced. The sensibility and ardour of his mind will not suffer him to travel on in the beaten and uniform track, along which the generality of mankind are satisfied to proceed. He often quits the common road for the unfrequented haunts of meditation; he is sometimes seduced from his course by pleasure, and lost in her flowery labyrinth; and sometimes disgusted with the roughness of the way, he leaves it in dejection, and seeks the cavern of despair.[11]

It is not a large step to relate this to Stockdale's own 'sensibility and ardour', and his attempt to move into the rhapsodic, heightened existence of the poet. It is equally clear (as has been discussed in the cases of Savage and Seward) that there is an inherent difficulty in this notion of the poetic vocation as an utter separation from the humdrum and often miserable quotidian; at the heart of Stockdale's failure as an author is the fact that there was no magic way in which the terms of his existence could be changed instantly and irrevocably, merely because he published prose and verse.

As an example of Stockdale's critical even-handedness, the conclusion to his account of Waller is interesting, especially in the light of his future works, where partiality would consistently undermine his judgement. It would be simplicity itself for Stockdale to have accused Waller of various sins of omission and general lack of consistency. Yet he takes a more balanced view of the public life of a poet who shifted allegiances more than most, and invited charges of mendacity and bad faith: 'his moral character will be viewed with lenity by those whose minds are actuated by humanity, and who are properly acquainted with their own failings; who consider the violence of the times in which he lived, and who are accustomed to think before they decide'.[12] Such a withholding of judgement refuses to draw easy conclusions from the fact that Waller, like many writers caught up in political arguments before or since, was not an exemplum of high-minded principle. This measured approach towards his subject would become increasingly rare in Stockdale's criticism, as shown by the brooding resentment of his account of the edition in the *Memoirs*: he tells us that the poet Richard Glover 'likes his Waller' (*Memoirs*, vol. II, p. 68), and there is certainly no evidence of any reaction other than approbation, yet, when describing his dislike of Johnson's *Lives of the Poets* (an area that would become Stockdale's King Charles's Head), the 'Life of Waller' is marked for opprobrium, not least because it makes too little mention of Stockdale's own efforts.[13] Hence, the reader can hardly take seriously the claim that Johnson's 'Waller' is 'written in a remarkably superficial, and careless manner'. Similarly, an advertisement which described it as 'supereminently excellent' leads Stockdale to make the unlikely claim that 'The booksellers, and their criticks probably threw out' this, in order 'to mortify the authour of these memoirs', as well as to boost sales (*Memoirs*, vol. II, pp. 199, 199–200). It is unfortunate that such paranoia should enter into the discussion of Stockdale's one critical work that appears to have raised absolutely no controversy.

His next work would see a return to his poetic ambitions. *The Poet*, published in 1773, was designed as Stockdale's poetic *magnum opus*; it stands out for its relative success, even if that was limited to its immediate decade. Yet it produced for the first time significant results in its reception, which Stockdale divides into 'the keen hostilities of resentment, and malignity' and 'the polite, and respectful attention of the learned; the elegant; and the fair' (*Memoirs*, vol. II, p. 78). It is a rather simplistic divide, and suggests a critical narrowness that Stockdale exhibits repeatedly almost as a reflex; though he was capable of far more sophisticated critical positions, his response to criticism almost always follows this strict binary. For Stockdale, critics of his poetry are never simply expressing their aesthetic differences, or finding his poetry wanting in comparison with the tradition to which it affixes itself. Instead, they are showing their resentment and envy. It is an opinion as unwavering as Anna Seward's criticisms of Johnson's slighting of his poetic contemporaries. Such a defensive attitude explains why 'malignity' is far from being the least repeated term in Stockdale's vocabulary. And it is as motiveless as the malignity of Coleridge's more famous example: after repeated iterations, it becomes clear that Stockdale has convinced himself that dislike of his work is proof of either inherent or circumstantial malice in the offending party.

Any malicious wounding was offset by the praise of David Garrick, who, upon reading the poem, writes back that "'I am in raptures with the poem; it is excellent indeed.'" This encourages Stockdale's 'delight in fame', and 'buoys him up, above all difficulties, and mortifications'. Even such bliss is disturbed, however: Garrick declined to receive the dedication of the poem, though Stockdale, whilst remarking that Garrick 'had not always a firm, and independent mind', assures the reader (unconvincingly) that this is not a comment on his refusal (*Memoirs*, vol. 11, pp. 78, 84). The reader of *The Poet* may well find Garrick's praise of it somewhat exaggerated. The poem celebrates the exalted poetic role: poets are different from other mortals; they follow different rules, and cannot be judged by common standards, therefore their productions and workings can only be understood by other members of the tribe. The eternal problem of delineating inspiration is thus side-stepped, and instead the utter distinction of the poetic identity is celebrated:

> Yet though the bliss inspired by nature's charms,
> The poet's breast with strongest influence warms;
> He oft exerts imagination's power
> Without the nymph, and the luxuriant bower;
> Trusts to his native energy of mind,
> And soars above the vulgar of mankind;
> Enjoys existence, wakes the genial strain,
> When souls inferiour only live to pain.
>
> (vol. 1, p. 10)

One of Stockdale's many self-inflicted misfortunes was his placing such a high value on his poetic abilities, when his literary criticism was his strongest suit. The problem, in part, is that his poetic models are so obvious as to make his verse a sort of wish fulfilment, aspiring towards the ideal that his heroes represent. In his criticism, this veneration is tempered to some extent by the practical need to examine and analyse; in his poetry, there is no such sense of constructive discipline to interfere.

The identification of Stockdale with his exalted predecessors is a given of *The Poet*, yet he faces a similar problem as Thomas Gray at the end of *The Progress of Poesy* (though for less intellectually considered reasons). Even given his confidence in his poetic abilities, Stockdale can hardly identify himself directly with the likes of Milton, Dryden, or Shakespeare. His solution is telling, and suggests that his own belief in the success of his poetic vocation is, to some extent, knowingly misplaced:

Early success 163

the figures he directly yearns to emulate in the poem are celebrated for their failure. First, there is Richard Savage:

> Though fortune frowned on Savage from his birth,
> Rather than doze a torpid son of earth,
> Proprietor of India's richest mine,
> I'd be that hapless favourite of the Nine:
> And on the ashes of a glass-house laid,
> But raised to heaven by each Aonian maid,
> My soul to rapture more than human wrought,
> By ardent genius, by excursive thought;
> Strongly inspired, and panting for renown,
> I would not envy kings the couch of down.
> (vol. 1, pp. 11–12)

The desire to be *like* Savage, in terms of possessing a rapturous poetic power, is not surprising, but it is hardly separable from being unrewarded (and in fact ruined), in material terms, for all this natural genius. The commonplace that the true poet cares little for worldly things becomes wilful, as Stockdale claims that he would like to emulate Savage's unhappy homelessness, as proof of integrity. It is a peculiar sentiment, as Stockdale almost seems to anticipate his own future failure; it implies that 'true' poetic genius always has to fly in the face of worldly adversity.

The pattern continues in the description of Stockdale's old hero, Charles XII. The somewhat absurd parallel of the undergraduate Stockdale with the failed conqueror is repeated, as misery traces its semblance in another's case: 'Anxious, his rise, meridian, and decline, / I view, and feel his varied fortune mine' (vol. 1, p. 27). But Stockdale is not, ostensibly, miserable in the poem, and the identification with 'Swedish Charles' is more jarring than that with Savage; the monarch was not a poet, so there must be another reason why Stockdale makes him an example:

> Successful greatness let the world descry,
> To greatness in misfortune, blind it's eye;
> I see him brightest in Pultowa's fray,
> Bursting in splendour through the gloomy day:
> I see him brightest, when in Bender's fort,
> He fights the army of a powerful court,
> A captive Swede alarming all the Porte.
> (vol. 1, pp. 28–9)

Not, perhaps, the finest poetic tribute ever paid to a monarch (Isaac D'Israeli would hold the lines up to mockery when reviewing the *Memoirs*, years later).[14] It is the oddity of the idea that is striking, however, beyond the vapidity of expression: Stockdale chooses to empathise with Charles at the moments of his greatest failure. Stockdale's obvious source is Johnson's well-known use of the same historical scenes in *The Vanity of Human Wishes*, where Charles's defeat at the battle of Poltava of 1709 ensures that 'The vanquish'd hero leaves his broken Bands / And shews his Miseries in distant lands.'[15] Instead of making Charles such a representative of human limitation, Stockdale salutes the courage of his failure, yet it is not that difficult to see this as a welcoming of it.

It is no surprise that the poem, despite ending on a rather tactless berating of the unthinking bourgeoisie for not having the superior imaginative capacity of the fortunate poetic brethren, cannot exemplify the advantages of this rarefied life. The abiding note is one of submerged but always potential failure, and the blame lies squarely with the malignancy of mankind, as in this description of the typical poet's fate:

> By harsh experience taught, at length they find
> The unrelenting nature of mankind;
> Are forced, their souls depressed with fortune's frown
> (A state unfit for works of high renown!)
> To animate the heart, to store the head,
> To barter genius for their daily bread.
>
> (vol. 1, p. 36)

There is a clumsiness about the absolute nature of the asserted definitions that the poem is built upon (poets are born and not made, and the public are naturally likely to revile them, being immutably of a different kind of sensibility). This makes it impossible for Stockdale to build any sense of contingency into his argument, but the result, inchoate as it is, harbours a considerable force of resentment, and anticipates his own repeated lack of success. This is not so much prophetic as a form of self-justification in advance: the 'unrelenting nature of mankind' is a defence of his own superiority that negates the possible success of his work, undermined as it consistently is by his misguided self-righteousness. In ratcheting up the acclaim that he demanded from his readers, whilst assuming that the majority of them would irrationally despise him, Stockdale ensured his own lack of success.

Critical rapture and railing

Although Stockdale's movements would be no more fixed over the ensuing years, the 1770s and 1780s stand out as the time when he was most likely to make his mark, given the number of literary and artistic friendships he had accumulated. That with Garrick seems to have been especially valuable, with Stockdale spending happy times at Garrick's seat at Hampton. Even this friendship is covered with Stockdale's strange carping, in the *Memoirs*, where he recalls Garrick's 'restless, and childish vanity' and posits that 'The human mind is thus, unfortunately, sometimes divided, and depressed; in all it's diversity of great abilities, provinces, and acquirements' (*Memoirs*, vol. II, p. 156). It is not the most self-conscious of remarks.[16]

In Garrick's library, Stockdale read, somewhat belatedly, the first volume of Joseph Warton's *Essay on the Writings and Genius of Pope* (1756), as important and influential a piece of literary criticism as anything contemporary. Warton's *Essay* was, by the 1770s, a respected work; its first volume provides a somewhat digressive commentary on Alexander Pope's early career, ending with the highest praise for *Eloisa to Abelard*. Warton's comment, in his dedication to Edward Young, that Pope was not of the most 'sublime' class of poets (meaning Milton, Spenser, and Shakespeare), being rather moral, or satiric, is a generic distinction that forms a very small part of his work as a whole, but it can only be presumed that Stockdale took it to be a deadly insult, and framed a response accordingly.[17]

That Stockdale revered Pope is clear, but even this does not fully explain his response to Warton. His *Inquiry into the Nature, and Genuine Laws of Poetry; Including a Particular Defence of the Writings, and Genius of Mr Pope* (1778) is so peculiar a work that 'criticism' seems too tame a description for it – it is a denunciation of Warton, from the first page to the last, excepting only those places where Stockdale forgets his ostensible target and hares off after another. Its tone is so intemperate that it calls to mind Isaac D'Israeli's mocking appraisal: 'Stockdale had, in truth, an excessive sensibility of temper, without any control over it ... His mind was so curved, that nothing could stand steadily upon it.'[18] The bluster of the *Inquiry* makes Stockdale's sincere passion for literature and sometimes very genuine powers of appreciation disappear far into the background, so that the reader is unable to distinguish them amongst the alternate rhapsody and ranting.

The explanation for this lack of discrimination can be found in the degree of Stockdale's admiration for Pope. His reverence is nowhere better shown than in his poetic memory of his visit to Pope's home:

> The fane of Twickenham oped; thy poet found
> The strong effects of consecrated ground:
> Now warmth, now chillness through my vitals crept;
> My heart's pulsation paused, and now it leapt.
> The spot was shown me where his ashes lie;
> I viewed the grave with reverential eye:

This outburst of enthusiasm concludes a few lines on: 'My mind's impressions met my listening ear; / And Echo said, – "The God of Pope is here."'[19] Given such feeling, Stockdale's reply to Warton was unlikely to be moderate. In the *Inquiry*, even the usual perfunctory dedication manages to be controversial and tactless, with a back-handed compliment to Stockdale's then patron, Lord George Germain.[20] The *Inquiry* is certainly not lacking in enthusiasm and passion. Warton, for Stockdale, is one of 'your men of mere erudition, your mechanical critics, [who] have presumed to publish their illiberal, and stupid remarks on this great and beautiful poet' (pp. 2–3). Warton represents a sort of debased academia: 'His moderate abilities have been perverted by promiscuous, and intemperate reading, by an undistinguishing, and servile admiration of the Ancients, and by an ignoble, and inordinate ambition of singularity' (p. 22). Stockdale personalises the argument, confronting Warton for his treachery:

> If my question brings you to a full sense of your demerit, you will make a recantation of your critical treason, not to me, but to an enlightened Publick, who admire, and venerate [Pope's] memory; and you will never again write, or speak disrespectfully of one of our first poets, to whom you would have crouched, if he had been alive, and whose acquaintance, at least from your literary vanity, and fear, you would have pronounced your greatest honour. (p. 25)

Such a bathetic tone could come from a scene in a bad novel. There is much of a similar strain in the *Inquiry*, and it reflects a towering fury rather than a critical argument.

Buried underneath such turmoil and rage are some very interesting points. Although Stockdale completely lacks a structured argument (making Warton's *Essay*, a notoriously digressive work, seem almost like a doctoral thesis in comparison), he hits upon points of great interest: Warton's theory that the test of great poetry is whether it can be transprosed or not is effectively questioned, showing Stockdale's keen attention to poetic effect: 'A particle may be so placed in a verse, that the sense of the Authour may be clear, and the idiom of our language may not be violated; yet even that particle, by a happy transposition, might acquire life, and energy, and give more animation, and lustre to the line.'[21] Stockdale's awareness of the subtlety of rhythmic movement and the intricacy of the workings of all significant poetry here shows itself. His aesthetic theory, though vague, is based upon the reception of the cumulative and yet spontaneous sensations of poetry by 'those on whose imaginations the complete style of the muse is warmly impressed, by the structure, and spirit of Poetry, and by the susceptibility of their own minds' (p. 20). This sense of the importance of poetic sympathy to the imagination is Stockdale's most attractive critical side.

Too often, though, it is covered by a dominating argumentative strain. After claiming that 'I like not to express myself in a manner very familiar to the writer whom I am refuting; in flaming hyperbole, and rapture' (p. 25), the reader is left to wonder what form Stockdale's more unbuttoned style might take. His 'flaming hyperbole' is counterpointed by a strain that would become more and more recurrent in his subsequent writings – a fear of contemporary decadence. Pope's zenith came 'after his glory had been thoroughly established by the admiration of his countrymen, and before luxury, and venality had ushered into England another age of barbarism' (pp. 3–4).

Portentous anxiety about the state of the world sits uneasily with Stockdale's ill-advised excursions into politics. Despite his complacent murmur that 'I scorn all national antipathy: if any man is, *I* have long become a citizen of the world' (*Memoirs*, vol. I, p. 106), Stockdale's contempt is often directed at the decadent French. He dislikes their 'sameness of disposition, and character; the arbitrary government of the nation; their frivolous, and mechanical manners (for they are a set of despicable apes of one another)' (p. 53). This is not, he assures us, motivated by the spirit of prejudice: 'If I harboured a blind, and universal partiality in favour of England, I should be severely censured by my own reason, and sentiments: for the narrow spirit of national prejudice is one of the many unmanly qualities for which I despise a Frenchman' (pp. 65–6).[22]

The *Inquiry* is a jumble of many parts; occasional moments suggest Stockdale's talent, but its many eccentricities dominate. It concludes with an 'Invocation to the Shade of Pope': 'Let me thank Thee for the consolation, for the pleasure, with which thy Muse hath alleviated my adverse life' (p. 182). It is not the last time that Stockdale will address the deceased subjects of his raptures. Stockdale's observance of Pope as a poetic deity, and his final prayer, 'that I shall obtain that mercy, and happiness, which were denied me in *this* unequal state' (p. 186), combine Pope's quasi-divinity with Stockdale's underlying pessimism and bitterness. It is a suitable ending, in every respect.

Stockdale records that no less a prose stylist than Edmund Burke read the *Inquiry* and paid him the following compliment: 'Sir, you write with a great deal of fire; which falls to the lot of very few men' (*Memoirs*, vol. II, p. 119). The painter and satirical poet George Huddesford, in his *Warley: A Satire* (1778), took a different view, describing how 'The whole tribe of fools, who the Dunciad compose, / Breath vengeance again in poor Percival's prose.' Huddesford at least shows that Stockdale was being noticed, if for the wrong reasons:

> Poor Percival Stockdale! who (dreadful to think on,)
> In Styx drench'd his goose quil instead of an inkhorn;
> With the fumes of the lake his mad brain over laid,
> Like Curl with the Cates of Corinna bewray'd;
> With critical Jaundice envelop'd his mind,
> And sightless himself, swears that Warton is blind.[23]

The caricature shows how the uncontrolled nature of Stockdale's writing invites parody. That Stockdale had utterly undermined his attack on Warton's supposed prejudice through the excesses of his own was clear, though one famous reader did not seem to agree.

Samuel Johnson's relationship with Stockdale was perhaps influenced by the older writer's knowledge of the harsh vicissitudes of the literary world; he appears to have treated Stockdale with compassion and aid. Boswell mentions 'the Rev. Mr. Stockdale, to whom [Johnson] was, upon many occasions, a kind protector'.[24] There is also the possibility of Stockdale being 'An authour of most anxious and restless vanity' of whom Johnson says 'there is not a young sapling upon Parnassus more severely blown about by every wind of criticism than that poor fellow'.[25] How then did Johnson view the *Inquiry*? In the admittedly coloured world of the *Memoirs*, Tom Davies told Stockdale of Johnson's comment: 'STOCKEY, said he to the company, is perfectly right; he has defended the cause of POPE with incontrovertible arguments, and with great eloquence.' But then Johnson tells him personally that 'the execution of your design is masterly; but I do not like your design of reducing my old friend, Jo. Warton, so low in the field of criticism'. Stockdale begins to question his rationale: 'Perhaps I was too indignant in my attack on very moderate parts; presuming to circumscribe; and indeed, to vilify, by depressing to mediocrity, instructive, elegant, spirited, and inventive genius: – but as I affix a species of profaneness, and impiety, to such an attempt, my most resentful animadversions on Dr. Warton, do not sit heavily on my conscience' (*Memoirs*, vol. II, pp. 120, 121). Stockdale almost admits that he has gone too far, only to fall back upon the religiosity of his supposed sanctification of Pope's memory.

The episode was to lead to more bitterness, since Stockdale wanted Johnson to mention the *Inquiry* in the 'Life of Pope', but Johnson eventually demurred, citing as a reason that Warton was a 'much older acquaintance'.[26] Yet this is only a small part of the story of how the *Lives of the Poets* would become a determining factor in the rest of Stockdale's life, for the wrong reasons, blowing his already brittle literary career disastrously off any normal course. In 1779, according to the *Memoirs*, the original choice by the booksellers of the writer for the edition that would become the *Lives of the Poets* was, it appears, not Johnson, but Stockdale, though 'I had made myself unpopular, by the imprudent, not by the unjust freedoms of my writings; – and I had some implacable and powerful enemies.' The result, inevitably, is success followed by a dashing of all hope: 'at a meeting of the booksellers, it was resolved, that *I* should be employed in preparing for the press, the intended edition of the english poets'. Yet, the booksellers were 'overruled and defeated by [William] STRAHAN's dislike of me', and backed 'the preponderating, and imperious weight of JOHNSON's name'.[27]

This new grievance ensured that a lot of the remainder of Stockdale's writing was dedicated to setting the record straight, correcting the misreadings and calumnies of Johnson in the *Lives*, and showing the world what form the collection should have taken under his own guidance. The fruits of his labours would eventually be published in 1807 as *Lectures on the Truly Eminent English Poets*, an attempt to claim back the credit supposedly stolen from him by the *Lives of the Poets*, but the wounding episode must have left its mark in other ways. Stockdale subsequently always had this example of treachery: Johnson, 'in his sentiments towards *me*, was divided between a benevolence to my interest, and a coldness to my fame' (*Memoirs*, vol. II, p. 128). For Stockdale, the former quality was rendered useless by the latter.

A gradual marginality

In the face of adversity, Stockdale was unyielding, convinced that his own abilities would be recognised and given their due, and yet often at the same time tentative, and quietly doubtful of this integral truth, no matter how many times he repeated it. On occasions, he seems dominated by his nervous depression. Around 1776, he recalls that a period of deep despondency led him to burn some of his unpublished poems. Recalling the event thirty years on, he somehow manages to put a cheerful slant on it:

> I am now glad, that like CORTES, I did not burn all my ships; to prevent my consecration in the temple of APOLLO; those active, and invincible yachts of glory; which, notwithstanding all the storms that they have suffered; notwithstanding all the invidious embargoes that have been laid upon them;

let malice permit me; and let generosity encourage me to hope; will yet be favoured with balmy, and friendly gales; and waft me to fame and to immortality. (*Memoirs*, vol. II, p. 110)

The telling mix of destruction and the invariable (and hardly convincing) pick-me-up suggests a tortured mixture of failure, and an exaggerated absolute self-belief. That such periods descended upon him is as much a result of the uncertainties of his material fortune, as of his intellectual one. After a spell as a naval chaplain, he finds himself in a brief turn as preacher in Grosvenor Chapel in 1779; he preaches, to a 'courtly' audience, a denunciation of the American War. This was later 'not forgiven by the stern primate of all ENGLAND' (*Memoirs*, vol. II, p. 207). In the same year he becomes tutor to the son of Lord Craven, resigning in 1780 supposedly because Lady Craven wanted him to be a prompter in her amateur theatricals, another instance where Stockdale's life resembles an eighteenth-century tragicomic novel (*Memoirs*, vol. II, p. 208). The pattern is of an at least annual movement, until November 1784 sees the award of the two livings of Lesbury and Longhoughton in Northumberland. These would form Stockdale's lasting ecclesiastical base, for all that he did everything in his power to spend as little time as possible in them. It may be that the livings were gained with the help of the new Prime Minister, William Pitt the Younger, to whom Stockdale dedicated the volume of sermons he published in the same year.

Stockdale's attitude towards his ecclesiastical duties was apparently so perfunctory, and the role played by the Church within his grand scheme of achieving literary fame so marginal, that his *Sermons* would not seem to demand much attention within his corpus of enthusiastic poetry, criticism, and general rodomontade. We have no way of knowing how much attention he lavished on them, but the dedication to Pitt sees him in familiar bullish mood:

> In literary enterprize, there is, sometimes, a high spirit of honourable adventure, which rises far above timidity or affected modesty, yet keeps as distinctly clear of the confines of arrogance or presumption. It can only be comprehended and exemplified by minds which are delicate, as well as ardent. By this spirit, I flatter myself that I am at present actuated.[28]

This self-flattery produces a stance of exclusivity that many would find presumptuous. Yet, for Stockdale, the tug of ambition justifies all: 'Mine, I own, is strong; and it's aim is noble: it has long been indefatigable and invincible, in aspiring to the level of intellectual merit' (*Sermons*, p. iv). The *Sermons* are more worthy because of the motives for which they were *not* written. He 'was not stimulated to write them either by interest or by vanity. While I devoted my time to them, my faculties were not invigorated, and brightened by the sanguine hopes of preferment, nor by the flattering consciousness that they were immediately intended for an elegant congregation' (p. vii). In this harsh world, separated from the benefits of favouritism, Stockdale begs to be humoured in his flights of fancy, which are those of a much afflicted poetic sensibility: 'As the pleasures of a Poet are extremely circumscribed, I know that your humanity will forgive me the luxuriance of imagination. Even a selfish and parsimonious world, when fortune spreads around us the horrors of perpetual Winter, would, surely, not preclude us from an Elysium of our own formation' (pp. xii–xiii).

It will be seen that Stockdale by 1784 had hardened into a state of stoicism in the face of the 'perpetual Winter' of fortune. This creeps into his sermons in rather overt ways. The first two sermons are 'On Prosperity and Adversity', a theme dear to his heart. Adversity is worse, for instance, 'especially if the mind of the sufferer is warm and sentimental; if it is peculiarly formed by nature to enjoy the charms of civilised, enlightened, and polished life; but hath been unfortunately thrown out of its orbit, by the violent workings of the apparent chaos of sublunary events' (pp. 7–8). This is as close to home as ingratitude, which 'is epidemical to the world; and it is one of the most infamous stigmas that we can apply to human nature' (p. 33). Praise is reserved for those 'great and unconquerable souls' who are

> maintaining a noble and vigorous opposition against adversity; and asserting the dignity and the powers of the mind, in defiance of the frowns and contempt of a prejudiced, vain, and luxurious age. I speak of those who have been bred in a liberal sphere, who have distinguished themselves by their mental faculties; but from a variety of causes, which operate in our uncertain and complicated life, have never obtained their merited reward. (p. 42)

The next subject is 'Self-Knowledge', and provides similar opportunities for his own experience to be reflected: 'Let us have but courage enough to retire frequently from that world, for our improvement in virtue; let us court the oracles of solitude, and we shall find that the tumultuous, the impetuous passions, will be hushed; that the fatal delusion, with regard to our real characters, which flows either from our own adulation, or from the adulation of others, will entirely vanish' (pp. 64–5). This sense of serene humility is not the most striking quality of Stockdale's literary works, and with the three sermons 'On Resignation to the Divine Will' he again preaches what he could not practise. Blaming others is wrong because 'if they would divest their minds of those narrow prejudices, of that extreme partiality to ourselves, with which we review our actions, they would find, in general, that most of the disagreeable circumstances, most of the painful events which embitter their existence, have originated from their own predicament' (p. 215). This could pass as a comment upon the tirade of unquestioning recriminations that make up Stockdale's later *Memoirs*. As it is, an odd digression on those whose virtue is not rewarded jars with the calm of the pulpit: 'A man's low estate (especially if he is distinguished by strength of intellect, and by the ornaments of the mind) such a man's *low* estate is *high* treason against the community' (p. 229). It is impossible for its speaker himself to obtain the benefits of this collection of wisdom; the ineffectuality of the whole, and a more gentle example of Stockdale's failure, is summed up by the reaction to the sermon 'On Humanity to the Animal Creation', a bravura performance against cruelty to animals, one of Stockdale's more endearing hobby-horses. (He would like the typical angler to 'suppose himself inhumanly dragged along in his own element, and deprived of life by that fatigue and pain, which extremely entertain *him*, in his aquatic prey' (p. 95).) Yet such righteous indignation fails to gain much response from his audience; a footnote informs us that when 'some of the lower class' of Richmond are asked about it, 'One shrugged up his shoulders, and said, *it was a good animal sermon*' (p. 110).[29]

Recrimination in adversity

Stockdale's abiding kindness to animals and hatred of the slave trade show his passions at their best, yet the chord that sounds increasingly loudly in his subsequent work is resentment at ingratitude. This can even be seen in the least likely place – his one venture into the world of drama, the tragedy, *Ximenes*, published in 1788. According to Stockdale, Mrs Pope (née Young) thought it 'too sublime for the stage', a view perhaps shared by the manager of Covent Garden Theatre, who rejected it (*Memoirs*, vol. II, p. 244). The origins of *Ximenes* can be found in Stockdale's previous sojourn in Gibraltar; at an impecunious point in the 1770s, Johnson had advised him to write a history of Spain, and 'drove me almost by force' to a bookseller, who was not interested. We also know that Stockdale wrote an unfinished history of Gibraltar which was sadly burnt by him in 1791, when he was 'oppressed' by 'misfortunes', and at 'a stage of the deepest dejection, and despondency'. Also included in the conflagration was 'my translation of Marsollier's Life of Cardinal Ximenes' (*Memoirs*, vol. II, p. 256). These undertakings show Stockdale's exceptional diligence, even if it was so often unavailing. Francisco Ximenes de Cisneros (1436–1517), Spanish Cardinal and Regent, a figure of considerable importance in political and intellectual terms, the founder of a university, and a man of legendary probity, could have appealed to Stockdale for a number of reasons. The translation of Marsollier's biography of 1684 would have provided Stockdale with the material of his play, and he offers a typical historical drama, with a few obvious additions.

To a modern reader, *Ximenes* appears to be almost completely devoid of human interest, being intrinsically undramatic. Some of Stockdale's lines do seem particularly risible. Ximenes, in conversation with the Moor Zaigri (the conversion of whom, and fulfilment of the romantic sub-plot, is the main 'action' of the play, such as it is), apologises to him for his lengthy speeches, with the wonderfully blunt 'If I'm prolix, excuse the fault of age.'[30] He need not worry, as Zaigri is enchanted by the old man: 'Oh! by thy eloquence, I'm led, in fancy, / To mansions worthy of seraphick spirits! / I almost blush that I revered the Koran!' (p. 34). Underneath the main theme of forgiveness and tolerance (with Ximenes's moral superiority overwhelming the cruelty of Torquemada and the Inquisition, and reconciling the warring passions of everybody else), familiar bugbears appear. The opening discussion of Ximenes describes how his 'genius'

> supersedes
> The *true* advantages of birth, and fortune;
> It conquers, with it's ardent perseverance,
> The prejudices, the malicious arts
> Of human kind; and with it's inspiration,
> Diverts, and breaks, the painted bubble, fashion,
> Admired, and followed, by the vulgar throng.
> (p. 4)

Stockdale's presiding hope of true talent being recognised and rewarded rears its head again. Similarly, the inclusion of the character of Audley, an English visitor to Granada, allows Ximenes to praise the matchless wonders of English liberty, from Magna Carta onwards, and for incongruous ruminations on human nature's failings: Audley's 'roughness' is a result of 'a mind susceptible' that has been confronted 'With envy, malice, insolence in power' (p. 38). He is reassured by Alonzo, Ximenes's secretary, who understands: 'Minds of blunt intellect, by fortune's caprice, / Held up to publick view, must ever hate / Superiour spirit, and superiour knowledge' (p. 40). Even the saintly Ximenes is moved, at times, to sound suspiciously like his author:

> – I've seen, I've known, I've felt this changeful world;
> It's many cares; it's toils; it's disappointments;

It's perfidy; it's black ingratitude:
Nought has it worth a wish, excepting virtue;
And that, for justice, must appeal above.

(p. 63)

The 'tragedy' of Ximenes is, not surprisingly in such a static drama, a muted one, but is no less heartfelt for that. Historically, Ximenes died from the effects of poison in November 1517, soon after allegedly receiving a letter from Charles V, thanking him for his efforts as regent, and allowing him to retire to his diocese. In Stockdale's play, this diplomatic snub becomes the tragic cause of the old man's demise, as he rails against Charles's letter, 'a dying lesson' that is 'big / With the deformity of human nature!' He asks why 'did not shame check his ingratitude' (pp. 116, 119). With this 'Ingratitude most barbarous' (p. 124), Stockdale's unperformed tragedy ends, exemplifying how easily his subject became dominated by the preoccupations of its author, to the detriment of both. An inconsequential play, its value lies in illustrating how deeply set Stockdale's prejudices had become; in an odd way they both energise his writing, and guarantee its continual lack of accomplishment and success.

The non-performance of *Ximenes* was followed by another Mediterranean misadventure of some duration.[31] On his return, Stockdale flitted between London and the North-East. 1792 found him living again in London, and the quixotic pursuit of literary fame was interrupted by an argument so self-aggrandising and petty that it is hard to believe that Stockdale found a publisher willing to pay for it to enter the public domain. If he did provide his own money for the publication of *Letters between Shute, Bishop of Durham, and Percival Stockdale: A Correspondence Interesting to Every Lover of Literature, Freedom, and Religion* (1792), then it was not wisely spent. The falling-out with Shute Barrington was, like most of Stockdale's quarrels, simple in origin, and its details kept alive only by Stockdale's paranoia and hopelessly misjudged sense of self-importance.

Earlier in 1792, in his 'Poetical Thoughts, and Views; On the Banks of the Wear', Stockdale had praised Barrington: amidst the over-familiar complaints of the mendacious world destroying poetic worth, the steadfast Bishop is an ally, and 'to the muse is shown / A candid glory circling Durham's Throne', which will help fulfil Stockdale's poetic success, when 'glory's warmth annihilates all woe'.[32] All this was to change when the living of Hartburn fell vacant; more remunerative than his present two posts, Hartburn was nevertheless still in the Northumberland that Stockdale rarely deigned to visit. The Bishop informs him that the living has already been given to someone else. Stockdale accuses him of lying, writes increasingly furious letters to him, and then publishes the one-sided correspondence as part of a threat to shame Barrington into decency.

It goes without saying, given this persiflage, that *Letters between Shute, Bishop of Durham, and Percival Stockdale* is completely lacking in dignity. It smacks of desperation, and Stockdale's ill-tempered 'Advertisement' admits that 'There is no object so dear to me as fair literary fame', a strange way to commence an ecclesiastical dispute, but an indication of the steps that Stockdale will take to keep hold of his crumbling status as an author. The controversy is thus literary criticism by other means, for all the claim that 'these letters partly flowed from my very just, and warrantable sentiments on long, implacable, but cowardly hostilities, with which I know that I have been persecuted by churchmen'. He has been accused of being 'splenetick', but refutes this by asserting the integrity of his intellectual journey:

> To aspire after renown by those attainments which most eminently adorn, and enable human nature; – in our efforts, in our conflicts, for glory, never fatally to yield to temporary interruptions, but always to rise superiour to adversity, to malignity, to ourselves ... these are not the characteristicks of a gloomy and splenetick, but of an open, and manly mind; and if I had not acted in this manner myself, I should pronounce it MAGNANIMITY.[33]

It does not matter what he pronounces it, of course, but there is a hidden acknowledgement that he is not always in command of the spirit of his writing; he is 'sensible that I have a peculiarity of mind, which I shall always wish to check, when it tends to that which is wrong; [and] which I shall always wish to indulge, when it dictates to me a singular, and noble morality' ('Preface', p. xiii). There is, however, lots of indulgence and no obvious control.

The pamphlet is also designed to give more than just an account of the argument with the Bishop; Stockdale appends the 'Poetical Thoughts, and Views; On the Banks of the Wear', making sure that his talents are fully visible. The public is the best judge, but 'hitherto, I have not been able, from a variety of hostile, and unfortunate circumstances, to take all the equitable advantages of their tribunal; to *them*, however, I hope, one day, to make a complete appeal; an appeal, which will amply avenge me (for I seek no revenge but glory) of malignant critics, and of more malignant priests' (p. xiv). He also adds a list of publications, for similar reasons: 'Many dark, and ungenerous means have been used to check the diffusion of my literary honours, which are dearer to me than my life. – Surely I am not impertinent to the publick, if I endeavour to attract that most honourable, and glorious attention, which the voice of nature tells my heart, that, in some degree, I deserve' (p. xxii). It is a self-contradictory and somewhat despairing appeal that could only be made by a writer in a state of advanced and unyielding delusion about the workings of the literary world.

This world is one he plays upon, referring to the verdicts of his famous friends to show how little he needs the validation of the Church: 'Episcopal praise would have been but vapid to a heart to which genius had been allowed, by a GARRICK, a JOHNSON, and a BURKE' (p. xxiii). The preface ends with an embarrassing apostrophe: 'Illustrious, and divine ROUSSEAU! Some friends, too generous to my fame, have discovered a similarity between thee and me! – In misfortunes, and in sufferings, I can see some resemblance between us' (p. xxvi). This continues the odd tendency of empathising with the adversity of heroes that had started with the unlikely undergraduate parallel with Charles XII. It is a strange way of signalling a kind of negative fame, the resemblance of failure covering the implication of deserving success.

The letters to the Bishop, his brief replies, and the running commentary supplied by Stockdale see him worked up into a tremendous and absurdly self-righteous state. The hyperbole of desperation makes Stockdale turn this latest setback into a metonym for his failed career; concomitantly, with a breakdown of logic, the living at Hartburn becomes a symbol of the inevitability of success, and the instant cure for all his ills. If placed there, Stockdale would be finally in a position to rebuff his many enemies and settle all quarrels. The Bishop can 'establish my fortune, my life; – my reputation, as an authour, and a clergyman' (p. 39). These are rather self-interested motives for a job application, and Barrington could hardly be blamed for turning down Stockdale's fervent request. When he informs him Hartburn is already disposed of, Stockdale accuses him of dissimulation. Barrington then makes an entirely reasonable point, expressing 'some surprise' at the inquiry, given that 'the severe climate' of Northumberland has been 'urged as a plea for non-residence' by Stockdale in his two present livings at Lesbury and Longhoughton (p. 14). This is brushed aside, as Stockdale takes the Bishop to task for not realising the solemn importance of this particular living in the advancement of his genius – he will willingly sacrifice the other two, in order to be given it. When it is obvious that even this largesse will not force the issue, Stockdale becomes more intemperate, and his letters turn into an extended apologia for the exalted nature of his literary vocation: 'my own compassion for unfortunate merit is, perhaps too romantick', he claims (p. 17), before offering the somewhat self-centred conclusion that

'Intellectual perseverance will establish my literary fame' and reveal the 'gross injustice' that has been 'done to me by mean and malevolent criticks' (pp. 22–3).

In fact, his ecclesiastical problems are a result of his literary talents: the man of genius has 'a natural splendour, which eclipses every artificial blaze' (p. 28), which has caused the clergy to resent and hate him. He compares himself to the poetic genius of Pope, having to deal with the worldliness of Oxford and Bolingbroke: 'I contemplate the beatified spirit of that immortal man, and the shades of MILTON, of DRYDEN, and of YOUNG, with rapture; – and I act to *you*, as I ought' (p. 50). There is a ludicrous final threat to publish the correspondence, unless he hears favourably from the Bishop, and the prediction that this appeal 'will *fairly* be imputed, not to the irritated, and vindictive spirit of *one* man; but to the cold, and inflexible mind of *another*' (p. 54). Stockdale ends by comparing his moral superiority to that of Alexander the Great and his forces, with Barrington in the role of Darius, the 'Persian monarch', backed only by slaves (p. 55). It is an unfortunate metaphor, though an appropriate end to a work that shows Stockdale in such a bad light as to produce sympathy, given the heightened sense of futility that must have been overcoming him, as his chance of literary fame moved even further away. Its absurdities were punished by lampoons and attacks, though the Bishop continued to be one of Stockdale's many targets for recrimination.[34]

A disgrace to English literature

The lack of discrimination and tact in Stockdale's approach to the argument with the Bishop of Durham shows a hardening; never particularly open to the critical views of others, the majority of his writings for the rest of his life would obsessively trace old quarrels and seek to vindicate himself. Barrington's 'fault' was ingratitude, and a failure to recognise the genius of Stockdale: by this time the critical treason of a more celebrated former friend had become the controlling impulse of Stockdale's literary life.

As the posthumous acclaim for Johnson's *Lives of the Poets* continued to grow after their completion in 1781, Stockdale reacted accordingly. There had been strong dissenting voices, but the place of the *Lives* as a central critical work must have seemed quite clear by 1794, when Stockdale began work on his *Lectures on the Truly Eminent English Poets*. Johnson's celebrity, after the publication of Boswell's *Life* in 1791, was great indeed;

Stockdale's literary place was as peripheral as ever. His attitude in writing his *Lectures* is shown in a letter to Edward Jerningham of 1793: in it, Stockdale describes his basic dislike of Johnson's *Lives*, their partiality, faults of selection, prejudices (both personal and political), arrogance, pomposity, and general wrong-headedness. They are (in a phrase that would become something of a mantra) 'a disgrace to English literature'.[35] The *Lectures* would take this strident critique and extend it very greatly (in terms of length, if not of tone) but they would not be completed for a number of years, as Stockdale's uncertain fortunes and friendships ensured various upheavals and travels, from London to Monmouth and Durham, until he became an unwilling resident in the North-East, in Durham and then Lesbury, from 1797.

He got the opportunity to practise his criticism of Johnson in 1794, when a prospective edition of James Thomson's *The Seasons* required annotation at short notice (*Memoirs*, vol. II, p. 275). Stockdale's annotation is not uneven in critical quality as much as in proportion. Whilst a great deal of the notes show wide reading, considerable knowledge, and a sometimes very acute poetic sympathy, the effect upon the reader is nonetheless odd, as criticisms of Johnson, starting off as asides, begin to predominate, until the notes end with (and turn into) a lengthy dismissal of the *Lives of the Poets*.

These notes exhibit genuine self-doubt about the value of his work: 'I am unavoidably limited in the extent of my Notes on the Seasons ... I am unfeignedly willing to acknowledge, that by the circumscription to which I must submit, more will be lost to my own private satisfaction, than to the information, or entertainment of the publick.'[36] Yet this changes to a far more confident sense of judgement whenever an excuse can be found for arraigning Johnson's critical crimes. Lord Lyttelton is one obvious instance: 'He was a mild, and benevolent man, an elegant scholar; a distinguished orator; an eminent writer both in verse and prose. JOHNSON is grossly unjust to his literary merit. But what attention is to be paid to the hypercritick, who tells us, that AKENSIDE's Odes will never be read?'[37] To clear the name of writers maligned by Johnson is something of a duty: 'I have taken this opportunity, with pleasure, to vindicate, in *some* degree, the transcendent merit, and fame of one of our first poets, from the arbitrary censures of a rude, vulgar and dogmatical chair.'[38] The suggestion is that Stockdale can only partially alleviate the damage that Johnson's criticism has done.

The final, long note offers an evaluative summary of Johnson's career: Stockdale is never so coloured by prejudice as to reject the whole of any significant author, and he likes the 'Preface' to the *Dictionary*, and *The Rambler*, which contains 'treasures' of knowledge and wisdom, but is too wordy (hardly a novel complaint). It seems likely that the earlier *Life of Savage* wins approbation because of Stockdale's interest in and partial identification with the subject. It is 'in every respect, an interesting, amiable, and beautiful production'. Moreover, Johnson 'has given proof to the world of his very uncommon poetical abilities'. But on the subject of the *Lives* Stockdale allows nothing. They showed

> that his faculties were on the decline, and that he was intoxicated with his consequence, and with his fame. As his intellect was losing its vigour, his political, and superstitious prejudices were gaining strength; and by *them*, not by judgement, and taste, he determined the merit, or demerit of his authours ... When the present busy, and paltry machinations of interest shall act no more; when the talents of the Departed, and of the Living shall be justly appreciated by posterity; it will be found that *those lives* are a Disgrace to English Literature.[39]

The edition of Thomson is not as eccentric as perhaps it could have been, if Stockdale had been able to give a loose to his critical talents, yet it also shows that such work was in some ways a skirmish in the larger war that Stockdale wanted to initiate with the effects of Johnson's criticism. That such an argument would not turn out well for him is indicated by an inevitable irony: the reader of the notes to the edition of Thomson, finding Johnson's *Lives* consistently denigrated, need only turn to the beginning of the edition to find such supposed critical malignancy and treason, as the 'Life' of Thomson used there is, inevitably, taken from Johnson.

The sporadic writing of the *Lectures* would continue until at least 1800. Before settling in Lesbury, Stockdale went to Durham in 1797, a quixotic move marked by his response to the fear of French invasion. He writes his topical poem on the subject, *The Invincible Island*, then rushes off to London to publish it at his own expense. For all that it is written to the moment, poor sales convince him 'that prejudice, and malignity, in my fate as an authour, seemed, indeed, to be invincible' (*Memoirs*, vol. II, p. 311). *The Invincible Island* shows a considerable falling-off in talent and intellectual resources. It offers as a subject only jingoism, and as a rationale only topicality: 'From human bliss no sounds discordant jar, / But faction's clamour, with it's wordy war' gives something of its flavour.[40] Stockdale dislikes the French, and salutes the British, in unedifying terms. He ends on an attempt at optimism, and the claim that England's genius will help to preserve his own:

> I feel; or seem to feel,
> Through all my frame the fine contagion steal;
> I feel the natural, ardent passion rise,
> To gain my country's praise; the poet's prize;
> (vol. 1, p. 348)

This places his immediate need for fame as the real purpose of his flattery. It is unusual to find a patriotic poem that so openly exhibits its own agenda. In this 'precarious world my life the sport', Stockdale more often falls back upon a melancholy note, seeing himself as the fortress that is under threat of invasion:

> Teach me, by virtuous discipline, to find
> A comprehensive kingdom, in my mind;
> There, with serene, yet with despotick reign,
> To guard the small but well-improved domain!
> (vol. 1, p. 350)

This is a strange metaphor, in that his serenity appears very far from invincible in these vulnerable appeals. For all the jingoism, Stockdale's personal confidence is not as abundant as the faith he places in his native land. It now seems unsurprising that the congenial and topical theme of the poem did not cover up its poetic limitations. In the *Memoirs*, Stockdale added a footnote to his account of the unhappy episode, saying that, for all the poem's failure in such propitious circumstances, 'still, something within me, calmly, yet distinctly told me that it *should* have been otherwise; therefore I proceed in my literary course' (*Memoirs*, vol. 11, p. 311). Such stubborn and determined self-deception both conceals and reveals the realisation that his influence in the London literary world (such as it was) had passed. He wrote to Porter that 'In my present state of life, I know not whether I wonder more at the spirits and alacrity with which I wrote and published the Invincible Island; or at the iron fate that Poem has experienced.' If this surprise at its failure and sense of the poem's value seem equally unlikely, then a preceding statement from the same letter suggests Stockdale's very real misery at his repeated mediocrity: 'This life is painful to me!'[41]

In 1800, Stockdale published a selection of poems, some of which have a streak of whimsical contemplation about his own literary fate. 'A Song' considers the inefficacy of all our worldly desires:

> Or does the bright poetic muse
> To nobler glory raise your views?
> Sagacious malice checks your aim,
> And poverty repels your flame[42]

Johnson's old model of literary struggle as 'Toil, envy, want' is personalised by the predictive wisdom of malicious forces. All, for Stockdale, is vanity: 'We're like Montgolfier's balloon', in that after soaring, troubles invariably make us 'To parent earth, at length, descend; / The trivial sport, and Wonder end.'[43] Yet perhaps the most interesting and incongruous aspect of the 1800 *Poems* is Stockdale's attempt to indulge in contemporary literary debate. It is built upon the premise that his taste will not be that of the fashions of the day, but he shows no sign of knowing what those fashions might be: 'DR PERCY'S *fits* are poetical *epilepsies*', he complains about the 'Hermit of Warkworth' as if it had been published recently, rather than in 1771. He likes Thomas Campbell, Crabbe, Scott, Robert Charles Dallas, and exclaims that 'I love the anacreon of MOORE', (p. xvi); he hates the impiety of Matthew Lewis's *The Monk*, and in a poem on William Wilberforce, laments that 'LEWIS, dead to virtue's fair renown, / Corrupts, with tales obscene, a tainted town' (p. 32). His taste is not uncommon, but the sense of a body of literature that has vitiated the sensibilities of the town is (with the exception of the lewd adventures of *The Monk*) left undescribed. His example reminds us that it was not uncommon for someone to live on into the nineteenth century and have little awareness of Wordsworth or Coleridge; the Romantic movement did not, for Stockdale, exist.[44] On the other hand, this also indicates his gradual removal from any real sense of contemporary literary culture; his remaining publications would be marked by this almost deliberate impression of living in the literary past.

The temple of English poetry

The *Poems* were dedicated to the Reverend William Beville with a design: through his help, 'I shall publickly give the lectures, in the metropolis, which I have, at length, almost finished, on our great ENGLISH POETS.'[45] The purpose of these *Lectures* is not obscure:

> In those lectures, which are written with a perfectly independent, and free, but not with a particle of a malignant mind, I have often praised, and admired, and I have too frequently had occasion to censure, and I trust, to refute, my illustrious predecessor, DR JOHNSON. The political and religious prejudices of that great man, in many instances, contaminate, and pervert his criticism ... he has profaned the most exalted, the sublimest altar of our PARNASSUS: he has violated the *sanctum santorum* of the temple of ENGLISH POETRY. (pp. 7–8)

The suggestion here that such animadversions on Johnson and the *Lives of the Poets* would be a secondary feature of the *Lectures on the Truly Eminent English Poets* is misleading. It was their main (and in many ways only) aim. The *Lectures*, when eventually published in 1807, would be the final product of Stockdale's long resentment over Johnson's *Lives* and the manner in which he had been apparently prevented from doing the job himself. Stockdale's long final work of literary criticism was designed to reverse the tide of literary fortune; it did next to nothing to question the justness of Johnson's fame, and less for Stockdale's desire for advancement or justification.

From the beginning of their composition, Stockdale presented the *Lectures* as simultaneously a work of lasting critical value, and as a way of rescuing his career and ensuring his own fame. 'I have great Literary ambition, and an original Literary plan in my mind', he tells Jane Porter, so much so that it is the only factor that will make him return to the malignant and envious scene that he so despises: 'nor would I ever again mix with the world, if I was not yet (to my shame be it written) infected with a passion for a very beautiful Phantom – Literary Glory!'[46] Yet the tone here is wistful – Stockdale knows that fame is a 'Phantom', and his desire for it almost childish; this awareness of the near-futility of the undertaking combines uneasily with Stockdale's need to assert himself one last time in the literary marketplace. The *Lectures* are the record of the resulting confusion of motive.

As a critical work, the unwieldy *Lectures* (1,263 pages in two volumes) contain, like most of Stockdale's later writing, moments of critical insight and heartfelt veneration, amidst long stretches of diatribe and misplaced justifications of arguments remote to the reader of 1807, let alone today. They represent the culmination of a particular response to Johnson, and Johnson's fame, that saw in the *Lives of the Poets* a misreading. They thus form a postscript to the often ferocious arguments over Johnson's *Lives*, but one so belated as to almost guarantee their own instant obsolescence, other than as a footnote to Johnson's growing fame. In Stockdale's *Memoirs*, the concluding lecture on Thomas Gray was written to 'vindicate' him from the 'gross injuries' received from Johnson (vol. II, p. 321), yet seems to have had the opposite effect, as indeed did the whole publication. Weinbrot has shown that amidst the commercial failure of the *Lectures*, their reception illustrates the almost antithetical result from that desired by Stockdale: he reminded readers of the value of Johnson's criticism, to the inevitable detriment of his own. As *The Edinburgh Review* described it, 'it is quite refreshing to meet with passages of [Johnson's] better sense and more dispassionate decisions, which our author quotes. The sentences of Johnson stand indeed with peculiar advantage in this insulated situation; and Mr Stockdale is entitled to the same sort of gratitude which we feel to a dull landlord who has invited us to dine with an interesting visitor.'[47] This back-handed compliment was hardly what Stockdale had wanted, but his response was defiant, if ineffectual: the 'indifferent success' of the *Lectures* 'has not proceeded from intellectual, and literary demerit; but from an impartial and free spirit, which, in this world, is a very unpropitious endowment' (*Memoirs*, vol. II, pp. 322–3).

The content of the *Lectures* reveals the uncertain state of Stockdale's fortunes throughout their composition: they are rambling, vehement, and uneven, both in length and quality, to a degree that would make them unsuitable for any form of public delivery. Stockdale apologises for their having taken thirteen years to write, for which his 'most afflicting nervous disorder' is to blame, along with other evils of old age.[48] He points out the relevance of the *Lectures* being on '"our TRULY eminent Poets;" for amongst the Poets of Dr. Johnson, there are names which have not the least pretensions to eminence' (*Lectures*, vol. I, p. ix). There is even a cheery declaration: 'To liberal, benevolent, and generous minds, whose good wishes I hope to deserve, I here honestly and openly declare that I am not a little ambitious of a literary immortality; and it would gratify me extremely to feel the rays of its orient lustre warm, and animate my languid frame before it descends to the tomb' (*Lectures*, vol. I, p. x). It is a hope that the *Lectures* themselves do little to fulfil. They are a vast lumber-room of Stockdale's hobby-horses, passions, and frustrations. Fundamentally they lack structure, and the course they follow is generated either by Stockdale's enthusiasms or, more often, his critical disputes. Reaction against Johnson, particularly, is their fulcrum, and too often they are built around a sense of grievance and complaint.

This also ensures that they are at their most balanced when dealing with authors outside the canon of the *Lives of the Poets*. The opening lectures, on Shakespeare and Spenser, show how engaging Stockdale could be when he did not have the Johnsonian mote in his eye. He likes the form of *The Faerie Queene*, for example, but dislikes allegory, which is 'for ever defeating the great ends of all genuine poetry' which are 'to strike, to charm, and to captivate' (*Lectures*, vol. I, p. 16). He also does not care for the allegorical model, 'the monstrous, and ridiculous fictions of Ariosto, which are too palpable and gross even to amuse a school-boy', or that Spenser 'mixes, and confounds the images of the Christian revelation with the heathen mythology' (*Lectures*, vol. I, pp. 17, 23). More familiar is his using an image of Spenser as the suffering artist, striving against fate: 'it must have been his consolation, it must have been his triumph, to have reflected, that a susceptible, and poetical soul, contending with poverty, oppression, and persecution; and emerging conquerour in that contest, is one of the finest painful conflicts, and victories that can be imagined' (*Lectures*, vol. 1, p. 28). It seems a willed self-portrait. A footnote shortly after shows Stockdale's veneration for Johnson in the days of his poverty and struggle: visiting him in 1773, he is surprised that Johnson has not many places to spend that Sunday: '"My dear Stockdale," said he with great emotion, "for many years of my life, I had *no* place to go to"' (*Lectures*, vol. 1, p. 29). This is part of Stockdale's sentimental identification with (and fetishisation of) the great artist as necessarily being in adversity; moreover, it becomes central to his reading of Johnson, in that before his fame and pension he represents a more authentic, sensitive critic. In similar vein, Stockdale never demurs from his verdict that the *Life of Savage* shows 'tender, and amiable benevolence' (*Memoirs*, vol. 11, p. 199), and refers to it in the *Lectures* as 'perhaps the masterpiece of its authour'.[49] The later Johnson, however, is distorted by comfort and adulation into his critical crimes of envy and malice in the *Lives*, 'when he was intoxicated with literary prosperity; when, with faculties in the decline; when, with a mind still powerful, but comparatively enfeebled, he endeavoured to injure the reputation, and the fame, of illustrious men' (*Lectures*, vol. 1, p. 102). Such moments are a reminder of the reason for the existence of the *Lectures* – Stockdale's anger at the apparent hegemony of Johnson's view of literary history. The problem is that he has little original to say about the subjects concerned, when not attacking his famous antagonist.

The result can be seen in the pleasant superficies of the lecture on Shakespeare, where he compliments past and present scholars, and disputes their identifications of works on the strengths of his own feelings, disagreeing with Johnson's low opinion of *The Merry Wives of Windsor* (Stockdale finds it 'perhaps, the first comedy in the English language'), telling Malone that there is little or none of Shakespeare in the trash of the three parts of *Henry VI*, or *Love's Labour's Lost*, and remarking on the 'tedious, and embarrassing measure' of the *Sonnets* (*Lectures*, vol. 1, pp. 60, 73–80, 81, 99). None of this is shocking, or particularly against the received view of the time, with regard to Shakespeare's poetry, but neither is it revealing or especially insightful. Stockdale's prose becomes more energised, and yet more predictable by the reappearance of a familiar foe, as he turns to Milton, 'the greatest, because the sublimest, of poets', unjust victim of the 'iniquity of Johnson' and his 'superficial, inconsistent, and ungenerous animadversions' (*Lectures*, vol. 1, pp. 101, 107, 134).

Stockdale's tactic in countering Johnson is to animadvert – he quotes from the *Lives* and subjects these passages to scrutiny; the result as literary criticism is dull and unconvincing: Stockdale reveals what he feels to be a contradiction or falsehood in Johnson, rejoices in proving his case, and repeats the exercise. The pity is that even in these works of his critical dotage, Stockdale can still convey the excitement and passion of great literature, as in his description of Satan's meeting with Sin and Death: 'The soul of the reader, too, blends with the tumult; and is vehemently moved with a mixed horrour, and transport of agitation.' He is also bold enough to echo Shelley and Blake (and anticipate William Empson and A. J. A. Waldock) in his view of Satan: 'though he is wicked, and rebellious, he is intrepid, and eloquent, throughout; he is the most active, and enterprising being in the poem'. And there are nuggets of literary history, as in Lyttelton's telling him of Pope's admission that he could not translate Homer into blank verse (*Lectures*, vol. 1, pp. 146, 155, 172–3). But the spirit of conflict with Johnson dominates, and it is a surprise when Stockdale relates simply that *Paradise Regained* 'is a poor performance' (vol. 1, p. 189), given how far the Milton lectures have moved from direct criticism of their subject, amongst all the accusation and refutation.

Stockdale's high esteem of Dryden is reflected in three lectures that add very little to Johnson's, or other previous criticism of the poet. Other than a preference for the major satires, and an absence of comment on late poems and translations, there is nothing in these conventional accounts that had not already been said. As Stockdale admits, Johnson's lives of Dryden and Pope are worthy and not automatically deserving of the title of blasphemies: although 'not without their characteristicks of singularity, arrogance, and cynicism', they 'almost do justice' to their subjects (*Lectures*, vol. 1, pp. 233, 234). Unfortunately, being in relative agreement with Johnson means Stockdale has nothing to argue against. Of his many digressions in these pages, the most notable is on the love of fame: 'the first; the honest; the avowed incentive of every man of genius, through all the literary progress of his life! It subjects the love of gain to moral, and intellectual dignity, and glory; – it thaws the frost of poverty; it blunts the shafts of persecution; it speeds the wing of the muse' (*Lectures*, vol. 1, p. 264). The most peculiar is a long apostrophe to the shade of Dryden, telling him of the malignance of Johnson's *Lives*, and their critical acceptance in the decadent contemporary world: 'Farewell, thou great and venerable poet! Thou art now in a state free from the various folly which

I have related to you' (*Lectures*, vol. 1, pp. 269–78, 277). The slip of 'folly' for 'follies' suggests the lack of care with which the *Lectures* entered the world, just as the insertion of this odd passage in itself evinces the absence of a careful editor or friendly reader to moderate Stockdale's excesses.

Stockdale's previous defence of Pope against Joseph Warton in 1778, in his *Inquiry into the Nature, and Genuine Laws of Poetry*, had shown his reverence for the poet (he apologetically quotes from it repeatedly and extensively in his two lectures on him).[50] He is at his best in his praise: 'There is nothing feeble; nothing superfluous, in the poetry of Pope; all is compressed; all is clear; all is polished; and it flames like the spear of Achilles. – He takes our hearts with a charming ambush; or his lines are arranged; they are marshalled for victory; he assails us with sentiments; with images; in firm, and splendid array' (*Lectures*, vol. 1, p. 412). His view of Pope's canon is not controversial, placing the *Iliad* translation and *The Rape of the Lock* on high, and having little interest in *The Dunciad*, whose 'perishable dramatis personae are not worthy of the muse of its authour' (*Lectures*, vol. 1, p. 513). There is a need to pick a fight with Johnson, who is 'particularly unjust' about the 'beautiful' *Essay on Man*, 'perhaps from his acrimony against Bolingbroke', and on the subject of Pope's 'capital production', *Eloisa to Abelard*, which 'has not obtained from Johnson the very high eulogy which it deserved' (*Lectures*, vol. 1, pp. 455, 482). At the end of the Pope lectures, Stockdale begs the reader not to think that he is 'under the influence of envy, and resentment' in his critical arguments, as 'Most faintly to apprehend that you think so hardly of me, would be injustice, and ingratitude to your liberality.' It is a strange way to cajole his readership, and suggests an insecurity that is not helped by the next page dwelling upon Johnson's treachery in not promoting Stockdale's *Inquiry* in the 'Life of Pope', and complimenting Warton instead (*Lectures*, vol. 1, pp. 533, 534).

The other subjects of the *Lectures* are Young, Thomson, Chatterton, and Gray. The near four hundred pages devoted to the defence of Chatterton are an anomaly, even in Stockdale's work, and are described as part of the Conclusion to this book. Stockdale's account of Young is helped by Herbert Croft's having written the bulk of Johnson's 'Life' of that poet; there is thus less contradiction and refutation, and a mainly level-headed relation of Young's poetic strengths and weaknesses. The latter are described with economy: 'By an overheated fancy, breaking through every pale of judgment, he sometimes loses himself in fustian, when he imagines that he has attained sublimity.' Young's problem is an 'epigrammatic passion; this inordinate love of laboured, and fantastic ornaments'.[51] The lecture on James Thomson allows Stockdale to recycle some of his contributions to the earlier edition. Otherwise, he is concerned mainly with showing the greatness of Thomson's moral character, in a way that chimes with his own exalted notion of the poet's existence: 'nothing forms the mind of man to true benevolence, and humanity, than a high enjoyment of what is good, in this life; and a long, and pungent experience of its evils. Of this severe, but salutary school, the poet seems particularly doomed to be a disciple, from his exquisite sensibility; and from his unequal, and iniquitous situations.'[52] None, for Stockdale, was more iniquitous than the fate of Gray after Johnson's criticism of him.

The two lectures on Gray are the summation of Stockdale's refutation of Johnson, angry pieces that show how little Stockdale has forgotten the critical smarts delivered by the 'Life of Gray' more than a quarter of a century before. Yet this signal fact of the passing of time also reveals the problem of Stockdale's misplaced fury: the many ripostes to Johnson over Gray in the 1780s (by Anna Seward, amongst others) at least dealt with recent literary history; the world had moved on, though Stockdale had not, and his designedly magisterial put-downs of Johnson are inflated and unbalanced screeds delivered to an empty room.[53]

Inevitably, Stockdale accuses his target through hyperbole: 'a great poet was never treated more unjustly, enviously, and malignantly, than *he* has been treated by Dr. Johnson'. He acknowledges that he is far from the first to mention this, but other critics 'were too complaisant; they payed too profound a deference to our Stagyrite' (*Lectures*, vol. II, pp. 538, 541). He will be blunter. Yet this promises more than it delivers too. The sad fact soon becomes pertinent that, short of disagreeing with Johnson, disputing the terms of his critique, or accusing him of lack of taste and judgement, Stockdale has nothing to add to these old arguments. Instead, the pattern is formed of his exalted claims for Gray being followed by part of Johnson's dismissal of him, and Stockdale's pained animadversion. It is no surprise that he wants to 'venture to assert, without hyperbolical compliment, that the *progress of poesy* is an ode which has not its superiour in the poetical world', or that, after quoting Johnson's criticism of its obscurity, Stockdale relates that its opening is 'perfectly intelligible, and clear to every one whose soul is susceptible; moderately informed; and untainted with spleen' (*Lectures*, vol. I, pp. 573, 578). For all the rapturous praise and exclamations of disgust, the lectures are half-hearted, and Stockdale plods his weary way without conviction; even the sarcasm is forced: 'I am now *obliged* to say something on the outrages on all the just and universally established laws of criticism, which are committed by

Johnson, in his remarks on this ode'. As ever, Stockdale is wounded enough to view dissenting criticism as a sin of fallen humanity: whereas Seward blamed malice and envy, Johnson's crushing summary of *The Progress of Poesy* and *The Bard* is 'an emphatical instance of a very selfish depravity, which is too common to human nature' (*Lectures*, vol. II, pp. 590, 612). But the major effect of reading about 'this literary Diogenes' who has 'thus contemptuously trampled on the magnificent apparel of our poetical Platos' (p. 594) is to wonder at the psychology of a writer who could, even with reduced vehemence in his dotage, produce so much criticism clouded by his dissension with another literary critic, without being apparently aware of how it had vitiated almost the entire enterprise.

If they had been produced swiftly and published in the 1790s, when arguments around Johnson had more immediacy, it is likely that the *Lectures on the Truly Eminent English Poets* would have been highly detrimental to Stockdale's literary reputation – not through their iconoclastic attack on a central literary figure, but for their incoherence, subjectivity, and superfluities. As it was, by 1807 Stockdale had so little reputation that the brief coverage of the *Lectures* was better than nothing. It is obvious that, although Johnson became its obsession, the project was an expression of Stockdale's belief in a poetic canon against the depravities of contemporary taste, and modern life in general; Johnson's rudeness about Gray was a symbol, for this elderly man, of a greater malaise:

> How long will a great part of a nation, celebrated for its intellectual strength, and acquirements, be the dupes of a superficial pedantry; – of its dry, and spiritless criticism; of its pusillanimous trimming; of its gross partiality, and malignant censure! – How long will the publick be dupes to the venal slaves of vanity and trade: to the unprincipled flatterers of dullness, and assassins of genius! (*Lectures*, vol. II, p. 624)

At such moments, Stockdale strays into the stirring superficialities of journalism for which his temperament was, in some ways, suited.

He concludes the *Lectures* by claiming that if the *Lives of the Poets* had not had the 'imperious authority' of Johnson's name, 'they would only have excited a momentary resentment; and been dismissed from farther attention, with a calm, and decisive contempt' (*Lectures*, vol. II, p. 656). It is a telling comment on how much Stockdale was affected by the success of such authority. If his conclusion is taken at face value, it might be considered that such insignificant critical trifles as the *Lives* hardly required refuting, especially not by an enormous, unwieldy work that was a loss-making failure. Stockdale never seems to have accepted that there was more to the *Lives* than Johnson's name and authority; the *Lectures* were his last attempt at asserting his own critical ability, and they were undermined both by their intellectual premises, and execution.

A delineation of failure

If the failure of the *Lectures* confirmed Stockdale's assumptions about the debased literary taste of the present age, then their companion piece, the *Memoirs* eventually published in 1809, provides a commentary on why he will not be given his due fame. Like so much of Stockdale's work, the *Memoirs* are alternately self-aggrandising and timorously unconfident; their span of over eight hundred pages may seem more than sufficient for most readers, but this represents a compression of Stockdale's original intention to describe his life minutely. At the start of the second volume, which finds him only up to the 1760s, he explains that this Shandean problem of narration means that he will be less detailed and more attentive to significant events of his career, as time is running out. Two hundred pages on, he announces the need for further concision: it is February 1804, and he has been ill and depressed all winter. Also, 'my expiring passion for public praise' means that he has lost the purpose of writing anyway; the rest will be a list of publications, and their contexts (*Memoirs*, vol. II, p. 201). This peculiar doubting of his own significance (after having expressed it many times in the preceding pages) is of course transitory: the *Memoirs* will go on to posit the inevitability of his future celebrity, but will equally then contradict themselves at moments of self-doubt. This inconstancy suggests that Stockdale was naturally unsure of his right to the merit he had so often claimed, and it makes the *Memoirs* an appropriately difficult, uneven work, veering from minute attention to very obscure quarrels, to passages where Stockdale assumes the reader to have lost interest.

The piecemeal nature of the *Memoirs* can be seen in the published dedication to Jane Porter, who had travelled up to Lesbury to help this undoubtedly difficult old man put the work in order. Porter had copied out the manuscript of the *Memoirs* when old age and 'a most afflicting nervous disorder' had again weakened his powers (*Memoirs*, vol. I, p. v). Yet this was written in 1805, and it would be four years before they appeared. Stockdale's hopes for the *Memoirs* were at times high: in London, when they were in press, he informed Jane Porter that 'I have considerably altered, and improved them. – I found it necessary to expunge a great deal; and I have enlarged, and confirmed, in different places, my sentiments on subjects of great importance', as well as giving extracts from poems, 'which I thought would be entertaining, and interesting to my readers; and of service to poetical fame'. He even wished that 'Before I return to Lesbury, I hope that I shall republish all my printed works.' Such optimism perhaps stemmed from his publisher: Longman and Rees 'take upon themselves all the expense of publication; and we are, in every edition equally to divide the profits'. Once the *Memoirs* were published, he was pleased to hear that the 'trade have taken a hundred copies'.[54]

The eventual published 'Preface' of 1808 shows a similar confidence: 'It is now six years since I wrote the memoirs which I am now going to publish. From that time to the present, I never looked at them. I have now reperused them with great care, and circumspection; a species of attention which has not timidly checked the freedom with which I always wish to write' (*Memoirs*, vol. 1, p. ix). He will 'vindicate that freedom', as 'not a particle of it resulted from the austerity, and remoteness of old age; from disappointed ambition; nor from that prejudice, and partiality for past times, which is often, without foundation, imputed to old men' (vol. 1, pp. ix–x). Instead, it comes from 'the absolute independence of my mind; from my constitutional, and habitual assertion of all important truth, without any unmanly fear of consequences; – a noble state of the soul, from which I will not ignominiously, and shamefully recede, in my old age; nor in my death' (vol. 1, p. x).

With the commencement of the *Memoirs* proper, the reader finds much the same message, albeit written six years previously: so, whilst Stockdale will write about contemporary literature 'as dispassionately, as if I had never been an authour myself', he turns, on the same page, to the 'degenerate republick of letters' (vol. 1, p. 7), keeping his dispassion well hidden: 'Our literature is debased with the characteristicks of the *general* depravity, and puerility of our taste' (vol. 1, p. 8). Another old staple then enters, in his paranoid conviction that he will never get a fair reception from the literary world: 'Not spleen, and disgust, but long, and incontrovertible experience has taught me to apprehend that the constitutional, and indefeasible right of an english writer to ingenuous, and unlimited criticism, will not so cheerfully be granted to *me*, as to others' (vol. 1, p. 10). The only remedy is the old ally, posterity: 'it may openly, and warmly acknowledge, that [my] ardent, and unsubmitting efforts, contributed, or *should* have contributed, to retard the moral, and literary corruption of their country' (vol. 1, p. 14).

Rather than being the intellectual redeemer of his vulgarised country, however, Stockdale's invocations to posterity in the *Memoirs* are as much

A delineation of failure 191

to convince himself as the reader, and although these two volumes provide an invaluable casebook of individual failure, they did little to rescue his reputation after the eccentric and largely unread *Lectures*. The *Memoirs* offer a running commentary on the misadventures that make up Stockdale's literary career; as such, they have an unintentional momentum of their own, as Isaac D'Israeli noted in a nasty, but not inaccurate review:

> such, however, is the prevalence of his ill stars, that, in the course of his whimsical and weary pilgrimage, he blunders from one pit-fall into another, with an alacrity, which, in minds inclined to scepticism, might almost excite a doubt of the justness of his unqualified pretensions to superior sagacity. These accidents he describes with such a face of rueful simplicity, and mixes up with so much grave drollery and merry pathos with all he says or does, that we are perpetually at a loss whether to laugh or cry.[55]

For D'Israeli, the self-important folly of the *Memoirs* was the culmination of a life that mistakenly refused to examine its own values and accept its own inherent limitations, particularly with regard to Stockdale's pretensions to write poetry:

> Much of the misery of his life has arisen from a fatal error concerning his talents: his friends unfortunately mistook his animal spirits for genius, and by directing them into the walk of poetry, bewildered him for ever. Though he never wrote a line beyond the powers of the bell-man, or the stone-cutter; though he confesses that all his verses have been received with negligence and contempt; yet the mediocrity, the absolute poverty of his genius, has not once occurred to him. While he is forgotten faster than he writes, he still dreams of 'immortality,' and confidently predicts that his ephemeral trifles, which passed unnoticed at their birth, will yet force attention, and descend with 'glory' to futurity! It is enough to give wisdom to the foolish, and seriousness to the giddy, to contemplate the afflicting picture of self-delusion so warm in the colouring, and so true to the life. Mr. Stockdale has embittered his days by a restless and tormenting thirst after waters which nature placed far beyond his reach; and which those who have tasted of them, have seldom found to be the purest draught of human felicity.[56]

It could be argued that Stockdale had reached too vulnerable an age to be subjected to such a bitter destruction of his supposed talents, yet D'Israeli, whilst he may lack tact and compassion, makes a valuable point about the essential problem of Stockdale's literary dream, and its attendant delusions. Despite the evidence, Stockdale never stopped believing that one single moment of acceptance into the literary world could redeem his existence; D'Israeli is acute in pointing out that it has signally failed to charm many of the greatly successful, or to alter (and simplify) the difficulties of their life, but less able to envisage why Stockdale could not face these shattering conclusions about the inefficacy of literary fame, and his own lack of qualification for it. Stockdale's failure to accept such contingencies is in one sense a failure of maturity; it is his greatest blindspot and his inspiration, keeping him going long after less committed aspirants would have given up. Yet without it, it is hard to avoid the conclusion that his long life on the fringes of English literary culture would have been even more tormented than he made it.

Ultimately, what did endure in him was an uneasy but resilient sense that things should have been otherwise: Stockdale's religious thinking was orthodox, and he dismissed what he saw as the gloomy injustices of Calvinism, but with difficulty: 'On looking back, at the present hour, on the completion of these memoirs, I recognise that they are shaded with many observations which are not to the honour of the human species', he writes, in 1808 (*Memoirs*, vol. II, p. 341). What hovers over all his writing is the painful possibility that the malice he sometimes attributes to human workings is actually ever-present, and that his fearless openness is an exception that his disingenuous fellow creatures have punished, without mercy: 'even the extreme predominance of the *bad*, cannot extinguish the *good* that there is in human nature', he claims (*Memoirs*, vol. I, p. 32), but he is not, ultimately, so sure. Even posterity, the last refuge, needs to be appealed to:

> When I shall be *thus* known to posterity, I doubt not that *their* impartial, and equitable judgment, will atone for the illiberality, and malice of my contemporaries; – they will probably think (notwithstanding my unfortunate ambition, while I lived) that I was entitled to literary honours, and rewards. – Such was the irresistible, and charming attraction; such was the bright magick, and enchantment of this pure, generous, and sublime employment; that it made a life, which in other respects, was melancholy, and oppressed; not only tolerable, but even desirable. (*Memoirs*, vol. II, pp. 332–3)

Is this the last self-delusion of the type delineated by D'Israeli? If so, it was a necessary one, like many such, and it seems wrong to deny Stockdale its efficacy. After all, he suffered enough for the 'bright magick' of the literary world. On one hand, it is hard to dispute Howard Weinbrot's judgement that 'The at once painfully varied and consistent nature of Stockdale's life was based as much on his overly generous estimate of his needs and talents as on the world's impatience with him.'[57] To not be aware of his own prejudices and their obvious motives is a grave flaw, and it makes much of Stockdale's work turgid in the extreme, with its endless self-righteous resentments. Walter Scott, who remembered seeing Stockdale flitting around London publishers, responded to the *Memoirs* thus:

This extraordinary effusion of egotism and vanity should be read by all who are visited by the folly of thinking highly of their own productions ... The judgements which this conceited cock-brained fidgetty man passes ... shew that there is no wound festers and rankles so deeply as what is inflicted on personal vanity.[58]

And yet, Stockdale had very little left to show for his endless enthusiasm for poetry, and small but undoubted talent as a literary critic, other than the vanity of resentment. His purpose today is certainly different from what he anticipated and desperately wanted: he reminds us of an arbitrary, capricious literary world – a world we can never fully understand unless we pay some small attention to the often laughable but also rather tragic non-careers of writers such as Stockdale. For all that Stockdale's writing is obsessed with the need for recognition and success, he is the exemplary record of a failure in the eighteenth century, because he was so detailed in recording his disappointments that they became, unwittingly, the subject of his many writings. As such, these works have become an invaluable record of the destructiveness of literary fame, and the immoderate need for the authority and self-definition that it conveys. For all the public bluster, there are small points where Stockdale admits how self-defeating his critical attitudes and defensiveness, his insecure need for fame, and his exaggerated responses to arguments have been. In a late letter to Porter, he acknowledges:

> When Pope's merit is disparaged, I am as much wounded as if my own was undervalued, afterward I think of it with mental pain; such is the foolish force of my nervous disorder. Its irritations produce many impressions unfavourable to moral happiness. I live in a continual war with myself.[59]

For all the weight of his reaction being placed upon his nervous illness, the last sentence has the poignancy of self-realisation rare in a writer so often strident in his demands for his questionable achievements to be celebrated. His sense of perpetual self-conflict humanises him: it makes the claims for his individual genius fade into something more nondescript and commonplace: in a peculiar paradox, the nature of Stockdale's failure both isolates and singles him out (though not in the way he wanted), and then returns his example to a more common sense of human limitation. The eccentricity of Stockdale does not prevent him from at points representing needs and desires shared by every creative and critical thinker: like the other figures discussed in this book, Stockdale both embodies many of the most important facets of eighteenth-century literary culture, and anticipates more Romantic and modern views of the artist, in ways which the Conclusion will discuss.

Conclusion

By the age of fifteen, Jamie Boswell, rather than being a moody teenager himself, had instead to cheer up his perpetually unhappy father. In October 1794, James Boswell senior was complaining (again) of his lack of a fixed place to do his family (and himself) justice and honour. His son pointed out that the successful placemen and pensioners he envied 'have not the fame of having been the biographer of Johnson or the conscious exultation of a man of genius'. Furthermore, would the strictly professional life of 'a rich, dull, plodding lawyer' have allowed his father to have been intimate with Rousseau, Voltaire, Garrick, and Goldsmith? It seemed unlikely: 'You cannot expect to be both at the same time. Every situation in life has its advantages and disadvantages.'[1] Only a man as consistently changeable as Boswell could get such advice from his young son: Boswell the famous biographer yearned for the slow stability of (what he imagined to be) the typical life of a successful man of property, power, and preferment. Concomitantly, Boswell the laird and advocate wanted the less tangible but more alluring fame of literary life. The melancholy that beset him throughout his career was both a symptom and cause of his inability to be satisfied with either course. Boswell's ambitions depended upon a sense of the absolute: either he escaped his father and the law and found a life in the pursuits of the imagination, or he inherited Auchinleck, and became a part of the family tradition he both needed and feared. The result, as so often, was an uncertain mixture of the two.

Boswell's endless inability to find contentment makes him a leading example of the inefficacy of the sort of fame hankered after by so many. Boswell's writings on Johnson found overwhelming success, but this did not translate into a change in his life: the publication of the *Life of Johnson* in 1791 would secure his literary immortality, but its contemporary acclaim and popularity did not see a happy Boswell resting on his laurels; instead, he remained the same insecure figure, fascinated by the idea of fulfilment, but unable to find it.

The inefficacy of literary fame

This is not at all surprising, even without Boswell's particular problems. If success was such a panacea, after all, then few writers would continue to produce after reaching a plateau of renown. The notion that literary fame is in itself a solution to (and a removal from) the everyday concerns and vicissitudes of existence is a naïve one, predicated on the mistaken notion that a relation to the world can be instantly altered; it seeks in literature an answer to problems that it cannot possibly provide. Moreover, examples of great writers who achieved fame and renown yet led lives of misery are legion. It is equally true that the posthumous fame of writers is often assailed by changes in fashion, or reconsiderations of the past; Anna Seward and Percival Stockdale should have realised this, as they spent so much ink on decrying the neglect, in their lifetimes, of past genius. Yet their devotion to the ideal of literature as a domain beyond the normal workings of the earthly world appears to have blinded them. Instead, their faith in literature as a quasi-religion motivated them to ignore the evidence to hand, and instead work towards a level of achievement and recognition that was beyond them.

Richard Savage is a different case, in expecting such recognition as due from his birthright; in doing so in a reckless and high-handed manner, with no consideration as to the questioning of his own talents, he incidentally contributed to the influential symbolic Romantic figure of the doomed author, so important to later ages. Equally accidentally, the disastrous career of William Dodd (who had a signal lack of pretension about the value of his mediocre writings) suggests how mutable the characteristics of success and failure could be, given that he was eulogised as an innocent victim and damned as a hypocrite, whilst a draconian judgement rendered his sudden literary success rather irrelevant.

In considering what conclusions can be drawn from the separate narratives of failure that this book offers, it is useful to envisage the ambitions of such largely disappointed writers, in their attempts at authorship. Savage seems to have conceived of the author as a surrogate for noble birth, hence his patrician belief that the true writer is a figure beyond criticism and worthy of respect and reward as a matter of due (just as the penurious hacks beneath him are naturally subject to ridicule for their paltry efforts to emulate his genius). It was a position which the downturn in his own circumstances failed to alter, and his death and subsequent fame (mainly through the hand of Johnson) ironically only lent more credence to his view of the author as a genius separate from the cavils of petty mortals. Dodd seems to have been immune to such high-minded concerns; his original works were products of both a genuine and far from uninformed literary bent (as witnessed by the success of his *Beauties of Shakespear*) or were more simple and less scholarly attempts to make money. When these latter availed him little, he concentrated on compilations and anthologies, contributing mundane homiletic writings that nonetheless sold better than his earlier, more consciously literary effusions. His representation (both in his last, despairing writings and in the works of his supporters) as a figure of sensibility and a martyr to injustice and cruelty seems far from sincere, yet was ironically his most successful attempt at striking a literary pose. Seward and Stockdale inherited Savage's notion of the author as an inspired being beyond the criticism of the less gifted; more importantly, they turned this into an often paranoid obsession with the injustices that assail 'true' authorship. This compromised their work, leaving them with a fatal inability for self-criticism.

Yet it should not be assumed that they were lone idealistic eccentrics in this respect, surrounded by hard-headed pragmatists. The end of the eighteenth century offers many examples of support for the idea of artistic genius as separate from (and at odds with) the world which is unable to appreciate its value. This can be seen in part through the growing genre of literary compilations, anecdotes, and ana, which often memorialise eccentricity and failure. Isaac D'Israeli's writings of the 1790s on the nature of the literary character view artistic talent as something often at odds with a culture unable to fully appreciate it. In *Curiosities of Literature*, there are many instances of genius suffering unnecessarily and unfairly because of the ignorance of the world, and a section on 'The Poverty of the Learned' makes clear that 'Fortune has rarely condescended to be the companion of Merit. Even in these enlightened times, men of letters have lived in obscurity, while their reputation was widely spread; and have perished in poverty, while their works were enriching the booksellers.' Amongst his examples are Savage selling 'that eccentric poem, *The Wanderer*' for £10, Milton parting with 'his immortal work' for the same sum, Thomas Otway starving to death, Chatterton not being able to afford a penny tart, and another familiar failure: 'Samuel Boyce, whose Poem on Creation ranks high in the scale of poetic excellence, was absolutely famished to death; and was found dead, in a garret, with a blanket thrown over his shoulders, and fastened by a skewer, with a pen in his hand!'[2] Like Chatterton on his bed after Wallis's painting, poor Boyse was fated to represent the indignity of failure like a muse, striking various melodramatic poses in his blanket.

Amongst such common complaints against fortune, though, a line is drawn, whereby it is possible to lament neglected and suffering genius,

The inefficacy of literary fame 197

without pretending that it is always a source of surprise or indeed unjustifiable, when applied to less talented subjects. Hence D'Israeli's later 1809 flyting of Stockdale's *Memoirs*, which amongst its ridicule has some sympathy for the misery produced by Stockdale's chaining himself to a poetic career for which he was far from suited. In very similar vein is the account of the Abbé de Marolles (1600–81), added to *Curiosities of Literature* in 1794, who is an exemplum of the thesis that 'There have been, in all the flourishing ages of literature, authors who, although little able to boast of literary talents, have unceasingly harassed the public; and have at length been remembered only by the number of wretched volumes their unhappy industry has produced.' The Abbé 'wrote about eighty volumes, which enjoy the same reputation, being all equally despised'. He was 'a most egregious scribbler. He was tormented with so violent a fit for publication, that he even printed lists and catalogues of his friends. I have seen, at the end of one of his works, a list of names of those persons who had given him books!'[3]

D'Israeli's short tale of the unfortunate Abbé is an interesting mixture of bathos and sympathy, and illustrates how narratives of failure are often used to make a serious point whilst simultaneously holding up their object to some scorn: it is the appeal of such narratives that they combine a moral warning against vanity (found famously at the end of Johnson's *Life of Savage*) with a less exalted tendency towards voyeurism. Thus, the Abbé 'exultingly told a poet, that his verses had cost him little: "They cost you what they are worth," replied the sarcastic critic' (p. 78), inspiring the reader to laugh at pretensions pricked whilst feeling pity for the insulted recipient. D'Israeli acknowledges the value of de Marolles's *Memoirs*, which serves (as Stockdale's similarly bitter autobiography will later do) as a warning against the folly of placing yourself in an arena where you are bound to fail. He quotes the Abbé's cautionary note that 'I do not advise any one of my relatives or friends to apply himself as I have done to study, and particularly to composing books, if he thinks that will add to his fame or fortune. I am persuaded that of all persons in the kingdom, none are more neglected than those who devote themselves entirely to letters' (p. 79). This caution is intended to be of relevance far beyond the hapless Abbé.

In another section, 'The Origin of Literary Journals', the rise of literary criticism is posited by D'Israeli as a necessity, given the 'multitude of *scribblers*' who have arisen during the growth of literary production:

> In the last century, it was a consolation, at least, for the unsuccessful writer, that he fell insensibly into oblivion. If he committed the *private* folly of printing what no one would purchase, he had only to settle the matter with his publisher: he was not arraigned at the *public* tribunal, as if he had

committed a crime of magnitude. But, in those times, the nation was little addicted to the cultivation of letters: the writers were then few, and the readers were not many. When, at length, a taste for literature spread itself through the body of the people, vanity induced the inexperienced and the ignorant to aspire to literary honours. To oppose these inroads into the haunts of the Muses, Periodical Criticism brandished its formidable weapon; and it was by the fall of others that our greatest geniuses have been taught to rise.[4]

Criticism is a valuable reaction against the development of indiscriminate writing, rather than a biased and self-serving institution, that refutes challenges to its hegemony. The difference is in perspective, of course: D'Israeli's lack of direct involvement meant that he had never been on the wrong critical end; yet such distance allows him to suggest that criticism generally adjudicates on literary merits with accuracy and proportion. Such a judgement is nowhere to be found in the writings of Stockdale or Seward (or Savage, for that matter), where writing that contradicts their vehemently held judgements is generally depicted as the result of partiality, want of taste, or deliberate malice.

D'Israeli points out that literary neglect is not necessarily a reflection on the weakness and bias of criticism, so much as the inferiority of talents; but he does argue, equally, that there are as many examples of genius and real merit destroyed by failure. A related idea of the author is that of genius overcoming adversity. The model for such a figure by the 1790s was Samuel Johnson.

Johnson's practical importance to the figures in this book is plain: the *Life of Savage* created an audience for the life and writing of its subject that would otherwise not have existed much beyond his own lifetime, as well as offering an account of a failed career that moved in sophistication well beyond simple hagiography or moral denunciation. The sensation of Dodd's case was augmented by Johnson's interventions on his behalf, which guaranteed Dodd a minor critical currency. As critical arbiter, and symbolic embodiment of a literary establishment that disagreed with their views, Johnson was the source of the anger and resentment that generated so many pages by Stockdale and Seward, becoming indeed such a *bête noire* as to control the direction of much of their criticism. Perhaps even more importantly, he had gone through a long struggle for recognition and literary fame, and succeeded; they, in different ways, had fought the same fight, and had not achieved the renown that they thought their talents deserved. As Johnson became the most famous writer in Britain, and a byword for literary genius, it is hard to see how this could not offend his former friend Stockdale, and his fellow author from Lichfield, Seward.

Above all, the canonisation of Johnson as the exemplary life of achievement through years of adversity left a template against which to measure his less successful contemporaries; the renowned moral and religious rectitude, the well-documented public persona, and the endless labours that produced the *Dictionary*, the edition of Shakespeare, and the *Lives of the Poets*, amongst others, meant that the comparison would hardly be in the favour of a figure such as Stockdale, obsessively carrying forward his grudge over the supposed contract of the *Lives*, or Seward, complaining repeatedly that Johnson's criticism was the product of envy and malice. By 1791, and the triumph of Boswell's *Life*, Johnson represented so much to the public as to be immune from such criticisms, which seemed petty by comparison (as indeed they often were). Johnson, after all, had suffered, survived, and succeeded, and whatever his faults and weaknesses, self-pity was not among them.

Boswell's *Life* competed with, conquered, and drew together the energy of the many biographical accounts of Johnson. As the resulting figure acquired mythic proportions, the effect on literary biography was profound. As Alvin Kernan describes it,

> His intense personality, in a way the first romantic artist, appears at exactly the right point in literary history in several ways, the kind of poor, strange, troubled person that the print business could attract and use as a Grub Street hack, and, at the same time, the type of individual who needed and could use print to satisfy certain existential needs of his own for bread, for status, for meaning.[5]

Perhaps most profoundly, in terms of failure, Johnson in the arc of Boswell's narrative had come through his struggles and found such meaning; by contrast, he had himself applied such a meaning to Savage's life, which in a less sympathetic account would have merely detailed a self-destructive man ignorant of his own weaknesses. Furthermore, the lengthy autobiographical self-justifications of Seward and Stockdale, published afterwards, evoke sympathy not from their finding meaning through their conquering (or even accepting) of adverse circumstance, but from their unintentional lack of the sort of awareness that was so important to Johnson's understanding of the relative values of success and failure.

Johnson's example symbolised, amongst many other things, a determined austerity of purpose that was all but impossible to emulate; moreover, when a figure such as Stockdale complained in his *Memoirs* of the universal injustices which had destroyed him, in comparison with the ideal of the writer as represented by Johnson, it came across as self-indulgence. In an imaginary conversation published in 1799, James Beattie projected

Johnson in dialogue with Joseph Addison, defending his severity of outlook and demeanour by positing its origin:

> You, Sir, passed your time in affluence, posterity, and ease; supported by the applause of literature, and the patronage of greatness; you were kind to others, for others were kind to you. My genius bloomed in a desert; and from that desert it was not drawn, till the winter of life had repressed its vigour, and tarnished its beauty. My days were spent in sickness and in sorrow; agitated by fruitless hope, and chilled by unforeseen disappointment.[6]

In Beattie's imagined Johnsonian cadences and parallelisms can be seen the strict idea of artistic integrity that Johnson had come to represent; the successful writer, it is implied, has to face adversity squarely and defeat it, though even this will not ensure their happiness. In contrast, the failed author is more concerned with enumerating their supposed injuries (to the point of making a fetish of them), than with acquiring this hard-won self-knowledge, and the perspective it gives on the vanity of human desires and ambitions. Moreover, narratives of failure follow a pattern whereby the material of a career is manipulated. The result is often an unintentional mixture of tragedy and comedy, a moral warning that also serves as entertainment. In a sense, all such narratives come out of the pocket of Johnson's *Life of Savage*, in that the attempt to inculcate a moral also contains and plays upon the fascination of the idea of failure, particularly its possible similarity to and yet distance from readers. Narratives of failure can be sentimentalised, or made into comic relief (or both), but all tend to take a similar route.

Failure and Romantic posterity

Whether the subject of academic criticism, or playing a different role in collections of anecdotes or ana, failure narratives are retold in a way that stresses the lack of achievement, the seemingly avoidable pain wrought by over-ambitiousness, and a misconception of both personal abilities and the worth of success. This is inevitable: given that narratives of success are built around epiphanies and significant turning points in a career, an attempt to make sense of failure will draw attention, conversely, to crucial factors or events which cause or anticipate the lack of fulfilment which will be the end of the story. The narratives offered by the subjects of this book all follow an ostensibly similar path, but each also contributes, in a distinctive way, to a cumulative picture of the failure to achieve and legitimate a particular type of success, usually embodied in the idea of authorship. All also offer, in different aspects, another characteristic of the failed writer, in adopting strategies that seem, in many ways, to be acts of defiance, but which are actually mechanisms of self-defence, ways of coping with the melancholy realisation that the success and fame for which they yearn will not arrive.

This book has argued that a leading quality of a certain kind of literary failure, one of the marks of an unfulfilled literary life, is the belief that the actions of an unjust and ungrateful world have deliberately denied the full range of human possibilities and talents from coming to fruition. This is usually less than plausible, but it has an erstwhile significance: in bemoaning the injustices that have frustrated and destroyed supposed genius and denied it fame, such writers contribute to the important Romantic transformation of the idea of authorship, whereby the very neglect and lack of fulfilment of a career becomes fetishised, and part of its appeal. In this view, an artist ought to be at odds with contemporary culture, and it would be a pejorative reflection if they were not.

In this sense, the very lack of fulfilment so evident in Seward's and Stockdale's autobiographical writings makes them as much of their time as *Lyrical Ballads* or *My First Acquaintance with Poets*. Their (somewhat accidental) relevance to contemporary critical ideas can be seen in the responses of Seward and Stockdale to the significant case of Thomas Chatterton, where the worldly failure and despairing death of the 'marvellous boy' is used (unsurprisingly) to represent the folly and malice of a corrupted critical establishment; Seward stops there, but Stockdale extends the argument, significantly, seeing the end of Chatterton as an expression of the more existential side of failure – the conviction, of experience over hope, that artistic contentment and fulfilment is as impossible to achieve in this life as earthly happiness. It goes without saying that such a response is in many ways a submerged statement of personal frustration and disappointment (and is anyway hardly universal – some artists were happy and successful; Stockdale's error was to assume that all of them should be made so by fame). Yet it is also one that shows how the times had (in one strange, accidental sense) caught up with Stockdale and with Seward, as it was becoming fashionable to lament the failures of tortured genius in a particular manner: this involved a melodramatic style alive to the tears of sensibility, and the assumption that the very proof of the genius of such failed careers was in their being thwarted, either by circumstance or malice.

In 1787, George Hardinge made the mistake of complimenting Horace Walpole in a letter to Seward, only to be told very firmly, 'do not expect that I can learn to esteem that fastidious and unfeeling being to whose insensibility we owe the extinction of the greatest poetic luminary, if we may judge from the brightness of its dawn, that ever rose in our, or perhaps in any other, hemisphere' (*Letters*, vol. I, pp. 370–1). George Gregory, the author of *The Life of Thomas Chatterton* (1789), accordingly received a warmer welcome, and was complimented on his 'ingenious book', an 'elegant, spirited, and valuable memoir of the most extraordinary genius which perhaps ever existed' (*Letters*, vol. III, p. 125). Samuel Holt Monk thought that Chatterton was a perfect example of Seward's literary view, as he 'filled the role of the genius oppressed by critics' and 'happily illustrated her conception of the poet'.[7] There is certainly an absence of discrimination in her writings on him; Walpole is eventually forgiven, posthumously, for not responding to Chatterton's appeal for patronage (and thus supposedly ensuring the desperate young bard's doom) via a back-handed note of commiseration: he must have had a total want of 'poetic fancy' – how else could he have failed to perceive 'the magnitude of that genius' (*Letters*, vol. VI, pp. 234–5)?

Seward came close to sarcasm in her treatment of Walpole; Stockdale did not indulge in such politeness. Even by the inconsistent standards and loaded premises of his *Lectures on the Truly Eminent English Poets*, the near four hundred pages dedicated to Chatterton in the second volume of that sprawling work are an oddity. The destruction of Chatterton by malicious forces is such a glaring injustice to Stockdale that he all but neglects criticism. The lectures proceed on a simple opposition between Chatterton, who, had he lived, would have become 'as great a poet as it was possible for human nature to produce', and 'would have excelled Dryden, and Shakespeare; and every poet, of every age, and nation', and 'the frozen, and evil genius of Walpole', which blighted him.[8] As usual, the overheated passions simplify the confusion of motives, so that Walpole's negligence in replying to Chatterton's request for help is interpreted not as mere high-handedness and disdain (or even indolence); instead, Stockdale implies that it was a deliberate act of villainy, and then admonishes Walpole over many pages for his brutality.[9]

The result says little about Chatterton, the childish (and thus wholly innocent) genius. Hero worship is combined with superfluous insults. Jacob Bryant, the chief (and mistaken) adherent for the authorship of Rowley rather than Chatterton, comes in for particular abuse, but even more amenable figures to the opinions of Stockdale, such as Thomas Tyrwhitt and George Gregory, are interrogated for daring to question any aspect of Chatterton's luminous brilliance, or for failing to understand that poetic insight is superior to any amount of musty scholarship. The magnification of the tragic demise of one unfortunate penurious poet embraces absurdity: Chatterton is compared to Stockdale's old hero

'Swedish Charles' and Alexander the Great (vol. II, p. 283). On the theological difficulties of Chatterton's suicide, Stockdale's solution is to stress the extent to which he was provoked, so much so that no less than the voice of God is imagined, forgiving him: '"There never was a more excessive sensibility than thine, since the creation of man: since *that* time, there never was a more excessive human obduracy than *that* which it was thy sublunary fate to encounter"' (vol. II, p. 276). It is not an underestimation of Chatterton's travails to suggest that this lacks perspective.

As the farrago continues, the suffering sensibility of Chatterton becomes an emblem of every unjustly neglected or unfairly criticised writer: Walpole has sinned against the future of the cultural world, as have the other 'tyrants and oppressours, in its immature greatness, of one of the first sublunary creatures of God' (vol. II, p. 435). Chatterton is made to symbolise the poetic vocation, not just in his innocence and inspiration, but also in his poverty: 'the cowardly animosity of the presumptuous, and unfeeling tribe is apt to be particularly hostile to departed genius; and in proportion as that genius was indigent, and great' (vol. II, p. 255). In a similar way that Savage's wanderings and privations became a model of the doomed but noble artist, Chatterton here resembles the Romantic poet, condemned to suffering because of the lazy prejudice and ignorance of critics and patrons. Yet his failure will, of course, be reversed by the justice of time and posterity, with the obvious implication that the same might happen to other, less gifted but still worthy aspirants to literary glory, such as the writer himself, 'fool that I am, myself, to fame, present, and posthumous' (vol. II, p. 274). True artistry thus unites in solidarity with his tragic life, which shows how suffering is strengthening: 'Genius may gain an additional, and propitious fire, from its determined, and heroick opposition to difficulties and distress', and can 'disappoint the triumphant, and satanick smile of envy'. This idea of triumph over adversity was evidently a solace to Stockdale in light of his own declining fortunes, but it tends to fetishise struggle and deprivation, as with his claim of a former friend: 'I have no doubt that Johnson was thus impelled, in the squalid, and solitary gloom of the temple; in his unprotected, unpensioned, unfashionable days; which were the days of his true dignity; of his true glory' (vol. II, pp. 531, 533), another attempt to celebrate the younger, authentic Samuel Johnson at the expense of the later success which supposedly corrupted his work. It is unlikely that the older Johnson would have agreed with him, and yearned for a return to the days of penury and endless struggle. But for Stockdale, the envisioning of such situations is a way of affirming his tireless faith in literature as an escape from life's inadequacies.

Stockdale's championing of Chatterton was in tune with the times, for it was during the years of composition of the *Lectures on the Truly Eminent English Poets* that the legend of Chatterton the genius destroyed by a heartless world was enshrined, not least by Coleridge's *Monody on the Death of Chatterton* and Wordsworth's *Resolution and Independence*.[10] This was a concomitant, in part, of the establishment of a cultural belief about genius that, whilst not invented by Romantic writers, came to its full prominence during that period. As Andrew Bennett has argued, it was 'by the early nineteenth century' that 'the figure of the neglected genius had become firmly established as a major, if contested element of poetics and aesthetics'. Moreover, 'by the mid-nineteenth century', and the full acceptance of Romantic tastes, assumptions 'concerning the contemporary neglect and posthumous recognition of the poet, were simply taken for granted'. The distinction, made often before, between lack of success in a lifetime, and the rediscovery of genius by a more understanding posterity, is thus turned into a norm, rather than an exception, in understanding the reception of works of art; as Bennett says, the 'Romantic period' is when 'a consensus develops regarding the nature of poets centred round textual survival, contemporary neglect, and the redemptive possibilities of a posthumous life'. In the most well-known texts of English Romantic poetics, the traditional distinction is repeatedly emphasised between two different kinds of poetic reception: an immediate and popular applause on the one hand, and an initial rejection of the artwork followed by more lasting and more worthwhile appreciation on the other.[11] It was not a distinction invented by Romantic poets, but rather inherited and popularised until it became an established cultural assumption that has (largely) remained embedded. In the Romantic period, Seward and Stockdale, eighteenth-century writers by inclination and taste, tried repeatedly to make this understanding of neglected genius a sort of imprimatur on their works, without much success. In some respects they tried too hard (Keats, after all, hoped to be among the English poets after his death, but did not yearn for such a fate on nearly every page of his correspondence). The laying out of their literary frustrations at such great and often tedious length meant that the reader became over-familiar with their claims. It was far easier to construct a myth of failed genius from the more fragmentary remains of Chatterton's life and work.

But another, far more significant if unwitting part played by Seward and Stockdale was that their works are part of the developing wider consciousness of failure, an attempt to explain away what an author knows to be the case, and at great length defend arguments that are already lost. The Romantic deification of neglected genius meant that there was a freedom in writing about an acknowledged lack of success, and that it could be done so self-consciously, in the knowledge that to place yourself as the sensitive victim of an unfeeling world was not in itself an embarrassment, but part of a wider cultural understanding of such cases. The often confessional writings of Hazlitt and De Quincey are obvious touchstones here. Yet the fact that both Stockdale's *Memoirs* and Seward's *Letters* appeared within two years of each other to a reception of amused condescension, disgust, and mockery suggests that even a literary world that was becoming more accepting of expressions of personal failings, and was able to transform them into something of grandeur and suffering, could not tolerate such lengthy self-justifications. It would seem that the development of neglected genius left no room for failure, unless it was the self-conscious creation of failure as an inherent part of autobiographical art, whereas Stockdale and Seward both attempted, more ingenuously, to simply state their cases. Once the tragedy of failure, and the inability to achieve became integral to understandings of the writings and lives of Byron, Keats, Shelley, and others, discussions of failure moved to a different level of critical consciousness, and writing about failure became an artistic mode in itself, leaving the protagonists of the present study behind, even if they contributed to this cultural shift, in different but significant ways.

Modern relativism, and the value of failure

The self-consciousness of literary failure as a genre has continued to follow the Romantic iconography of doomed genius, but in ways which have moved beyond the frustrations of a Stockdale or the belief in emotional and artistic nobility of a Richard Savage. Stockdale designed his writings as a defiant apologia for his talents, but by the twentieth century, it became acceptable to construct works entirely around your inability to achieve. In a recent introduction to a collection of extracts of writings connecting failure with modern and contemporary art, Lisa Le Feuvre makes this clear. Failure 'has been the source of a productive and generative drive since at least the first stirrings of the modernist era ... For an artist to place a work into the world is to lose control. What does refusal mean? Who are the arbiters of taste? Failure here becomes a pivotal term, rejected by one group, embraced by another.' Moreover, if 'failure is released from being a judgmental term, and success deemed overrated, the embrace of failure can become an act of bravery, of daring to go beyond normal practices and enter a realm of not-knowing'.[12] This is a long way from Stockdale's exhortations to posterity to reward him for his sufferings as a writer – in itself a plea for a sense of providence to right the wrongs of the sublunary world, just as the benevolent deity will reward Chatterton's earthly trials in the afterlife. Instead of a search for meaning and value that will give some purpose to a life otherwise spent in intellectual pursuits which have not been their own reward, failure has come to embody its own meaning, in a less evaluative critical world, through its very existence. This can be related to modern views of art as a process, possibly fragmentary and incomplete, rather than an organic unity, and the related shift in artistic temperament towards creation for its own sake, rather than coherence, given that expression of an envisaged artistic ideal is itself impossible. In terms of style, if not content, it is the world of Samuel Beckett rather than Samuel Johnson.

By contrast, for the eighteenth and early nineteenth centuries, the metaphysical side of literary failure represented a very real problem, a more general lack of closure and the inability to fulfil something lasting, concrete, and satisfying. Narratives of failure were both a moral warning, and a reminder of the general uncertainty of pretensions, artistic and otherwise. Walter Scott's perspective, with which this study began, was of the necessity of warding off the vanity and self-pity endemic to those who are obsessed with literary success, and fail to fulfil themselves – without it you could be doomed to a life, like Savage, Stockdale, and Seward, of always aspiring, but never remotely reaching the contentment or satisfaction that you desperately need. Failure is thus a *memento mori* for the literary career, at a time when the model of authorial fame is shifting: the eighteenth century saw writers increasingly measured economically, and often found wanting, in terms of material success, hence the need for the appreciation of posterity to compensate for the absence of fame in a lifetime.

To a general audience, cases of literary failure have encouraged both voyeurism and entertainment, but also no little pity at such self-generated ineffectuality, and the related blight of a life. To the literary historian, they have tended to be overlooked, treated mostly as curios, or evidence of sociological causation (the excesses and exigencies of authors), but their actual value is far more significant. They give a fuller and more striking representation of the idea of authorship – especially of the centrality of the allure of fame, and the impossibility of attaining it – than can often be found elsewhere. In the unread works of these mostly forgotten writers, and in the small, cumulative vexations and travails that record their lack of success, we are offered glimpses into a literary world that is both particular and universal: the inability of the artistic grasp to match the reach, and the wilful suspension of self-criticism will always be with us, but the subjects of this book illustrate such concepts with particular allure and vividness. Most importantly, they also dramatise a number of central debates and conflicts within the role and status of authorship in their own time and after.

To look at examples of literary failure is to introduce a new subculture of British literature, one that in some ways tells us more about the details and characteristics of literary history than the substantially smaller group of writers who succeed, and have been absorbed into regular critical attention. Such study also reconfigures the nature of literary fame, by stressing the ever-present number of those who could not have it, and by showing why this was often the case; moreover, the workings of literary reception do not become less arbitrary and more rational from such scrutiny, even when posterity's rejection of these writers is entirely explicable. The literary world of this book is one of near exponential growth of authorship, and such overproduction has been shown to be accompanied by the often delusive and self-destructive need for literary fame of those who could least understand why they were rejected by such a market. Lastly, the examples of this book explicitly show the different stages of the transformation of the idea of authorship towards a Romantic and post-Romantic mode (and cliché), where the genius of artistry is often necessarily at odds with their contemporary culture, and it is to be expected that posterity alone will recognise it. Such a shift is embryonic in the life (and bohemian example) of Savage, and the sentimental narrative of Dodd, and has started to be accepted by the time of the frustrated remonstrance of Seward and Stockdale.

Such posthumous significance would be little consolation to such seekers of the everlasting renown of literary fame, but to be such examples (albeit of your own lack of fulfilment) in the annals of literature is arguably a better fate than the utter obscurity of many writers, in all ages. On the other hand, the failed artist could wish to be forgotten, rather than illuminated only occasionally in comparison with the successful. Yet given that, in an existential sense, the satisfaction of vanity is all but impossible (and even posthumous fame will still come under examination and be open to question and re-evaluation), it is the only one that is on offer, and one that places failed writers in the distinguished ranks of those who do not feel that they have fulfilled themselves – a group encompassing many more categories than mere authors, and likely to be perpetually augmented, even as the terms by which they are understood change over the years.

Notes

Introduction: motion without progress

1 Sir Walter Scott, 'Introduction' to *Chronicles of the Canongate*, ed. Claire Lamont (Edinburgh University Press, 2000), p. 9. For discussions of the putative motives behind Scott's anonymity, see Seamus Cooney, 'Scott's Anonymity – Its Motives and Consequences', *Studies in Scottish Literature* 10 (1973), 207–19, and Claire Lamont, 'Walter Scott and the Unmasking of Harlequin', in *Authorship, Commerce and the Public: Scenes of Writing, 1750–1850*, ed. Emma Clery, Carolyn Franklin, and Peter Garside (Basingstoke: Palgrave Macmillan, 2002), pp. 54–66. An indication of the problems plaguing Scott and his associates at the time can be found in Edgar Johnson, *Sir Walter Scott: The Great Unknown*, 2 vols. (London: Hamilton, 1970), vol. II, pp. 1021–36.
2 *The Journal of Sir Walter Scott* (Edinburgh: David Douglas, 1891), 12 December 1827, p. 496.
3 Scott, 'Introduction' to *Chronicles of the Canongate*, pp. 9–10.
4 *The Cambridge Edition of the Works of Jonathan Swift*, vol. I, *A Tale of a Tub and Other Works*, ed. Marcus Walsh (Cambridge University Press, 2010), p. 23.
5 The general outline of Cowper's depression is well known, through a great deal of critical commentary. See James King, *William Cowper* (Durham, NC: Duke University Press, 1986), pp. 43–51, and 86–94, for bald outlines of his breakdowns of 1763 and 1773, and subsequent alienation. For a relation of Cowper's alienation and religious failure to the poetry of his final decade see Adam Rounce, 'Cowper's Ends', in *Romanticism and Millenarianism*, ed. Tim Fulford (Basingstoke: Palgrave, 2002), pp. 23–36.
6 As Sarah Jordan suggests, Cowper did not see himself as a professional writer, except for his Homer translations: writing was more often a means of distraction, or task given by God, which he usually failed to perform in his own estimation. *The Anxieties of Idleness* (Lewisburg, PA: Bucknell University Press, 2003), pp. 182, 187–90.
7 Martha Woodmansee, *The Author, Art, and the Market: Rereading the History of Aesthetics* (New York, NY: Columbia University Press, 1994), pp. 36, 37, part of a longer discussion on individual genius and its relationship to emergent ideas of copyright, as applicable to German culture (see pp. 35–55).

Notes to pages 10–15

8 Dustin Griffin, *Literary Patronage in England, 1650–1800* (Cambridge University Press, 1996), p. 10.
9 Brean S. Hammond, *Professional Imaginative Writing in England, 1670–1740: 'Hackney for Bread'* (Oxford: Clarendon Press, 1997), pp. 5, 23.
10 Mark Rose, *Authors and Owners: The Invention of Copyright* (Cambridge, MA: Harvard University Press, 1993), pp. 6, 118, 119. For a more local discussion of copyright and literary ownership in the mid-century, and the differing conceptions of Johnson and Young regarding such ownership, see Linda Zionkowski, 'Aesthetics, Copyright, and "The Goods of the Mind"', *British Journal for Eighteenth-Century Studies* 15 (1992), 163–74.
11 *Authors and Owners*, p. 119. Linda Zionkowski, 'Territorial Disputes in the Republic of Letters: Canon Formation and the Literary Profession', *The Eighteenth Century: Theory and Interpretation* 31 (1990), 3–22, pp. 4, 5.
12 'Territorial Disputes', pp. 13, 17.
13 Frank Donoghue, *The Fame Machine: Book Reviewing and Eighteenth-Century Literary Careers* (Palo Alto, CA: Stanford University Press, 1996), pp. 2, 17.
14 Pat Rogers, *Grub Street: Studies in a Subculture* (London: Methuen, 1972), p. 377. Rogers's investigation of the 'Grub Street myth' (pp. 363–404), and the misuse by later writers of the examples of Boyse and Savage, amongst others, is the most important modern account of the separation of failed authors from the conditions of their existence into legend.
15 'Samuel Boyse', in *The Lives of the Poets of Great Britain and Ireland*, ed. Theophilus Cibber, 5 vols. (London, 1753), vol. V, pp. 160–76, pp. 168–9. Written by Robert Shiels, this is the fullest account of Boyse's difficult career, and the model that was followed in abbreviated form in the *Annual Register for 1764* (1765), pp. 54–8, and elsewhere. It is possible that Shiels got information from Samuel Johnson, who confirmed to John Nichols that he had redeemed Boyse's clothes (Nichols, *Select Collection of Poems* (vol. VIII [1782], p. 288)). For more on the edition, see William R. Keast, 'Johnson and Cibber's *Lives of the Poets*, 1753', in *Restoration and Eighteenth-Century Literature*, ed. Carroll Camden (University of Chicago Press, 1963), pp. 89–101.
16 Hester Lynch Piozzi, *Anecdotes of the Late Samuel Johnson* (1786), in *Johnsonian Miscellanies*, ed. George Birkbeck Hill, 2 vols. (Oxford: Clarendon Press, 1897), vol. I, p. 228.
17 John Nichols, *Literary Anecdotes of the Eighteenth Century*, 9 vols. (London, 1812–16), vol. IX, p. 777.
18 Shiels, 'Samuel Boyse', p. 170, noting with outrage that the supposedly dying Boyse would run, somewhat inevitably, into his surprised acquaintances soon afterward. These details are also covered, disapprovingly, by Sir John Hawkins. See *The Life of Samuel Johnson*, ed. O M Brack Jr (University of Georgia Press, 2009), p. 160.
19 Shiels, 'Samuel Boyse', p. 166.
20 Rogers, *Grub Street*, p. 371.
21 David Hume, 'Of the Rise and Progress of the Arts and Sciences', in *Essays, Moral and Political*, 2 vols. (Edinburgh, 1742), vol. II, p. 97.

22 James Beattie, *Dissertations Moral and Critical* (Edinburgh, 1783), pp. 146, 148.
23 *The Life and Errors of John Dunton, Late Citizen of London, Written by Himself in Solitude* (London, 1705), p. 243.
24 *Dunton's Journal. Part I. or, The Whipping-Post: Being a Satyr upon Every Body* (London, 1706), pp. 32–3.
25 James Ralph, *The Case of Authors by Profession* (London, 1758), p. 71.
26 Robert W. Kenny, 'Ralph's *Case of Authors:* Its Influence on Goldsmith and Isaac D'Israeli', *Publications of the Modern Language Association* 52 (1937), 104–13, p. 109.
27 Oliver Goldsmith, *An Enquiry into the Present State of Polite Learning in Europe* (London, 1759), p. 2. Goldsmith's own position in the *Enquiry* is complicated by his own complaints about the sufferings of authorship, the most extreme of which were removed from the second edition of 1774. See the account by Donoghue in *The Fame Machine*, pp. 88–94.
28 'Preface' to *A Dictionary of the English Language* (1755), repr. in *The Yale Edition of the Works of Samuel Johnson*, vol. XVIII, *Johnson on the English Language*, ed. Gwin J. Kolb and Robert DeMaria Jr (New Haven, CT: Yale University Press, 2005), pp. 99–100.
29 'Preface' to the *Dictionary*, p. 100. *The Yale Edition of the Works of Samuel Johnson*, vol. XVI, *Rasselas and Other Tales*, ed. Gwin J. Kolb (New Haven, CT: Yale University Press, 1990), p. 109. Johnson's own perceived idleness is related by Sarah Jordan to the sense of mental (and spiritual) vacuity that 'Johnson mentions so often in his conversation and writings, which both lured and deeply terrified him', in a discussion of his 'very strong sense of the *misery* of idleness and its attendant boredom, a misery which seems to disturb him more than the sins boredom occasions' (*The Anxieties of Idleness*, pp. 154–5).
30 'Preface' to the *Dictionary*, p. 113.
31 Review (1757) of Soame Jenyns, *A Free Enquiry into the Nature and Origin of Evil*, repr. in *Johnson: Prose and Poetry*, ed. Mona Wilson (London: Hart-Davis, 1966), p. 365.
32 *Idler* 88, in *The Yale Edition of the Works of Samuel Johnson*, vol. II, *The Idler and The Adventurer*, ed. W. J. Bate, J. M. Bullitt, and L. F. Powell (New Haven, CT: Yale University Press, 1963), pp. 274–5.
33 'Preface' to *The Works of William Shakespeare*, in *The Yale Edition of the Works of Samuel Johnson*, vols. VII and VIII, *Johnson on Shakespeare*, ed. Arthur Sherbo (New Haven, CT: Yale University Press, 1969), vol. VII, p. 99.
34 Charlotte Lennox, *The Female Quixote*, ed. Margaret Dalziel (Oxford University Press, 1989), pp. 379, 380. On the question of the authorship of this Johnsonian chapter, I follow Duncan Isles, in his appendix to this edition, who suggests that there 'appears to be nothing in it that a good writer familiar with Johnson's style could not have achieved', but that Lennox was 'heavily influenced by his ideas and phraseology' (p. 422). For a more recent summary, see Susan Carlile and O M Brack Jr, 'Samuel Johnson's Contribution to Charlotte Lennox's *The Female Quixote*', *Yale University Library Gazette* 77 (2003), 166–73.

35 *Adventurer* 115, in *The Yale Edition of the Works of Samuel Johnson*, vol. II, *The Idler and The Adventurer*, ed. W. J. Bate, J. M. Bullitt, and L. F. Powell (New Haven, CT: Yale University Press, 1963), pp. 457, 458, 459.
36 Isaac D'Israeli, *An Essay on the Manners and Genius of the Literary Character* (London, 1795), p. 4.

1 An author to be let

1 *The Life of Mr. Richard Savage* (London, 1727), p. 3. The authorship of this pamphlet, written to support Savage after his conviction for murder, is conjectural; Clarence Tracy thinks it likely to have been written by Thomas Cooke, as well as Charles Beckingham (the latter identified by Johnson). See *The Artificial Bastard: A Biography of Richard Savage* (University of Toronto Press, 1953), pp. 90–1.
2 Samuel Johnson, *The Life of Savage*, ed. Clarence Tracy (Oxford: Clarendon Press, 1971), p. 140.
3 Theophilus Cibber, *The Lives of the Poets*, 5 vols. (London, 1753), vol. V, pp. 32–66, p. 32.
4 Much of the literature on Johnson's relationship with Savage supports Robert Folkenflik's conclusion that the *Life of Savage* is 'finer and richer than a merely tragic or satiric interpretation of Savage would be for its refusal to reduce Savage's life to either'. *Samuel Johnson, Biographer* (Ithaca, NY: Cornell University Press, 1978), p. 213. For a brief account of the effect and influence of Johnson's work, see Paul K. Alkon, 'The Intention and Reception of Johnson's *Life of Savage*', *Modern Philology* 72 (1974), 139–150.
5 Hawkins, *The Life of Samuel Johnson*, p. 33.
6 Tracy, *The Artificial Bastard*, p. vii.
7 The fullest account of the background to Savage's claims, including the affair between Lady Macclesfield and Earl Rivers, and Savage's alleged subsequent finding of his birthright, is in Tracy, *The Artificial Bastard*, pp. 9–27. The most recent is in Freya Johnston's excellent entry in the *Oxford Dictionary of National Biography*. For a brief, useful summary of the different versions, see Richard Holmes, *Dr Johnson & Mr Savage* (London: Hodder & Stoughton, 1993), pp. 233–5. The theory of unconscious imposture was first offered to Boswell by Francis Cockayne Cust (nephew of Lord Tyrconnel, and a descendant of Lady Macclesfield). See James Boswell, *Life of Johnson*, ed. George Birkbeck Hill, rev. and enlarged L. F. Powell, 6 vols. (Oxford: Clarendon Press, 1934–50), vol. I, p. 172; Tracy, *Artificial Bastard*, pp. 26–7; and Johnston, *ODNB*.
8 John A. Dussinger, '"The Solemn Magnificence of a Stupendous Ruin": Richard Savage, Poet Manqué', in *Fresh Reflections on Samuel Johnson*, ed. Prem Nath (New York, NY: Whitston Publishing, 1987), pp. 167–82, p. 167.
9 Tracy, *Artificial Bastard*, pp. 13, 30–1, quoting *Weekly Packet*, 5–12 November 1715, and James Sutherland in the *Times Literary Supplement*, 1 January 1938, p. 12.

10 Richard Savage, 'To the Right Honourable *George*, Lord Lansdown', Dedication to *Love in a Veil* (London, 1719), A2^{r-v}.
11 Tracy describes it as 'a bumbling piece of legislation' that 'created an artificial bastard by attaching the stigma of illegitimacy to a child born in wedlock, and deprived him by law of his natural right of inheritance' (*Artificial Bastard*, pp. 12–13). Despite the subsequent status of Lady Macclesfield after the divorce as Anne Brett, I continue to refer to her throughout this chapter by her former name (as did Savage and his supporters) to avoid confusion.
12 'Preface', *Miscellaneous Poems and Translations, by Several Hands, Published by Richard Savage, Son of the late Earl Rivers*, 1st edn (London, 1726), repr. in *The Poetical Works of Richard Savage*, ed. Clarence Tracy (Cambridge University Press, 1962), pp. 64, 63. All subsequent references to Savage's poems are from this edition, unless otherwise stated, and are cited as *Poetical Works*, with page reference. The preface was withdrawn, presumably at the instigation of Lady Macclesfield or her relations. See Tracy, *Artificial Bastard*, pp. 76–7. For the relationship between Savage and Hill's circle, see Christine Gerrard, *Aaron Hill: The Muses' Projector* (Oxford University Press, 2003), pp. 64–7, 93–100, where details support the suggestion that 'Savage benefited immeasurably from Hill's wide range of social contacts in the literary establishment' (p. 64).
13 Dustin Griffin, *Literary Patronage in England, 1650–1800* (Cambridge University Press, 1996), pp. 179–80.
14 For Savage's creation of himself as a writer, and the extent to which his whole career was an 'autobiographical enterprise', see Hal Gladfelder, 'The Hard Work of Doing Nothing: Richard Savage's Parallel Lives', *Modern Language Quarterly* 64 (2003), 445–72, p. 452, though in seeing Savage's self-fashioning as akin to that of a Wildean dandy or a playful post-modernist, Gladfelder underestimates the needs (both metaphysical and material) of Savage, and the undoubted pain and privations that he endured.
15 For the attribution and dating of these poems, see *Poetical Works*, pp. 15–16.
16 Christine Gerrard, *The Patriot Opposition to Walpole: Politics, Poetry, and National Myth, 1725–1742* (Oxford University Press, 1994), p. 234. Emotional Jacobitism is a useful concept because of the amount of times that, whilst not identifying directly with the Jacobite cause, Savage invokes it, usually with unconscious reference to his own career as akin to that of a prince in exile. An obvious example is his inveighing in his poem 'On False Historians' against the rumours of James II's child being smuggled into the bedchamber at birth, to frustrate Protestant hopes: 'Is a prince born? What birth more base believ'd? / Or, what's more strange, his mother ne'er conceiv'd' (*Poetical Works*, p. 241). This is more successful as an indirect reminder of the denial of Savage's own supposedly noble birth than as a critique of trends of historicism.
17 See Tracy, *Artificial Bastard*, pp. 3–4, 53.
18 'Verses Sent to Aaron Hill, Esq. with the *Tragedy of Sir Thomas Overbury*, Expecting Him to Correct it', *Poetical Works*, pp. 47–8. Theophilus Cibber also had a hand in revising the play, as Savage admitted in his inimical fashion:

Notes to pages 37–50

according to Johnson, Savage had to 'admit, with whatever Reluctance, the Emendations of Mr. *Cibber*, which he always considered as the disgrace of his Performance' (*Life*, p. 22).
19 Richard Savage, *Sir Thomas Overbury: A Tragedy*, in *The Works of Richard Savage*, 2 vols. (London 1777), vol. I, p. 155. All other page references are to this edition. Tracy, *Artificial Bastard*, pp. 50, 51.
20 *Life*, p. 10. The alleged kidnapping is also mentioned in the section dealing with Rivers and Lady Macclesfield in Eliza Haywood's sensationalised *roman à clef*, *Memoirs of a Certain Island* (London, 1724), pp. 157–87. For the misogynistic depictions of his mother by Savage and Johnson (and a suggestive association between bastardry and writing), see Felicity Nussbaum, *Torrid Zones: Maternity, Sexuality, and Empire in Eighteenth-Century English Narratives* (Baltimore, MD: Johns Hopkins University Press, 1995), pp. 53–66.
21 '*The* PICTURE. *To Mr* DYER, *when in the Country*', *Poetical Works*, p. 57.
22 James L. Clifford, *Young Samuel Johnson* (London: Heinemann, 1955), p. 201.
23 See Johnson, *Life*, pp. 21–2, where he concludes that the imperfections of the play therefore 'must rather excite Pity than provoke Censure'.
24 Griffin, *Literary Patronage*, pp. 169, 170, 174, 177, 182, 184.
25 For the poem's background, see Tracy, *Artificial Bastard*, p. 81. He points out the typical unfortunate error made by Savage, who 'had been clumsy enough to link the names of George I and George II, who, as everybody knew, hated each other'.
26 See the highly partial accounts in the *Life* of 1727, and Johnson (*Life*, pp. 30–8), and the more forensic readings of Tracy (*Artificial Bastard*, pp. 82–93), and Richard Holmes (*Dr Johnson and Mr Savage*, pp. 100–32).
27 Tracy, *Artificial Bastard*, p. 88.
28 See Tracy, *Artificial Bastard*, pp. 93, 95–6, for external evidence of such a break between Tyrconnel and Lady Macclesfield, and the unlikelihood of Tyrconnel's patronage being dependent on Savage keeping quiet about his claim after the publication of 'The Bastard', as had been argued by Johnson, *Life*, p. 44, and more recently by Holmes, *Dr Johnson and Mr Savage*, pp. 136–9.
29 This letter shows why Savage has always attracted attention as more of a spectacle than a writer: addressed to the '*Right Honourable* BRUTE, *and* BOOBY', it ends 'I defy and despise you. I am, your determined adversary, R.S.' It was passed on by Francis Cockayne Cust to Boswell, who was the first to print it. *Life of Johnson*, vol. I, p. 161.
30 Dussinger, '"The Solemn Magnificence of a Stupendous Ruin"', p. 170.
31 Dussinger, '"The Solemn Magnificence of a Stupendous Ruin"', p. 174. Tracy finds other moments (such as the bard in Canto III who has been cheated of an inheritance) where Savage's experience is writ large in the poem. *Artificial Bastard*, pp. 99–100.
32 Tracy, *Artificial Bastard*, p. 103.
33 For Savage's helping Pope, see Johnson, *Life*, pp. 50–1, and Tracy, *Artificial Bastard*, pp. 105–8. Two years later, *The Grub-Street Journal* advertised the

second part of *An Author to be Lett*, which never appeared. It was revised and enlarged when reprinted in *A Collection of Pieces in Verse and Prose, Which have been Publish'd on Occasion of the DUNCIAD* (London, 1731), a collection which Tracy thinks that Savage might have edited (*Artificial Bastard*, pp. 108, 110).

34 Richard Savage, *An Author to be Lett* (London, 1729), A2^v, italics reversed.
35 *The Yale Edition of the Works of Samuel Johnson*, vol. VI, *Poems*, ed. E. J. McAdam and George Milne (New Haven, CT: Yale University Press, 1964), p. 56. The headnote (p. 47) explains the difficulty of identifying Thales in *London* with Savage, given that Johnson's version of Juvenal predates any intention of Savage to leave London (p. 47); see also Thomas Kaminski, 'Was Savage "Thales"?' *Bulletin of Research for the Humanities* 85 (1982), 322–35. Richard Holmes is convinced of the identification, despite the evidence to the contrary (*Dr Johnson and Mr Savage*, pp. 177–83).
36 Tracy, *Artificial Bastard*, p. 115. A similar suggestion was made by Hal Gladfelder: 'Savage's ridicule for his subject's poverty and criminal entanglements seems almost pathological in light of Hackney's close resemblance to his author.' See 'The Hard Work of Doing Nothing: Richard Savage's Parallel Lives', *Modern Language Quarterly* 64 (2003), 445–72, p. 460.
37 Gladfelder, 'The Hard Work of Doing Nothing', p. 468.
38 *Life*, p. 103. Savage's arrangements with publishers were, unsurprisingly, not of the ordinary. Tracy describes how Savage's poems were published simultaneously in both *The London Magazine* and *The Gentleman's Magazine* in the 1730s, in (he speculates) a drive by the editors for publicity for the chimerical collected edition. *Artificial Bastard*, p. 121.
39 *Life*, p. 61. See pp. 59–62 for Johnson's patient summary of the failure of the relationship; Tracy suggests that the 'real cause' was Savage's 'electioneering in the interest of Tyrconnel's political opponents' (*Artificial Bastard*, p. 130). Savage remembered Tyrconnel's supposed ingratitude towards him enough to blot out his compliments to him in his own copy of *The Wanderer*.
40 Steven D. Scherwatzky, '"Complicated Virtue": The Politics of Samuel Johnson's *Life of Savage*', *Eighteenth-Century Life* 25 (2001), 80–93, p. 84.
41 *Life*, p. 86. For a summary of the original dispute which supposedly inspired the poem, see Tracy's note to *Life*, p. 84, and *Artificial Bastard*, pp. 127–9, where he traces the origins of Savage's 'immoderate and ill-advised attack' on Edmund Gibson, Bishop of London (p. 127).
42 See Tracy, *Artificial Bastard*, pp. 124–5, for the poem's background. It is indeed, as he says, remarkable (and lucky for Savage) that Queen Caroline kept his annuity after the poem dedicated to her son appeared.
43 In a letter to Thomas Birch (BL Sloane MS 4318) of September 1738 describing his being struck off the pension list after the Queen's death, a postscript hopes Birch has not forgotten to lend Elizabeth Carter *An Author to be Lett*. Savage also sent her an annotated copy of the anonymous 1727 *Life* in 1739. For this unlikely friendship, see Tracy, *Artificial Bastard*, pp. 135–6.

44 *Life*, p. 113. Johnson also notes that Savage thought the letter would be used against him by Lady Macclesfield's relatives in future, particularly in hypothetical reply to his planned (but never written) 'Account of the Treatment he had received' from them (p. 114).
45 Letter of 18 May 1739, in *The Correspondence of Alexander Pope*, ed. George Sherburn, 5 vols. (Oxford: Clarendon Press, 1956), vol. IV, p. 180.
46 See Johnson, *Life*, pp. 110–11. Savage began the revisions to *Overbury*, but the script was unfinished at his death. See Tracy, *Artificial Bastard*, pp. 143–4.
47 Tracy, *Artificial Bastard*, p. 133. See also Pope's letter on Savage's misplaced independence, of 17 December 1739 (*Correspondence*, vol. IV, p. 210).
48 *Life*, p. 116. Savage's anger at the '*Perfidiousness*' of the subscribers led him to imagine that they planned to exploit the profits of the revised *Overbury* behind his back; this ludicrous suggestion and his wider conduct led almost all of them but Pope to discontinue their support. See Tracy, *Artificial Bastard*, p. 144, and Pope's exasperated letter to Savage: 'What Mortal would take your Play, or your business with Lord T. out of your hands, if you could come and attend it yourself?' (15 September 1742, *Correspondence*, vol. IV, p. 418).
49 Writing to Allen (December 1742), Pope was 'vexed at this wrongheaded fool' (*Correspondence*, vol. IV, p. 431). Later that month he tells the same correspondent that he is made 'peevish' by 'Savage's strange behaviour', but still was 'in haste to relieve him, tho I think nothing will relieve him' (27 December 1742, *Correspondence*, vol. IV, p. 433).
50 *The Gentleman's Magazine* XII (1742), p. 597.
51 Johnson describes his descent into penury (*Life*, pp. 119–20), and his lodging 'in the Garret of an obscure Inn' (p. 120). As a posthumous account of Savage's time in Bristol recorded, this was the White Lion on St Thomas Street, significantly beyond Bristol Bridge and the city boundaries, thus leaving him beyond the powers of the bailiffs. *The Gentleman's Magazine* LVII (1787), pp. 1040–1.
52 *Life*, p. 124. Johnson proposes that the refusal indicated that Savage 'thought he had been before too burthensome to him'; Tracy, that it shows Savage again 'drawing that fine line between acceptable and unacceptable charities' (*Artificial Bastard*, p. 149). It is also possible that, in a strange way, Savage liked imprisonment: it appealed to his desire for spectacle and his sense that the martyrdom involved was a form of self-justification.
53 Bristol's Newgate Prison was on the spot now home to The Galleries shopping centre (a location that seems all too appropriate for confinement). A plaque on the Union Street entrance marks Savage's death.
54 Letter to Mr Strong, 19 June 1743, *The Gentleman's Magazine* LVII (1787), p. 1040. Abel Dagge was the keeper of Newgate.
55 Letter of 19 June 1743, *The Gentleman's Magazine* LVII (1787), p. 1040.
56 *The Gentleman's Magazine* LVII (1787), p. 1041.

Notes to pages 69–73

2 The exemplary failure of Dr Dodd

1 Sir John Hawkins, *The Life of Samuel Johnson*, p. 355. The potential thief was George Steevens. See Michael Bundock, 'Did John Hawkins Steal Johnson's Diary?', *Age of Johnson* 21 (2012), 77–92, for the most objective analysis of the episode.
2 Richard Porson, *A Panegyrical Epistle on Hawkins v. Johnson* (1787), repr. in *Johnsonian Miscellanies*, vol. II, p. 131.
3 Boswell, *Life of Johnson*, vol. III, p. 167.
4 'Histories of the Tête-à-Tête annex'd', *The Town and Country Magazine* V (1773), p. 681. Henrietta Battier, 'An Elegy on the Unfortunate Dr Dodd', in *The Protected Fugitives: A Collection of Miscellaneous Poems* (Dublin, 1791), p. 169.
5 Paul Baines, *The House of Forgery in Eighteenth-Century Britain* (Aldershot: Ashgate, 1999), p. 130.
6 The frequency of reprints of Dodd's most popular works (leaving aside other volumes and anthologies) after his death into the twentieth century is striking: of his anthologies, *The Beauties of Shakespear* ran to thirty-two editions, *Reflections on Death* to twenty-six, and *Thoughts in Prison* to twenty-nine. See A. D. Barker, 'Samuel Johnson and the Campaign to Save William Dodd', *Harvard Library Bulletin* 31 (1983), 147–80, p. 147.
7 John Nichols, *Literary Anecdotes of the Eighteenth Century*, 9 vols. (London, 1812–16), vol. II, p. 381.
8 A. D. Barker, 'The Early Career of William Dodd', *Transactions of the Cambridge Bibliographical Society* 8 (1982), 217–35, p. 220.
9 William Dodd, *Poems* (London, 1767), p. 13. All further references are to this edition, unless otherwise stated.
10 Gerald Howson, *The Macaroni Parson: The Life of the Unfortunate Dr Dodd* (London: Hutchinson, 1973), p. 48.
11 For this edition, see the discussions in Simon Jarvis, *Scholars and Gentlemen: Shakespearean Textual Criticism and Representations of Scholarly Labour, 1725–1765* (Oxford: Clarendon Press, 1995), pp. 107–28; Marcus Walsh, *Shakespeare, Milton, and Eighteenth-Century Literary Editing* (Cambridge University Press, 1997), pp. 149–65; and Adam Rounce, '"A Clamour Too Loud to be Distinct": William Warburton's Literary Squabbles', *Age of Johnson* 16 (2005), 199–217.
12 *A New Book of the Dunciad* (London, 1750), pp. 1–2.
13 Warburton suggested changing the speech at the opening of *1 Henry IV* from 'No more the thirsty entrance of this soil / Shall damp her lips' to 'trempe her lips' ('This nonsense should be read *Shall* TREMPE, *i.e.* moisten'). *The Works of William Shakespeare*, ed. William Warburton, 8 vols. (London, 1747), vol. IV, p. 97. Johnson quoted and refuted Warburton's own 'nonsense' in his edition. See *The Plays of William Shakespeare*, ed. Samuel Johnson, 8 vols. (London, 1765), vol. IV, p. 110. To 'narrify' was a conjecture of Warburton's for *Coriolanus* (*Works*, vol. VI, p. 541).

Notes to pages 74–83

14 Details of Dodd's time in London, plays, marriage, and trouble with his father come from his old college friend John Duncombe's *Historical Memoirs of the Life and Writings of the Late Rev. William Dodd* (London, 1777), pp. 4–7.
15 Barker, 'Samuel Johnson and the Campaign to Save William Dodd', p. 147.
16 Edwin E. Willoughby, 'A Deadly Edition of Shakespeare', *Shakespeare Quarterly* 5 (1954), 351–7, pp. 351–2. 'The Unfortunate Dr. Dodd', *Essays by Divers Hands* XXIX (1958), 124–43, p. 126. Howson, *Macaroni Parson*, p. 33.
17 William Dodd, *The Beauties of Shakespear*, 2 vols. (London, 1752), vol. I, p. vii.
18 Dodd quotes Act 1, Scene 2, ll. 100–11, 'For once, upon a raw and gusty day, . . . Caesar cried, 'Help me, Cassius, or I sink!' I have adjusted the text and scene to that in the Arden Shakespeare's *Julius Caesar*, ed. David Daniell (London: Methuen, 1998), pp. 169–70.
19 Percy Fitzgerald, *A Famous Forgery: Being the Story of "the Unfortunate" Doctor Dodd* (London: Chapman and Hall, 1865), p. 15. Barker, 'The Early Career of William Dodd', p. 226. Howson, *Macaroni Parson*, p. 40.
20 *The Sisters: or, the History of Lucy and Caroline Sanson, Entrusted to a False Friend*, 2 vols. (London, 1754), vol. I, p. iii.
21 Henry Fielding, *The History of Tom Jones, A Foundling. The Wesleyan Edition of the Works of Henry Fielding*, ed. Fredson Bowers and Martin C. Battestin (Middletown, CT: Wesleyan University Press, 1975), Book VII, Chapter 6, p. 346.
22 Compare 'She set her huge arms a-kembo: *Hoh*! Madam, let me tell you, I am amazed at your freedoms with my character!' Samuel Richardson, *Clarissa, or, The History of a Young Lady*, ed. Angus Ross (Harmondsworth: Penguin, 1985), Letter 256, p. 882.
23 See Howson, *Macaroni Parson*, pp. 72–4, who surmises that Dodd hoped to get the then five-year-old Prince of Wales in attendance, thus encouraging his own hopes of gaining a tutorship in the royal household; four pews were reserved for the Queen and her retinue. Dodd relinquished the Chapel in 1776, at the height of his financial problems.
24 Charlotte Papendick, *The Court and Private Life of Queen Charlotte*, 2 vols. (London, 1887), vol. I, p. 81, quoted in Willoughby, 'The Unfortunate Dr. Dodd', p. 133. Papendick would be one of the many who visited Dodd's cell as a shrine after his death, kissing the furniture where he wrote his last words. See Howson, *Macaroni Parson*, p. 227.
25 *The Correspondence of Horace Walpole*, ed. W. S. Lewis *et al.*, 48 vols. (New Haven, CT: Yale University Press, 1937–83), vol. IX, p. 274.
26 Barker, 'The Early Career of William Dodd', p. 219, 'Samuel Johnson and the Campaign to Save William Dodd', p. 155. *Thoughts of a Citizen of London on the Conduct of Dr. Dodd* (London, 1777), p. 31.
27 *The Christian Magazine*, June 1760, quoted in Duncombe, *Historical Memoirs*, pp. 11–12.
28 Duncombe, *Historical Memoirs*, p. 12. For Dodd's later review of his own poems, see Howson, *Macaroni Parson*, p. 60.

218   *Notes to pages 84–91*

29 William Dodd, *Reflections on Death*, 5th edn (London, 1777), 'Advertisement', A4ʳ (italics reversed). *The Monthly Review* XXVII (April 1763), pp. 311–12, quoted in Barker, 'Samuel Johnson and the Campaign to Save William Dodd', p. 147.
30 William Dodd, *Reflections on Death* (London, 1763), p. 166.
31 Isaac Reed, *An Impartial Account of the Life and Writings of Dr William Dodd* (London, 1777), pp. 46–7.
32 *Poems*, A1ʳ, p. 10.
33 *A Famous Forgery*, pp. 59–60.
34 *A Famous Forgery*, p. 61. The identification is by Fitzgerald, pp. 23–4.
35 *A Famous Forgery*, p. 36.
36 'Histories of the Tête-à-Tête annex'd', *The Town and Country Magazine* V (1773), pp. 681, 682–3, 683. For Fitzgerald's identification, see *A Famous Forgery*, p. 95.
37 Horace Walpole, *Last Journals*, 2 vols. (London: Bodley Head, 1910), vol. I, p. 285. Dodd had been a critic of Methodism since the 1750s. He corresponded with John Wesley in 1763, and published a sermon, *Caution Against Methodism, or Unity Recommended*, which Wesley refuted two years later. This did not stop Wesley visiting Dodd twice in prison. See Howson, *Macaroni Parson*, pp. 52–5, 136, 137.
38 Duncombe, *Historical Memoirs*, pp. 40–1. Howson (*Macaroni Parson*, pp. 97–8) estimates the annual worth of St George's at £1,500, and points out that Dodd had recently taken a house in Mayfair, and was (according to the gossip of *The Town and Country Magazine*) besieged by creditors.
39 Walpole, to Lady Ossory, 29 January 1774, *The Correspondence of Horace Walpole*, vol. XXXII, p. 185. Innuendoes concerning Dodd and women were not new: in 1764, in his satire *The Times*, Charles Churchill had mockingly described how 'to Wellclose-square' (in the vicinity of the Magdalen Chapel) 'Fine fresh young strumpets (for Dodd preaches there) / Flock for subsistence'. *The Poetical Works of Charles Churchill*, ed. Douglas Grant (Oxford: Clarendon Press, 1956), p. 356.
40 Duncombe, *Historical Memoirs*, p. 42. Reed, *Impartial Account*, pp. 41–2. For a tangled and unlikely version of the affair offered by Dodd in the aftermath, see Howson, *Macaroni Parson*, p. 99.
41 Samuel Foote, *The Cozeners* (London, 1774), p. 24.
42 Howson, *Macaroni Parson*, pp. 104, 105. Howson claims that this was after Dodd had left Chesterfield in 1774 (and was therefore gambling away the money the Earl had given him) but offers no source. The obituary in *The Town and Country Magazine* IX (July 1777) places the event later: 'it is certain he visited Paris last summer' (that is, 1776), where 'he made a very gay appearance, and was particularly conspicuous at the horse races upon the *Plaine de Sablons*' (pp. 374–5).
43 Reed, *Impartial Account*, pp. 49–50. Barker, 'The Early Career of William Dodd', p. 229. For specific analysis of Dodd's annotated copy of Shakespeare, see Willoughby, 'A Deadly Edition of Shakespeare', pp. 355–6 (though

Notes to pages 91–3

Willoughby was the only modern critic to believe in the Shakespeare edition as a probability – see 'The Unfortunate Dr. Dodd', p. 137). Isaac Reed remarked that 'A writer in the Gentleman's Magazine for April' claimed to have 'seen various printed sheets of this intended edition of Shakespeare, with specimens of the type in which the work was to have been executed' (*Impartial Account*, p. 108). So did another correspondent: see *The Gentleman's Magazine* XLVII (1777), pp. 116, 172. Barker suggests, very plausibly, that these were at best samples for a possible subscription ('Early Career', p. 229). Dodd's general need for funds at this point is also signalled by his advertising a proposal for a subscription for a history of free-masonry. See Willoughby, 'A Deadly Edition', p. 353.

44 *The Town and Country Magazine* IX (July 1777), p. 375.
45 Willoughby, 'The Unfortunate Dr. Dodd', p. 135. John J. Burke has calculated this as being analogous to $500,000 (at the rate of 1991), and makes the germane comparison with Johnson, who managed to support himself and his tribe of mendicants on a pension of £300, and that only after 1762. See 'Crime and Punishment in 1777: The Execution of the Reverend Dr. William Dodd and Its Impact upon His Contemporaries', in *Executions and the British Experience from the Seventeenth to the Twentieth Century*, ed. William B. Thesing (Folkestone: Macfarland, 1991), pp. 59–75, pp. 62, 73.
46 *Macaroni Parson*, p. 110. Howson calculates that, given the average life expectancy of a further thirty-three years for Chesterfield, the annuity and interest would (unless the lump sum was paid back) have raised £23,100 in repayment.
47 Barker, 'Samuel Johnson and the Campaign to Save William Dodd', p. 151. This is the most succinct account, though there are important additional details in Howson, *Macaroni Parson*, pp. 108–21.
48 *Old Bailey Proceedings Online* (www.oldbaileyonline.org), ref. T17770219-1, 19 February 1777.
49 Barker, 'Samuel Johnson and the Campaign to Save William Dodd', p. 152. It was at this time that Manley is supposed to have left Dodd alone with the bond, and thus presented an obvious opportunity for him to throw it into the fire. See Howson, *Macaroni Parson*, pp. 117–18.
50 See Howson's narrative, compiled from the reports, in *Macaroni Parson*, pp. 118–21. Fitzgerald describes the 'odious' celebrity with which Chesterfield enjoyed having 'hung a parson' (*A Famous Forgery*, p. 108).
51 Baines, *The House of Forgery*, p. 126.
52 Robert Anderson, *The Life of Samuel Johnson* (London, 1795), p. 364.
53 Barker, 'Samuel Johnson and the Campaign to Save William Dodd', p. 152. For Manley's deception, see Howson, *Macaroni Parson*, pp. 141–3, 150–1.
54 The details of Dodd's trial were widely reported and published. I have quoted from the *Old Bailey Proceedings Online* (www.oldbaileyonline.org), February 1777, trial of William Dodd (T17770219-1), and, of the many print sources, William Jackson, *The New and Complete Newgate Calendar*, 6 vols. (London, 1795), vol. V, p. 216.

55 Fitzgerald, *A Famous Forgery*, p. 119.
56 A report on this is in *The Gentleman's Magazine* XLVII (April 1777), p. 193. See *Newgate Calendar*, vol. v, pp. 218–19, and Howson, *Macaroni Parson*, pp. 151, 177, for the extraordinarily high-handed manner in which the tribunal treated the legal problem. The question of Robertson's evidence was submerged beneath the general appeal for clemency, but it remains shocking how little equity Dodd received, not least in the light of his social position and relative celebrity.
57 Fitzgerald describes how the jury wanted clemency, and presented a petition as soon as sentence had been passed (*A Famous Forgery*, p. 133). Barker, drawing on the *Memoirs* of Sir Nathaniel Wraxall, has an excellent description of the King's meeting with the Privy Council, and Mansfield's intransigence ('Samuel Johnson and the Campaign to Save William Dodd', p. 165).
58 *Old Bailey Proceedings Online*, T17770219-1. *Newgate Calendar*, vol. v, p. 220.
59 A good summary of the coverage can be found in Baines, *The House of Forgery*, pp. 135–6.
60 *The Malefactor's Register, or, the Newgate and Tyburn Calendar*, 5 vols. (London, 1779), vol. v, pp. 224–5.
61 Walpole, *Last Journals*, vol. I, p. 285, vol. II, pp. 32, 33, 34.
62 *Last Journals*, vol. II, p. 34. Dodd had written a brief introduction to *A Familiar Explanation of the Poetical Works of Milton* (London, 1762), a glossary that utilises the notes from Newton's popular 1749 edition of *Paradise Lost*.
63 Hawkins, *The Life of Samuel Johnson*, p. 312. Hawkins also gives an account of Dodd's fecklessness and promiscuity, gained through his acquaintance with Dodd's brother-in-law, who 'rented some land of me' (p. 261). Fitzgerald mentions the story, with no other source (*A Famous Forgery*, p. 47). No record of this relation has been located, to my knowledge; I am grateful to O M Brack Jr, the scholarly authority on Hawkins, for confirming this absence in correspondence.
64 Hawkins, *Life*, p. 313. Fitzgerald, *A Famous Forgery*, p. 2.
65 *Papers Written by Dr. Johnson and Dr. Dodd in 1777*, ed. R. W. Chapman (Oxford: Clarendon Press, 1926), p. xiv.
66 Boswell, *Life of Johnson*, vol. III, p. 141. Johnson's motives have been much discussed; Walter Jackson Bate's psychoanalytic approach related Johnson's attitude in the episode to the 'mysterious disgrace Johnson's brother, Nathaniel, had brought on himself (*Samuel Johnson* (London: Hogarth, 1984), p. 524). What happened to Johnson's brother is likely to remain obscure, but it has often been inferred that his death (which could have been suicide) followed an episode in which Nathaniel seems to have been guilty of some sort of financial misdemeanour, such as forgery. The more pragmatic view is offered by Robert DeMaria: 'Dodd's situation was for Johnson an image of the human condition, and he used appeals to morality like those in his other sermons and the *Rambler*.' *The Life of Samuel Johnson* (Oxford: Blackwell, 1994), p. 277.

67 Anderson, *Life of Johnson*, p. 365.
68 Johnson, letter to Charles Jenkinson, Friday 20 June 1777, and letter to Lady Harrington, Wednesday 25 June 1777. *The Letters of Samuel Johnson*, ed. Bruce Redford, 5 vols. (Oxford: Clarendon Press, 1992), vol. III, pp. 29, 32.
69 For the petition, see Fitzgerald, *A Famous Forgery*, p. 135, and Howson, *Macaroni Parson*, p. 209. Johnson's text is from the draft of 'The Petition of the City of London to His Majesty, in Favour of Dr. Dodd', in Boswell, *Life of Johnson*, vol. III, p. 143.
70 Johnson, letter to William Dodd, Thursday 26 June 1777, *Letters*, vol. III, p. 33.
71 Johnson, letter to James Boswell, Saturday 28 June 1777, *Letters*, vol. III, p. 35.
72 Boswell, *Life of Johnson*, vol. IV, pp. 208–9.
73 *Thoughts of a Citizen of London on the Conduct of Dr. Dodd* (London, 1777), p. 24.
74 Baines, *The House of Forgery*, p. 141.
75 The Countess's peculiar letter is quoted at length in the *Thoughts of a Citizen of London*, pp. 38–9. Letter of 20 July 1777, in *Letters from Elizabeth Carter to Mrs Montagu*, ed. William Pennington, 3 vols. (London: Rivington, 1817), vol. III, pp. 27, 26–7.
76 Howson, *Macaroni Parson*, p. 203, quoting from John Taylor, *Records of My Life*, 2 vols. (London, 1832), vol. II, pp. 250–1.
77 Butler would later write indignantly to disprove claims that the poem was written by Johnson, producing the manuscript. See *The Gentleman's Magazine* LXIII (March 1793), pp. 233–4, and Baines, *The House of Forgery*, pp. 139–40.
78 William Dodd, *Thoughts in Prison* (London, 1777), 'Advertisement', p. i.
79 Howson, *Macaroni Parson*, p. 160. Barker, 'Early Career', pp. 217, 218. Fitzgerald, *A Famous Forgery*, pp. 124, 125.
80 *Thoughts in Prison*, p. 6. The correct reference is to *Paradise Lost*, Book V, l. 543 (though the counting here is by tens of lines, as was common in the eighteenth century). It is of course possible that Weedon Butler added the footnotes, though he showed little inclination to make such additions in his other works for Dodd; nor does this alter the incongruity of the references in this context. For Fitzgerald's comment, see *A Famous Forgery*, p. 125.
81 Boswell, *Life of Johnson*, vol. III, p. 270.
82 *The Adventures of a Hackney Coach* (London, 1781), p. 196. This popular novel has been attributed to Dorothy Kilner. See Freya Johnston, 'Little Lives: An Eighteenth-Century Sub-Genre', *Cambridge Quarterly* 32 (2003), 143–60, pp. 143, 144.
83 *The Memoirs of Sir Philip Thicknesse*, 3 vols. (Dublin, 1788–91), vol. I, pp. 221–2.
84 Walpole, *Last Journals*, vol. II, p. 32.
85 John Villette, *A Genuine Account of the Behaviour and Dying Words of William Dodd* (London, 1777), pp. 17, 18.
86 Letter to Selwyn by Anthony Morris Storer, in J. H. Jesse, *George Selwyn and His Contemporaries*, 3 vols. (London, 1901), vol. III, pp. 197–8.

87 Walpole, *Last Journals*, vol. II, p. 36.
88 Fitzgerald, writing relatively soon after, described how the story was 'worked into an effective Surrey melodrama, not many years back ... the Doctor's tastes for dissipation afforded an opportunity of introducing Ranelagh and other effective scenes of amusement. "Doctor Dodd" had a long run.' *A Famous Forgery*, p. 245.

3 Anna Seward's cruel times

1 *Letters of Anna Seward, Written Between the Years 1784 and 1807*, 6 vols. (Edinburgh: Constable, 1811), vol. I, p. 66. Hereafter cited as *Letters*, with volume and page number.
2 *The Journals and Correspondence of Thomas Sedgwick Whalley, D. D.*, ed. Hill Wickham, 2 vols. (London: Richard Bentley, 1863), vol. I, p. 348.
3 Norma Clarke, 'Anna Seward: Swan, Duckling or Goose?', in *British Women's Writing in the Long Eighteenth Century: Authorship, Politics and History*, ed. Jennie Batchelor and Cora Kaplan (Basingstoke: Palgrave Macmillan, 2005), pp. 34–47, p. 41. *The Rise and Fall of the Woman of Letters* (London: Pimlico, 2004), p. 10.
4 *The Autobiography, Time, Opinions, and Contemporaries of Sir Egerton Brydges, Bart.*, 2 vols. (London: Cochrane and M'Crone, 1834), vol. I, p. 57.
5 Samuel Holt Monk, 'Anna Seward and the Romantic Poets: A Study in Taste', in *Wordsworth and Coleridge: Studies in Honour of George McLean Harper*, ed. Earl Leslie Griggs (Princeton University Press, 1939), pp. 118–34, pp. 118, 121, 119, 120, 122, 123.
6 Clarke, 'Swan, Duckling or Goose?', pp. 35, 37, 38. *Rise and Fall*, p. 12. John Brewer, *The Pleasures of the Imagination: English Culture in the Eighteenth Century* (London: HarperCollins, 1997), p. 589.
7 Teresa Barnard, *Anna Seward: A Constructed Life, A Critical Biography* (Aldershot: Ashgate, 2009), p. 3. Although the present chapter disagrees with Barnard about the level of Seward's achievement and the degree to which censorship damaged it, this is a valuably detailed study of critical sympathy.
8 Claudia Thomas Kairoff, *Anna Seward and the End of the Eighteenth Century* (Baltimore, MD: Johns Hopkins University Press, 2012), pp. 1, 3, x.
9 Clarke, *Rise and Fall*, pp. 18, 12, 17. 'Swan, Duckling or Goose?', p. 37. Seward left Constable, the publisher, with twelve volumes of letters, adding that 'voluminous as is the collection, it does not include a twelfth part of my epistolary writing' (*Letters*, vol. I, pp. v–vi). On being asked in 1811 if he had read her *Letters*, Scott remembered his Shakespeare: 'God knows I had enough of them when she lived, for she did not imitate the ancient Romans in brevity.' *The Letters of Sir Walter Scott*, ed. Herbert Grierson, 12 vols. (London: Constable, 1932), vol. III, p. 17.
10 James L. Clifford, 'The Authenticity of Anna Seward's Published Correspondence', *Modern Philology* 39 (1941), 113–22, p. 113.

Notes to pages 113–21 223

11 Clifford, 'Authenticity', pp. 115, 119. The published version appeared in *Letters*, vol. II, pp. 39–46.
12 Seward later remarks again how Piozzi has managed to 'extract almost all the corrosive particles from the old growler's letters' and on the 'care with which Mrs Piozzi weeded them of the prejudicial and malevolent passages' (*Letters*, vol. II, pp. 102, 346), amongst the very frequent animadversions on Johnson in her correspondence.
13 Clarke, *Rise and Fall*, p. 51. Brewer, *Pleasures*, p. 604.
14 *The Poetical Works of Anna Seward*, ed. Walter Scott, 3 vols. (Edinburgh: Ballantyne, 1810), vol. I, p. xxxv.
15 For Jane West and Bishop Percy see *Illustrations of the Literary History of the Eighteenth Century*, ed. John Nichols, 8 vols. (London, 1817–58), vol. VIII, pp. 427–32. Brydges, *Autobiography*, vol. I, p. 57. Clarke, 'Swan, Duckling or Goose?', p. 37. *Letters*, 'Advertisement', vol. I, p. vii.
16 Clarke, 'Swan, Duckling or Goose?', p. 36.
17 'Written in the Title Page of a Volume Containing Mr Jephson's Tragedies', *The Poetical Works of Anna Seward*, ed. Walter Scott, 3 vols. (Edinburgh, 1810), vol. II, p. 133. All further references to Seward's poetry are cited from this edition, unless otherwise stated.
18 M. Severin Peterson, *Robert Jephson (1736–1803): A Study of His Life and Works* (University of Nebraska Press, 1930). Seward wrote a prologue for Jephson's *Braganza* (1775).
19 *Letters*, vol. I, p. 243. For the myth of 'poor Collins' see Richard Wendorf, *William Collins and Eighteenth-Century British Poetry* (University of Minnesota Press, 1981), pp. 7–11.
20 Margaret Ashmun, *The Singing Swan: An Account of Anna Seward* (New Haven, CT: Yale University Press, 1931), p. 153.
21 *The Poetical Works*, vol. I, pp. xxiii–xxiv.
22 Ashmun, *Singing Swan*, p. 227.
23 Seward's love of Gray even allowed her to include him in a digression in her *Memoirs* of Erasmus Darwin, where (apropos of very little) we are reminded that Gray wrote 'those two great Odes which place him first at the goal of the Lyric Muse'. *Memoirs of the Life of Dr. Darwin, Chiefly During His Residence at Lichfield* (London: Joseph Johnson, 1804), p. 419.
24 Brewer, *Pleasures*, p. 609. Ashmun, *Singing Swan*, p. 218.
25 Brewer, *Pleasures*, p. 611.
26 *Memoirs of the Life of Dr. Darwin*, p. 383.
27 In 1786, Seward responded to *The Gentleman's Magazine*'s praise of Smith's sonnets as 'superior to Shakespeare's and Milton's': 'All the lines that are not the lines of others are weak and unimpressive; and these hedge-flowers to be preferred, by a critical dictator, to the roses and amaranths of the two first poets the world has produced!!! – It makes one sick' (*Letters*, vol. II, pp. 162, 163). Two years later, she found other plagiarisms in Smith (*Letters*, vol. II, pp. 162–4, 216–17). Kairoff argues that this conflict is part of Seward's larger defence of the Miltonic sonnet tradition. See *Anna Seward*, pp. 166–70.

28 *Poetical Works*, vol. I, pp. xii–xiii.
29 For Seward's anger over not getting the Cook medal, see *Letters*, vol. III, pp. 60, 59, 32.
30 See J. G. Lockhart, *Memoirs of the Life of Sir Walter Scott*, 2nd edn, 10 vols. (Edinburgh: Cadell, 1839), vol. II, p. 328. He also records that Constable helped Scott 'by allowing him to draw his pen through Miss Seward's extravagant eulogies on himself and his poetry' (vol. III, p. 298). On 18 March 1810, Scott wrote to Joanna Baillie that he was 'submitting to edit [Seward's] posthumous poetry most of which is absolutely execrable', though the emphasis should perhaps be placed on the 'posthumous' here, in that Scott suggests that Seward's swelling of the materials had not enhanced them. *The Letters of Sir Walter Scott*, vol. II, pp. 314–15.
31 For Lady Miller's assemblies and poetic games, see Kairoff, *Anna Seward*, pp. 34–40, and Gavin Turner, *Christopher Anstey: A Life in Eighteenth-Century Bath* (Bristol: Broadcast Books, 2005), pp. 62–71.
32 Kairoff, *Anna Seward*, p. 89.
33 *Poetical Works*, vol. I, p. xx. Ashmun, *Singing Swan*, p. 13, where Darwin is blamed for 'that ornateness which disfigured the maturer writings of Miss Seward, and made them too often an object of ridicule instead of discriminating praise'.
34 Ashmun, *Singing Swan*, pp. 10, 14, 281.
35 Seward's disagreeable impression of Porter during the episode is recorded in the letters attached to *Poetical Works*, vol. I, pp. cxiii–cxxv.
36 For Wright, and the misnaming of Temple, see Teresa Barnard, *Anna Seward*, pp. 59–62.
37 *Poetical Works*, vol. I, pp. clxxxiii–clxxxiv. Bizarrely, Temple's wife would write to Seward in 1796, claiming that her husband had been infatuated with her for thirty years; in a ludicrous scene, he then visits her, only to run away before she can receive him. See *Letters*, vol. IV, pp. 215–19, 271–5, and Ashmun, *Singing Swan*, pp. 220–4. Seward also tells Mrs Temple of her subsequent attachment to one Cornet Vyse (*Letters*, vol. IV, pp. 177–80). Barnard describes the efforts of Mrs Temple to inveigle her way into Seward's affections as a form of emotional (and ultimately financial) blackmail. See *Anna Seward*, pp. 62–4.
38 Ashmun, *Singing Swan*, p. 26.
39 Barnard, *Anna Seward*, p. 5.
40 *Journals and Correspondence of Thomas Sedgwick Whalley*, vol. I, p. 324. For the relationship see also Ashmun, *Singing Swan*, pp. 178–87, and Barnard, *Anna Seward*, pp. 85–90. Hill Wickham described it in his memoirs of Whalley as 'a platonic affection' whereby 'no slur was cast on her character' (vol. I, p. 13). In an undated letter of 1811, Scott wrote rather more suggestively that 'as for the scandal' between Seward 'and the Vicar Saville, she herself told a female friend, who told me, there was not a word of truth in it, – and I believe her; for she added candidly, she did not know what might have

happened if Saville had not been more afraid of the devil than she was!' *The Letters of Sir Walter Scott*, vol. III, p. 29.
41 Clarke, *Rise and Fall*, p. 38.
42 *Anna Seward*, pp. 202, 204. Kairoff's account of the relationship (pp. 201–8) is very useful, as is Barnard's biographical research: see her *Anna Seward*, p. 82, for the mysterious estrangement.
43 Clarke, 'Swan, Duckling or Goose?', pp. 34–5. Kairoff, *Anna Seward*, p. 206.
44 *Journals and Correspondence of Thomas Sedgwick Whalley*, vol. II, p. 56. In similar vein, Sonnets XXXI–XXXII of Seward's sequence of 1799 rail against Edgeworth, 'That specious false-one, by whose cruel wiles / I lost thy amity' (*Poetical Works*, vol. II, p. 153).
45 Ashmun, *Singing Swan*, p. 125. Kairoff, *Anna Seward*, pp. 10, 118. For Kairoff's account of the influences on the poem, and its generic flexibility and experimentation, see pp. 117–18, 121–31.
46 *Hyper-Criticism on Miss Seward's Louisa* (London, 1785), pp. 5, 6.
47 The suggested emendation to *Macbeth* involves part of a passage quoted in *Hyper-Criticism*, p. 26:

———Light thickens, and the crow
Makes wing to th' rocking wood

'In all editions, *rocking* is written *rooky* wood ... A rook being only a larger species of crow, it would not be much worse writing to say, the crow makes wing to th' *crowy* wood. The doubtless real adjective intended was *rocking*, which, making the night stormy, increases the horror' (*Letters*, vol. V, p. 310).
48 *Hyper-Criticism*, pp. 30–1. Other evidence confirming the likelihood of Seward's authorship includes the admonition that 'Mr Stevens's beautiful poem RETIREMENT, was one of the compositions so inconsiderately censured by the Critical Reviewers' (p. 30). The poetry of William Bagshot Stevens, the Master of Repton School and a friend of Erasmus Darwin, was one of Seward's many hobby-horses: in the *Letters*, Seward complained about the neglect of this poem to Stevens (vol. V, p. 286), and to others (vol. I, p. 162), and told Stevens of his genius (vol. I, p. 280; vol. IV, pp. 200–1), and in a verse 'Epistle' (*Poetical Works*, vol. II, pp. 165–71). She also wrote the epitaph for his monument in Repton Church after his death in 1800 (*Poetical Works*, vol. II, p. 194; *Letters*, vol. V, pp. 379–81). According to Egerton Brydges, Stevens 'Caught something of [Seward's] fondness for big words and glitter' (*Autobiography*, vol. I, p. 55).
49 Ashmun, *Singing Swan*, pp. 203, 119, 123.
50 Brewer, *Pleasures*, pp. 586, 588. Kairoff, *Anna Seward*, p. 186. These 'perspectives' do not entirely convince: they include gender, with the suggestion that 'Johnson omitted women from his *Lives of the Poets*', whereas the poets included were of course decided by the bookseller's consortium, with slight additions by Johnson. See *The Lives of the Poets*, ed. Roger Lonsdale, 4 vols. (Oxford University Press, 2006), vol. I, pp. 8–9.
51 See Kairoff, *Anna Seward*, pp. 262–3, for the related idea of Johnson as a father figure to Seward.

52 Kairoff, *Anna Seward*, p. 242.
53 For Cowper's response, see the letter of 31 October 1779, in *The Letters and Prose Writings of William* Cowper, ed. James King and Charles Ryskamp, 5 vols. (Oxford: Clarendon Press, 1979), vol. I, p. 5. The degree of Seward's feeling may be gauged by her mentioning Johnson's 'piqued pride and personal soreness', and how 'he hated the man for his party, and his poetry for its pre-eminence' (*Letters*, vol. IV, p. 132). Moreover 'he endeavours to do away, collectively, all his reluctant praise' of *Paradise Lost* 'by observing that no person closes its pages with the desire of recurring to them; – that its perusal is always a task, never a pleasure – to that effect'. Needless to say, Seward puts the most negative slant possible on this 'impudent falsehood' (vol. IV, p. 133).
54 *Letters*, vol. II, p. 209. Weston's protracted argument with Seward has been selected in *Pope Versus Dryden: A Controversy in Letters to The Gentleman's Magazine*, ed. Gretchen M. Foster (University of Victoria, 1989).
55 Seward's many poetic comments upon Johnson, some direct, some in passing, include 'Verses to the Rev. William Mason, on His Silence Respecting Dr Johnson's Unjust Criticisms upon Mr Gray's Works, in *The Lives of the Poets*' (*Poetical Works*, vol. II, pp. 179–80; Seward had wondered why Mason did not respond to the 'Life of Gray' – see *Letters*, vol. II, p. 68); 'To Charles Simpson, Esq. Barrister; With Thos. Warton's Edition of Milton's Lesser Poems' (vol. III, pp. 57–8); 'To the Right Honourable the Marchioness of Donegall, with Mr Hayley's Life of Milton' (vol. III, pp. 119–20); 'On the Posthumous Fame of Doctor Johnson' (vol. III, p. 189); Sonnet LXXVI, 'The Critics of Dr Johnson's School' (vol. III, p. 197).
56 The relevant letters were reprinted in *Illustrations of the Literary History of the Eighteenth Century*, vol. VII, pp. 321–65. Boswell's last word was that 'My fair antagonist's fertile fancy has men and things enough to employ itself upon, without vainly aspiring to be the judge of Johnson. She will permit me, in perfect good humour, to call to her recollection a verse in very ancient poetry: "I do not exercise myself in great matters, which are too high for me"' (p. 362).
57 For accounts of their acquaintance, see Donna Heiland, 'Swan Songs: The Correspondence of Anna Seward and James Boswell', *Modern Philology* 90 (1993), 381–91, and James D. Woolley, 'Johnson as Despot: Anna Seward's Rejected Contribution to Boswell's *Life*', *Modern Philology* 70 (1972), 140–5.
58 *Letters*, vol. I, pp. 100–3. Seward's account is also reprinted in Woolley, 'Johnson as Despot', pp. 142–3.
59 Woolley, 'Johnson as Despot', p. 145.
60 Ashmun, *Singing Swan*, pp. 275, 276. For Jane West, see *Illustrations of the Literary History of the Eighteenth Century*, vol. VIII, p. 430.
61 As well as those mentions of him already cited, Seward's obituary of Johnson appeared in *The General Evening Post* (27 December 1784). It established her view – of the genius of his prose, the greatness of the moral writings, particularly *The Rambler*, and of the jealousy that allegedly motivated the *Lives of the Poets*. Such points are repeated throughout her writings: in the

Letters, vol. I, pp. 10, 35, 50–1, 54, 67, 135; vol. II, pp. 26, 40, 44, 78, 146–8; vol. III, pp. 43, 90–1, 111, 169, 214, 223, 241, 307–8, 319, 331, 350, 352, 353, 377; vol. IV, pp. 52, 54–6, 57–8, 85, 132–3, 154, 159, 183, 197, 213, 319; vol. V, pp. 30–1, 89, 118–19, 187, 273; vol. VI, pp. 261, 277. In the letters attached to Scott's edition of her *Poetical Works*, there are comments (pp. lxx, lxxviii) and a discussion of the superiority of *The Rambler* over *The Spectator* (pp. lxxxviii–ciii). He also appears in her contributions to the *Journals and Correspondence of Thomas Sedgwick Whalley*, vol. I, pp. 416–17. In the *Memoirs of Darwin*, Seward claims that 'Biography of recently departed Eminence is apt to want characteristic truth', citing Boswell's and Piozzi's versions of Johnson, and attacks the *Lives of the Poets* (pp. viii–xi). Johnson also pops up sporadically in the descriptions of Lichfield (pp. 68, 71, 75–7).

62 *Memoirs of Darwin*, pp. 19, 34. She recalled his misanthropy (and its offence to her sociability) in similar terms in *Letters*, vol. II, p. 330.

63 Her initial admiration for *The Task* (*Letters*, vol. I, p. 92) was soon tempered: 'The sublime, though gloomy, fires of Young, with the corrosive ones of Churchill, stream blended through its later pages. The author seems almost as religious as the former, and quite as ill-natured as the latter. Shield me from saints who look upon the world as a den of fools and knaves' (vol. I, p. 112). As well as the poetic 'Remonstrance Addressed to William Cowper, in 1788, On the Sarcasms Levelled at National Gratitude in *The Task*' (*Poetical Works*, vol. III, pp. 5–14), there is questioning of Cowper's Calvinism: 'I cannot think that the oblations of such mere parasites in religion can be acceptable as those of the benevolent man, whose piety is the result of blended gratitude to his Maker, and of kindling esteem and love for whatever is great and worthy in man' (*Letters*, vol. I, p. 184). Seward had told Whalley that she looked forward to Cowper's Homer translation, as he could not insert his 'malignance' into it. *Journals and Correspondence of Thomas Sedgwick Whalley*, vol. II, p. 26. There are other frequent remarks on Cowper throughout the *Letters*: *The Task* is inferior to Gray's *Descent of Odin*, possibly Crowe's *Lewesdon Hill* and Southey's *Joan of Arc* (vol. V, pp. 319, 321, 322–3). The fault is Calvinism, which has made Cowper 'morose and reasonless' (vol. V, p. 326).

64 She complains to Hayley, on the publication of his *Life of Cowper*, that his subject had been 'ignobly attentive to the works of poetic genius which have adorned his country from Milton's time to the present', as he does not appear to have read Chatterton or *The Pleasures of Imagination* (*Letters*, vol. VI, pp. 61–2), and that 'his judgment' was 'perverted by jealous prejudice against the compositions of contemporary genius' (vol. VI, p. 159). For her, the suggestion that Cowper only liked his school-fellow Charles Churchill amongst recent poets amounts to a scandal which totally compromises his judgement (vol. VI, pp. 166–7).

65 *Letters*, vol. I, p. 114. Seward used the same argument in two sonnets from her collection of 1799, where she defended the modern 'lyric galaxy' against those critics whose 'dull spirits feel not the fine glow / Enthusiasm breathes' (*Poetical Works*, vol. II, pp. 142, 143).

66 *Letters*, vol. I, p. 207. Hardinge was the most contentious of her correspondents, as can be seen from Seward's replies. 'You say I want temper in argument. It certainly exhausts my patience to see a man of ability, with an air of unappealable decision, perpetually pronouncing in *modern* poets *that* to be obscure, which is clear as day-light' (*Letters*, vol. I, p. 229). Her attempts to convince Hardinge of his inability to recognise self-evident beauty were doomed to failure. As Clarke says, Hardinge 'repeatedly disagreed' and was dropped (*Rise and Fall*, p. 49).
67 Ashmun, *Singing Swan*, p. 97.
68 *Letters*, vol. I, pp. 22, 29. 'Verses Written in the Blank Leaves of Mr Hayley's Poems, Presented by A. Seward, to Wm Grove, Esq. of Lichfield, 1793' (*Poetical Works*, vol. II, p. 135); 'On Seeing Mr Hayley's Works Invidiously Criticized in the Public Prints of the Year 1783' (*Poetical Works*, vol. II, p. 139).
69 *Letters*, vol. II, pp. 86–7. Hayley is repeatedly placed in exalted poetic company by Seward. See *Letters*, vol. II, p. 290; vol. V, pp. 48–9, 188, 192.
70 Ashmun, *Singing Swan*, p. 168. For Seward's account of Mrs Hayley's death, see *Letters*, vol. V, pp. 21–5 (a remarkable letter, considering Seward has 'a severe return of my haemorrhage').
71 *Letters*, vol. IV, p. 46. In fact, Hayley had been forced to tone down his original comments by the publisher. He eventually published two editions of the *Life* – one with works (1794) and one separate (1796). By 1803, and Hayley's *Life of Cowper*, their friendship had cooled enough for Seward to complain to Whalley, 'what a miserable business has Mr Hayley made of his tedious and servile-styled biography'. *Journals and Correspondence of Thomas Sedgwick Whalley*, vol. II, p. 244.
72 *Letters*, vol. I, pp. 108, 189. Her view that Dryden was eclipsed by modern poets seemed to have strengthened, as she would later write of Dryden's 'slovenly vulgarities, and wild absurdities' (vol. II, p. 211), and that 'No writer of genius disgusts me half so often, both by sins of omission and commission in his poetry, and by eternal self-contradictions and false precepts in his criticisms'. He was 'that unprincipled man, and most unequal poet' and it has been 'surely the fashion to hold him much too high', seeing that he has 'been excelled in every separate order of verse', including 'in elegy by Gray, and by Mason' (*Letters*, vol. V, p. 349; vol. VI, pp. 26, 27). For similar remarks see vol. IV, p. 331; vol. V, pp. 307–8, 312, 316, 408); vol. VI, pp. 258–9, 306–7.
73 *Letters*, vol. I, p. 57. See also vol. I, pp. 54–8, 67–8. A sonnet praises Sargent's (admittedly rare) ability to 'mineral scenes display' (*Poetical Works*, vol. II, p. 183).
74 *Letters*, vol. II, p. 365. In the *Memoirs of Darwin*, Gray is better than Pindar, and an educative tool: 'Ah! When will our schools and universities exchange classical partiality for patriotism, and become just to the exalted merits of the English Poets?' (pp. 421–2).
75 *Letters*, vol. I, p. 195. Later, Seward claims that Mason's 'Epistle from an Unfortunate Elector of Hanover to His Friend, Mr Pinchbeck' in 'strength of fancy, happiness of classic allusion, keenness of covert reproach, and poetic

Notes to pages 142–51

magnificence of style, exceeds any poetic satire I have read – not excepting even Pope's' (*Letters*, vol. IV, p. 363).

76 *Letters*, vol. III, pp. 4, 5, 153, 154–5. For Seward's claims, see 'Verses Written in Dr Darwin's Botanic Garden Near Lichfield, July, 1778', and accompanying note (*Poetical Works*, vol. I, pp. 1–4). For more on this 'disingenuous suppression' of her authorship, see *Memoirs of Darwin*, pp. xxi, 128–32, and Kairoff, *Anna Seward*, pp. 235–7.

77 *Memoirs of Darwin*, p. 180. The analysis of the poem covers pp. 166–382 of the 432-page book.

78 *Memoirs of Darwin*, pp. 406, 408. For Seward's retraction of Darwin's comment in *The Edinburgh Review*, April 1804, see *Letters*, vol. VI, pp. 135–6.

79 For Johnson's envy, see *Letters*, vol. VI, p. 277; the joy of her first reading, vol. VI, p. 316. The early letter is in *Poetical Works*, vol. I, p. lvii. For the chiding of Sophia Weston, and attributing the bombast to Macpherson, vol. I, pp. 240, 263; her final affirmation of Macpherson's genius, vol. VI, p. 315. Characteristically, Seward thought that Ossian must have 'sublimity', despite the doubters, because of Gray's high opinion of it (vol. II, p. 259).

80 For Godwin, see *Letters*, vol. IV, pp. 211, 228–9; vol. V, pp. 67–74 (including Humphrey Repton's odd plan for a continuation of *Caleb Williams*, which misses the point of the original exceedingly well), and 241–4; *St Leon* is praised in vol. V, pp. 275, 289–90, 296, 369–70. For an account of Seward's marginalia, see Aileen Douglas, 'Anna Seward's Annotated Copy of *Caleb Williams*', *Princeton University Library Chronicle* 49 (1987), 74–7.

81 *Letters*, vol. IV, pp. 295, 298, 312 (where for all his genius, Southey is 'in design a parricide').

82 Monk, 'Anna Seward and the Romantic Poets: A Study in Taste', pp. 133–4.

83 Brewer, *Pleasures*, p. 584. Monk, 'Anna Seward and the Romantic Poets: A Study in Taste', p. 130.

84 See Barnard, *Anna Seward*, p. 148. Scott, *Poetical Works*, vol. I, p. xvii.

85 For the description of Eyam and William Mompesson's letters during the plague of 1666 see *Poetical Works*, vol. I, pp. cliii–clxxxv; for Thomas Seward's last visit of 1783, see *Letters*, vol. II, pp. 68–9.

86 For the context and reception of the poem, see Ashmun, *Singing Swan*, pp. 213–17, and Barnard, *Anna Seward*, pp. 64–5.

87 Seward's desired form of publication is reprinted in the 'Advertisement', *Letters*, vol. I, pp. v–vi. Southey claimed that the publisher had thus ruined Seward's intended discretion towards living friends and acquaintances, arguing, for example, that the 'strange part of her own history relative to Col. Taylor [i.e. Temple] and his wife were never meant to be made public while they lived' (quoted by Ashmun, *Singing Swan*, p. 272).

88 Barnard, *Anna Seward*, pp. 168, 165. For censorship, see pp. 162–5.

89 For Anderson and her own reaction, see Ashmun, *Singing Swan*, pp. 274, 277. Barnard, *Anna Seward*, p. 168.

90 For Percy, see *Illustrations of the Literary History of the Eighteenth Century*, vol. VIII, p. 432. *Journals and Correspondence of Thomas Sedgwick Whalley*,

vol. I, p. 15. Hayley's remonstrance is in *The Letters of Sir Walter Scott*, vol. II, p. 513n.

91 Hardinge agreed with his correspondent Lady Knowles on the affectations of Seward's writing: 'Your critique upon Miss Seward is just, but oh that I had nothing worse to urge against her than her inflation of style in prose! In verse, I think she had gifted powers; but there too she was too fond of new or quaint words or phrases. In prose I think her the essence of a monstrous taste. But she had no heart; her behaviour to me, which I *must* expose to the world, was a base and cruel perfidy.' Letter of 12 November 1815, in *Illustrations of the Literary History of the Eighteenth Century*, vol. III, p. 815.

92 Ashmun, *Singing Swan*, p. 281.

93 Clarke, 'Swan, Duckling or Goose?', p. 41. *Rise and Fall*, pp. 21, 18.

4 Percival Stockdale's alternative literary history

1 Percival Stockdale, *A Letter to the Honourable and Right Reverend the Lord Bishop of Durham, on the Slave-Trade: to which are added Observations on the Late Parliamentary Debate on that Subject* (Durham, 1799).

2 *A Letter to the Reverend Percival Stockdale* (Booksellers of York, Newcastle, Durham and Neighbouring Towns, 1799), p. 23.

3 Howard Weinbrot, 'Samuel Johnson, Percival Stockdale, and Brick-bats from Grubstreet', *Huntington Library Quarterly* 56 (1993), 105–34, p. 111. This is a rare and invaluable modern account of Stockdale.

4 Percival Stockdale, *Memoirs of the Life and Writings of Percival Stockdale, Containing Many Interesting Anecdotes of the Illustrious Men with Whom He Was Connected, Written by Himself*, 2 vols. (London, 1809), vol. I, pp. 34, 35.

5 Percival Stockdale to Jane Porter, 10 October 1808, Houghton Library, Harvard University, MS Eng 1250 (92). Subsequent references to this collection are by class and letter number.

6 See *Memoirs*, vol. I, pp. 162–4, for Stockdale's inveighing against his relations for not helping him on this occasion.

7 *The Poetical Works of Percival Stockdale*, 2 vols. (London, 1810), vol. I, pp. 377–8. All references to Stockdale's poetry are to this edition, unless otherwise stated. For his account of the accident and writing of the poem, see *Memoirs*, vol. II, p. 290, and his letter to Porter of 29 May 1794, Houghton, MS Eng 1250 (3), where the cause of the trouble is his companions' drunken excitement: Stockdale, 'the example of Temperance suffered most', and his friend, the inebriated Mr Selby, received a 'severe' blow to the head, 'which he well deserved'.

8 The unlikely parallel of their careers is in *Memoirs*, vol. I, pp. 269–77. Years later, Stockdale's conversation with Samuel Johnson gives an example of Stockdale's hero worship, and Johnson's amusing hard-headedness: Stockdale (perhaps uneasily recalling rumours about the monarch's sexuality) observed that it was odd that 'Swedish Charles' 'had no commerce with women. "Sir," (answered the Stagyrite of ENGLAND, in his usual decisive tone and manner) "a man who is busy, has no *occasion* for women."' (*Memoirs*, vol. I, p. 255).

Notes to pages 158–66

9 Letter to Edward Jerningham, 19 July 1785. Henry E. Huntington Library, MSS JE 93, quoted by Weinbrot, 'Brick-bats from Grubstreet', p. 109. Weinbrot comments on the aftermath of this unhappy liaison: 'Stockdale was happiest when he thought his wife dead and was shocked when she reappeared and invaded his "asylum." He bought her exclusion from his home with a £50 per year allowance' (p. 131).

10 *Memoirs*, vol. II, pp. 57, 42. In 1800, reprinting a chorus from the translation, Stockdale made one of his repeated pronouncements on how posterity would rescue his work: 'Many operatives of time are slow, but they are ultimately sure, and permanently decisive. I hope that my translation of that beautiful poem, will hereafter make some impression in the minds of my countrymen; when prejudice, and malignity shall be defeated by truth, and justice.' 'Chorus to the Second Act of TASSO'S AMINTA', *Poems, by Percival Stockdale* (London, 1800), p. 9.

11 'Life' of Waller, in *The Works of Edmund Waller*, ed. Percival Stockdale (London, 1772), p. i.

12 'Life' of Waller, p. lxv.

13 Johnson does quote from Stockdale, Waller's 'last, ingenious biographer' and notes his sensible advice not to judge Waller's political wavering too harshly, as like most people, 'his character included not the poet, the orator, and the hero'. Samuel Johnson, 'Life of Waller', *The Lives of the Poets*, ed. Roger Lonsdale, vol. II, p. 38. According to Stockdale, Johnson had promised to mention him, yet 'takes but a very transient, and anonymous notice' of it (*Memoirs*, vol. II, p. 123). Stockdale's animus with Johnson and the *Lives* eventually reached the point where no mention of it would be sufficient.

14 Isaac D'Israeli, review of *The Memoirs of the Life and Writings of Percival Stockdale*, *Quarterly Review* 1 (1809), 371–86, p. 378.

15 Samuel Johnson, *The Complete English Poems*, ed. J. D. Fleeman (Harmondsworth: Penguin, 1971), p. 88.

16 The *Memoirs* are littered with such moments. In relating Johnson's quarrel with Garrick, Stockdale makes it Johnson's fault for his 'rudeness and insolence'; he 'meanly envied' Garrick's fame (vol. II, p. 187). By this time, Johnson's success made him the greatest reproach of all to the failed writer. Similarly (and comically, to the reader who has waded through Stockdale's endless petty recriminations), Edmund Burke 'was apt to be disconcerted, and thrown into unguarded passion, by trifling rubs, or oppositions' (vol. II, p. 130). Gibbon's 'face, and person were the reverse of graceful; and there was a stiffness, and solemnity in his *social*, which resembled the form of his *literary* manner' (vol. II, p. 112).

17 For the critical history of Warton's *Essay*, see the 'Introduction' to *Alexander Pope and His Critics*, ed. Adam Rounce, 3 vols. (London: Routledge, 2003), vol. I, pp. xxvii–xxxiii.

18 Isaac D'Israeli, *Calamities of Authors*, 2 vols. (London, 1812), vol. II, p. 319.

19 Percival Stockdale, 'To Henry Collingwood Selby, Esquire', *Poetical Works*, vol. II, p. 289.

20 Germain, who had been Camp Commander at Brompton, in 1757, while Stockdale was still in the army, was an important figure, being Lord Commissioner of Trade and Plantations, and Secretary of State for the Colonies. In this latter role he was instrumental in the ongoing War of Independence, which Stockdale disapproved of with his usual vehemence. Stockdale begins by saying that he is dedicating the work to him because of Germain's literary talents and appreciation, and because his father, the Earl of Dorset, had known Pope: 'These are the motives that dictated this Address to your Lordship: – not my gratitude, as an Englishman, for the progress, or rather continuation, of our unconstitutional, sanguinary and destructive continental war, over which *you* preside; not very auspiciously to your political reputation. – I pay this homage to the polite scholar, and to the orator; not a particle of my respect is intended for the Minister.' *An Inquiry into the Nature, and Genuine Laws of Poetry; Including a Particular Defence of the Writings, and Genius of Mr Pope* (1778), repr. in *Alexander Pope and His Critics*, vol. III, pp. v–vi. The questionable tact of this is rejected by Stockdale in his *Memoirs*: it 'was short, independent and manly', and won him favour from Germain for its honesty (vol. II, p. 125). Germain later recommended Stockdale for an ecclesiastical living to the Governor of Jamaica, but he had yet to become ordained, and thus could not take it up. Johnson wrote to Robert Lowth, then Bishop of London, in 1780 to try and help his ordination, but without success. See *The Letters of Samuel Johnson*, ed. Bruce Redford, 5 vols. (Oxford: Clarendon Press, 1992), vol. III, pp. 286–7, 291. As Weinbrot wryly suggests, Germain's 'willingness to find Stockdale a place in Jamaica may have had more than one motive' ('Brick-bats from Grubstreet', p. 107).

21 See the *Inquiry*, p. 7, and pp. 5–22, for the full debate. John Hardy, 'Stockdale's Defence of Pope', *Review of English Studies* 18 (1967), 49–54, has an analysis of Stockdale's refutation of this part of Warton's argument; Hardy speculates that 'in writing his ['Life of Pope'] Johnson at least remembered a previous defence of Pope whose author seemed already to have answered Warton effectively' (p. 54). Even given Stockdale's rebuttal of the theory (hardly the centrepiece of Warton's thesis), it is hard to see how the rest of his argument is 'effective', by any critical standard.

22 Stockdale's bellicose nationalism is also apparent in the 'Preface' to his translation of *The Amyntas of Tasso* (London, 1770), with mention of 'Boileau, one of the contemptible French rhymers'; Stockdale is 'only ambitious to please Englishmen. I shall despise the impertinent censure of any pedantick Italian' (pp. x–xi, xix).

23 George Huddesford, *Warley: A Satire, Part the Second* (London, 1778), pp. 14–15.

24 Boswell, *Life of Johnson*, vol. II, p. 113.

25 Boswell, *Life of Johnson*, vol. IV, p. 319. For the identification of Stockdale, see Weinbrot, 'Brick-bats from Grubstreet', pp. 132–3.

26 *Memoirs*, vol. II, pp. 123–4. He claims he was compelled by a 'friend' to write a 'long, and rather a pathetick letter' beseeching Johnson to include him.

27 *Memoirs*, vol. II, pp. 194, 195. Weinbrot ('Brick-bats from Grubstreet', p. 114) suggests that the very Johnsonian authority of the earlier 'Life of Waller' would have been one factor in the decision of the consortium to take on Stockdale; one wonders if the violence of the *Inquiry* would have played a part in the opposite sense. It became Stockdale's most significant single resentment, with the added implication that Johnson had been complicit in underhand business, since when Stockdale confronted him about it, 'he was perfectly silent' (*Memoirs*, vol. II, p. 197).
28 Percival Stockdale, *Sermons on Important and Interesting Subjects* (London: John Stockdale, 1784), p. iii.
29 Stockdale claimed that his 'ardent defence of humanity to the animal creation' offended the Archbishop of Canterbury (*Memoirs*, vol. II, p. 80).
30 *Ximenes; a Tragedy* (London, 1788), p. 33.
31 This was a sojourn to Tangier (at the invitation of Mr Matra, the Consul) via Gibraltar; it is marked by 'coldness of behaviour' and rudeness towards him, until the Consul's 'vile and disgusting behaviour' leads him to reprise his role as naval chaplain, leaving almost instantly because of the 'shockingly blasphemous and obscene' language of the officers. He goes to Algiers, and returns via France. This pointless and rather tragic farce lasted from 1788 to 1790, and was Stockdale's last elaborate journey. See *Memoirs*, vol. II, pp. 249–70.
32 *Poetical Works*, vol. II, pp. 185, 173.
33 *Letters between Shute, Bishop of Durham, and Percival Stockdale: A Correspondence Interesting to Every Lover of Literature, Freedom, and Religion* (London: J. Ridgway, 1792), 'Advertisement', A^r, A^{r-v}, A3^v–4^r.
34 As well as the admonitory *A Letter to P. S. on the Publication of His Pretended Correspondence with the Lord Bishop of Durham* (London, 1792), there is also the facetious versification of *An Humble, Introductory, Prefatory, Adulatory, Consolatory, Admonitory Epistolary, Address Indeed! To P— S–d–e, a Very Pious And Meek Divine Truly!!!* (Newcastle, 1792).
35 The letter is reprinted by Weinbrot, in 'Brick-bats from Grubstreet', pp. 127–9.
36 James Thomson, *The Seasons*, ed. Percival Stockdale (London: A. Hamilton, 1793), note to 'Spring' (end of section).
37 *The Seasons*, note to 'Spring', l. 900.
38 *The Seasons*, note to 'Summer' (opening of section).
39 *The Seasons*, final note.
40 *Poetical Works*, vol. I, p. 344.
41 Letter to Porter, 9 June 1798, Houghton, Eng MS 1520 (33).
42 'A Song' ['Do great achievements fire'], *Poems* (1800), p. 14. The poem was written in 1784.
43 'A Song', p. 15.
44 Stockdale would later inveigh against the criticism of Coleridge, specifically his having the 'impudence to assert' that Dryden's *Alexander's Feast* 'is little better than an old ballad', and that Pope is a 'good versifier'. He and Southey are 'two publick clowns'. Letter to Porter, 14 March 1809, Houghton, Eng MS 1520 (93).

45 Dedication to *Poems* (1800), p. 7. This is dated 4 March 1800; in a letter to Jerningham of 22 June 1801, as Weinbrot points out, Stockdale complains that 'the world is not prepared generously to receive my lectures' ('Brick-bats from Grubstreet', p. 118). The unlikely hope of giving the *Lectures* in public seems to have receded by this later date, possibly due to lack of encouragement, though not presumably from Porter, who would take over their publication from the increasingly infirm Stockdale, and help see them through the press by 1807. It is also unclear when they were completed: the letters to Porter detail Stockdale's progress while trapped in Monmouth. He still hopes that the *Lectures*, if finished, might produce 'emolument and fame', but is wary of the nature of the latter, which has 'hitherto treacherously, and cruelly, eluded my grasp'. By December 1795, he had finished Spenser and Shakespeare, and was writing on Milton: 'I am traversing Earth, and Chaos, Heaven and Hell, with that astonishing; with that god-like Poet. My literary ambition is, again, all alive.' This is finished by 14 December, when he writes of his servant Molly, who, hearing him often recite the names of Milton and Johnson, 'asked me if they were the men who near London, not very long ago, fought a great Boxing-match'. January and February have him planning to write on Dryden in this 'vile welch hole'. Dryden was completed by August 1796, Pope by December, and Thomson by August 1797. See letters to Jane Porter, Houghton, MS Eng 1520 (10, 16, 17, 18, 19, 22, 26, 31). There are repeated references in letters of 1802 to the final chronological lecture on Gray, but some of the lectures on Chatterton may well have been added after, along with other tinkering.

46 Letters to Jane Porter, 4 January 1795, 27 December 1796, Houghton, Eng MS 1520 (7, 26).

47 Review of *Lectures on the Truly Eminent English Poets*, *The Edinburgh Review* 12 (April 1808), 62–82, p. 77 (attributed to Thomas Campbell). For the reception of the *Lectures*, see Weinbrot, 'Brick-bats from Grubstreet', pp. 122–5.

48 Stockdale, *Lectures on the Truly Eminent English Poets*, 2 vols. (London: Longman, 1807), vol. 1, p. viii. Hereafter referred to as *Lectures*, with volume and page number. The italics are reversed in all the following prefatory quotations.

49 *Lectures*, vol. 1, p. 235. It is worth noting that Johnson's very sympathetic expression of both the problems which had benighted Savage, and the ways in which Savage could not admit that many of these were self-inflicted, is not dissimilar to the long pattern of self-delusion that runs through Stockdale's work, and that his appreciation of the *Life of Savage* may have had more motives than he realised.

50 Passages from 'the little book, to which I begin to fear that I have too frequently referred' (*Lectures*, vol. 1, p. 461) can be found on pp. 426–7, 429–36, 456–60, 461–2, and 525–6. Stockdale does, to be fair, 'wish nothing expunged from it but my too warm resentment against the worthy Dr. Warton, in my zeal for Pope' (p. 525).

51 *Lectures*, vol. 1, pp. 546, 553. The Young lectures also show Stockdale's talent for humorous anecdote, which was not indulged enough (because usually

submerged beneath his disputes). He records that Young asked Pope for a motto to *Night Thoughts*, and received the great man's reply: 'I had intended for the motto to my Essay on Man; – *Know thyself.* I think the motto to *your* Night-Thoughts should be; – *Go, hang thyself* (p. 607).

52 *Lectures*, vol. II, p. 80. Stockdale quotes from the notes to his edition of Thomson on pp. 108–9, 110–15, 120–3.

53 Apart from the references to Anna Seward in this study, for the reception of Johnson's 'Life of Gray', see W. Powell Jones, 'Johnson and Gray: A Study in Literary Antagonism', *Modern Philology* 56 (1959), 243–53, and Roger Lonsdale, 'Gray and Johnson: The Biographical Problem', in *Fearful Joy: Papers from the Thomas Gray Bicentenary Conference at Carleton University*, ed. James Downey and Ben Jones (Montreal: McGill-Queen's University Press, 1974), pp. 66–84.

54 Letters to Jane Porter, 31 October 1808, 23 March 1809, Houghton, Eng MS 1520 (92, 94).

55 Isaac D'Israeli, review of *The Memoirs of the Life and Writings of Percival Stockdale*, *Quarterly Review* I (1809), 371–86, p. 372. Stockdale read this: ' what injustice has been done to them in a new quarterly review'. Letter to Jane Porter, 26 July 1809, Houghton, Eng MS 1520 (98).

56 D'Israeli, *Quarterly Review* I (1809), p. 386.

57 Weinbrot, 'Brick-bats from Grubstreet', p. 109.

58 Quoted in W. M. Parker, 'Bibliography: Scott's Marginalia, III', *Times Literary Supplement* (5 October 1940), p. 8.

59 Letter to Jane Porter, 20 April 1809, Houghton, Eng MS 1520 (96).

Conclusion

1 Letter of 18 October 1794, Boswell Papers, C353. Quoted by Peter Martin, *A Life of James Boswell* (London: Phoenix Press, 2000), p. 545.

2 Isaac D'Israeli, *Curiosities of Literature* (London, 1791), pp. 60, 63.

3 D'Israeli, *Curiosities of Literature*, 2nd edn, 2 vols. (London, 1794), vol. II, pp. 79, 76–7, 77.

4 *Curiosities of Literature* (1791), pp. 95–6.

5 Alvin Kernan, *Samuel Johnson and the Impact of Print* (Princeton University Press, 1989), p. 114. Also pertinent is Kernan's description of Johnson's role as biographer, in the *Lives of the Poets*: 'once Johnson had written their lives, isolated them from other kinds of lives not involved with poetry, and linked them to one another in the stabilizing context of literary history, their reality as writers, as well as that of the writer in general, was strongly reinforced' (p. 109).

6 James Beattie, 'Dialogues of the Dead', in *The Minstrel: With Some Other Poems, to Which Are Now Added, Miscellanies*, 2 vols. (London, 1799), vol. II, pp. 158–9.

7 Monk, 'Anna Seward and the Romantic Poets: A Study in Taste', p. 129. Seward claimed that Chatterton 'stood unparalleled' by 'any child of sixteen that was ever born for the glory of human intellect' (*Letters*, vol. VI, p. 247).

8 Stockdale, *Lectures on the Truly Eminent English Poets*, vol. II, pp. 148, 469, 163.
9 The small part of the diatribe devoted to direct literary criticism can be found in *Lectures*, vol. II, pp. 316–34, wherein a comparison with *Piers Plowman* sees Stockdale apologise for quoting 'this wretched stuff', an interesting reminder of the low status of much medieval literature into the nineteenth century (p. 327).
10 For Chatterton's Romantic reception, see Maria Grazia Lolla, '"Truth Sacrifising to the Muses": The Rowley Controversy and the Genesis of the Romantic Chatterton', and David Fairer, 'Chatterton's Poetic Afterlife, 1770–1794: A Context for Coleridge's *Monody*', in *Thomas Chatterton and Romantic Culture*, ed. Nick Groom (Basingstoke: Macmillan, 1999), pp. 151–71, 228–52; and Daniel Cook, 'Antiquaries to Romantics: A Reception History of Thomas Chatterton' (PhD thesis, University of Cambridge, 2008).
11 Andrew Bennett, *Romantic Poetry and the Culture of Posterity* (Cambridge University Press, 1999), pp. 53, 55–6, 17, 21. Bennett explores this partly through Coleridge's distinction between fame and reputation (pp. 55–61).
12 *Failure* (Documents of Contemporary Art), ed. Lisa Le Feuvre (London: Whitechapel Gallery, 2010), pp. 12, 13.

Bibliography

Primary

The Adventures of a Hackney Coach. London, 1781.
Anderson, Robert, *The Life of Samuel Johnson.* London, 1795.
Battier, Henrietta, *The Protected Fugitives: A Collection of Miscellaneous Poems.* Dublin, 1791.
Beattie, James, *Dissertations Moral and Critical.* Edinburgh, 1783.
The Minstrel: With Some Other Poems, to Which Are Now Added, Miscellanies, 2 vols. London, 1799.
Birkbeck Hill, George, ed., *Johnsonian Miscellanies,* 2 vols. Oxford: Clarendon Press, 1897.
Boswell, James, *Life of Johnson,* ed. George Birkbeck Hill, rev. and enlarged L. F. Powell, 6 vols. Oxford: Clarendon Press, 1934–50.
Brydges, Sir Egerton, *The Autobiography, Time, Opinions, and Contemporaries of Sir Egerton Brydges, Bart.,* 2 vols. London: Cochrane and M'Crone, 1834.
Carter, Elizabeth, *Letters from Elizabeth Carter to Mrs Montagu,* ed. William Pennington, 3 vols. London: Rivington, 1817.
Churchill, Charles, *The Poetical Works of Charles Churchill,* ed. Douglas Grant. Oxford: Clarendon Press, 1956.
Cibber, Theophilus, ed., *The Lives of the Poets of Great Britain and Ireland,* 5 vols. London, 1753.
Cowper, William, *The Letters and Prose Writings of William Cowper,* ed. James King and Charles Ryskamp, 5 vols. Oxford: Clarendon Press, 1979.
D'Israeli, Isaac, *Calamities of Authors,* 2 vols. London, 1812.
Curiosities of Literature. London, 1791.
Curiosities of Literature, 2nd edn, 2 vols. London, 1794.
An Essay on the Manners and Genius of the Literary Character. London, 1795.
Dodd, William, *The Beauties of Shakespear,* 2 vols. London, 1752.
'Introduction', *A Familiar Explanation of the Poetical Works of Milton.* London, 1762.
A New Book of the Dunciad. London, 1750.
Papers Written by Dr. Johnson and Dr. Dodd in 1777, ed. R. W. Chapman. Oxford: Clarendon Press, 1926.
Poems. London, 1767.

Reflections on Death. London, 1763.
Reflections on Death, 5th edn. London, 1777.
The Sisters. or, the History of Lucy and Caroline Sanson, Entrusted to a False Friend, 2 vols. London, 1754.
Thoughts in Prison. London, 1777.
Duncombe, John, *Historical Memoirs of the Life and Writings of the Late Rev. William Dodd*. London, 1777.
Dunton, John, *Dunton's Journal. Part I. or, The Whipping-Post: Being a Satyr upon Every Body*. London, 1706.
The Life and Errors of John Dunton, Late Citizen of London, Written by Himself in Solitude. London, 1705.
Fielding, Henry, *The History of Tom Jones, A Foundling. The Wesleyan Edition of the Works of Henry Fielding*, ed. Fredson Bowers and Martin C. Battestin. Middletown, CT: Wesleyan University Press, 1975.
Foote, Samuel, *The Cozeners*. London, 1774.
Foster, Gretchen M., ed., *Pope Versus Dryden: A Controversy in Letters to The Gentleman's Magazine*. University of Victoria, 1989.
Goldsmith, Oliver, *An Enquiry into the Present State of Polite Learning in Europe*. London, 1759.
Hawkins, Sir John, *The Life of Samuel Johnson*, ed. O M Brack Jr. University of Georgia Press, 2009.
Haywood, Eliza, *Memoirs of a Certain Island*. London, 1724.
'Histories of the Tête-à-Tête annex'd', *The Town and Country Magazine* v, 1773.
Huddesford, George, *Warley: A Satire, Part the Second*. London, 1778.
An Humble, Introductory, Prefatory, Adulatory, Consolatory, Admonitory Epistolary, Address Indeed! To P— S–d–e, a Very Pious And Meek Divine Truly!!! Newcastle, 1792.
Hume, David, *Essays, Moral and Political*, 2 vols. Edinburgh, 1742.
Jackson, William, *The New and Complete Newgate Calendar*, 6 vols. London, 1795.
Johnson, Samuel, *The Complete English Poems*, ed. J. D. Fleeman. Harmondsworth: Penguin, 1971.
The Letters of Samuel Johnson, ed. Bruce Redford, 5 vols. Oxford: Clarendon Press, 1992.
The Life of Savage, ed. Clarence Tracy. Oxford: Clarendon Press, 1971.
The Lives of the Poets, ed. Roger Lonsdale, 4 vols. Oxford University Press, 2006.
ed., *The Plays of William Shakespeare*, 8 vols. London, 1765.
Johnson: Prose and Poetry, ed. Mona Wilson. London: Hart-Davis, 1966.
The Yale Edition of the Works of Samuel Johnson, vol. II, *The Idler and The Adventurer*, ed. W. J. Bate, J. M. Bullitt, and L. F. Powell. New Haven, CT: Yale University Press, 1963.
The Yale Edition of the Works of Samuel Johnson, vol. XVIII, *Johnson on the English Language*, ed. Gwin J. Kolb and Robert DeMaria Jr. New Haven, CT: Yale University Press, 2005.

The Yale Edition of the Works of Samuel Johnson, vols. VII and VIII, *Johnson on Shakespeare*, ed. Arthur Sherbo. New Haven, CT: Yale University Press, 1969.
The Yale Edition of the Works of Samuel Johnson, vol. VI, *Poems*, ed. E. J. McAdam and George Milne. New Haven, CT: Yale University Press, 1964.
The Yale Edition of the Works of Samuel Johnson, vol. XVI, *Rasselas and Other Tales*, ed. Gwin J. Kolb. New Haven, CT: Yale University Press, 1990.
Lennox, Charlotte, *The Female Quixote*, ed. Margaret Dalziel. Oxford University Press, 1989.
A Letter to P. S. on the Publication of His Pretended Correspondence with the Lord Bishop of Durham. London, 1792.
A Letter to the Reverend Percival Stockdale. Booksellers of York, Newcastle, Durham and Neighbouring Towns, 1799.
The Life of Mr. Richard Savage. London, 1727.
The Malefactor's Register, or, the Newgate and Tyburn Calendar, 5 vols. London, 1779.
Nichols, John, ed., *Illustrations of the Literary History of the Eighteenth Century*, 8 vols. London, 1817–58.
Literary Anecdotes of the Eighteenth Century, 9 vols. London, 1812–16.
ed., *Select Collection of Poems*, 8 vols. London, 1782.
Old Bailey Proceedings Online (www.oldbaileyonline.org, version 6.0, 17 April 2011), 19 February 1777 (T17770219-1).
Pope, Alexander, *The Correspondence of Alexander Pope*, ed. George Sherburn, 5 vols. Oxford: Clarendon Press, 1956.
Ralph, James, *The Case of Authors by Profession*. London, 1758.
Reed, Isaac, *An Impartial Account of the Life and Writings of Dr William Dodd*. London, 1777.
Richardson, Samuel, *Clarissa, or, The History of a Young Lady*, ed. Angus Ross. Harmondsworth: Penguin, 1985.
Rounce, Adam, ed., *Alexander Pope and His Critics*, 3 vols. London: Routledge, 2003.
Savage, Richard, *An Author to be Lett*. London, 1729.
Love in a Veil. London, 1719.
The Poetical Works of Richard Savage, ed. Clarence Tracy. Cambridge University Press, 1962.
The Works of Richard Savage, 2 vols. London 1777.
Scott, Sir Walter, *Chronicles of the Canongate*, ed. Claire Lamont. Edinburgh University Press, 2000.
The Journal of Sir Walter Scott. Edinburgh: David Douglas, 1891.
The Letters of Sir Walter Scott, ed. Herbert Grierson, 12 vols. London: Constable, 1932.
[Seward, Anna,] *Hyper-Criticism on Miss Seward's Louisa*. London, 1785.
Seward, Anna, *Letters of Anna Seward, Written Between the Years 1784 and 1807*, 6 vols. Edinburgh: Constable, 1811.

Memoirs of the Life of Dr. Darwin, Chiefly During His Residence at Lichfield. London: Joseph Johnson, 1804.
The Poetical Works of Anna Seward, ed. Walter Scott, 3 vols. Edinburgh: Ballantyne, 1810.
Shakespeare, William, *Julius Caesar*, ed. David Daniell. London: Methuen, 1998.
Stockdale, Percival, *An Inquiry into the Nature, and Genuine Laws of Poetry; Including a Particular Defence of the Writings, and Genius of Mr Pope*. 1778.
Lectures on the Truly Eminent English Poets, 2 vols. London: Longman, 1807.
A Letter to the Honourable and Right Reverend the Lord Bishop of Durham, on the Slave-Trade: to which are added Observations on the Late Parliamentary Debate on that Subject. Durham, 1799.
Letters of Percival Stockdale to Jane Porter, Houghton Library, Harvard University, MS Eng 1250.
Letters between Shute, Bishop of Durham, and Percival Stockdale: A Correspondence Interesting to Every Lover of Literature, Freedom, and Religion. London: J. Ridgway, 1792.
Memoirs of the Life and Writings of Percival Stockdale, Containing Many Interesting Anecdotes of the Illustrious Men with Whom He Was Connected, Written by Himself, 2 vols. London, 1809.
Poems, by Percival Stockdale. London, 1800.
The Poetical Works of Percival Stockdale, 2 vols. London, 1810.
Sermons on Important and Interesting Subjects. London: John Stockdale, 1784
Ximenes; a Tragedy. London, 1788.
Swift, Jonathan, *The Cambridge Edition of the Works of Jonathan Swift, A Tale of a Tub and Other Works*, ed. Marcus Walsh. Cambridge University Press, 2010.
Taylor, John, *Records of My Life*, 2 vols. London, 1832.
Thicknesse, Sir Philip, *The Memoirs of Sir Philip Thicknesse*, 3 vols. Dublin, 1788–91.
Thomson, James, *The Seasons*, ed. Percival Stockdale. London: A. Hamilton, 1793.
Thoughts of a Citizen of London on the Conduct of Dr. Dodd. London, 1777.
Villette, John, *A Genuine Account of the Behaviour and Dying Words of William Dodd*. London, 1777.
Waller, Edmund, *The Works of Edmund Waller*, ed. Percival Stockdale. London, 1772.
Walpole, Horace, *The Correspondence of Horace Walpole*, ed. W. S. Lewis *et al.*, 48 vols. New Haven, CT: Yale University Press, 1937–83.
Last Journals, 2 vols. London: Bodley Head, 1910.
Warburton, William, ed., *The Works of William Shakespeare*, 8 vols. London, 1747.
Whalley, Thomas, *The Journals and Correspondence of Thomas Sedgwick Whalley, D. D.*, ed. Hill Wickham, 2 vols. London: Richard Bentley, 1863.

Secondary

Alkon, Paul K., 'The Intention and Reception of Johnson's *Life of Savage*', *Modern Philology* 72 (1974), 139–50.
Ashmun, Margaret, *The Singing Swan: An Account of Anna Seward*. New Haven, CT: Yale University Press, 1931.
Backscheider, Paula, *Eighteenth-Century Women Poets and Their Poetry: Inventing Agency, Inventing Genre*. Baltimore, MD: Johns Hopkins University Press, 2005.
Baines, Paul, *The House of Forgery in Eighteenth-Century Britain*. Aldershot: Ashgate, 1999.
Barker, A. D., 'Samuel Johnson and the Campaign to Save William Dodd', *Harvard Library Bulletin* 31 (1983), 147–80.
 'The Early Career of William Dodd', *Transactions of the Cambridge Bibliographical Society* 8 (1982), 217–35.
Barnard, Teresa, *Anna Seward: A Constructed Life, A Critical Biography*. Aldershot: Ashgate, 2009.
Bate, Walter Jackson, *Samuel Johnson*. London: Hogarth, 1984.
Bennett, Andrew, *Romantic Poetry and the Culture of Posterity*. Cambridge University Press, 1999.
Braudy, Leo, *The Frenzy of Renown: Fame and Its History*. London: Vintage, 1997.
Brewer, John, *The Pleasures of the Imagination: English Culture in the Eighteenth Century*. London: HarperCollins, 1997.
Bundock, Michael, 'Did John Hawkins Steal Johnson's Diary?', *Age of Johnson* 21 (2012), 77–92.
Burke, John J., 'Crime and Punishment in 1777: The Execution of the Reverend Dr. William Dodd and Its Impact upon His Contemporaries', in *Executions and the British Experience from the Seventeenth to the Twentieth Century*, ed. William B. Thesing. Folkestone: Macfarland, 1991, pp. 59–75.
[Campbell, Thomas,] review of *Lectures on the Truly Eminent English Poets*, *The Edinburgh Review* 12 (April 1808), 62–82.
Carlile, Susan, and O M Brack Jr, 'Samuel Johnson's Contribution to Charlotte Lennox's *The Female Quixote*', *Yale University Library Gazette* 77 (2003), 166–73.
Clarke, Norma, 'Anna Seward: Swan, Duckling or Goose?', in *British Women's Writing in the Long Eighteenth Century: Authorship, Politics and History*, ed. Jennie Batchelor and Cora Kaplan. Basingstoke: Palgrave Macmillan, 2005, pp. 34–47.
 The Rise and Fall of the Woman of Letters. London: Pimlico, 2004.
Clifford, James L., 'The Authenticity of Anna Seward's Published Correspondence', *Modern Philology* 39 (1941), 113–22.
 Young Samuel Johnson. London: Heinemann, 1955.
Cook, Daniel, 'Antiquaries to Romantics: A Reception History of Thomas Chatterton', PhD thesis, University of Cambridge, 2008.

Cooney, Seamus, 'Scott's Anonymity – Its Motives and Consequences', *Studies in Scottish Literature* 10 (1973), 207–19,
Curran, Stuart, 'Anna Seward and the Dynamics of Female Friendship', in *Romantic Women Poets: Genre and Gender*, ed. Lilla Maria Crisafulli and Cecilia Pietropoli. Amsterdam: Rodopi, 2007, pp. 11–21.
D'Israeli, Isaac, review of *The Memoirs of the Life and Writings of Percival Stockdale*, *Quarterly Review* 1 (1809), 371–86.
DeMaria Jr, Robert, *The Life of Samuel Johnson*. Oxford: Blackwell, 1994.
Donoghue, Frank, *The Fame Machine: Book Reviewing and Eighteenth-Century Literary Careers*. Palo Alto, CA: Stanford University Press, 1996.
Douglas, Aileen, 'Anna Seward's Annotated Copy of *Caleb Williams*', *Princeton University Library Chronicle* 49 (1987), 74–7.
Dussinger, John A., '"The Solemn Magnificence of a Stupendous Ruin": Richard Savage, Poet Manqué', in *Fresh Reflections on Samuel Johnson*, ed. Prem Nath. New York, NY: Whitston Publishing, 1987, pp. 167–82.
Fitzgerald, Percy, *A Famous Forgery: Being the Story of "the Unfortunate" Doctor Dodd*. London: Chapman and Hall, 1865.
Folkenflik, Robert, *Samuel Johnson, Biographer*. Ithaca, NY: Cornell University Press, 1978.
Gerrard, Christine, *Aaron Hill: The Muses' Projector*. Oxford University Press, 2003.
  The Patriot Opposition to Walpole: Politics, Poetry, and National Myth, 1725–1742. Oxford University Press, 1994.
Gladfelder, Hal, 'The Hard Work of Doing Nothing: Richard Savage's Parallel Lives', *Modern Language Quarterly* 64 (2003), 445–72.
Griffin, Dustin, *Literary Patronage in England, 1650–1800*. Cambridge University Press, 1996.
Groom, Nick, ed., *Thomas Chatterton and Romantic Culture*. Basingstoke: Macmillan, 1999.
Hammond, Brean S., *Professional Imaginative Writing in England, 1670–1740: 'Hackney for Bread'*. Oxford: Clarendon Press, 1997.
Hardy, John, 'Stockdale's Defence of Pope', *Review of English Studies* 18 (1967), 49–54.
Heiland, Donna, 'Swan Songs: The Correspondence of Anna Seward and James Boswell', *Modern Philology* 90 (1993), 381–91.
Holmes, Richard, *Dr Johnson & Mr Savage*. London: Hodder & Stoughton, 1993.
Howson, Gerald, *The Macaroni Parson: The Life of the Unfortunate Dr Dodd*. London: Hutchinson, 1973.
Jarvis, Simon, *Scholars and Gentlemen: Shakespearean Textual Criticism and Representations of Scholarly Labour, 1725–1765*. Oxford: Clarendon Press, 1995.
Jesse, J. H., *George Selwyn and His Contemporaries*, 3 vols. London, 1901.
Johnson, Edgar, *Sir Walter Scott: The Great Unknown*, 2 vols. London: Hamilton, 1970.
Johnston, Freya, 'Little Lives: An Eighteenth-Century Sub-Genre', *Cambridge Quarterly* 32 (2003), 143–60.

Jordan, Sarah, *The Anxieties of Idleness*. Lewisburg, PA: Bucknell University Press, 2003.
Kairoff, Claudia Thomas, *Anna Seward and the End of the Eighteenth Century*. Baltimore, MD: Johns Hopkins University Press, 2012.
Kaminski, Thomas, 'Was Savage "Thales"?' *Bulletin of Research for the Humanities* 85 (1982), 322–5.
Keast, William R., 'Johnson and Cibber's Lives of the Poets, 1753', in *Restoration and Eighteenth-Century Literature*, ed. Carroll Camden. University of Chicago Press, 1963, pp. 89–101.
Kenny, Robert W., 'Ralph's *Case of Authors:* Its Influence on Goldsmith and Isaac D'Israeli', *Publications of the Modern Language Association* 52 (1937), 104–13.
Kernan, Alvin, *Samuel Johnson and the Impact of Print*. Princeton University Press, 1989.
King, James, *William Cowper*. Durham, NC: Duke University Press, 1986.
Lamont, Claire, 'Walter Scott and the Unmasking of Harlequin', in *Authorship, Commerce and the Public: Scenes of Writing, 1750–1850*, ed. Emma Clery, Carolyn Franklin, and Peter Garside. Basingstoke: Palgrave Macmillan, 2002, pp. 54–66.
Le Feuvre, Lisa, ed., *Failure*. London: Whitechapel Gallery, 2010.
Lockhart, J. G., *Memoirs of the Life of Sir Walter Scott*, 2nd edn, 10 vols. Edinburgh: Cadell, 1839.
Lonsdale, Roger, 'Gray and Johnson: The Biographical Problem', in *Fearful Joy: Papers from the Thomas Gray Bicentenary Conference at Carleton University*, ed. James Downey and Ben Jones. Montreal: McGill-Queen's University Press, 1974, pp. 66–84.
Martin, Peter, *A Life of James Boswell*. London: Phoenix Press, 2000.
Mitchell, C. J., 'The Spread and Fluctuation of Eighteen-Century Printing', *Studies in Voltaire and the Eighteenth Century* 230 (1985), 305–21.
Monk, Samuel Holt, 'Anna Seward and the Romantic Poets: A Study in Taste', in *Wordsworth and Coleridge: Studies in Honour of George McLean Harper*, ed. Earl Leslie Griggs. Princeton University Press, 1939, pp. 118–34.
Nussbaum, Felicity, *Torrid Zones: Maternity, Sexuality, and Empire in Eighteenth-Century English Narratives*. Baltimore, MD: Johns Hopkins University Press, 1995.
Papendick, Charlotte, *The Court and Private Life of Queen Charlotte*, 2 vols. London, 1887.
Parker, W. M., 'Bibliography: Scott's Marginalia, III', *Times Literary Supplement*, 5 October 1940, p. 8.
Peterson, M. Severin, *Robert Jephson 1736–1803: A Study of His Life and Works*. University of Nebraska Press, 1930.
Powell Jones, W., 'Johnson and Gray: A Study in Literary Antagonism', *Modern Philology* 56 (1959), 243–53.
Rogers, Pat, *Grub Street: Studies in a Subculture*. London: Methuen, 1972.
Rose, Mark, *Authors and Owners: The Invention of Copyright*. Cambridge, MA: Harvard University Press, 1993.

Rounce, Adam, '"A Clamour Too Loud to be Distinct": William Warburton's Literary Squabbles', *Age of Johnson* 16 (2005), 199–217.
'Cowper's Ends', in *Romanticism and Millenarianism*, ed. Tim Fulford. Basingstoke: Palgrave, 2002, pp. 23–36.
Scherwatzky, Steven D., '"Complicated Virtue": The Politics of Samuel Johnson's *Life of Savage*', *Eighteenth-Century Life* 25 (2001), 80–93.
Staves, Susan, *A Literary History of Women's Writing in Britain, 1660–1789*. Cambridge University Press, 2006.
Tracy, Clarence, *The Artificial Bastard: A Biography of Richard Savage*. University of Toronto Press, 1953.
Turner, Gavin, *Christopher Anstey: A Life in Eighteenth-Century Bath*. Bristol: Broadcast Books, 2005.
Walsh, Marcus, *Shakespeare, Milton, and Eighteenth-Century Literary Editing*. Cambridge University Press, 1997.
Weinbrot, Howard, 'Samuel Johnson, Percival Stockdale, and Brick-bats from Grubstreet', *Huntington Literary Quarterly* 56 (1993), 105–34.
Wendorf, Richard, *William Collins and Eighteenth-Century British Poetry*. University of Minnesota Press, 1981.
Willoughby, Edwin E., 'A Deadly Edition of Shakespeare', *Shakespeare Quarterly* 5 (1954), 351–7.
'The Unfortunate Dr. Dodd', *Essays by Divers Hands* xxix (1958), 124–43.
Wood, Gillen, 'The Female Pensoroso: Anna Seward, Sociable Poetry, and the Handelian Consensus', *Modern Language Quarterly* 67 (2006), 451–77.
Woodmansee, Martha, *The Author, Art, and the Market: Rereading the History of Aesthetics*. New York, NY: Columbia University Press, 1994.
Woolley, James D., 'Johnson as Despot: Anna Seward's Rejected Contribution to Boswell's *Life*', *Modern Philology* 70 (1972), 140–5.
Zionkowski, Linda, 'Aesthetics, Copyright, and "The Goods of the Mind"', *British Journal for Eighteenth-Century Studies* 15 (1992), 163–74.
'Territorial Disputes in the Republic of Letters: Canon Formation and the Literary Profession', *The Eighteenth Century: Theory and Interpretation* 31 (1990), 3–22.

Index

Addison, Joseph, 200
  Cato, 37
The Adventures of a Hackney Coach, 105
Akenside, Mark, *The Pleasures of Imagination*, 142
Alexander the Great
  Stockdale compares Chatterton to, 203
  Stockdale compares himself to, 177
Allen, Ralph, 59
Anderson, Robert, 93, 97, 151
Ashmun, Margaret, 116, 118–19, 122–4, 129, 138, 140, 151
Athenian Mercury. See Dunton, John

Baines, Paul, 70, 99
Banks, Joseph, 121
Barker, A. D., 71, 77, 82, 91, 101
Barnard, Teresa, 112, 125, 150–1
Barrington, Shute (Bishop of Durham), 154
Bate, Walter Jackson, 220
Battier, Henrietta, 70
Beattie, James, 17, 22
  'On Memory and Imagination', 16
  'Dialogues of the Dead', 199
Beckett, Samuel, 206
Bennett, Andrew, 204
Berryman, John, 'Dream Song 14', 23
Beville, William, 181
Blake, William, 185
Boswell, James, 134, 137–8, 194
  Life of Johnson, 97–8, 137, 168, 194, 199
  The Journal of a Tour to the Hebrides, 137
Boswell, Jamie, 194
Boyse, Samuel, 12–15, 21, 25, 55, 196
  Deity, 13–14
Brewer, John, 112, 114, 119, 132, 144
Brooke, Frances, 109
Bryant, Jacob, 202
Brydges, Egerton, 114
  Memoirs, 111
Bundock, Michael, 216

Burke, Edmund, 159, 167
Butler, Weedon, 100

Campbell, Thomas, 181
Caroline, Queen, 45, 56
Carter, Elizabeth, 99
Cary, Henry, 135, 145
Cave, Edward, 63, 71
Chapman, R. W., 97
Charles V, 174
Charles XII, 'Swedish Charles', 157, 163, 203, 230
Chatterton, Thomas, 8, 68, 132, 196, 201–4
Chaucer, Geoffrey, 145
  The Canterbury Tales, 13
Chesterfield, 5th Earl of (Philip Stanhope), 6, 70, 89–91, 93, 103
Christian Magazine, 81, 100
Churchill, Charles, 120, 158
Cibber, Colley, 56, 72
Clarke, Norma, 110–11, 114–15, 124, 126, 152
Clifford, James L., 40, 112, 114
Coleridge, Samuel Taylor, 161, 181
  Monody on the Death of Chatterton, 204
Collins, William, 116, 135
Constable, Archibald, 150
Cook, Captain James, 121
Cooper, Lucy, 78
Cowper, William, 4, 135, 139, 153, 208
  The Task, 120, 139
Crabbe, George, 181
Critical Review, 159
Croft, Herbert, 186
Crowe, William, *Lewesdon Hill*, 120
Cumberland, Richard, writes epilogue for Savage's play, 36

Dagge, Abel, 65
Dallas, Robert Charles, 181
Darwin, Erasmus, 110, 123
  The Botanic Garden, 120, 141
  The Loves of the Plants, 141

245

Davies, Tom, 159–60, 168
Day, Thomas, 139
De Quincey, Thomas, 205
Defoe, Daniel, *Robinson Crusoe*, 17
DeMaria Jr, Robert, 220
Denham, Sir John, *Cooper's Hill*, 42
D'Israeli, Isaac, 25–7, 165, 198
  Curiosities of Literature, 25, 196–7
  review of Stockdale's *Memoirs*, 163, 191
Dodd, William, 6, 25, 69–108, 195
  African eclogues, 71
  attempted simony, 90
  The Beauties of Shakespear, 74–7, 105, 196
  Commentary on the Bible, 101
  confesses, 92
  'Diggon Davy's Resolution on the Death of His Last Cow', 71
  'Elegy on the Death of His Royal Highness the Prince of Wales', 73
  forgery and discovery, 91–4
  fulsome dedication to Archbishop Secker, 83
  The Hymns of Callimachus, 74
  as 'Macaroni Parson', 70
  and Magdalen Chapel, 82
  'Moral Pastorals', 87
  A New Book of the Dunciad, 72
  ordination, 74
  'Petition of the City of London', 97
  Poems (1767), 74, 86–8
  poetry, 72
  possible Shakespeare edition, 91
  posthumous success of works, 216
  Reflections on Death, 84–5
  sentenced to death, 94
  'Sir Roger de Coverly', 74, 100
  The Sisters, 77–81, 100
  success of works, 71
  'The Syracusan', 74
  Thoughts in Prison, 100–4, 108
  'To the Author of Tristram Shandy, on the Publication of His Third and Fourth Volumes', 87
  trial and conviction, 93
  The Wisdom and Goodness of God in the Vegetable Creation, 83
  writes glowing review of own work, 83
Dodington, George 'Bubb', 44
Dodsley, Robert, *Miscellany*, 123
Donoghue, Frank, 11
Dryden, John, 120, 131, 135, 141, 145, 162, 185
Duncombe, William, 83, 89
  Historical Memoirs, 81–2
Dunton, John, 18, 20
  The Life and Errors, 18
  The Whipping-Post, 18

Dussinger, John, 31, 47, 49
Dyer, John, 39

Edgeworth, Richard Lovell, 125
  Seward on, 127
Edinburgh Review, 182
Edwards, Thomas, *Canons of Criticism*, 73
Empson, William, 185

Fenton, Elijah, 160
Fielding, Henry, 11, 78
  Tom Jones, 13, 79
Fitzgerald, Percy, 77, 89, 94, 96, 101
Fletcher, John, finances Dodd's bond, 91
Foote, Samuel, *The Cozeners*, 90
Frederick, Prince of Wales, 58

Garrick, David, 108, 159, 164
  praises Stockdale, 162
Gentleman's Magazine, 61, 111, 119, 135, 137, 141
Germain, Lord George, 166, 232
Gerrard, Christine, 35, 67
Gessner, Salomon, *Idyllen*, 87
Gibbon, Edward, 159
Gladfelder, Hal, 54
Glover, Richard, 161
God (the Christian), Stockdale imagines him forgiving Chatterton's suicide, 203
Godwin, William, 143
  Caleb Williams, 143
  Life of Chaucer, 145
  St Leon, 143
Goldsmith, Oliver, 11, 159
  Enquiry into the Present State of Learning, 20
Gordon, Duchess of, 13
Gray, Thomas, 7, 115, 131–2, 135, 139, 141, 159, 182, 187
  Elegy Written in a Country Churchyard, 127
  The Bard, 119, 188
  The Progress of Poesy, 119, 162, 188
Gregory, George, 202
  Life of Chatterton, 202
Griffin, Dustin, 10, 41

Halifax, 2nd Earl of (George Montagu-Dunk), 71
Hammond, Brean, 10
Hardinge, George, 116, 135, 139, 141, 151, 201
Harris, Thomas, 100
Harry, Jenny, 137
Hawkesworth, John, 159
Hawkins, Sir John, 30, 66, 96, 98
  Life of Samuel Johnson, 30, 96

Hayley, William, 120, 122, 134–5, 139–41, 145, 151, 153
  Life of Cowper, 138
  The Triumph of Music, 140
Hazlitt, William, 205
Hill, Aaron, 33
Hinton, John, 159
Howard, Lady Frances, 37
Howson, Gerald, 72, 75, 77, 100–1
Huddesford, George, *Warley*, 167
Hume, David, 'Of the Rise and Progress of the Arts and Sciences', 15
Huntington, Lady, 99

Jeffrey, Francis, 150
Jenkinson, Charles, 97
Jenyns, Soame, 22
Jephson, Robert, 115, 119
Jerningham, Edward, 178
Johnson, Samuel, 5–8, 11, 13, 15, 20–5, 31, 45, 54, 61–2, 69, 94, 104, 108–9, 113, 121, 138–40, 142, 156, 159, 182, 187, 195, 199, 206
  Adventurer, 24
  Dictionary, 21, 179
  edition of Shakespeare, 23, 73, 75
  helps Dodd, 97–8
  Idler, 22
  Irene, 135
  Life of Savage, 5, 15, 28–9, 31, 37–8, 44, 49, 51–3, 55, 58–60, 179, 184, 197–8, 200
  Lives of the Poets, 7, 132, 134–6, 138, 148, 153, 161, 169, 177–9, 182–3, 185, 188, 231
  selection of poets for, 225
  London, 52
  praises Stockdale, 168
  Rambler, 179
  Rasselas, 21, 116
  repeatedly criticised in Stockdale's *Lectures*, 181–9
  The Vanity of Human Wishes, 157, 164
Jones, Bridget, addressed poetically by Savage, 61

Kairoff, Claudia Thomas, 112, 123, 126, 132, 134
Keats, John, 204
Kernan, Alvin, 199
Knowles, Mary, 137

Le Feuvre, Lisa, 205
Lennox, Charlotte, *The Female Quixote*, 23
Lewis, Matthew, *The Monk*, 181
Life of Savage (anon), 28, 34, 45
The Loves of the Triangles, 142
Lyttelton, 1st Baron (George Lyttelton), 178, 185

Macclesfield, Lady (Anne Brett), 5, 28, 31–2, 37–9, 45, 48
Mackenzie, Henry
  The Man of Feeling, 70, 107
  Ossian poems, commission of 1805, 143
Macpherson, James, Ossian poems, 142, 145
Malone, Edmond, 116, 184
Manley, John, reveals Dodd's forgery, 92
Mansfield, Lord Chief Justice, 93
Marolles, Abbé de, 197
Marsollier, Jacques, 173
Mason, William, 135–6, 141
Miller, Lady Anna, Batheaston poetry contest, 122
Milton, John, 115, 132, 135, 139, 159, 162, 165, 184
  Comus, 131
  Lycidas, 109
  'Methought I saw my late espoused Saint', 128
  shorter poems, 118
Monk, Samuel Holt, 111, 144, 202
Montagu, Elizabeth, 99
Monthly Review, 130
Moore, Thomas, 181
Morning Chronicle, 100
Mrs Read
  Savage's Bristol landlady, 62
  'Madam Wolf bitch', 62

Newton, Thomas, 95
Nichols, John, 71

Ogle, George, 13
Otway, Thomas, 196
  Venice Preserved, 76
Overbury, Sir Thomas, 37, 103

Papendick, Charlotte, 82
Paradise Lost, 51, 79, 102, 142
Paradise Regained, 185
patronage, 33
Percy, Thomas, 114, 151
  'Hermit of Warkworth', 181
Perkins, Mary (wife of William Dodd), 74
Piozzi, Hester Lynch, 113, 119, 143
Pitt, William, the Younger, 170
Pope, Alexander, 9, 12, 44, 52, 55, 58–9, 61, 117, 120, 135, 140, 159, 165, 167–8, 185
  The Dunciad, 9, 50–1, 186
  Eloisa to Abelard, 72, 129, 165, 186
  An Essay on Man, 186
  gets Grub Street gossip from Savage, 41
  Homer translation, 185–6
  The Rape of the Lock, 186
Porson, Richard, 70
Porter, Jane, 182, 189

Porter, Joseph, 124
Porter, Lucy, 121

Raleigh, Sir Walter, 103
Ralph, James, 20
  The Case of Authors by Profession, 19
Reed, Isaac, on Dodd, 85
Richardson, Samuel, 77, 129
  Clarissa, 80
Rivers, 4th Earl (Richard Savage), 5, 28, 31–2
Robertson, Lewis, 91
Rogers, Pat, 12, 14
Rose, Mark, 11

Sandwich, 4th Earl of (John Montagu), 74
Sargent, John, *The Mine*, 141
Saunders, William, 61
Savage, Richard, 5, 8–9, 13, 21, 23, 25, 28–68, 163, 195
  An Author to be Lett, 50–5
  The Authors of the Town, 41, 43, 50
  'The Bastard', 33, 46–7, 50
  emotional Jacobitism, 67
  final letters from prison, 65
  'London and Bristol Delineated', 63–4
  Love in a Veil, 32
  'Of Public Spirit in Public Works', 58
  'A Poem, Sacred to the Glorious Memory of Our Late Most Gracious Sovereign', 44
  'The Progress of a Divine', 57
  Sir Thomas Overbury, 36–40, 59, 100
  supposed Jacobitism, 32, 35
  'To a Young Gentleman, a Painter', 39
  'Volunteer Laureat', 56
  The Wanderer, 44, 47–50, 196
Saville, John, 124
  and Seward, 124–5
Scherwatzky, Steven, 56
Scott, Sir Walter, 1, 15, 114, 120, 123, 143–5, 150, 152, 181, 192, 206
  Chronicles of the Canongate, 1–2
  edits Seward's poetry, 122
  Journal, 1
  on Seward, 118
Selwyn, George, 106
Seward, Anna, 7, 109–53, 159, 161, 187, 195, 201
  death of sister, 124
  desire for fame, 117–18
  Elegy on Captain Cook, 111, 122, 133
  'Epistle to Nathaniel Lister', 121
  Eyam, 148, 150
  'Honora, an Elegy', 126
  and Honora Sneyd, 125–8
  Hyper-Criticism on Miss Seward's Louisa, 130, 132

  ideas of literary envy, 115–16
  'Inscribed on the blank leaves of the Poem Madoc', 144
  on Johnson, 132–8, 226
  Letters, 109, 115, 117–21, 130, 132–40, 143–6, 150, 152–3, 202, 205
    badly received, 151
  'Llangollen Vale', 119, 148
  Louisa, 111, 128–32, 145
  'Love Elegies and Epistles', 125
  Memoirs of Erasmus Darwin, 120, 142
  'On Reading a Description of Pope's Gardens', 118
  Original Sonnets, 148–50
  Poetical Works, 122
  prose style, 114
Seward, Thomas, 123–4
Shakespeare, William, 162, 165, 184
  Henry VI, 184
  King Lear, 47
  Love's Labour's Lost, 184
  Measure for Measure, 90
  The Merry Wives of Windsor, 184
  Sonnets (Stockdale's low opinion of), 184
  The Tempest, 76
Shelley, Percy Bysshe, 185
Shenstone, William, 131
Sheridan, Richard Brinsley, 36
Shiels, Robert, 13, 15, 28–9
Sinclair, James, 45
Smith, Charlotte, Seward accuses of plagiarism, 121
Sneyd, Honora, 125, 148
Somerset, Earl of (Robert Carr), 37
Southey, Robert, 120, 143, 145
  Joan of Arc, 143
  Madoc, 143
Spenser, Edmund, 131, 144, 165
  The Faerie Queene, 183
St James' Chronicle, 90
Sterne, Laurence, *Tristram Shandy*, 87
Stevens, William Bagshot, 225
Stockdale, Percival, 7, 10, 23, 154–93, 195
  apostrophe to the shade of Dryden, 185
  argument with Shute Barrington, 174–7
  attacked by 'Veritas', 154
  attacks cruelty to animals, 172
  awarded livings, 170
  burns history of Gibraltar, 172
  burns unpublished works, 169
  chosen to edit the *Lives of the Poets*, 169
  Churchill Defended. A Poem Addressed to the Minority, 158
  compares himself to Alexander the Great, 177
  The Constituents, 158

edition of Thomson's *The Seasons*, 178
edition of Waller, 8, 161
An Inquiry into the Nature, and Genuine Laws of Poetry, 165–8, 186
The Invincible Island, 179–80
on Johnson's former poverty, 184
Johnson's neighbour, 160
Lectures on the Truly Eminent English Poets, 155, 169, 177, 181–9, 202
Letters between Shute, Bishop of Durham, and Percival Stockdale, 174
Memoirs, 155–7, 159, 161, 167–8, 170, 172, 183, 189–93, 197, 205
nervous illness, 156
on *Night Thoughts*, 235
ordination, 158
'The Poet', 161–4
poetic reverence of Pope, 166
'Poetical Thoughts, and Views', 174
Sermons, 172
'A Song', 180
Tasso's *Amyntas*, 159
tutor to Lord Craven's son, 170
unhappy marriage, 158
'Verses Addressed to Oxford', 157
Ximenes, 174
Stokes, Anna Rogers, 137
Storer, Anthony Morris, 106
Suckling, Sir John, *Goblins*, 76
Swift, Jonathan, 4
A Tale of a Tub, 4, 9

Temple, Captain (alias Taylor), 124, 224
Temple, William Johnson, on Stockdale's marriage, 158
Thicknesse, Philip, 105
Thomson, James, 187
influence on Savage, 47
Thoughts of a Citizen of London on the Conduct of Dr. Dodd, 98
Todd, Henry J., 144
Town and Country Magazine, 89
Tracey, Robert 'Beau', 78
Tracy, Clarence, 31, 37, 45, 50, 53, 59
Tyrconnel, Lord, 45, 50, 52
Tyrwhitt, Thomas, 202

Universal Magazine, 159

Villette, John (Ordinary of Newgate), 106

Wagner, Richard, *Das Rheingold*, 141
Waldock, A. J. A., 185
Waller, Edmund, 159
Wallis, Henry, *Death of Chatterton*, 196
Walpole, Horace, 89, 95, 105, 107, 201–2
on Dodd's preaching, 82
Warburton, William, 75
The Divine Legation of Moses Demonstrated, 73
edition of Pope, 72
edition of Shakespeare, 72
Warton, Joseph, 186
An Essay on the Writings and Genius of Pope, 165
Warton, Thomas, edition of Milton's shorter poems, 109
Wedgwood, Josiah, 117
Weinbrot, Howard, 155, 158, 192
West, Jane, 114, 138
Weston, Joseph, 135
Weston, Sophia, 143
Whalley, Thomas Sedgwick, 117, 120, 130, 143, 151
Wickham, Hill, 151
Wilberforce, William, 181
Wilkes, John, 158
Willoughby, Edwin, 75
Woodfall, William, 100
Woodmansee, Martha, 10
Woolley, James, 138
Wordsworth, William, 144, 181
Poems of 1807, 144
Resolution and Independence, 204
Wortley Montagu, Lady Mary, 120
Wright, Major John, 124

Ximenes, Francisco de Cisneros, 173

Young, Edward, 186
Night Thoughts, 142
The Universal Passion, 41

Zionkowski, Linda, 11